First World War
and Army of Occupation
War Diary
France, Belgium and Germany

30 DIVISION
89 Infantry Brigade
Royal Inniskilling Fusiliers 7/8th Battalion,
Prince of Wales's Volunteers (South Lancashire Regiment)
2nd Battalion,
London Regiment 2/17 Battalion,
Brigade Machine Gun Company,
Brigade Trench Mortar Battery
17 September 1915 - 31 August 1916

WO95/2336

The Naval & Military Press Ltd
www.nmarchive.com
Published in association with The National Archives

Published by

The Naval & Military Press Ltd

Unit 10 Ridgewood Industrial Park,

Uckfield, East Sussex,

TN22 5QE England

Tel: +44 (0) 1825 749494

www.naval-military-press.com

www.nmarchive.com

This diary has been reprinted in facsimile from the original. Any imperfections are inevitably reproduced and the quality may fall short of modern type and cartographic standards.

© **Crown Copyright**
Images reproduced by permission of The National Archives, London, England, 2015.

Contents

Document type	Place/Title	Date From	Date To
Heading	30th Division 89th Infy Bde 7-8th In Inniskilling Fus Jun 1918-Sep 1919 From 16 Div 49 Bde.		
Map	France.		
Miscellaneous	Trench Map.		
Heading	War Diary Of 7/8th Battalion Inniskilling Fusiliers. 1st June 1918. 30th June 1918 Sep 1919 Vol 29		
War Diary	Frencq.	01/06/1918	26/06/1918
War Diary	Steenbecque.	30/06/1918	30/06/1918
Heading	War Diary Of 7/8th Battn R Innis Fus July 1st 1918 July 31st 1918 Vol 30		
War Diary	Steenbecque.	01/07/1918	03/07/1918
War Diary	Westrove.	03/07/1918	08/07/1918
War Diary	Le-Paradis	08/07/1918	08/07/1918
War Diary	Nordpeene.	09/07/1918	09/07/1918
War Diary	Steenvoorde.	10/07/1918	31/07/1918
War Diary	Steenbecque.	01/07/1918	05/07/1918
War Diary	Steenvoorde.	18/07/1918	29/07/1918
Heading	War Diary Of 7/8th Battalion Royal Inniskilling Fusiliers From 1st To 31st August. 1918. Vol 31		
War Diary	Steenvoorde.	01/08/1918	01/08/1918
War Diary	Boeschepe Ref.Sheet 27 SE & 28 S.W. 1/20,000.	09/08/1918	10/08/1918
War Diary	Ref.Berthen & Meteren 27 S.E Position Map 1/20,000.	10/08/1918	20/08/1918
War Diary	Ref. Special Locre Sheet.	21/08/1918	24/08/1918
War Diary	Ref. Locre 10,000 & Sheet 27 1/40,000.	25/08/1918	26/08/1918
War Diary	Ref. Sheet 27 SE V 28 S.W 1/20,000.	31/08/1918	31/08/1918
Heading	War Diary Of 7/8 (S). Battn R. Innis Fus From 1-9-18 To 30-9-18. Vol 32		
Heading	War Diary Of 7/8 (S) Bn. Royal Inniskilling Fusiliers From 1st Sept 1918 To 30th Sept 1918.		
War Diary	Ref 27.S.E & 28.S.W. (Combined Sheet) Edition F.	01/09/1918	20/09/1918
War Diary	Ploegsteert Edition 5c (Local) And 27 S.E & 28 Sheet (Combined Sheet) Edition 1.	22/09/1918	25/09/1918
War Diary	Ploegsteert Edition 5c (Local)	25/09/1918	27/09/1918
War Diary	Ref. Belgium & Part Of France Sheet 28 S.W.	28/09/1918	29/09/1918
War Diary	Ploegsteert Edition 5c (Local).	29/09/1918	30/09/1918
Heading	War Diary Of 7/8th Battalion Royal Inniskilling Fusiliers From 1st To 31st October, 1918. Vol 36.		
War Diary	M. 35.d.85.50 Sheet 28.	01/10/1918	05/10/1918
War Diary	Sheet 28 SE P.12.d.6.8.	05/10/1918	11/10/1918
War Diary	O.25. Central Sheet 28.	11/10/1918	16/10/1918
War Diary	Sheet 28 Q 19.	18/10/1918	18/10/1918
War Diary	Sheet 28 & 29 1/40,000.	19/10/1918	31/10/1918
Heading	War Diary Of 7/8th Battn. Royal Inniskilling Fusiliers Nov 1st To Nov 30th 1918 Vol 37.		
War Diary	Sheet 28 & 29 1/40,000	01/11/1918	04/11/1918
War Diary	Sheet 29 1/40,000	04/11/1918	09/11/1918
War Diary	Tournai 5 1/20,0000.	10/11/1918	11/11/1918
War Diary	Sheet 30	14/11/1918	14/11/1918
War Diary	Sheet 29 1/40,000	16/11/1918	17/11/1918
War Diary	Tournai 5	28/11/1918	28/11/1918

War Diary	Tournai & Hazebrouck	29/11/1918	29/11/1918
War Diary	Hazebrouck 5 A	30/11/1918	30/11/1918
Heading	War Diary Of 7/8th Bn. Royal Inniskilling Fus. Dec 1st To Dec 31st 1918 Vol 38		
War Diary	Sheet Hazebrouck 5A.	01/12/1918	31/12/1918
War Diary	Sheet Hazebrouck.	01/01/1919	11/01/1919
Heading	War Diary Of 7/8th Bn. Royal Inniskilling Fusiliers From 1st February, 1919 To 28th February, 1919 Vol 40.		
War Diary	Boulogne.	01/02/1919	25/02/1919
War Diary	Boulogne	10/02/1919	10/02/1919
War Diary	St. Martin Camp.Boulogne.	01/03/1919	31/03/1919
War Diary	St. Martin Camp. Boulogne.	03/03/1919	31/03/1919
War Diary	St. Martin Camp. Boulogne.	01/03/1919	29/03/1919
War Diary	St. Martin Camp, Boulogne.	11/04/1919	25/04/1919
War Diary	St. Martin Camp, Boulogne.	01/04/1919	28/04/1919
War Diary	Saint Martin Camp, Boulogne.	04/05/1919	24/05/1919
War Diary		15/05/1919	24/05/1919
War Diary		25/04/1919	25/04/1919
War Diary	Saint Martin Camp, Boulogne.	02/06/1919	11/06/1919
War Diary	Saint Martin Camp, Boulogne.	09/07/1919	09/07/1919
War Diary		08/07/1919	08/07/1919
War Diary	St. Martin Camp.	01/08/1919	20/08/1919
War Diary	Henriville Camp.	28/08/1919	29/08/1919
War Diary		02/08/1919	20/08/1919
War Diary		01/08/1919	07/08/1919
War Diary	Henriville Camp.	26/09/1919	26/09/1919
War Diary		04/09/1919	26/09/1919
Heading	30th Division 89th Infy Bde 2nd Bn Sth Lancs Regt Jly 1918- Mar 1919 From 25 Div 75 Bde.		
Heading	War Diary 2nd Battn. S. Lancs Regt. 1st-31st July 1918 N.W. 1919 Vol 46		
Heading	2nd Battalion South Lancashire Regiment War Diary 1st To 31st July 1918. 12 Page.		
War Diary		01/07/1918	31/07/1918
Heading	War Diary 2nd South Lancashire Regt. 1st To 31st August 1918 Vol 47.		
War Diary		01/08/1918	31/08/1918
Heading	War Diary Of 2nd Battn S. Lancs Regt From 1-9-18 To 30-9-18 Vol 48.		
Heading	2nd Battalion South Lancashire Regiment War Diary 1st To 30th September 1915.		
War Diary		01/09/1918	30/09/1918
Heading	2nd Battalion South Lancashire Regt War Diary 1st To 31st Oct 1918. Vol 52		
War Diary		01/10/1918	31/10/1918
Heading	2nd. Battalion South Lancashire Regiment. War Diary 1st To 30th November 1918 Vol 53.		
War Diary		01/11/1918	30/11/1918
Heading	2nd Battalion South Lancashire Regiment. War Diary 1st To 31st December 1918 Vol 52.		
War Diary		01/12/1918	31/12/1918
Heading	2nd Battalion South Lancashire Regiment War Diary 1st To 31st January 1919 Vol 53.		
War Diary		01/01/1919	31/01/1919

Heading	War Diary Of 2nd. Bn. South Lancs. Regt. From 1st February, 1919 To 28th February, 1919. Vol 54.		
War Diary		01/02/1919	31/03/1919
Heading	30th Division 89th Infy Bde 2/17 Bn London Regt 1918 Jun 1919 Sep From Egypt 60 Div 180 Bde.		
Heading	War Diary Of The 2/17th Battalion London Regiment From 1st June 1918 To 30th June 1918 Vol 1.		
War Diary	Kantara.	01/06/1918	15/06/1918
War Diary	Alexandria.	16/06/1918	18/06/1918
War Diary	At Sea.	19/06/1918	21/06/1918
War Diary	Toranto	22/06/1918	24/06/1918
War Diary	In Train.	25/06/1918	30/06/1918
War Diary	Ouest Mont.	30/06/1918	30/06/1918
Heading	War Diary Of 2/17th Battn London Regiment 1st-31st July 1918 Vol 2.		
Heading	War Diary Of 2/17th Battalion London Regiment From 1st July 1918 To 31st July 1918.		
War Diary	Ouest Mont.	01/07/1918	09/07/1918
War Diary	Sheet 27. 1/40,000 Q 8c 87d.	10/07/1918	10/07/1918
War Diary	Q 8c & 7d.	11/07/1918	31/07/1918
Heading	War Diary Of 2/17th Battalion London Regiment From 1st August 1918 To 31st August 1918 Vol 3.		
War Diary	Q 12c 9.6 & R 3c.	01/08/1918	01/08/1918
War Diary	Combined Sheet 27 S.E & 28 S.W	02/08/1918	02/08/1918
War Diary	Le Carreaux.	03/08/1918	10/08/1918
War Diary	Boeschepe Combined Sheet 27 S.E. & 28 S.W. R.9 b & d	11/08/1918	20/08/1918
War Diary	Koudekot Sector.	21/08/1918	27/08/1918
War Diary	Locre 1/10000.	28/08/1918	31/08/1918
Heading	War Diary Of 2/17th Battn London Regt. From 1-9-18 To 30-9-18. Vol 4.		
Heading	War Diary Of 2/17th Battalion London Regiment From 1st September 1918 To 30 September 1918		
War Diary	S 5a 2.3.	01/09/1918	01/09/1918
War Diary	M 34 d.	01/09/1918	01/09/1918
War Diary	S 12c.	02/09/1918	02/09/1918
War Diary	T 1a	03/09/1918	06/09/1918
War Diary	S 4 b 9.2.	07/09/1918	08/09/1918
War Diary	T 6c.5.3.	09/09/1918	15/09/1918
War Diary	M 28 C.	15/09/1918	15/09/1918
War Diary	Boeschepe.	16/09/1918	18/09/1918
War Diary	M 26 a.	19/09/1918	19/09/1918
War Diary	M 20a 15 85.	20/09/1918	22/09/1918
War Diary	M 35c b2.	23/09/1918	25/09/1918
War Diary	N 27 d 1.7.	26/09/1918	29/09/1918
War Diary	O26d Z.Z.	30/09/1918	30/09/1918
Heading	War Diary Of 2/17th Battalion London Regt. 1st October 1918-31st October 1918 Vol 5.		
War Diary	O26d 22	01/10/1918	01/10/1918
War Diary	O30d 49	02/10/1918	05/10/1918
War Diary	P 12d 6.8.	05/10/1918	07/10/1918
War Diary	P 22 & 9.3.	08/10/1918	12/10/1918
War Diary	O 19 d 7.2.	12/10/1918	18/10/1918
War Diary	Q 21a 2.1.	18/10/1918	19/10/1918
War Diary	X 4 C. 3.5.	19/10/1918	20/10/1918
War Diary	S 7a 3.2.	20/10/1918	21/10/1918

War Diary	U 25d 0.3.	21/10/1918	21/10/1918
War Diary	C 3 C 8.6.	21/10/1918	21/10/1918
War Diary	C 4 a 2.0.	21/10/1918	21/10/1918
War Diary	U 26 d 99.	22/10/1918	22/10/1918
War Diary	C 4 a 5.2.	23/10/1918	23/10/1918
War Diary	C 4 a 2.0.	23/10/1918	23/10/1918
War Diary	C 4 a 5.2.	23/10/1918	24/10/1918
War Diary	C 4 a 5.2.	23/10/1918	23/10/1918
War Diary	C 9 d 7.8.	24/10/1918	24/10/1918
War Diary	C 4 a 3.6.	24/10/1918	24/10/1918
War Diary	C 4 a 2.0.	24/10/1918	24/10/1918
War Diary	C 4 a 6.2.	25/10/1918	25/10/1918
War Diary	C 4 a 2.0.	25/10/1918	26/10/1918
War Diary	U 26 C 8.8.	27/10/1918	27/10/1918
War Diary	U 29c 9.4.	28/10/1918	28/10/1918
War Diary	T 2a 1.9.	29/10/1918	31/10/1918
Heading	War Diary Of 2/17th Battalion London Regiment From 1st Nov 1918 To 31 Nov 1918.		
War Diary	S 12c 4.4.	01/11/1918	04/11/1918
War Diary	P. 25a 4.3.	04/11/1918	04/11/1918
War Diary	O 18 & 2.1.	05/11/1918	06/11/1918
War Diary	U 6 d 3.6.	07/11/1918	07/11/1918
War Diary	V 14 d 3.7.	08/11/1918	08/11/1918
War Diary	V 15 a 4.9.	08/11/1918	08/11/1918
War Diary	V 15 a.4.3.	09/11/1918	09/11/1918
War Diary	D 6 b 7.6.	09/11/1918	09/11/1918
War Diary	F6 a 0.5.	10/11/1918	10/11/1918
War Diary	A 1 b 2.9.	10/11/1918	11/11/1918
War Diary	T 27 b 5.8.	11/11/1918	14/11/1918
War Diary	X 27 d 7.6.	15/11/1918	16/11/1918
War Diary	U 6 a 8.8.	17/11/1918	17/11/1918
War Diary	T 14 a 3.5.	18/11/1918	30/11/1918
Heading	War Diary Of 2/17th Battalion London Regiment From December 1st 1918 To December 31st 1918 Vol 7.		
War Diary	In The Field.	01/12/1918	31/12/1918
Heading	War Diary Of 2/17th Battalion London Regiment. From 1st January 1919. To. 31st January 1919. Vol 8.		
War Diary	In The Field.	01/01/1919	31/01/1919
Heading	War Diary Of 2/17th Bn. London Regiment. From 1st February, 1919 To 28th February, 1919. Vol 9.		
Heading	War Diary Of 2/17th Battalion London Regiment. From 1st February, 1919. To: 28th February, 1919.		
War Diary	Boulogne.	01/02/1919	28/02/1919
Heading	War Diary Of 2/17th Battalion London Regiment. From 1st March, 1919 to 31st March, 1919. Vol 10.		
War Diary	Boulogne.	01/03/1919	05/03/1919
War Diary	Boulogne.	06/04/1919	31/04/1919
Heading	War Diary Of 2/17th Battalion London Regiment. From. 1st April, 1919. To. 30th April, 1919. Vol 11.		
War Diary	Boulogne.	01/04/1919	29/09/1919
Heading	30th Division 89th Infy Bde 89th Machine Gun Coy. Mar 1916-Feb 1918.		
War Diary	Havre.	11/03/1916	13/03/1916
War Diary	Sailly Laurette.	14/03/1916	14/03/1916
War Diary	La Houssoye.	18/03/1916	26/03/1916
War Diary	Sailly Laurette.	29/03/1916	29/03/1916

Miscellaneous	89 Coy. Machine Gun Corps. From Officer Commanding 89th Coy Machine Gun Corps To. O/c A.G.S. Office The Base.	31/03/1916	31/03/1916
War Diary	Sailly-Laurette.	07/04/1916	30/04/1916
Miscellaneous	From:- O.C. 89 Coy Machine Gun Corp To:- D.A.G. 36 Echelon	02/05/1916	02/05/1916
Miscellaneous	Appendix T. Vol 2 War Diary Of 89th Coy Machine Gun Corp For April. 1916	00/04/1916	00/04/1916
Miscellaneous	From:- Officer Commanding 89th Coy Machine Gun Corps.	31/05/1916	31/05/1916
War Diary	Bray (Coy H.Q.).	30/04/1916	30/04/1916
War Diary	Z Sector.	01/05/1916	29/05/1916
Miscellaneous	War Diary (Reference Appendix 2). 89th Coy Machine Gun Corps.		
Miscellaneous	Appendix No IV Of War Diary Of 89 Coy-Machine Gun Corps. Vol III May 1916 Opertions Order No 5 By Capt J H Roxburgh	26/05/1916	26/05/1916
Operation(al) Order(s)	Appendix No V Of War Diary Of 89 Coy-Machine Gun Corps Opertions Order No 6 By Capt J H Roxburgh	26/05/1916	26/05/1916
Map			
Miscellaneous	From:- Officer Commanding 89th Coy Machine Gun Corps.	01/07/1916	01/07/1916
War Diary	Ailly-Sur-Somme.	31/05/1916	11/06/1916
War Diary	Corbie.	12/06/1916	12/06/1916
War Diary	Etinehem.	13/06/1916	13/06/1916
War Diary	Bray.	16/06/1916	18/06/1916
War Diary	Maricourt.	19/06/1916	29/06/1916
War Diary		30/09/1916	30/09/1916
Miscellaneous	From:- Officer Commanding 89 Coy Machine Gun Corps.	04/08/1916	04/08/1916
War Diary	Maricourt.	01/07/1916	01/07/1916
War Diary	Dones Redoubt.	01/07/1916	05/07/1916
War Diary	Bois Des Tailles.	05/07/1916	08/07/1916
War Diary	Ceylon Wood.	08/07/1916	09/07/1916
War Diary	Dones Redoubt.	10/07/1916	13/07/1916
War Diary	Bois Des Tailles.	13/07/1916	13/07/1916
War Diary	Corbie.	14/07/1916	19/07/1916
War Diary	Happy Valley.	19/07/1916	20/07/1916
War Diary	F 15 a 18.	22/07/1916	31/07/1916
Heading	89th Brigade. 30th Division. 89th Machine Gun Company August 1916.		
Miscellaneous	Headquarters, 89th Inf. Bde.	03/09/1916	03/09/1916
War Diary	F 15a 18 Meaulte 62 O.N.E 2 1/10,000.	01/08/1916	02/08/1916
War Diary	Huppy.	02/08/1916	03/08/1916
War Diary	Q 20 a.	04/08/1916	06/08/1916
War Diary	R 7 C.	09/08/1916	17/08/1916
War Diary	Levertanndy.	18/08/1916	24/08/1916
War Diary	Gorre.	26/08/1916	31/08/1916
Heading	War Diary Of 89 Machine Gun Coy For The Month Of September 1916 Volume VII.		
Miscellaneous	Headquarters, 89th Inf. Bde.	01/10/1916	01/10/1916
War Diary	Gorre.	01/09/1916	07/09/1916
War Diary	X 30 & 91.	07/09/1916	07/09/1916
War Diary	W 22 d 23.	13/09/1916	14/09/1916
War Diary	Essars.	15/09/1916	16/09/1916

War Diary	La Miquellerie	16/09/1916	18/09/1916
War Diary	Bretel.	18/09/1916	21/09/1916
War Diary	Vignacourt.	21/09/1916	28/09/1916
Heading	War Diary Of The 89th Machine Gun Company For The Month Of October 1916 Volume VIII.		
War Diary	Vignacourt.	01/10/1916	04/10/1916
War Diary	Dernancourt.	05/10/1916	10/10/1916
War Diary	S 21b.	10/10/1916	10/10/1916
War Diary	M 36 b 5.6.	10/10/1916	11/11/1916
War Diary	M 36 a 59.	11/10/1916	13/10/1916
War Diary	M 36.c 2.5.	14/10/1916	14/10/1916
War Diary	S 21 b.	15/10/1916	16/10/1916
War Diary	M 30 d 8.5.	16/10/1916	22/10/1916
War Diary	S 19 c.	23/10/1916	24/10/1916
War Diary	Buire.	25/10/1916	27/10/1916
War Diary	Caumesnil.	28/10/1916	28/10/1916
War Diary	Pommiers.	29/10/1916	30/10/1916
War Diary	Berles-Au-Bois.	31/10/1916	31/10/1916
Heading	War Diary Of 89 Machine Gun Company For The Month Of November 1916 Volume IX Appendies VII &VIII Vol 9.		
War Diary	W 16 c 6.8.	01/11/1916	30/11/1916
Operation(al) Order(s)	89 Machine Gun Company. Operation Order No. 6. by Captain J.H. Roxburgh. Appendix VII.	18/11/1916	18/11/1916
Map	Appendix VIII.		
Heading	War Diary Of 89th Machine Gun Company For The Month Of December 1916 Volume X.		
War Diary	Berles.-Au-Bois.	01/12/1916	01/12/1916
War Diary	W 15c.6.8.	01/12/1916	27/12/1916
War Diary	W 15 d 2.2.	28/12/1916	31/12/1916
Operation(al) Order(s)	89th. Machine Gun Coy. Operation Order No. 7. by Captain, J.H. Roxburgh. Appendix X.	11/12/1916	11/12/1916
Operation(al) Order(s)	Appendix To 89th. Machine Gun Company Operation Order No. 7. by Captain J.H. Roxburgh.		
Heading	War Diary Of 89th Machine Gun Company January 1917 Volume XI.		
War Diary	Berles-Au-Bois.		
War Diary	W 15 C 6.8.	01/01/1917	08/01/1917
War Diary	B 29 C 4.8.	09/01/1917	25/01/1917
Operation(al) Order(s)	89th. Machine Gun Company. Operation Order No. 8. by Captain J.H. Roxburgh.	06/01/1917	06/01/1917
Heading	War Diary Of The 89th Machine Gun Company-M.G.C. For The Month Of February. Volume XII Vol 12		
Miscellaneous	Headquarters, 89th Infantry Brigade.	02/03/1917	02/03/1917
War Diary	Caumesnil.		
War Diary	B 29 C 4.8.	01/02/1917	01/02/1917
War Diary	Warluzel.	03/02/1917	04/02/1917
War Diary	Monchiet.	05/02/1917	05/02/1917
War Diary	Beaumetz.	06/02/1917	07/02/1917
War Diary	M 8 & 8.5.	07/02/1917	28/02/1917
Map	Appendix XI to War Diary Of 89th Machine Gun Company Vol XII For February 1917.		
Heading	War Diary Of the 89th Coy Machine Gun Corps. For The Month Of March 1917. Volume XIII.		
War Diary	Agny-M.8.b.8.5.	01/03/1917	10/03/1917

Type	Description	From	To
War Diary	M.8.b.8.5.	11/03/1917	22/03/1917
War Diary	Lefermont.	22/03/1917	23/03/1917
War Diary	Fermont.	24/03/1917	31/03/1917
Heading	War Diary Of 89th Machine Gun Company For The Month Of April 1917 Volume XIV.		
War Diary	Bailleulmont.	01/04/1917	06/04/1917
War Diary	Blaireville.	07/04/1917	08/04/1917
War Diary	S 4.c.80.15.	08/04/1917	10/04/1917
War Diary	S 12 b 8.7.	10/04/1917	10/04/1917
War Diary	N 32 c 5.3.	10/04/1917	12/04/1917
War Diary	S 3.c.8.2 Blaireville.	12/04/1917	13/04/1917
War Diary	Basseux.	13/04/1917	14/04/1917
War Diary	Couin.	14/04/1917	21/04/1917
War Diary	Achicourt.	22/04/1917	23/04/1917
War Diary	M 11d 6.8	24/04/1917	24/04/1917
War Diary	N 27 a 4.7.	24/04/1917	26/04/1917
War Diary	N 29 C.A.3.80.	26/04/1917	27/04/1917
War Diary	N 27 a 4.7.	27/04/1917	28/04/1917
War Diary	M 11d 6.8.	28/04/1917	28/04/1917
War Diary	Framecourt.	29/04/1917	30/04/1917
Heading	War Diary Of 89th Machine Gun Company For Month Of May 1917. Vol 15.		
War Diary	Framecourt.	01/05/1917	03/05/1917
War Diary	Buire.	03/05/1917	03/05/1917
War Diary	Haravesnes.	04/05/1917	15/05/1917
War Diary	Framecourt.	20/05/1917	20/05/1917
War Diary	Conteville	21/05/1917	22/05/1917
War Diary	Lespresses.	22/05/1917	23/05/1917
War Diary	Thiennes.	24/05/1917	24/05/1917
War Diary	Caestre.	25/05/1917	26/05/1917
War Diary	Watou.	26/05/1917	26/05/1917
War Diary	Brandhoek.	27/05/1917	28/05/1917
War Diary	Ypres.	28/05/1917	30/05/1917
Heading	War Diary Of The 89th Machine Gun Coy for the Month of June 1917 Volume 16.		
Miscellaneous	Headquarters, 89th Inf. Bde.	03/07/1917	03/07/1917
War Diary	Ypres.	01/06/1917	09/06/1917
War Diary	K18a9.9.	10/06/1917	22/06/1917
War Diary	H.33.d.2.8.	23/06/1917	27/06/1917
War Diary	H.30.a.90.05.	27/06/1917	30/06/1917
Heading	War Diary Of The 89th Machine Gun Company For The Month Of July 1917. Volume XVII Appendix XI. Vol. 17.		
War Diary	H.30.a.90.05.	01/07/1917	07/07/1917
War Diary	G.24.c.8.8.	07/07/1917	07/07/1917
War Diary	Notre Dame Farm.	08/07/1917	19/07/1917
War Diary	Le Temple.	24/07/1917	24/07/1917
War Diary	Dallington Camp	25/07/1917	28/07/1917
War Diary	Palace Camp.	29/07/1917	30/07/1917
Operation(al) Order(s)	89th Machine Gun Coy. Operation Orders No. 10. By Captain J.H. Roxburgh. Appendix XI. To War Diary Vol. XVII. For July 1917.	23/07/1917	23/07/1917
Operation(al) Order(s)	89th Coy. Machine Gun Corps. Operation Order No. 10.		
Operation(al) Order(s)	89th Machine Gun Company-Operation Order No. 10. Appendix. B.		

Operation(al) Order(s)	89th Coy Machine Gun Corps-Operation Orders No. 10. Appendix "C".		
Heading	War Diary.		
Miscellaneous	Fire Organization Table.		
Heading	War Diary Of The 89th Company Machine Gun Corps For The Month Of August 1917 Volume XVIII.		
War Diary	I.17.d.1.1.	31/07/1917	04/08/1917
War Diary	G.24.b.30.	04/08/1917	04/08/1917
War Diary	Eecke.	05/08/1917	07/08/1917
War Diary	Merris.	09/08/1917	09/08/1917
War Diary	S.8.b.8.6.	10/08/1917	23/08/1917
War Diary	Dranoutre.	23/08/1917	28/08/1917
War Diary	N.31.d.8.7.	29/08/1917	31/08/1917
Heading	War Diary Of 89th Machine Gun Company For The Month Of September 1917 Volume XIX.		
War Diary	N.31.d.8.7.	01/09/1917	02/09/1917
War Diary	C.9.a.7.2.	03/09/1917	04/09/1917
War Diary	O.15.b.96.70.	05/09/1917	30/09/1917
Operation(al) Order(s)	89 M.G. Coy. Operation Order No. 11. By Capt. J.H. Roxburgh.	19/09/1917	19/09/1917
Miscellaneous	Details For 89 M.G. Coy-6 Guns In Flanking Arrange Of 30th Divn.		
Miscellaneous	S.O.S. Barrage. 89 M.G. Coy Appendix XIII		
Heading	War Diary Of The 89th Machine Gun Company For The Month Of October 1917 Volume XX.		
Miscellaneous	Headquarters. 89th Inf. Bde.	01/11/1917	01/11/1917
War Diary	O.15b.96.70.	01/10/1917	31/10/1917
Heading	War Diary Of The 89th Machine Gun Company For The Month Of November 1917 Volume XXI.		
War Diary	O.15 b.96.70.	01/11/1917	14/11/1917
War Diary	Locre.	15/11/1917	16/11/1917
War Diary	J.24.d.7.8.	17/11/1917	26/11/1917
War Diary	Stirling Castle.	27/11/1917	27/11/1917
War Diary	J.19.b.5.9.	27/11/1917	30/11/1917
Heading	War Diary Of The 89th Machine Gun Company For the Month of December 1917 Vol XXII.		
War Diary		01/12/1917	31/12/1917
Heading	War Diary Of The 89th Machine Gun Company For The Month Of January 1918 Volume XXIII.		
War Diary		01/01/1918	07/01/1918
War Diary	Heuringhem.	08/01/1918	11/01/1918
War Diary	Cachy.	12/01/1918	13/01/1918
War Diary	Guillaucourt-Vrely.	14/01/1918	18/01/1918
War Diary	Guerbigny.	19/01/1918	19/01/1918
War Diary	Beaulieu Les.	20/01/1918	20/01/1918
War Diary	Fongrine.	21/01/1918	31/01/1918
Heading	89th Coy M.G.C. War Diary Vol XXIV.		
War Diary		01/02/1918	28/02/1918
Heading	3 Army Troops 30 Div 89 Bde. 89 Trench Mortar Bt/ 1915 Sep To 1916 Apl		
Heading	3rd Army 89th Trench Mortar Batty Vol I Sept 15		
War Diary	In The Field.	17/09/1915	30/09/1915
War Diary	Poulainville.	12/04/1916	19/04/1916
War Diary	Sailly-Laurette	19/04/1916	29/04/1916
War Diary	Maricourt.	29/04/1916	25/05/1916
War Diary	Ailly Sur Somme.	26/05/1916	26/05/1916

War Diary	Maricourt.	18/05/1916	21/05/1916
War Diary	Mericourt Loc.	25/05/1916	25/05/1916
War Diary	Ailly-Sur-Somme.	26/05/1916	12/06/1916
War Diary	Heilly.	12/06/1916	12/06/1916
War Diary	Etinehem.	12/06/1916	15/06/1916
War Diary	Maricourt.	16/06/1916	30/06/1916
War Diary	Trenches N Of Maricourt.	01/07/1916	01/07/1916
War Diary	Bois Des Tailles.	05/07/1916	05/07/1916
War Diary	Trigger Wood.	08/07/1916	08/07/1916
War Diary	Maricourt.	09/07/1916	13/07/1916
War Diary	Bois Des Tailles.	13/07/1916	13/07/1916
War Diary	Corbie.	14/07/1916	14/07/1916
War Diary	Happy Valley.	19/07/1916	19/07/1916
War Diary	Citadel.	20/07/1916	29/07/1916
War Diary	Trenches.	29/07/1916	30/07/1916
War Diary	Citadel.	31/07/1916	31/07/1916
War Diary	Battle Of The Somme By B. Newton Lieut.		
War Diary	Battle Of The Somme By B. Newton Lieut.	01/07/1916	04/07/1916
War Diary	Battle Of The Somme By Capt. B. Newton	30/07/1916	30/07/1916
Heading	War Diary Of 89th Trench Mortar Battery For The Month Of August 1916 Volume 3.		
War Diary	Citadel.	02/08/1916	03/08/1916
War Diary	Merville.	04/08/1916	04/08/1916
War Diary	Calonne.	04/08/1916	09/08/1916
War Diary	Fosse.	09/08/1916	18/08/1916
War Diary	Pont L' Hinges	20/08/1916	26/08/1916
War Diary	Gorre.	27/08/1916	31/08/1916
War Diary	Trenches Givenchy Sector.	27/08/1916	31/08/1916

30TH DIVISION
09TH INFY BDE

7-8TH BN INNISKILLING FUS.
JUN 1918-SEP 1919

From 16 DIV
49 BDE

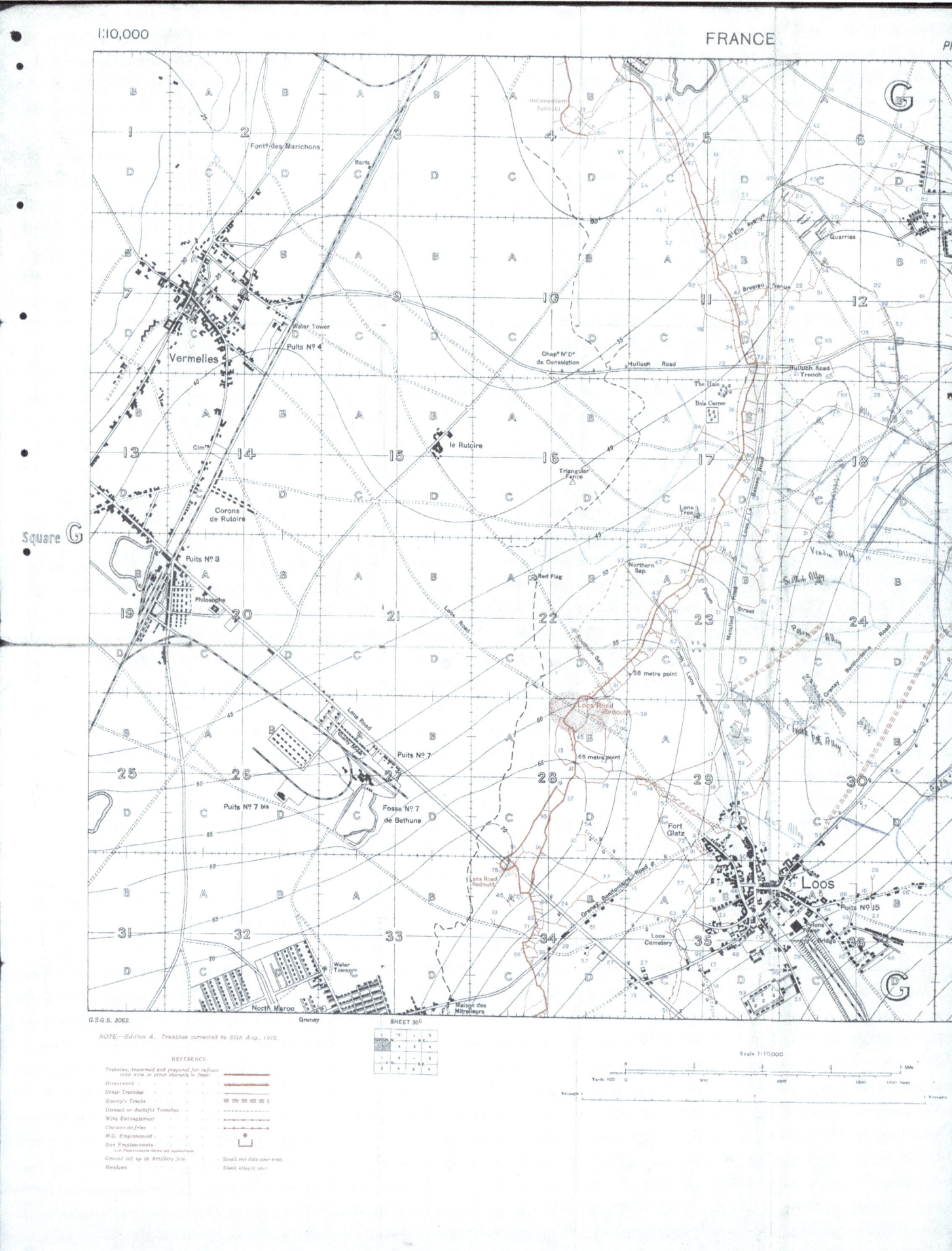

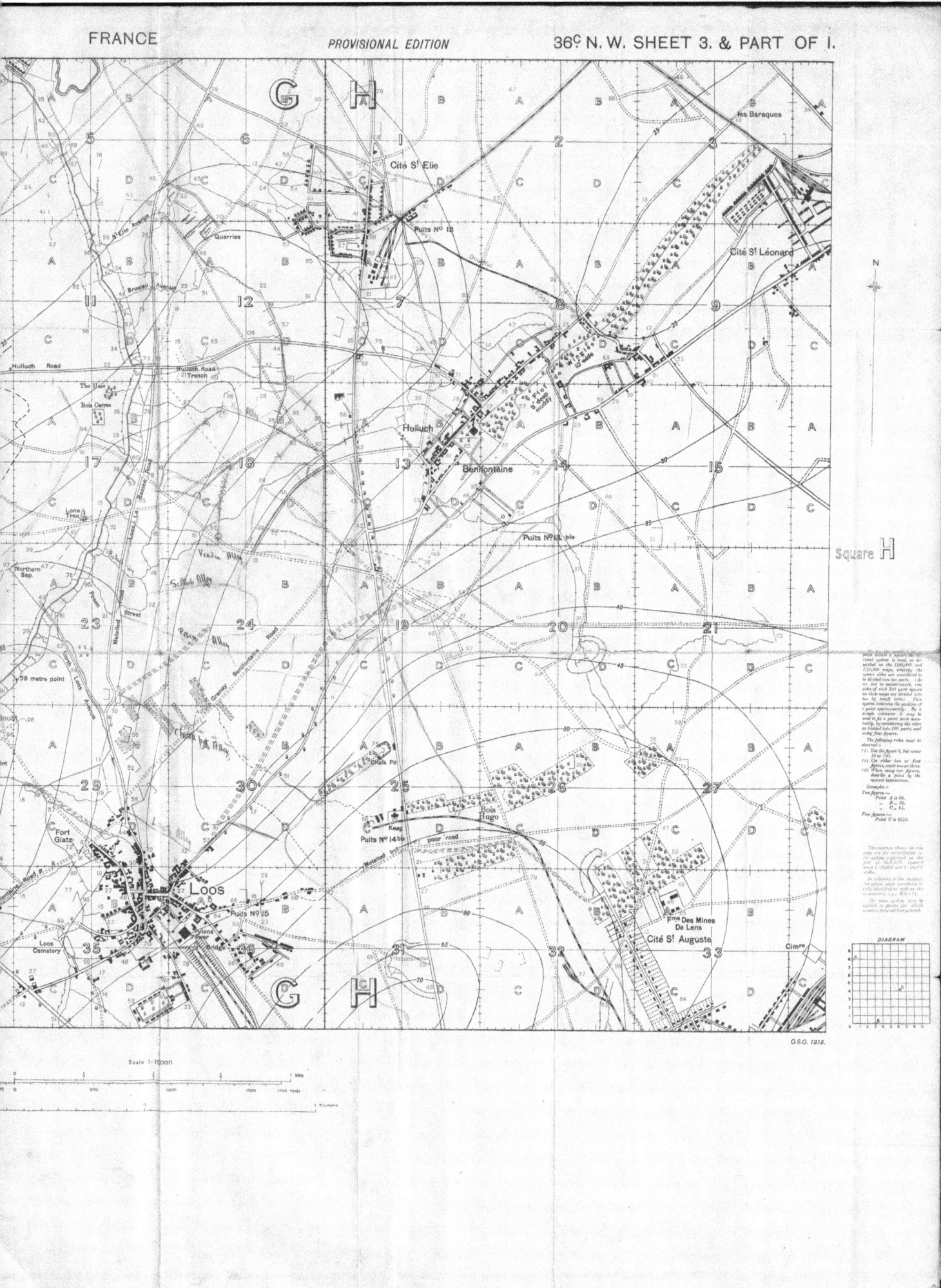

TRENCH MAP.

SHEET 36c N.W. 3 AND PART OF 4.

Scale 1 : 10,000

INDEX TO ADJOINING SHEETS.

CONFIDENTIAL

WAR DIARY

OF

7/8TH BATTALLION INNISKILLING FUSILIERS.

1st June 1918.

Army Form C. 2118.

WAR DIARY
or
INTELLIGENCE SUMMARY

(Erase heading not required.) 7/8th Royal Inniskilling Fusiliers

June 1918.

Place	Date	Hour	Summary of Events and Information	Remarks and references to Appendices
FRANCE	June 19th 1918		Training Staff still at FRENCQ Training Americans	
	20th		Training Staff moved to BERNULLES and took over training of 318th Regt. A.E.F.	
	23rd		Training Staff moved to STEENBECQUE and took over from 8th Bn Rifle Brigade 18 Officers and 357 O.R's and commenced work on G.H.Q. Lide designation of Bn 7/8th Royal Inniskilling Fusiliers (Reinforcing Bn)	
STEENBECQUE	30th		Battalion still at STEENBECQUE.	

Officers Joining
Lieut Col R.A. Impie C.M.G. M.O.D. Joined Bn 3.6.18
2 Lieut M.J. Danis M.C. Joined Bn 3.6.18
2 Lieut J.W.K. Wilkinson Joined Bn 10.6.18
Capt J.A.N. Bolton Joined Bn 12.6.18

Officers Quitting
Lieut. Col. R.A. Impie C.M.G. M.O.D. Invalided to Hospl 7/6/18
Capt L.A.W. French admitted to Hospl 12/6/18

C. Neal Captain
O.C. 7/8th (Rein) Bn Royal Inniskilling Fusiliers

Confidential

9830 — 76

War Diary
of
7/8th Battn. R. Innis. Fus.

July 1st 1918

July 31st 1918

Army Form C. 2118.

WAR DIARY
or
INTELLIGENCE SUMMARY.
(Erase heading not required.)

7/8th Royal Inniskilling Fusiliers / July 1918.

Instructions regarding War Diaries and Intelligence Summaries are contained in F. S. Regs., Part II. and the Staff Manual respectively. Title pages will be prepared in manuscript.

Place	Date	Hour	Summary of Events and Information	Remarks and references to Appendices
STEENBECQUE	1st to 3rd		Battalion still at STEENBECQUE working on G.H.Q. Line	
WESTROVE	3rd		Battalion moved by bus to WESTROVE.	
"	3rd to 6th		The time was spent in reorganising the Battalion	
LE-PARADIS	8th		Battalion marched to LE-PARADIS.	
NORDPEENE	9th		Battalion marched to NORD PEENE.	
STEENVOORDE	10th		Battalion marched to STEENVOORDE-AREA	
"	12th		The Battalion assembled on the WESTON MOLEN and VLENVICKHOVE Sector on the night 12/13th.	
"	13th		The Battalion less 1 Company moved back into Corps Reserve	
"	13th to 16th		Battalion still in Corps Reserve training Specialists etc.	
"	17th & 18th		The Battalion assembled less one Company on the WESTON MOLEN and VLENVICKHOVE SECTOR on the night 17/18th	
"	18th		The Battalion less 1 Company moved back into Corps Reserve.	
"	19th		Lieut Col R.A. Irvine C.M.G. D.S.O. returned from sick leave and assumed command of Bn.	
"	19th		'B' Company relieved 'D' Company in BERTHEN LINE	
"	19th to 24th		Battalion still in Corps Reserve training Specialists etc.	
"	25th		'B' Company was relieved by 2nd Coy in BERTHEN LINE and marched back to Camp	
"	26th		'C' Company was relieved in BERTHEN LINE and marched back to Camp	
"	26th to 31st		Battalion still in Corps Reserve training	
			Casualties	
			5 O.R.s Killed	
			8 " Wounded.	

Army Form C. 2118.

WAR DIARY
or
INTELLIGENCE SUMMARY.
(Erase heading not required.)

Instructions regarding War Diaries and Intelligence Summaries are contained in F. S. Regs., Part II. and the Staff Manual respectively. Title pages will be prepared in manuscript.

7/8th Royal Inniskilling Fusiliers   July 1918

Place	Date	Hour	Summary of Events and Information	Remarks and references to Appendices
STEENBECQUE	1-7-18		Officers Joining	
			2/Lieut R W Davison	
			2/Lieut H P Hunter	
			2/Lieut W Burke	
			1/Lieut W J Irwin	
			" A Green	
			" 2/H White	
			" W Mulligan	
			" H Haigh	
			2/Lieut W McCourt	
	5-7-18		Capt J A W Gough from Hospl	
STEENVOORDE	18-7-18		Lieut Col R A Irons CMG DSO from Sick Leave	
	28-7-18		Capt W M Knight	
	29-7-18		2/Lieut E R Anderson	
	"		" R Byers	
	"		2/Lieut H C May	

Officers Quitting

2/Lieut L Lyth to 2nd Notts Derby 12-7-18
Lieut E R Anderson to Base 18-7-18
" H Frame " 18-7-18
" R Byers " 18-7-18
" R J Boardley " 18-7-18
2/Lieut H C May " 18-7-18
" L J Marr 2nd Roy W Fus 20-7-18
" H Capel 8th North Staff 20-7-18

OXXX Major
for OC 7/8th Royal Inniskilling Fusiliers

Army Form C. 2118.

WAR DIARY
or
INTELLIGENCE SUMMARY.

VOL 31

War Diary
of
7/8th Battalion Royal Inniskilling Fusiliers
from 1st to 31st August, 1918

12.0
7 inst

Army Form C. 2118.

WAR DIARY
or
INTELLIGENCE SUMMARY.
(Erase heading not required.)

August 1918

Place	Date	Hour	Summary of Events and Information	Remarks and references to Appendices
STEENVOORDE	18/8		The Battalion in training near STEENVOORDE.	
BOESCHEPE 9th Aug. Ref. Sheet 27.S.E.+28.S.W. 1/20,000	9th Aug		The Battalion moved into Right Divisional Reserve (BOESCHEPE) on night of 9/10th August. "A" and "B" Coys. occupied area R.10.c. Central to R.11.a.3.5. "C" Coy. occupied R.9.b.9.9 to R.9.b.9.4. and "D" Coy. occupied position R.9.a.9.9 to R.9.a. Central. Transport Lines and Details remained at Q.10.c.6.9.	
Ref: BERTHEN 10.F VIETEREN 27 S.E. London Sheet 1/50,000	14/8		The Battalion relieved 17th Bn. Royal Scots in Support position (MONT NOIR) and MONT VIDAIGNE on night of 14th August. P.6.12. Order of march D, B, C and A Coys. "B" & "D" Coys. moving off at 4 p.m. and "A" and "C" Coys. moving off at 4.15 p.m. with 10 minutes interval between Coys., and 200 yards between Platoons.	
	19/20/8		Battalion relieved 7/8th London Regiment in front line on night of 19/20th August. "B" Coy. on Right front, "C" Coy. on Left front, "A" Coy. in support, "D" Coy. in Reserve. Battalion H.Q. M.29.b.9.3.	
Ref: SPECIAL LOCRE SHEET	21/8		At 1 a.m. on the morning of the 21st. "A" Coy. assembled on the line M.34.d.5.2. to M.34.b.5.2. the assembly was carried out quickly and very quietly and the enemy had no indication of our intentions. Two Platoons were in the front line and two in support. At the same time one Platoon of "B" Company assembled on the Sunken track at S.+ L Central (Bavast) The barrage started at 2.5. am. and from 2.20 to 2.25am	SG*

WAR DIARY or INTELLIGENCE SUMMARY

Army Form C. 2118.

Sheet 2

August 1918.

Place	Date	Hour	Summary of Events and Information	Remarks and references to Appendices
N.E. of SPECIAL LOOS B SHEET	21st		89th L.T.M. Battery fired on CABARET and trench junction at M.34.d.85.65. The advance started at 2.50 a.m. and all objectives were quickly gained. On the left about M.34.d.9.9. an enemy machine gun post offered some opposition but the post was rushed, the gun captured and the team killed or captured. On the rest of the front the enemy seems to have withdrawn under our barrage fire, and little opposition was encountered. A Company have consolidated x posts held by two new Lewis gun posts as follows:- M.34.d.9.3. M.34.d.95.45. M.34.d.95.65. and M.34.d.95.85. There are being rapidly wired and consolidated. The finding of a certain amount of enemy ammunition was due to the hurrying. The remaining two platoons of the Company held to the support trench approximately on the line M.34.d.7.0. - M.34.d.5.7. - M.34.d.8.9. This trench is left with 2nd Battalion South Lancs on the left. B Company have consolidated 2 Rifle section posts and 2 Lewis gun posts as follows:- S.4.b.7.7. - S.4.b.75.85. - M.34.d.5.0. and M.34.d.8.2. (south of Road junction) to trench with original line on the right. ENEMY	

Army Form C. 2118.

WAR DIARY
or
INTELLIGENCE SUMMARY.
(Erase heading not required.)

Sheet 3   August 1918

Place	Date	Hour	Summary of Events and Information	Remarks and references to Appendices
RET. SPECIAL LOOSE SHEET	21st		ENEMY. Patrols report the neighbourhood of our posts and the CABARET clear of the enemy. An enemy post was located at S.5.a.1.8. A bombing attack made on this post was abandoned as the enemy was found to be in strength and sufficient men to capture the post could not be spared from the consolidation parties. "A" Company captured 4 prisoners and 1 machine gun. Runner service was relied on to be slow, and it was to the enemy barrage was repeatedly cut, consequently reports came through slowly.	
	21/22nd		On the night of the 21/22nd August the KEMDEKOT sector was held by the Battalion with "B" and "A" Coys in the front line and "C" and "D" Coys in support. During the night a very heavy barrage was put down on the front line about 3 a.m. but the only infantry action which took place was a small bombing raid on the right Company, which was successfully repulsed.	
	22nd		The day of the 22nd passed quietly, and that night an inter-Coy relief took place, "D" Coy relieving "A" Coy, and "C" Coy relieved "B" Coy in the front line.	

Army Form C. 2118.

WAR DIARY
or
INTELLIGENCE SUMMARY.

Sheet 4

(Erase heading not required.)

Place	Date	Hour	Summary of Events and Information	Remarks and references to Appendices
REF. SPECIAL LOORE SHEET	23/24/4		On the night of the 23/24th the Battalion was ordered to take over the front line then held by the 2nd S. Lancs. Regt. on the S.E. of MOWBRAY WOOD. Front line posts from M.35.a.5.8 - M.35.a.8.2. and support line on the wood M.35.0.0.2 - M.35.0.2.5. "D" Coy was ordered to carry out the relief, 1 platoon going to the front line and 1 platoon in support. At 1 a.m. just before the relief was completed the enemy suddenly put down a very heavy barrage of artillery, trench mortars and machine guns on the front line and back areas. The posts on the right of the new sector, and this battalion's original left post S. of the River DOUVE were rushed, the Outlying Commander of the 2nd S. Lancs Coy was wounded, and consequently there was a certain amount of confusion. The enemy having penetrated on the right of the new line, tried to work his way round behind the left hand posts. He was not taught to the last; one was knocked out by a direct hit from a shell, and one containing Lewis gunner was seen firing his gun to the last. The other line South of the DOUVE formed a defensive flank, and assisted by the left front posts in MOWBRAY WOOD succeeded in keeping off the enemy when the situation became quiet about 3 a.m. Officers commanding "D" Coy satisfied himself that his original front line South of the DOUVE	

Army Form C. 2118.

WAR DIARY
or
INTELLIGENCE SUMMARY.
(Erase heading not required.)

Sheet 5

August 1916

Place	Date	Hour	Summary of Events and Information	Remarks and references to Appendices
REF: SPECIAL LOCRE SHEET	03/9/16		DOUVE was free of the enemy. Having heard nothing to indicate that the relief was complete in MOWBRAY WOOD, he went over to that part of the front. He found that a number of his own men, and that the area (incl. our killed and wounded, several were missing, but the area was) cleared of the enemy so far as he could see. Two patrols on the left of the front line remained on "red" by the Battalion and one by the 2nd South Lancs. There were no men in the support line. By this time it was dawn, and further troop movements were impossible. The front line was held by the crew of the Lewis gun on the left flank of MOWBRAY WOOD and by the offensive patrol south of the Pur. DOUVE. As the total strength of "B" Coy. was now only about 68, orders were issued to "A" Coy. to take over the front and support lines in MOWBRAY WOOD, one platoon in front line and one in support, one in the assembly trenches at STARLING FARM and the fourth at LOCRE CHATEAU. "D" Coy. re-established the line south of the DOUVE to the CABARET, one platoon in the front line and one in support S.E. of KOUDEKOT. This operation was completed at 1 p.m. on the night of the 24/25/7 D Coy. casualties were about 27 in all including 9 reported	

Army Form C. 2118.

Sheet 6

WAR DIARY
or
INTELLIGENCE SUMMARY.
(Erase heading not required.)

August 1918

Place	Date	Hour	Summary of Events and Information	Remarks and references to Appendices
REF. LOCRE 10,000 + SHEET 27 1/40,000	25/26th		The Battalion was relieved by 2/17th London Regt on the night of 25/26th August, and proceeded to BOESCHEPE where they were billeted. On 28th Augt. the Brig-Major Lt Col. R.A. Browne C.M.G., D.S.O. took over Command of 69th Infantry Brigade. Major C. O'Healy M.C. assumed temporary Command of the Battalion.	
REF. SHEET 27 S.E. & 28 S.W. 1/20,000	31st		On the night of the 31st the Battalion moved into Brigade Support on MONT VIDAIGNE, and relieved the 2nd South Lancs. Regt.	

Newfough
Major

For Officer Commanding 7/8 Bn. The Inniskilling Fus.

9837 89/30

13.0
8 sheets

Confidential

War Diary

of

7/8 (S) Battn. R. Innis. Fus.

From 1-9-18
To 30-9-18

War Diary of
7/8 (D) Bn. Royal Inniskilling Fusiliers
from 1st Sept 1918 to 30th Sept 1918.

WAR DIARY / INTELLIGENCE SUMMARY

Army Form C. 2118.

7/8th Royal Innis. Fus.

Place	Date	Hour	Summary of Events and Information	Remarks and references to Appendices
R.S.F. 27.S.E & 28.S.W. 1/2 (Contoured Sheet) EDITION 1ᴮ	Sept 1/2		S.A.A. The Battalion moved from [ ] + took up position at A Coy (Left) + B Coy (Right) — the front line from T.7 to 6.5 to T.18.a.39.	
		4.15 P.M.	C Coy — Support at T.12.a.39. – 9.9.3 by — Reserve at INKERMAN CAMP. The B. Batt. was ordered to attack NEUVE EGLISE and take up a position about 1500ˣ front and one Coy to support + one Coy — Reserve. Bn attack on a two Coy front and H.Q. was at T.14.a.29. Lt. [illegible] + attacked NEUVE EGLISE + Regt. Bank note — front road at T.18.a.39. Having entrained occupied road within 30ˣ of NEUVE E.G./25 when seven of companies organised for the G. final objective. Companies worked their way forward but failed to reach line.	
		9.30 A.M.	A Coy was then with T.9.c.2.3. — T.14.d.9.5. B Coy came up — support of B, the reached but the right Coy (B) was outflanked. The attack was the right from the road near met by Lewis m.g. fire. As its flank was in the air and down to E. T.14.6 – 7.7.5 — T.14 t.5.7 had to make D Coy was then ordered to support B by one Coy the 2nd L. known as of Brigadier General came to Bn H.Q. at T.14.a.2 + supervised the attack on an attack was ordered at once. Meanwhile Patrols from A + B Coys secured touch with the enemy. It was 1.45 A.M.	

Army Form C. 2118.

WAR DIARY
or
INTELLIGENCE SUMMARY.
(Erase heading not required.)

1/8th R. Irwin. Inn.

Instructions regarding War Diaries and Intelligence Summaries are contained in F. S. Regs., Part II. and the Staff Manual respectively. Title pages will be prepared in manuscript.

Place	Date	Hour	Summary of Events and Information	Remarks and references to Appendices
REF: 27.S.15 + 28 S.W (COMBINED SHEET) EDITION 1 B	2nd		At 2.30 A.M. A & B Coys attacked & were supported by C & D Coys attacked r— mile & heavy M.G. fire from tied planks above the village and enabled A & B Coys mostly on line T.15.b.3.8 — T.15.6.9.1 — T.15.c.6.9 — T.14.d.9.5. These companies were now on the line – D Company dug in support at T.14.d.2.6. at 5.30 A.M. on the 2nd April. T.15.d. (Batt HQrs) took over the line & the Batt moved into ~~T.1~~ appx T.1.d.	
	3rd		The Batt moved to S.4.d. and went in Bde Reserve.	
	5th		Batt was in Bde Reserve. Operations were to take place had Fine Batt cancelled.	
	6th		Batt march to E.M.346 1.9. where training was carried out.	
	8th /17		Batt relieved 9th London Devons in what was subsequently known as the NEUVE EGLISE LINE. A & B Coy went to Front Line. The former was Frontwork from N.33.6.36.5 N.27.d.1.8. The latter from N.32.6.4.5 N.33.6.3.6. C Coy was in support Front Line from N.32.6.4.5 to N.33.a.7.3. D Coy was in support in area N.32.6. Batt. H.Q. was at N.31.a.7.3. Intermittently heavy shelling and bombardment which Bn Scout & Bridge for intermittently heavy shelling the town passed without incident.	

D. D. & L., London, E.C.
(A8001) Wt. W1771/M2931 750,000 5/17 Sch. 52 Forms C.2118/14

Army Form C. 2118.

WAR DIARY
or
INTELLIGENCE SUMMARY. 7/8th Royal Innis. Fus.
(Erase heading not required.)

Instructions regarding War Diaries and Intelligence Summaries are contained in F. S. Regs., Part II. and the Staff Manual respectively. Title pages will be prepared in manuscript.

Place	Date	Hour	Summary of Events and Information	Remarks and references to Appendices
REF 27.S.E & 28.S.W (Combined Sheet) EDITION 1.B	14th		Batt was relieved in the NEUVE EGLISE LINE by the 16th Cheshire Regt. and marched to WEST OUTRE (in area M.15.a.2.8).	
"	15th		Drainage was carried out.	
"	16th		Lt Col. Irvine, having handed over command of Bayonet to Brig. Gen. Laurie, resumed command of the Batt.	
"	17th		Brig. Gen. Laurie inspected the Battalion.	
"	18th		Drainage was continued.	
"	19th		— DO —	
"	20th		The Batt. relieved the 9/16 London Regt in area about ULSTER CAMP, KRUDEKOT (M.34.d.) LOCRE CHATEAU (M.34.b.) A Coy was on ULSTER CAMP, (O. by) was in KRUDEKOT area, C.D Coys in LOCRECHATEAU area & H.Q. and ULSTER CAMP. D.L.B. attacked. Tramway line was used in supply [M.22/23]	
PLOEGSTEERT EDITION 5C (LOCAL) and 27.S.E & 28.S.W (Combined Sheet) EDITION 1.B	21st 22nd 23rd		The Batt. moved into the Right Sub Sector from U.I.C.57 to U.I.A.5.0. A Coy was in front line on the left from U.I.C.57 to U.I.C.8.5. B Coy was front line from U.I.C.8.5 to U.I.A.5.0. D Coy in support at T.B.C. central & C Coy in Reserve at T.B.d. central. On the night of 24/25th, B Coy relieved A Coy and D Coy relieved B Coy. C Coy and and enemy patrol which was driven in by our patrol Scissors Piperoman Hy Coy farm. D Coy sent out a strong patrol	

Army Form C. 2118.

WAR DIARY
INTELLIGENCE SUMMARY. 7/8th Royal Innis. Fus.

(Erase heading not required.)

Instructions regarding War Diaries and Intelligence Summaries are contained in F. S. Regs., Part II. and the Staff Manual respectively. Title pages will be prepared in manuscript.

Place	Date	Hour	Summary of Events and Information	Remarks and references to Appendices
PLOEGSTEERT EDITION 5C (LOCAL)	25/26		which seemed to foreman and 1 machine gun.	
	26/27		B Coy sent in a strong patrol without encountering any of the enemy. It travelled about 1700x - front of the patrol. During the time complete supremacy of No MAN'S LAND was secured.	
	26/27.		The Batt was relieved by the 91st London Regt. moved into ULSTER CAMP area. Bn H.Q. Who at ULSTER CAMP; and A Coy also. C + D Coys were situated at LOCRE CHATEAU area. B Coy was in KUDEKOT area about M 34.d.2.5. — M 34.d.7.2. and remained in rest until the evening of the 29th Sept.	
REF. BELGIUM PART OF FRANCE SHEET 28 S.W.	28/29th		The Batt moved into Bde. Reserve on the NEUVE EGLISE LINE. Bn. H.Q. was in LINDENHOEK DUGOUTS at N.27 central. A coy was in dugouts at N.27.d. B. by in area N.33.6. C.by - SUNKEN ROAD at N.27c + N.33.a. D.by in area about N.33.a. + N.33.c.	
PLOEGSTEERT EDITION 5C (LOCAL)	29 ✓		The Bn moved on to the WULVERGHEM RIDGE. H.Q.d RE FARM.	
	30 ✗		Batt at above position	

3/9/18.

R M Hardy Major
7/8 R. Innis. Fus.

Army Form C. 2118.

WAR DIARY
or
INTELLIGENCE SUMMARY.
(Erase heading not required.)

7/8th R[oyal] Innis[killing] Fus[iliers]

Place	Date	Hour	Summary of Events and Information	Remarks and references to Appendices
	3/9/18		Officers Joined 2/Lt R.H. Ingham 6/9/18 2/Lt Grt. Hickman L.W. — " — Lt J.P. Orwin 24/9/18 2/Lt m.P. Boyd — " — 2/Lt D.J. Statham — " — 2/Lt J.L. Colwell 20/9/18	
			Officer Casualties. 2/Lt E.H. Shaw 9/9/18 wounded " H.P. Hindle — " — 2/Lt N.L. McCant — " — 2/Lt J.W. Burke 29/9/18 killed " J.H. Barr — " — " " R. Irvine — " — " Hospital. Lt. J.A. Jamieson 18/9/18 Capt. J.W. Marks M.C. 8/9/18	
			C.H. Keely Major 7/8 R. Innis Fus.	

Army Form C. 2118.

WAR DIARY
or
INTELLIGENCE SUMMARY.

(Erase heading not required.)

War Diary
of
7/8th Battalion Royal Inniskilling Fusiliers

from 1st to 31st October, 1918.

WAR DIARY
INTELLIGENCE SUMMARY

Army Form C. 2118.

October 1918

Place	Date	Hour	Summary of Events and Information	Remarks and references to Appendices
M.35.d.85.50 SHEET 28	1/2/3/4		The Battalion in position on WULVERGHEM RIDGE, in Reserve, with Battalion Headquarters at P.E. FARM M.35.d.85.50.	
SHEET 28 & 8/9 P.12.c.6.8	5/6		The Battalion moved into the line relieving the 5th A. & S. Highlanders and one Coy. of the K.O.S.B., D and C Coys. being in frontline from Q.13.b.30.55 to Q.8.c.7.4 with dividing line at Q.9.d.7.3, C Coy. being on the right. A Coy. in Support at P.18. Central and B Coy. in Reserve at P.12.c. Battalion Headquarters at P.12.d.6.8.	
— —	11th		On 11th instant the enemy bombarded Bn Headquarters with H.E. and mustard gas shells from about 2h.m. until 8h.m. The Commanding Officer, Lieut Col J.A. Burne, C.M.G., D.S.O., Captain J.S. Thompson M.C. Acting Adjutant, Lieut E.A. Woulfe, Signal Officer, Captain D. Roche O.C. and Captain M.J. McMahon M.O. U.S.A. were all removed to hospital suffering from gas poison as also will 6th Lieuts of the Headquarters, Captain P.C. Holmes took over Command of Battalion in absence of Major C.J. Healy, M.C. on leave.	
	11/12th		The Battalion was relieved on night of 11/12th October and	

WAR DIARY
or
INTELLIGENCE SUMMARY

(Erase heading not required.)

Army Form C. 2118.

October 1918

Place	Date	Hour	Summary of Events and Information	Remarks and references to Appendices
O.25. Central SHEET 28	11/12		moved to the village of WYTCHAETE. The Battalion moved to HOUTHEM	
	16th		The Battalion moved to area G.19.	
SHEET 28	18th		The Battalion moved to the area STERHOEK, PSTITZER, LEDRUN, CORNET, PETIT CORNIL	
SHEET 28 & 29 1/40,000	19th		The Battalion moved to area ROLLEGHEM, LE COMPAS, TOMBROEK. Battalion moved into Brigade Reserve in area about T.18.6 and T.24.	
"	20th		Battalion moved into area about T.30 and U.35. Major C.L. Healy M.C. assumed command of Battalion	
"	23rd		on his return from leave, and is authorized to wear the badges of rank of Lieut Colonel. Captain R.C.E	
"	"		Hahns took over the duties of 2nd in Command.	
" - O.31	25th		The Battalion moved into area O.31 Central Headquarters at O.31.d.30.40.	
" - "	28th			
	31st		Headquarters moved to O.31.6.2.4.	

C.L. Healy
Lieut Colonel
Commanding 7/8 Bn R. Inniskilling Fus.

WAR DIARY

OF

7/8th BATTN. ROYAL INNISKILLING FUSILIERS

Nov. 1st To Nov. 30th 1918

Army Form C. 2118.

WAR DIARY
or
INTELLIGENCE SUMMARY.
(Erase heading not required.)

November 1918

Instructions regarding War Diaries and Intelligence Summaries are contained in F. S. Regs., Part II. and the Staff Manual respectively. Title pages will be prepared in manuscript.

Place	Date	Hour	Summary of Events and Information	Remarks and references to Appendices
Sheet 28 & 29 Y.30000	1/11		The Battalion in positions at O.31. with Battalion Headquarters at O.31. b.2.4.	
Sheet 29 Y.30000	4/11		The Battalion moved into the line relieving the 3/4 London Regt and 2/5 London Regt with forward companies through P.25, P.20, & P.21 and outposts on the line of the R. L'ivesse. Battalion Headquarters at P.26. b.50.65.	
"	7/11		The Battalion were relieved on the line by the 12th Batt. Norfolk Regt and proceeded to area about O.31, 34 & 37.	
"	9th		Battalion moved forward to HEESTERT-MOEN-KLIJTTE area	
"	10th		Battalion moved to WATTRIPONT and then on to RENAIX area.	
TOURNAI 5 Y.30000	11th		The Battalion arrived at 7 a.m. to move forward to establish an outpost line in front of GHOY leaving through the 3/4 London Regt & 2nd Batt Sixth Essex Regt. At 8.30 a.m. orders in the march were received so that the Armistice had been signed and hostilities would cease at 11 a.m. Previous to the hour the 9th Dragoon Guards passed through us to form an outpost line, which was withdrawn by us in the afternoon. Battalion headquarters at GHY.	
Sheet 30 & 38	14th		Battalion moved back to RENAIX	
Sheet 29 Z.30000	16th		Battalion moved to ST JENOIS	
"	17th		Battalion moved to LINGHE	
TOURNAI 5	20th		Battalion moved to LINSELLES being the first stage on a five days march to WALLON-CAPEL area	

Army Form C. 2118.

WAR DIARY
or
INTELLIGENCE SUMMARY.
(Erase heading not required.)

Instructions regarding War Diaries and Intelligence Summaries are contained in F.S. Regs., Part II. and the Staff Manual respectively. Title pages will be prepared in manuscript.

Place	Date	Hour	Summary of Events and Information	Remarks and references to Appendices
TOURNAI / HAZEBROUCK	29		Battalion continued moved to FUNQUEREAU	
HAZEBROUCK	30		Battalion continued moved to LA GORGUE. The following Officers reinforcements joined the Battalion	
			2/Lieut S. Hilbo	
			" A. Garner	
			" S.P. Kibby	
			" A. Franklin	
			" L. Mead	
			" J.M. Lambert	
			" J.N. Sherwood	

A.P. Healy Lieut-Colonel.
Commanding 11th Battn. Royal Inniskilling Fusiliers

WW 38

WAR DIARY

OF

7/8th Bn. ROYAL INNISKILLING FUS.

Dec 1st to Dec 31st 1916

WAR DIARY
or
INTELLIGENCE SUMMARY.

Army Form C. 2118.

December 1918

Place	Date	Hour	Summary of Events and Information	Remarks and references to Appendices
Sheet HAZEBROUCK 5A	1 Dec 18		Battalion moved to ST VENANT.	
	2 Dec 18		Battalion arrived at WALLON CAPPEL, being the destination, after a march of 5 days	
			Battalion inspected by G.O.C. 89th Infantry Brigade	
	21 Dec		Battalion still at WALLON CAPPEL	
	31 Dec			
			Officers Joining 2/Lieut W.H. Stephens reported for duty	
			" E. Moore " "	
			Capt R.V. Hope " "	
			2/Lieut J.H. Edwards " "	
			2/Lieut J.S. Farmer " "	
			Officers Quitting	
			1/Lieut A. Harris M.C. transferred to England sick 22/11/16	
			Capt F.A.N. Bolton on Sick Leave and ordered Medical Board.	

O.V. Neely Lieut. Col.
Commanding 1/6th Batt. Royal Inniskilling Fusiliers

7/8 R. Inniskilling Fus.
January 1919

WAR DIARY
or
INTELLIGENCE SUMMARY

Army Form C. 2118.

Place	Date	Hour	Summary of Events and Information	Remarks and references to Appendices
HAZEBROUCK	1919 1 Jany		Battalion still at WALLON-CAPPEL	
	11 Jany		Battalion moved to WARDRECQUES	
	11 Jany		Battalion entrained at EBBLINGHEM en route for BOULOGNE to be employed on Demobilization work, at St Martin Camp. ("B"Bn),("C" & "D" Coys being attd to 2nd Batln. South Lancs Regt. for duty at Ostrohove Camp.) (Signed)	
			Officers leaving:	
			1 Major R.B. Ralston (gone sick) for duty	
			Officers Quitting:	
			Capt. J. M. Toms having been ordered Medical Board on Short of the strength 29/1/19	
			2/Lt. C.J. Moore having proceeded to England on Leave on Expiration 24/1/19 reckoned off strength	
			2/Lieut. J.B. Ruckley posted to join 2nd Batn. R. Dublin Fus on 20/1/19 & struck off strength	
			W.S. Holmes, Major	
			Commanding 7&8th Battn R. Inniskilling Fus	

CONFIDENTIAL.

WAR DIARY OF

7/8th Bn. Royal Inniskilling Fusiliers

FROM 1st February, 1919 TO 28th February, 1919.

CONFIDENTIAL.

Army Form C. 2118.

WAR DIARY
or
INTELLIGENCE SUMMARY.
(Erase heading not required.)

February 1919

Instructions regarding War Diaries and Intelligence Summaries are contained in F. S. Regs., Part II. and the Staff Manual respectively. Title pages will be prepared in manuscript.

Place	Date	Hour	Summary of Events and Information	Remarks and references to Appendices
Boulogne	1st	1919	Battalion still at BOULOGNE (St MARTIN CAMP) carrying out the duties of demobilization. D Company transferred from OSTROHOVE CAMP to St MARTIN CAMP. C Company attached to 2/South Lancs kept for duty at OSTROHOVE CAMP. Officers Joining Capt & S.C. Gifford Lieut Burtip M.C. " Taylor V M.C. 2/Lt Cockell E.C. " Wright A.F. " Shaw H.R. M.C. " Proudfoot G.R. " Buswell G.G. " Dopres H.J. " McConnell W.R. Lieut J. P. Quinn rejoined from Hospital 18.2.19	
	10th		Officers Quitting Lieut R. Green to Eng for demobilization 14.2.19 2/Lt H.A. Powell " " " " " J.A. Sherwood " " " " " G.H. Aylward " " " " Lieut J. Haigh M.C. Evacuated to England 26.2.19	

R.C. Holcroft Fn. Lt Col
Commanding 18th Royal Innikillings Fus

Army Form C. 2118.

WAR DIARY
or
INTELLIGENCE SUMMARY.
(Erase heading not required.)

Instructions regarding War Diaries and Intelligence Summaries are contained in F. S. Regs., Part II. and the Staff Manual respectively. Title pages will be prepared in manuscript.

Place	Date	Hour	Summary of Events and Information	Remarks and references to Appendices
St.Martin Camp. BOULOGNE.	1/3/19 to 31/3/19.		The Battalion during the month was still carrying on Demobilization duties at St.Martin Camp, Boulogne. Reinforcements arrived from the 1st, 2nd, 5th, 6th, 9th and 13th Battalions Royal Inniskilling Fusiliers and also from the 5th Bn. Royal Irish Fusiliers.	
			The following Officers joined the Battalion :-	
	3/3/19.		Lieut.W.Grentham. 2nd Lieut. D.B.Walker. 2nd Lieut. W.C.Phipps. 2nd Lieut.J.E.Phillips. Captain E.N.Flook. 2nd Lieut. J.Ellison. 2nd Lieut. D.Nicholls.	
	5/3/19.		Captain G.R.Roche Kelly. 2nd Lieut.G.E.Brown. 2nd Lieut. J.E.O'Neill. 2nd Lieut. G.L.Chambers. 2nd Lieut.J.W.Hart.	
	24/3/19.		Captain (T/Major) J.Tynan, D.S.O.	
	26/3/19.		2nd Lieut. J.J.Morris, M.M.	
	27/3/19.		Capt. D.T.Figgis. Capt. G.H.Gallogly. 2nd Lieut. J.Carroll, M.C. Lieut.A.E.Browne. Capt. W.A.Beattie, M.C. 2nd Lieut.P.J.T.Cator. 2nd Lieut. P.L.Davis. Lieut.H.B.Reynell. 2nd Lieut.J.Thornton. 2nd Lieut.L.Ward,D.C.M. 2nd Lieut. G.E.Chiplin. 2nd Lieut. J.G.Nicholls. 2nd Lieut.T.J.Gallagher.	
	31/3/19.		2nd Lieut. H.Stevens.	
			The following Officers were struck off strength :-	
	1/3/19.		a/Capt.J.Haigh, M.C. Evacuated to England "Sick".	
	13/3/19.		2nd Lieut.W.Mead. To England for demobilization.	
	27/3/19.		" A.Garner. " " " "	
	29/3/19.		Lieut.J.P.Quinn. " " " "	

.... Lieut.Col.
Commanding 7/8th Bn.Royal Inniskilling Fusiliers.

Army Form C. 2118.

WAR DIARY
or
INTELLIGENCE SUMMARY.
(Erase heading not required.)

Place	Date	Hour	Summary of Events and Information	Remarks and references to Appendices
St.Martin Camp, BOULOGNE.	11/4/19. 25/4/19.		The Battalion during the month in question was still at St.Martin Camp, Boulogne, carrying on Demobilization duties. "B" Company at OSTROHOVE CAMP rejoined Battalion at St.Martin Camp. "C" Company moved to St. Omer to be employed on Guard duties, etc.	
	1/4/19.		The following Officers joined the Battalion :- Lieut. R.H.Spurgin. 2nd Lieut. A.F.Folley.	
	7/4/19. 21/4/19. 28/4/19.		The following Officers were struck off strength :- 2nd Lieut. J.E. Furner. To England for demobilization. Lieut.A/Capt. W.G.Groombridge proceeded to England on 2 months leave prior to joining Reg.Army. 2nd Lieut. J.Carroll, M.C. ditto. " T.J.Gallagher. ditto.	

R.H...... Lieut.Colonel,
Commanding 7/8th Bn. Royal Inniskilling Fusiliers.

WAR DIARY
or
INTELLIGENCE SUMMARY.

(Erase heading not required.)

Army Form C. 2118.

Place	Date	Hour	Summary of Events and Information	Remarks and references to Appendices
Saint Martin Camp, Boulogne.			During the month in question, the Battalion was situated at St.Martin Camp, Boulogne, carrying on Demobilization duties, "Q" Company remaining at Saint Omer.	
			The following officers joined during the month :-	
	4/5/19.		Captain G.H.R.Lyndon, M.C. Captain W.Moore, M.C.	
	21/5/19.		Lieut. W.Geraghty, P.	
			The undermentioned were struck off strength.-	
	23/5/19.		Major J.Tynan, D.S.O. proceeded to take over Command of 7th R.Irish Rgt.	
	24/5/19.		Lieut.J.Taylor, M.C. " join 17th R.Sussex Rgt.	
	15/5/19.		2nd Lieut. J.K.Cassells evacuated and S. of S.	
	24/5/19		" C.G.Brown to England for demobilisation.	
	25/4/19		Captain A.V.Myles. To join Russian Expeditionary Force 25/4/19.	

..................Lieut.Colonel,

Commanding 7/8th Battalion Royal Inniskilling Fusiliers.

Army Form C. 2118.

WAR DIARY
or
INTELLIGENCE SUMMARY.
(Erase heading not required.)

7/8 R. Inniskilling

Instructions regarding War Diaries and Intelligence Summaries are contained in F. S. Regs., Part II. and the Staff Manual respectively. Title pages will be prepared in manuscript.

Place	Date	Hour	Summary of Events and Information	Remarks and references to Appendices
Saint Martin Camp, BOULOGNE.	June		During the month in question, the Battalion was situated at St.Martin Camp, Boulogne, carrying on Demobilization Duties, "Q" Company remaining at Saint Omer. The following Officers were struck off strength :-	
	2.6.19.		2nd Lieut. S.B.Kibbey, proceeded to England form demobilization.	
	4.6.19.		Captain R.C.E.Holmes " "	
	11.6.19.		2nd Lieut. S.Kelso " "	

...................Lieut.Colonel,

Commanding 7/8th Bn.Royal Inniskilling Fusiliers.

WAR DIARY
or
INTELLIGENCE SUMMARY.

(Erase heading not required.)

Army Form C. 2118.

7/8 R.Innis. Fusiliers 30

Place	Date	Hour	Summary of Events and Information	Remarks and references to Appendices
Saint Martin Camp, BOULOGNE.			During the month in question, the Battalion was situated at St.Martin Camp, Boulogne, carrying on Demobilization Duties, "C" Company remaining at St Omer.	
	9/7/19.		The following Officer joined during the month :- Captain E.D.Morrison M.C.	
	8/7/19.		The following Officer was struck off the strength :- 2nd Lieut G.H.Coleman.	

29/7/19.

Lieut. Colonel
Commdg 7/8 R.Innis. Fusiliers

Army Form C. 2118.

WAR DIARY
or
INTELLIGENCE SUMMARY.
(Erase heading not required.)

Instructions regarding War Diaries and Intelligence Summaries are contained in F. S. Regs., Part II. and the Staff Manual respectively. Title pages will be prepared in manuscript.

Place	Date	Hour	Summary of Events and Information	Remarks and references to Appendices
St.Martin Camp.	1.8.19.		The Battalion continued carrying on Demobilization Duties at St.Martin Camp, Boulogne, "C" Company remaining at St.Omer.	
	20.8.19.		The Battalion ceased to be employed on Demobilization Duties at St.Martin Camp, and moved to Henriville Camp, Boulogne, "C" Company remaining at St.Omer.	
Henriville Camp.	22.8.19.		Major A.J.W.Fitzmaurice took over command of the Battalion vice Lieut.Colonel C.F.Healy, M.C. on leave to U.K.	
	24.8.19.		The Battalion was presented with the King's Colour by Brig. General Ramsey, C.B., C.M.G., D.S.O. The following Officers were on parade:— Major A.J.W.Fitzmaurice, Capt. J.Shuly M.C. Capt. A.I.Philpot. Capt. N.Robson M.C. Capt. J.Berry. 2nd.Lieut.J.F.Caldwell. 2nd.Lieut.D.V.Sheehan. Lieut.R.Keays. The parade consisted of 81 other Ranks. The Colours were consecrated by the Rev. Father C.O'Rorke,H.C.,C.F.	
			The following Officers reported for Duty.	
	2.8.19.		Major A.J.W.Fitzmaurice. Captain J.Sherry.	
	30.8.19.			
			The following Officer Rejoined.	
	1.8.19.		2nd.Lieut. H.R.Shawe,M.C.	
	7.8.19.		Captain G.Kennedy.	

 ....Major,
Commdg. 7/8th. Bn. The Royal Inniskilling Fusiliers.

Army Form C. 2118.

WAR DIARY
or
INTELLIGENCE SUMMARY.
(Erase heading not required).

Instructions regarding War Diaries and Intelligence Summaries are contained in F. S. Regs., Part II. and the Staff Manual respectively. Title pages will be prepared in manuscript.

Place	Date	Hour	Summary of Events and Information	Remarks and references to Appendices
Henriville Camp.	26.9.19.		The Cadre proceeded to U.K. consisting of 5 Officers and 40 other ranks	
			The following Officers quitted.	
	4.9.19.		Captain J.J.Barry proceeded to England for demob.	
	11.9.19.		2nd Lt. G.R.Proudfoot. " " " " "	
	12.9.19.		Captain G.E.B.Lyndon. " " " " "	
	14.9.19.		Lieut. J.C.Eastbury " duty with No.37 Labour Company.	
			" G.O.Burige M.C. " " " 58 " "	
			" T.V.Browne " " " 61 " "	
			2nds D.B.Walker " " " 58 " "	
			" W.R.McConnell " " " 65 " "	
			" W.C.Phipps " " " 61 " "	
			" J.W.Hart " " " 51 " "	
			" W.Draper " " " 59 " "	
	15.9.19.		Captain W.Moore M.C. transferred to D.D.O.S.5th Area	
	16.9.19.		Lieut. W.A.Beattie M.C. " " South Lancashire Regt.	
	19.9.19.		" A.E.Browne transferred to No.513 P.O.W.Company	
			" P.J.T.Oster " " " 61 Labour "	
			" H.B.Reynell " " " 51 " "	
			" N.W.Gore Hickman " " " 51 " "	
	21.9.19.		2nd Lt. J.L.Chambers " " " 65 " "	
	26.9.19.		Lt.Col. O.F.Healy M.C. proceeded to U.K.for demob.	
			Captain A.E.Balfour " " " " "	
			Lieut. R.W.Davison M.C. " " " " "	
			" A.J.Wright " " " " "	
			" W.Grantham " " " " "	

.... Major,
Commanding 7/8th Bn. Royal Inniskilling Fusiliers.

30TH DIVISION
89TH INFY BDE

2ND BN STH LANCS REGT
JLY 1918-MAR 1919

FROM 25 DN
75 BDE

Confidential

Vol 46

War Diary

2nd Battn. S. Lanc. Regt

47A
15 sheets

1st–31st July 1918

2nd Battalion South Lancashire Regiment

War diary.

1st to 31st July 1916

12 pages.

Army Form C. 2118.

WAR DIARY
or
INTELLIGENCE SUMMARY.
(Erase heading not required.)

Instructions regarding War Diaries and Intelligence Summaries are contained in F. S. Regs., Part II. and the Staff Manual respectively. Title pages will be prepared in manuscript.

Place	Date 1918	Hour	Summary of Events and Information	Remarks and references to Appendices
	Monday 1 July		Battalion arrived by march route at BAYENGHEM about 4 am and enjoyed billets.	
			All rest during the day. Battalion now in 89th Infantry Brigade, 30th Division.	
	Tuesday 2 July		Fine day. Training in progress. Battalion inspected by Brig. Gen. R.M. CURRIE. D.S.O. Commanding 89th Inf. Bde.	
	Wednesday 3 July		Fine day. Dispositions unchanged. Training continues.	
			Transport of Battalion inspected by B.G. to 89th Inf. Bde.	
			Lieut. A.L. CLAYDON rejoined.	
			His rendezvous officer also joined.	
			2nd Lieuts. JOHN BROWN — WILLIAM HENRY DUTTON — RICHARD WILLIAM WREN — S. Lan R	
	Thursday 4 July		Very fine day. Dispositions unchanged. Training continues.	
			Lieut. A FERGUSON M.C. rejoined from 75th Inf. Bde.	

Army Form C. 2118.

WAR DIARY
or
INTELLIGENCE SUMMARY.
(Erase heading not required.)

Instructions regarding War Diaries and Intelligence Summaries are contained in F. S. Regs., Part II. and the Staff Manual respectively. Title pages will be prepared in manuscript.

Place	Date	Hour	Summary of Events and Information	Remarks and references to Appendices
	1918			
	Friday 5 July		This day - Inspection workgroups - training continues	
			Undermentioned officers join Colony.	
			2nd Lieut. EDMUND BARDSLEY	
			PETER JOSEPH NOLAN } S. Lan. R.	
			CHARLES GORDON HARRISON.	
	Saturday 6 July		This day Inspection workgroups. Training continues.	
			2nd Lieut ANDREW MORROW S. Lan. R. joins.	
			R.H PRICE proceeds to VII Days Brigade School	
			Lieut. F. KIRBY assumes temporary charge of Battalion transport vice Lieut W.O.NEWSHAM to hosp.	
	Sunday 7 July		This day Inspection workgroups. Divine Service - Training continues.	
			Division in area of Battalion Transport.	

A6945 Wt. W11421/M1160 350,000 12/16 D. D. & L. Forms/C/2118/14.

WAR DIARY or INTELLIGENCE SUMMARY.

Army Form C. 2118.

(Erase heading not required.)

Instructions regarding War Diaries and Intelligence Summaries are contained in F. S. Regs., Part II. and the Staff Manual respectively. Title pages will be prepared in manuscript.

Place	Date	Hour	Summary of Events and Information	Remarks and references to Appendices
	1915			
	Monday 5 July		Very hot day. Battalion left BAYENGHEM at 11 am marching via WATTEN – ST. MOMELIN – NIEURLET to BOONEGHEM arriving about 3.30 pm and occupied billets. Orders received for march to be continued tomorrow.	
	Sunday 9 July		Battalion left BOONEGHEM at 8.30 am marching via BUYSSCHEURE – OOST HOUCK and bivouacing about 1 mile west of NOORDPEENE. The march was continued in the evening, Battalion moving off at 8.30 pm marching via LUYTPEENE – BAVINCHOVE – OXELAERE – and passing over east of CASSEL – STEENVOORDE – Very hot and dusty during both marches.	
	Wednesday 10 July		Battalion arrived 3/4 mile west of EECKE about 2 am and bivouaced. All officers reconnoitred the BERTHEN (2000 yds) LINE during the afternoon – Remainder of Battalion on rest. Turn stays up 5 about 4 pm when heavy thunderstorm came on – Heavy rain at frequent intervals – Very wet night.	

WAR DIARY
or
INTELLIGENCE SUMMARY.
(Erase heading not required.)

Army Form C. 2118.

Place	Date	Hour	Summary of Events and Information	Remarks and references to Appendices
	Thursday 11 July 1918		Weather very unsettled - Frequent heavy showers. Dispositions unchanged. Training continues. About 7 pm orders were received for Battalion to be prepared to move at two hours notice. 2nd Lieut ERNEST GEORGE MAYHALL & 2nd Lieut K. joined.	
	Friday 12 July		Rather boisterous day with frequent heavy showers. 2nd/Lieut K.M. BOURNE 9th reported from Division. 2nd Lieut DEAN and NORMAN commanding "A" Company. 2nd Lieut E. HARRISON proceeded to Senior Army School, LE TOUQUET. Battalion moved forward to occupy the BERTHEN LINE under following arrangements. "B" Company left bivouac at 1.30 pm and moved forward, taking up a thousand yards of the line. "C" and "D" companies [... 10.30 pm?] Remainder of Battalion left bivouac at 10-30 pm.	
	Saturday 13 July		"A" "B" and "D" companies in position by about 3 am - the position as occupied by the Battalion was reported to Bde Brigade commander after which the companies	

Army Form C. 2118.

WAR DIARY
or
INTELLIGENCE SUMMARY.
(Erase heading not required.)

Instructions regarding War Diaries and Intelligence Summaries are contained in F. S. Regs., Part II. and the Staff Manual respectively. Title pages will be prepared in manuscript.

Place	Date	Hour	Summary of Events and Information	Remarks and references to Appendices
5.				
	Saturday 13 July 1918		Less one platoon each, returned to bivouac – Third party arrived	
			about 9 a.m. Last about 11-30 a.m. – At rest during the day –	
			6. Company remainder in position taken up yesterday and the platoons of	
			A, B and D movement in Bertles Line. Weather much improved.	
	Sunday 14 July		Very unsettled day – much heavy rain on frequent intervals –	
			During the morning the Platoons of A, B and D companies returned to Battn. bivouac.	
			Weather dispatch unchanged – Troops at rest.	
			2nd Lieut W. H. DUTTON proceeded to 2nd. Army musketry School to courses of instruction –	
			During the evening a message was received from 41th. Stat[ionary] Hospital to the effect	
			that 2nd Lieut. E. TICKLE had been seriously ill and dead, but no details were given.	
			This Officer had proceeded to a course of instruction at 5th Army musketry	
			School on 2nd July –	
	Monday 15 July		Still close day – Battalion inspected by Second Army Commander General Sir	
			[H]erbert to O. Plumer – General disposition unchanged. All quiet.	

WARDIARY
or
INTELLIGENCE SUMMARY.
(Erase heading not required.)

Army Form C. 2118.

Place	Date	Hour	Summary of Events and Information	Remarks and references to Appendices
	Monday 15 July /18		Our Platoon each of A, B and D companies moved to BERTHEN LINE during the night to positions taken up on 13th. — No change in position of C Company. — One Lieut F. THOMAS, Middlesex Regt attached to the Battn, as signal officer.	
	Tuesday 16 July		About 12.30am enemy long range guns opened fire and between that hour and 2.30am about 20 shells pitches in the vicinity of Battalion Hqrs — two within 20 yards — but no damage was done — About 5.30am a Tenaji Minnenwerfer commenced to continual rapid fire about 7.30am — believed about 6am and remainder of day fire — 'D' Platoon which went forward last night arrived in position by 3am — During the morning the Commanding Officer and Company Commander himself to the BERTHEN Line to meet the Division Commander who inspected the positions and Lieut E. BARDSLEY moved 15 × 18 boys gas school for instruction. Training continues. J. C. CLARK admitted to hospital — One Platoon each of A, B and D Companies left bivouacs about 11 pm to relieve those in	

Edward Martin

WAR DIARY or INTELLIGENCE SUMMARY

Army Form C. 2118.

Place	Date	Hour	Summary of Events and Information	Remarks and references to Appendices
	Tuesday 16 July 1918	About 11.15 pm	enemy long range guns again opened fire - believe that shrapnel	
		11.45 pm	15 shells were fired but these pitched much nearer EECKE and the Battalion was not disturbed.	
	Wednesday 17 July		Religious service at 9.10 am of companies arrived in Bivouac about 7 am - Routine duties done day.	
			Joined the Battalion Rev LEONARD JAMES JACKSON C.F. attached to the Battalion - Training continues during the day	
		About 10.30 pm	orders were received for Battalion to proceed in battle order to a position of readiness about R.5 Central 1 mile NNE east of BOESCHEPPE - Left bivouac about midnight -	
	Thursday 18 July		During the march to position of readiness the Battalion - Owing to short amount of artillery moving about 1 am - Position in east of Battalion was rapid one did not arrive in position till about 5 am - Battalion slept afterwards & A. Coy. in a farm about 1000 yards west of position which earlier has been taken, and were interrupted was served about 6.30 am -	

A6945 Wt. W14422/M1160 350,000 12/16 D. D. & L. Forms/C./2118/14.

Army Form C. 2118.

WAR DIARY
or
INTELLIGENCE SUMMARY.
(Erase heading not required.)

Place	Date	Hour	Summary of Events and Information	Remarks and references to Appendices
	1918			
	Thursday 18 July		About 1 am. "C" Company returned to original position, and remainder of Battalion returned to original bivouac areas about 3 am. At rest during remainder of day.	
			2nd Lieut. T. A. BEARD proceeded to Machine Gun Training Centre Grantham.	
			No. 10019 L/Sgt. FRED BOAST proceeded to 5th South Lancashire Regt. for return commission as 2nd Lieut.	
	Friday 19. July		Fine day. General dispositions unchanged. During the afternoon "D" Company relieved "C" Company in forward area.	
	Saturday 20 July		Very unsettled day. Heavy rain during the afternoon — no change in dispositions of Battalion.	
			2nd Lieut. VICTOR ISBELL WATSON & 2nd Lieut. E. HARRISON joined the Battalion from course of instruction.	
	Sunday 21 July		Fine day. Very strong wind. Rather cold evening and night. Dispositions unchanged. Training exercises. Divine Service.	

Army Form C. 2118.

WAR DIARY
or
INTELLIGENCE SUMMARY.
(Erase heading not required.)

Place	Date	Hour	Summary of Events and Information	Remarks and references to Appendices
	1918			
	Monday 22 July		Fine day. Disposition unchanged. Training continues. Battalion attended a gas demonstration during the afternoon. Rain commenced about 9 pm and continues intermittently throughout the night. Village of EECKE and vicinity shelled by enemy intermittently at frequent intervals from 10 pm.	
	Tuesday 23 July		Shelling continued till about 3 am. Continuous heavy rain from about 10 am to about 4 pm. Still and unsettled during remainder of day. Very positions inspection by Brigade Commander cancelled on account of bad weather conditions. 2nd Lieut. E. BARDSLEY rejoins from 2d Corps School.	
	Wednesday 24 July		Fine bright day. Dispositions unchanged. Training continues. Lieut A. FERGUSON M.C. attached to Headquarters 89th Inf. Bde.	
	Thursday 25 July		Fine day. No change in dispositions. Training continues. Coy Commanders reports from detached positions in vicinity of BERTHEN LINE.	

Army Form C. 2118.

WAR DIARY
or
INTELLIGENCE SUMMARY.
(Erase heading not required.)

Instructions regarding War Diaries and Intelligence Summaries are contained in F. S. Regs., Part II. and the Staff Manual respectively. Title pages will be prepared in manuscript.

Place	Date 1915	Hour	Summary of Events and Information	Remarks and references to Appendices
	Friday 16 July		Still wet day. Disposition unchanged. Training continues. Demonstration in use of 'S.O.S.' rifle grenades given to the Battalion. 2nd Lieut. D. J. SILK proceeded to 2nd Army Bombing School.	
	Saturday 17 July		Very wet. Cheerless day. Disposition unchanged. 2nd Lieut. W. H. DUTTON returned from 2nd Army Musketry School.	
	Sunday 18 July		Weather improved but still unsettled. Disposition unchanged. Training suspended. Divine Service. No. 4 Platoon "A" Company under 2nd Lieut. E. G. MAYHALL proceeded to Division Headquarters at CASSELL for guard duties. 10001/Pain ARTHUR PERCIVAL VERNON PIGOT, D. Son W. joined.	
	Monday 19 July		2nd Lieut. J. BROWN proceeded this morning to 2nd Army Musketry School, LUMBRES. Fine day. Disposition unchanged. Training continues.	

Army Form C. 2118.

WAR DIARY
or
INTELLIGENCE SUMMARY.
(Erase heading not required.)

Instructions regarding War Diaries and Intelligence Summaries are contained in F. S. Regs., Part II. and the Staff Manual respectively. Title pages will be prepared in manuscript.

Place	Date	Hour	Summary of Events and Information	Remarks and references to Appendices
11	Sunday 30 July		Very fine day - rather hazy - No change in disposition - Training continues Par of Battalion baths at Bergues baths	
	Wednesday 31 July		Very fine day - Training continues - Disposition unchanged Lieut. F KIRBY proceeds to 35th Battalion M.G.C. for duty as Transport Officer Lieut. W.O. NEESHAM resumed duty as Battalion Transport Officer Bathing completed - Very considerable aerial activity during the night. The undermentioned Officers were present with the Battalion today:- Lieut. F.A. Owen - Bn. H. Qrs. and Lieut. E. Barclay a. Coy Lieut. & J. Blackburn b. Coy Major L. J. Booth M.C. 2/c. Quartermaster Captn. H.W. Bourne M.C. Secundy a Coy 2nd Lieut. M.H. Brennan a Coy " a L Blagdon b " W.H. Sutton b " " E. Hannan b Coy B.J. Hannan b " Captn. S. J. Jackson Chaplain H.V. Kitching b " " F.A. Sacramento Act. Adjt. H.V. Savin a "	

Army Form C. 2118.

WAR DIARY
or
INTELLIGENCE SUMMARY.
(Erase heading not required.)

Instructions regarding War Diaries and Intelligence Summaries are contained in F. S. Regs., Part II. and the Staff Manual respectively. Title pages will be prepared in manuscript.

Place	Date	Hour	Summary of Events and Information	Remarks and references to Appendices
	1918			
Beaurainville	31 July		Sh /o/c & S. Mather. Command Roll. 2nd Lieut O. Morgan. B. Coy	
Continued			Major & R. Watt. Roll Id. Qrs. Lieut W.O. Wareham. Transport Officer.	
			2nd Lieut P. J. Nolan. D. Coy. Loopn A.V.J. Viger. Bombing & Coy	
			Lt. Bradley. do. 2nd Lieut J. Baird. D. Coy	
			Lieut L. Snider (U.S.R.) Musketry Officer. Major A. J. Starkie. Bn. Hd. Qrs.	
			Captain J. Lund. Asst. Bombing. B. Coy. 2nd Lieut F. Thomas. " "	
			Lieut W. Jarvis. B. Coy " 2nd Lieut J. G. Watson. B. Coy.	
			2nd Lt. W. H. Wren. Roll. Hd Qrs.	
			The undermentioned on the Strength of the Battalion were detached as detail —	
			2nd Lieut J. Brown. 2nd Army Musketry School. Lieut. E. Brocklehurst. 69. Bde. Hd. Qrs.	
			" to blake Hospital. Q. Surgeon MC " "	
			" L Taylor " 2nd " E. S. Marshall - 30 Div Guard.	
			" " " Lieut E. Sandys. 112 Bde H.Q.	
			" W. H. Brown. VIII Corps Signal School. 2nd Lt. S. B. K. 2nd Army Scouting School	
			2nd Lt. W. Sharple MC Lewis MG. Omnials. 53	
			Feeding Strength - all ranks - 787.	
			J. W. Millar	
			Commanding 2. South Lancashire Regt	

Army Form C. 2118.

WAR DIARY
or
INTELLIGENCE SUMMARY.
(Erase heading not required.)

War Diary

2nd South Lancashire Regt.

1st to 31st August 1918

48A

WAR DIARY
or
INTELLIGENCE SUMMARY.

Army Form C. 2118.

W.O.N

Place	Date 1915	Hour	Summary of Events and Information	Remarks and references to Appendices
Merckeghem	Thursday 1. August		Very fine hot day. Disposition unchanged. Training continues. Battalion completed today 1st issue of 36 Lewis guns - 8 per company and 4 for special anti-aircraft work. Enormous aerial activity from about 10 am to 5 about midnight. Many hostile machines passed over Battalion bivouac moving in a Westerly direction.	
	Friday 2. August		Very hot day. Disposition unchanged. Training impossible. 2nd Lieuts T.C. CLARKE and L. FRYER rejoined from hospital. Lieut. W. TOMS admitted to hospital. Lieut. E.T. SANDIFORD transferred to 35th Div. Signals Company.	
	Saturday 3. August		Unsettled day. Frequent showers. Disposition unchanged. Training continues. 2nd Lieuts V.I. WATSON, H.V. KITCHING and P.T. NOLAN proceeded to 10th Corps School at MERCKEGHEM.	

Army Form C. 2118.

W.O.N-

WAR DIARY
or
INTELLIGENCE SUMMARY.

(Erase heading not required.)

Instructions regarding War Diaries and Intelligence Summaries are contained in F. S. Regs., Part II. and the Staff Manual respectively. Title pages will be prepared in manuscript.

Place	Date 1918	Hour	Summary of Events and Information	Remarks and references to Appendices
	Sunday 4 August		Fine day. Dispositions unchanged. Training progresses. Divine Service terminations Parade Service held in connection with a party of Belgian Warrant Officers N.C. Officers and men under command of Major S.T. BOAST MC who attended a Parade Service of Second Army at TERDEGHEM — Remainder of Battalion attended a Brigade Parade Service.	
	Monday 5 August		Dull unsettled day. No change in disposition – training continued. Heavy rain commenced about 8 p.m. and continued throughout the night	
	Tuesday 6 August		Unsettled day. Very windy. Disposition unchanged. Batt⁰ engaged in tactical exercise Capt & Adjt J.R. BEALE M.C. rejoined	
	Wednesday 7 August		Major S.T. BOAST M.C. D.C.M. proceeded to U.K. on 30 days leave. Capt J.R. BEALE M.C. assumed duties of Adjutant Fine day. Training continued	

cont⁰

Army Form C. 2118.

WAR DIARY
or
INTELLIGENCE SUMMARY.
(Erase heading not required.)

W.O.N-

Place	Date	Hour	Summary of Events and Information	Remarks and references to Appendices
	Wednesday 7th Aug 1918 (continued)		Warning orders issued to Batt⁹ to be prepared to move into SUPPORT line on night of 8/9 August — and to front line on night of 9/10 Aug	
MONT VIDAIGNE sector				
	Thursday 8 Aug		Fine day. Training continued during morning. Brigade Eliminating Competition for the I. Corps held during the morning. – The Batt⁹ was successful in winning the team (Limbers, 1 Water Cart and 1 Cooker) and the single [number events] Batt⁹ moved forward by companies into SUPPORT line – MONT VIDAIGNE in relief of the 16th H.L.I. – first company moving off at 6 p.m., a distance of 200 yds being maintained between platoons, ten minutes intervals between companies – Guides, 1 for Bn Hd Qrs and 1 per platoon met Batt⁹ near LANCET FARM R11.c.80.90. (Sheet 27.S.E.9 & S.W.) 3 (20,000), at 10.15 pm and conducted them to MONT VIDAIGNE – Batt⁹ Head Qrs were established at M.21.a.50.30 – Companies were distributed around MONT VIDAIGNE sector in dugouts and shelters. (cont⁹)	

Army Form C. 2118.

W.O.N.

WAR DIARY
or
INTELLIGENCE SUMMARY.
(Erase heading not required.)

Instructions regarding War Diaries and Intelligence Summaries are contained in F. S. Regs., Part II. and the Staff Manual respectively. Title pages will be prepared in manuscript.

Place	Date	Hour	Summary of Events and Information	Remarks and references to Appendices
#1	Thursday 8 Aug 1918 (continued)		Transport and Administrative details moved into Bivouac at Q.10.c.05.45 relieving the 18⁶ H.L.I. Dark night 2/Lieut L.FRYER admitted Hospital	
	Friday 9 August		Relief completed about 1.30pm – no casualties. Quiet day – Fine – Desultory shelling by enemy around the sector occupied by Batt. Batt moved forward to front line about 11pm in relief of the 17ᵗʰ Bn ROYAL SCOTS. Dark night. Capt K.MILBOURNE M.C. Lieut F.AARON and 34 other ranks were detailed as working party under 171ˢᵗ Tunnelling Coy	

A6945 Wt. W1422/M1160 350,000 12/16 D. D. & L. Forms/C./2118/14.

WAR DIARY
or
INTELLIGENCE SUMMARY.
(Erase heading not required.)

Army Form C. 2118.

Place	Date	Hour	Summary of Events and Information	Remarks and references to Appendices
	1918			
	Saturday 10 Aug		The relief completed at 3.30am — no casualties	
			Companies were disposed as follows :—	
			C Coy RIGHT FRONT	
			D " LEFT FRONT	
			A " RIGHT SUPPORT	
			B " LEFT SUPPORT	
			Bn Hd Qrs M27 & H (Sheet 27 s.e. 1:26 s.w. 1:20000)	
			Our artillery carried out harassing fire at intervals throughout the day — Slight retaliatory shelling by enemy	
			Fine bright day — visibility good	
			The Divisional General visited the line during the afternoon and the Brigadier General during the evening	
			Enemy shelled back areas at frequent intervals throughout the day and night — no damage and no casualties	
			2/Lieut WATSON rejoined from X Corps School. 2/Lieut GEORGE FRANCIS PEERS, and Lieut BRETHERTON WILLIAM WALTER MAITLAND. South Lancashire Regt joined casualties 10R guard	

Army Form C. 2118.

W.O.N.

WAR DIARY
or
INTELLIGENCE SUMMARY.
(Erase heading not required.)

Instructions regarding War Diaries and Intelligence Summaries are contained in F. S. Regs., Part II. and the Staff Manual respectively. Title pages will be prepared in manuscript.

Place	Date	Hour	Summary of Events and Information	Remarks and references to Appendices
	1918			
	Sunday 11 August		Fine bright day — no change in disposition — visibility good. Occasional shelling by enemy to which our artillery replied — Situation normal — no casualties. 2/Lieut D.J. SILK rejoined from 2nd Army School of Scouting. Fine night	
	Monday 12 August		Fine day. Slight hostile shelling during early hours of morning and enemy aircraft bombing in vicinity of line — quiet remainder of morning — visibility good. "A" "B" Coys moved forward to front line in relief of "C" "D" Coys — "C" "D" Coys moving back to support. Disposition as follows "A" Coy — RIGHT FRONT "B" LEFT FRONT "C" RIGHT SUPPORT "D" LEFT SUPPORT. Fairly quiet night — Casualties 1 Other Rank wounded (Shell Shock). Rations taken up by transport in usual manner.	

Army Form C. 2118.

W.O.N

WAR DIARY
or
INTELLIGENCE SUMMARY.
(Erase heading not required.)

Instructions regarding War Diaries and Intelligence Summaries are contained in F. S. Regs., Part II. and the Staff Manual respectively. Title pages will be prepared in manuscript.

Place	Date	Hour	Summary of Events and Information	Remarks and references to Appendices
Tuesday	13 August 1918		Relief completed about 3.30 am - no casualties - slight hostile shelling during relief	
			Fine bright day - visibility good	
			1 Other Rank wounded	
			Lieut. W HARRISON and 25 Other Ranks patrolled forwards HOOGGRAF # CABT with object of occupying it should enemy dispositions admit. This was unsuccessful and the patrol withdrew without any casualties.	
Wednesday	14 Aug		Fine bright day - no change in disposition	
			At dusk 2 patrols were sent forward. - One to reconnoitre disused trench in front of right company - This trench was found to be unoccupied. The second patrol went forward to reconnoitre NO MANS LAND but found nothing of importance	
			A reconnaissance patrol was also made by the Act. Adjutant,	
			(Capt J.F. LOCKINGTON) (Cont.)	

Army Form C. 2118.

W.O.N

WAR DIARY
or
INTELLIGENCE SUMMARY.
(Erase heading not required.)

Place	Date 1918	Hour	Summary of Events and Information	Remarks and references to Appendices
	Wednesday 14th August (cont'd)		Batt: were relieved by the 2/17 LONDON REGT – Relief commenced about 11 p.m. – During the relief the enemy shelled the sector around Bn. Hd. Qrs very heavily, but no casualties were caused. On completion of relief Batt: moved back to Brigade Reserve and occupied billets in BOESCHEPE. Lieut CARRIL HECTOR NICHOLSON SIMON joined for duty.	
	Thursday 15th Aug		Relief completed about 3a.m. at which time Batt: was disposed as under. Bn. H.Qrs. R.H.C.H.1. A & B Coy. R.10. central } Map Ref. Sheet 27 C " R.9. B & 6. } (Eastern half) 1/20000 D " R.9. a. 9. 5. Companies were at rest during remainder of day. Fine bright clear day (cont'd)	

Army Form C. 2118.

W.O.N.

WAR DIARY
or
INTELLIGENCE SUMMARY.
(Erase heading not required.)

Place	Date	Hour	Summary of Events and Information	Remarks and references to Appendices
	Thursday 15 Aug 1918 (Con'd)		Batt⁰ practised a wire cutting scheme from 10 pm	
			Lieut A L CLAYDON, the Band and 5 O.R. proceeded to Dunavoral Reception Camp ARNEKE — This party is proceeding to 2nd Army Rest Camp AUDRESELLES on 16th inst.	
	Friday 16 Aug		Fine bright day — no change in disposition	
			Batt⁰ returned from wire cutting scheme about 1 a.m.	
			Batt⁰ bathed at GODEWAERSVELDE during the day	
			Batt⁰ under 48 hours notice for special operations	
			Fine clear night	

Army Form C. 2118.

WON.

WAR DIARY
or
INTELLIGENCE SUMMARY.
(Erase heading not required.)

Place	Date 1918	Hour	Summary of Events and Information	Remarks and references to Appendices
10	Saturday 17th August		Dull day – windy	
			No change in disposition – Companies at training	
			Battn now under 36 hours notice for the "special operations"	
			Dull cloudy night, slight rain	
	Sunday 18th Aug		Fine day – Disposition unchanged.	
			Company training continued	
			Battn practised a special operation from about 8 p.m	
			Slight hostile shelling around sector occupied by "A"&"B" Coys during the night	
			no casualties	
			Dark night.	
			2/Lieut J. BROWN rejoined from 2nd Army Musketry School	
			2/Lieut L. FRYER discharged Hospital	

Army Form C. 2118.

W.O.N.

WAR DIARY
or
INTELLIGENCE SUMMARY.
(Erase heading not required.)

Place	Date	Hour	Summary of Events and Information	Remarks and references to Appendices
11	1918			
	Monday 19th Aug		Fine bright day – Companies at training during morning. 2/Lt D J SILK admitted Hospital. Orders received to attack LOCRE/WOFTN RIDGE on night 20/21 Aug. In connection with the above operations "B"Coy moved forward to SUPPORT LINE at MONT VIDAIGNE commencing with "A" Coy at 9 pm followed by "B""C". "D" and "HD" Coys at 15 minutes intervals. – Dress – Battle Order. 2/Lieut R H PRICE rejoined from VII Corps Signal School. 2/Lieut FRED BOAST joined on re posting from 1/5 SOUTH LANCASHIRE REGT.	
	Tuesday 20th August		Relief completed about 2.30am. no casualties. Disposition same as on 8th inst. Quiet day – usual shelling by both sides. At 10 25 p.m. the Batt" moved forward from its position by platoons at six minute intervals. – "A" Coy (Capt K M BOURNE M.C.) was leading followed by one platoon of "B" Coy as a wiring platoon – "C" Coy (Capt A P V PIGOT) followed with another platoon of "B" Coy as a wiring platoon. – Behind these came the remaining two platoons of "B" Coy, one as carrying party for "A" Coy and one for "C" Coy. "B" Coy was commanded by Capt T SNEE-ESCOTT. Attached to each of the attacking Coys "HD" Q's were two Batt" Observers whose duty it [con'd]	

WAR DIARY
or
INTELLIGENCE SUMMARY.

Army Form C. 2118.

W.O.N.

Place	Date 1918	Hour	Summary of Events and Information	Remarks and references to Appendices
	Tuesday 20th Aug cont'd		was to run out a tape line from the position of deployment to the Bay Bat Q's at the final objective. — A party of six signallers was attached to the right company whose duty it was to run out a wire from the line of deployment to the final objective (a line having been previously run out from Batt. Hd Qrs to the line of deployment), and to fix a camp which could communicate with Bn Hd Qrs. The line of deployment was taped out before the arrival of the attacking companies and guides met these companies at LOCRE CHATEAU GATES. The deployment started at 11.30 pm along a line running from M.3.H.&.20.6.5 to M.26.d.55.45. Lieut G.F. PEERS admitted hospital from Canvas — Lieut W. TOMS — discharged hospital	
	Wednesday 21st Aug		All troops were in position by 1 a.m. — The carrying parties picked up YUKON packs holding 1 coil wire, 6 screw pickets and 1 Lewis gun drum from the dump at M.28.c.25.30 — Each of these men also carried an extra bandolier of S.A.A. The carrying platoons made 2 journeys returning after the completion of the first journey to a dump at M.28.d.20.15. for a second load. The attack was made with the object of capturing the LOCRE HOF FARM RIDGE cont'd	

Army Form C. 2118.

W.O. N:

WAR DIARY
or
INTELLIGENCE SUMMARY.
(Erase heading not required.)

Place	Date 1918	Hour	Summary of Events and Information	Remarks and references to Appendices
Wednesday	21st August (cont'd)		On the right the 7/8th Bn INNISKILLING FUSILIERS and on the left the 2/14th LONDON REGT (LONDON SCOTTISH) co-operated in the attack. - The Batt's objective was the position with its right about M35 c 35,90 and its left about M35 b 20 H6. The Batt" attacked on a 400 yds frontage with two companies in the front line each having two platoons in the front line and two platoons in rear as "moppers up", who formed the support line on reaching the objective. In rear of each company came a wiring platoon and in rear of these again a carrying platoon. At 4.55 a.m. the barrage opened 150 yds in front of the leading companies and moved forward 100 yds every four minutes. The enemy barrage came down about 50 yds in rear of the deployed troops. The attacking companies moved forward close up to our barrage fire - They met with a certain amount of resistance from enemy machine guns, but not much from enemy shell fire. - The enemy barrage was not serious. The final objectives were all reached 32 minutes after ZERO and consolidation was begun immediately. About 50 prisoners and 3 machine guns were captured. (Cont'd)	

Army Form C. 2118.

W.O.N.

WAR DIARY
or
INTELLIGENCE SUMMARY.
(Erase heading not required.)

Instructions regarding War Diaries and Intelligence Summaries are contained in F. S. Regs., Par. II. and the Staff Manual respectively. Title pages will be prepared in manuscript.

Place	Date 1918	Hour	Summary of Events and Information	Remarks and references to Appendices
14	Wednesday 21st August		Casualties during the operations were light. After objectives had been taken the enemy were very quiet, but from 9 a.m. onwards our new line and approaches were heavily shelled. - This shelling continued practically all day and about 10 pm the enemy counter attacked putting down a very heavy barrage on Our left post was captured, but a counter attack immediately restored the situation	
	Thursday 22nd August		In spite of very heavy shelling and under great difficulties an inter company relief was commenced about 11 a.m. - This was effected successfully and the relief completed about 11 a.m. Companies were disposed as follows :- FRONT LINE 'D' Coy :- SUPPORT LINE 'B' Coy CLOSE RESERVE LINE - 2 platoons 'A' & 2 platoons 'C' Coy:- RESERVE LINE 2 platoons 'A' & 2 platoons 'C' During the day there were heavy bursts of shell fire but the enemy showed no inclination to attack. Orders were received at 11 a.m. stating that half the Battn front would be taken over by the Brigade on our left The relief was carried out by the 2/15th LONDON REGT. and completed by 12 m.n. Cont/o	

A6945 Wt. W14422/M1160 350,000 12/16 D. D. & L. Forms/C./2118/14.

Army Form C. 2118.

WO N~

15

WAR DIARY
or
INTELLIGENCE SUMMARY.
(Erase heading not required.)

Instructions regarding War Diaries and Intelligence Summaries are contained in F. S. Regs., Part II. and the Staff Manual respectively. Title pages will be prepared in manuscript.

Place	Date 1918	Hour	Summary of Events and Information	Remarks and references to Appendices
Thursday	22nd Aug		Dispositions after relief	
(continued)			FRONT LINE – 2 platoons D Coy. SUPPORT LINE – 2 platoons D Coy.	
			OLD FRONT LINE – 2 platoons B ": BLUE LINE – 2 platoons B Coy.	
			SUPPORT LINE (MONT VIDAIGNE) A and C Coys.	
Friday	23rd Aug		Fine clear day.	
			Enemy very quiet – very little hostile shelling.	
			Orders were received that the 1/6 Bn. INNISKILLING FUSILIERS would take over the front and support lines now held by B & D Coys. – The relief was commenced about 11pm but when nearly completed the enemy launched another counter attack.	
			2/Lt J.D. SILK discharged hospital	

Army Form C. 2118.

W.O.N.

WAR DIARY
or
INTELLIGENCE SUMMARY.
(Erase heading not required.)

Place	Date 1918	Hour	Summary of Events and Information	Remarks and references to Appendices
Saturday	24 August		About 1 a.m. a party of the enemy was seen approaching our lines, but as they had their hands up, they were not fired on as it was thought that they were going to surrender. As soon as they had reached our first posts, the enemy put down a heavy barrage and this party in conjunction with other enemy parties bombed our posts, but after an hours severe fighting they were driven off. The situation was very unsettled for some time but about 4.30 a.m. it was found that our line was still intact and the relief was then completed. "C" Companies and Bn Hd Qrs were now all around MONT VIDAIGNE in SUPPORT. Remainder of day was very quiet – Companies at rest during day. The total operations casualties through the operations from 21st to 24th were:— Killed 2/Lieut H Y LARSEN 21st Aug.; 2/Lieut W MAITLAND Wounded 21st Aug.; 2/Lieut E G MAYHALL Wounded 21st Aug.; Lieut F A AROM Killed 23rd Aug.; Capt S B SCHWABE MC Wounded 23rd "; Other Ranks Killed – 18; Wounded 91; Missing 22; Total 131	

Army Form C. 2118.

W.O.N

WAR DIARY
or
INTELLIGENCE SUMMARY.
(Erase heading not required.)

Instructions regarding War Diaries and Intelligence Summaries are contained in F. S. Regs., Part II. and the Staff Manual respectively. Title pages will be prepared in manuscript.

Place	Date	Hour	Summary of Events and Information	Remarks and references to Appendices
Sunday	25 August 1916		Fine day. No change in disposition - Companies at rest during day - Slight hostile shelling - 2/Lieuts E BARDSLEY and A MORROW wounded (gas shell) Fine clear night	
Monday	26 August		Fine day. Dispositions of B, C + D companies unchanged. A Coy moved down to BOESCHEPE arriving there about 11 am and were accomodated in billets on BOESCHEPE - BERTHEN road. Very quiet day	

WAR DIARY
or
INTELLIGENCE SUMMARY.

(Erase heading not required.)

Army Form C. 2118.

Place	Date	Hour	Summary of Events and Information	Remarks and references to Appendices
18	1918			
Tuesday	27 August		Fine clear day — No change in disposition — Batt" at rest	
			Usual hostile shelling around sector occupied by Batt"	
			2/Lieut JOHN MAILLY ⎫	
			Lieut GEORGE KERBALL PARRINGTON ⎬ SOUTH LANCASHIRE REGIMENT joined	
			2/Lieut KENNETH MORRIS HARPUR ⎭	
Wednesday	28 August		Fairly quiet day —	
			16 Coy moved down to BOESCHEPE in relief of a Coy who moved back to	
			MONT VIDAIGNE Relief completed by 10 pm	
			Fine clear night.	
			2/Lieut SIDNEY JACKSON SOUTH LANCASHIRE REGT joined	

Army Form C. 2118.

WAR DIARY
or
INTELLIGENCE SUMMARY.
(Erase heading not required.)

Place	Date 1918	Hour	Summary of Events and Information	Remarks and references to Appendices
Thursday	29th August		Fine day. Disposition unchanged	
			6 Coy bathed at GODEWAERSVELDE during the day	
			Quiet night	
			Lieut WILLIAM JOHN OWEN SOUTH LANCASHIRE REGT joined	
			2/Lieut F. BOAST proceeded to U.K. on leave	
Friday	30 August		Fine day. Very quiet during day	
			About 3pm a message was received from the Division on our right that	
			the enemy were evacuating their positions and the Batt⁰ were ordered to	
			stand to. 6 Coy going from BOESCHEPE. About 5pm it was noticed that the	
			enemy were vacating their positions in front of our line. The 2/17 LONDON REGT	
			moved forward and the Batt⁰ moved down from MONT VIDAIGNE about 10	
			p.m. and occupied our old front line	
			Very wet night	
			2/Lieuts ARTHUR SEWARD JAMES HAROLD SANDERSON EDWARD JONES	
			SOUTH LANCASHIRE REGT joined	

Army Form C. 2118.

WAR DIARY
or
INTELLIGENCE SUMMARY.
(Erase heading not required.)

Place	Date	Hour	Summary of Events and Information	Remarks and references to Appendices
Saturday 1918	31st Aug		About 5am Batt: received orders to move forward in support to the 2/17 LONDON REGT - The advance was very slow and snipers holding the advance up. These were cleared up eventually and by 6pm the Batt: occupied a line E. of DRANOUTRE. The rations were taken up to KOUDEKOT CABARET arriving there about 11pm - Transport and QM Stores moved forward to M I H B.C. (Sheet 27 S.E. q 28 S.W. combined) Recd C H N SYMON proceeded to 2nd Army Central School. X Corps Horse show held at TERDEGHEM. 1st Prize for best turned-out limbered waggon - awarded to battalion - also 1st prize for best turned-out mounted N.C.O. No 6670 Sgt W. PARRY and No 1490 Pte G. Moss (driver) - were recipients of prizes -	

Wmbourne Capt
for Lieut-Colonel
Commanding 2Bn South Lancashire Regt.

Confidential

Alan Drury

2nd Battn 1 Lancers Regt

From 1-9-18
To 30-9-18

VOL 48
89/30

A.D.
49A
15 sheets

2nd Battalion South Lancashire Regiment

1st to 30th September 1918

War diary.

12 Pages.

WAR DIARY
or
INTELLIGENCE SUMMARY.
(Erase heading not required.)

Army Form C. 2118.

Place	Date	Hour	Summary of Events and Information	Remarks and references to Appendices
Sunday	1 Sept 1918		During the early morning the Battalion was relieved by 7/8 Innskilling Fusiliers – Relief parties were sent back to KOUDEKOT CABARET area when about 4 a.m. – During the morning orders were received for the Battalion move to relieve our own troops G.H.C – There were then subsequently cancelled and the Battalion moved forward in support to the Innskillings who were attacking NEUVE EGLISE – During the operations a shell fell amongst Headquarters resulting in Capt T.R.BEALL M.C. Adjutant and 3 other ranks – Sergt T.MALLIN D.C.M. M.M. was also killed – Battalion were taken up by lorries and moved to HILLSIDE CAMP where Battalion was now established – Lieut T.N HARPUR wounded –	
Monday	2 Sept		Battalion reached HILLSIDE CAMP about 2 a.m – Battalion remained here till about 1.30 when it moved back to RESERVE LINE at T1/c.S.E of DRANOUTRE. This move was that our Battalion did not come in near relation till 6/m – Transport and details were formed to ULSTER CAMP about 1000 yards West of DRANOUTRE. Acting Captain F.J. LOCKINGTON assumed duty as acting Adjutant.	

Signed M.P. D.&L., London, E.C
(10404) Wt W 3509/P.73 750,000 3/17 B 2788 F-rms/C2118/16

Army Form C. 2118.

WAR DIARY
or
INTELLIGENCE SUMMARY.
(Erase heading not required.)

Instructions regarding War Diaries and Intelligence Summaries are contained in F. S. Regs., Part II. and the Staff Manual respectively. Title pages will be prepared in manuscript.

Place	Date 1916	Hour	Summary of Events and Information	Remarks and references to Appendices
Tuesday 3rd			Fine day – Sniper hostile shelling around Battalion area – Enemy in afternoon shelled Ravines, on ridge, and ground about SSE. one mile S.W. of DRANOUTRE – Being Battalion being relieved – Few casualties in trenches and some O.R.s – Fairly quiet day –	
Wednesday 4th			Fine clear day – Dispositions unchanged – Battalion engaged on working and fatigue parties.	
Thursday		5 A	Dispositions unchanged – Battalion work continued – Orders received during the afternoon for Brigade to move forward in connection with impending operations. There was no intelligence received. Fine clear night – there was nothing in vicinity of Battalion –	
Friday 5th		10 A	Fine clear day – Sunny – During the morning Brigade work continued – Later in Battalion moved back to support Trenches, relieving 2/23 LONDON REGT. 81st Brigade, at KOUDEKOT, one mile West of DRANOUTRE, arriving about 7 P.M. and employed known there – Fine clear night –	

WAR DIARY
or
INTELLIGENCE SUMMARY.
(Erase heading not required.)

Army Form C. 2118.

Instructions regarding War Diaries and Intelligence Summaries are contained in F. S. Regs., Part II. and the Staff Manual respectively. Title pages will be prepared in manuscript.

Place	Date	Hour	Summary of Events and Information	Remarks and references to Appendices
Sunday	1/8/16	7a.	No change in disposition - Companies in training - Warning orders for Battalion to be prepared to move forward - Reconnoissancy Officers and Company Commanders went forward to reconnoitre Sector to be occupied. Fine warm weather.	
Sunday		6 N.	Very miserable day - Battalion moves forward to front line system to relieve 5/16 London Regt. heavy thunder & rain storm commencing at 8 pm. Bombardments rain storm every now —	
Monday	9 th.		After heavy rain commenced about 1 am an intense 18th shrap 5cm and ammunition dump explosion & very frequent heavy showers. Relief complete by 2. 45 am by which time Battalion was disposed as under —	
			"A" Company - Left front }	
			"B" " - " " } North East of	
			"C" " - Right " } WULVERGHEM -	
			"D" to Companies - Reserve	
			1 man wounded during relief - movement slow owing to rain — General situation quiet - though rain commenced about 6pm and continued throughout the night - Enemy the early part of the night hostile artillery very active	

Army Form C. 2118.

WAR DIARY
or
INTELLIGENCE SUMMARY.
(Erase heading not required.)

Instructions regarding War Diaries and Intelligence Summaries are contained in F. S. Regs., Part II. and the Staff Manual respectively. Title pages will be prepared in manuscript.

4

Place	Date	Hour	Summary of Events and Information	Remarks and references to Appendices
Monday continued	9/4		in Battalion area en route leaving from transport lines.	
	10/4		After stand to Company moved forward to fill a gap in front line from right of "B" Company to SPRING WALK about 1000 yards East of WULVERGHEM. Two men wounded.	
Tuesday	10/4		Stormy mud all day. This proved to dry up the rest our men, but the others were in a very bad state. All rounds were not ammunition. Subaltern Allesley throughout the day and one night. One main trench. 2nd Lieut. T.C. CLARKE sent to hospital slightly frozen. Heavy rain during the night.	
Wednesday	11/4		Elliots after midnight "A" Company were found in relief of "B". Latter withdrawn to Support. Relief completed by 2.30 a.m. Heavy rain fell about 7 p.m.	
Thursday	12/4		Very wet and heavy rain throughout the day. Situation very difficult owing to this Company. "A" - advanced its line about 150 yards and our right Company. "C" - extended its line about 50 yards to the right with a view to forming defensive line. Write on flanks.	Sgt. 9/4 R. Queens (R. W. Surrey) 3rd & 5th Div [General Situation fairly quiet. Mount intermittent Shelling.] Remain Vfy.

(10340) Wt W3500/P713 750,000 3/15 H & S 8388 Forms/C2118/36 2/14. D. D. & L., London, E.C.

WAR DIARY
or
INTELLIGENCE SUMMARY.
(Erase heading not required.)

Army Form C. 2118.

Place	Date	Hour	Summary of Events and Information	Remarks and references to Appendices
	Friday 13th		Slight improvement in weather conditions - Train during the day. General disposition of Battalion unchanged - A Coy on our left was [?] in [?] from B Company but no further to see into front with the Germans on our right - Q Company which advanced to his last nights establishn a further [?] post - About midnight enemy attempted a raid on our rifle post but was driven off - Shrapnel to rifle posts Artillery active - Battalion remained night and to move to BOESCHEPE area on 15th.	
	Saturday 14th		Weather much unsettled - Heavy rain during our night. Disposition of Battalion unchanged during the day. Situation fairly quiet. Battalion relieved at night by 2/23rd London Regt. - Relief commenced about 11pm -	
	Sunday 15th		SOS running up to about 4am - Relief completed at 2.15am - Bn_hutst withdrew as relieved and proceeded to Bivouac at M31.d.3.5 - KOUDEKOT last had arriving about 4am - all ranks were very tired and wet, as in its position occupied it was not possible to obtain much rest - Battalion had bivouac about 3.30pm arr marched to area West of BOESCHEPE arriving about 6.30pm being accommodated in huts -	

WAR DIARY or INTELLIGENCE SUMMARY

Army Form C. 2118.

Place	Date	Hour	Summary of Events and Information	Remarks and references to Appendices
Monday	16.7		Stand from day. - Battalion at rest. Transport moved to BANGLE FARM - R17 k.2.5. about 1½ miles S.E. of BOESCHEPE. Just before leaving KOUDEKOT area the gun teams occupied by Brigade Transport were heavily shelled by enemy - a number of casualties were sustained by personnel & Battalion transport & air our Coys.	
Tuesday	17.7		Battalion near FLETRE from about 2 a.m. to 4.30 a.m. - Then during remainder of day - Inspection of Battalion unchanged.	
Wednesday	18.7		This day - Inspection unchanged - Training in progress - B and D Companies inspected by B.S.G.6. Brigade Parade during the afternoon for the presentation by Corps Commander of ribbands to n.c.o. & officers, men.	
Thursday	19.7		This day - Orders received for Battalion to move to MONT ROUGE, about 1½ miles S.E. of WESTOUTRE, this afternoon. Last company moved off at 4.30 p.m. Last company arrived at 5.30 p.m. Companies were independently - 100 yards between platoons. Last party arrived at new station about 7 p.m. - Battalion in bivouac. Transvia bivouac known as 3/10.7. Shan down Wigh.	

Army Form C. 2118.

WAR DIARY
or
INTELLIGENCE SUMMARY.
(Erase heading not required.)

Instructions regarding War Diaries and Intelligence Summaries are contained in F. S. Regs., Part II. and the Staff Manual respectively. Title pages will be prepared in manuscript.

Place	Date	Hour	Summary of Events and Information	Remarks and references to Appendices
Scherpenberg	20th		Fine day. Dispositions unchanged. Other half Battalion employed as Special working parties under R.E. - remainder as training.	
Scherpenberg	21st		Fine day. Dispositions unchanged - Training continued - Warning order received for Battalion to be prepared to move forward tomorrow.	
Scherpenberg	22nd		Battalion left MONT ROUGE in the evening for front lines. First half moved "A" about 4 p.m. - Last party about 5.30 p.m. Fine during the day but rain commenced about 4.30 p.m. and continues. Parade for burial service.
Senior Subaltern T.D. MATHER posted to command 2/23rd London Regt. Captain K.W. BOURNE was assumed Company commander of the Battalion. Major A.J. STATHER transferred to D.R.C. for course as S.I. Inspector.	
	23rd		Relief completed by 12.45 am. Battalion having taken over Bn. Sector line by 1/6th Yorkshire Regt. and 2/23rd London Regt. - Companies dispose as follows - D. Left front - B. Right front - A. Support - C. Reserve. Hants in Ntambo - Sept 14th Yorkshire Regt. - 3rd Int. Nights 1/8th Gunnestelling Zero - 30 -	

Army Form C. 2118.

WAR DIARY
or
INTELLIGENCE SUMMARY.
(Erase heading not required.)

Instructions regarding War Diaries and Intelligence Summaries are contained in F. S. Regs., Part II. and the Staff Manual respectively. Title pages will be prepared in manuscript.

Place	Date	Hour	Summary of Events and Information	Remarks and references to Appendices
	Monday 23rd 1916		Enemy mortar shewed activity. Considerable artillery activity. Buffalo lorries forward during the night 22/23rd as usual. This day Brigadier made short visit. Considerable experience in the evening in getting supplies forward owing to annual of Battalion transport being overcrowded. During the night 23/24 a change in disposition of Battalion was carried out as follows in front line:— D. Company Left. — A. Centre. — D. Wright. — each with two platoons and two platoons in support. — C. Company Reserve. — A few companies sent brushes out well in front and after enemy patrols from front companies in touch with the enemy, withdrawn to own line.	
	Tuesday 24th.		Fine day. Enemy disposition unchanged. — Situation normal. — 2nd Lieut. E. JONES transferred to 69/2 T.M.B. Strong wind during the night.	
	Wednesday 25th.		A raid on MORTAR FARM, about 1½ miles N.N.E. of WULVERGHEM, by four platoons of B. Company took place shortly after midnight 24–25th. One platoon under command of 2nd Lieut. E. G. HARRISON, from the top of B. Company were held up by machine gun and rifle fire in the vicinity of MORTAR FARM —	

Army Form C. 2118.

WAR DIARY
or
INTELLIGENCE SUMMARY.
(Erase heading not required.)

Instructions regarding War Diaries and Intelligence Summaries are contained in F. S. Regs., Part II. and the Staff Manual respectively. Title pages will be prepared in manuscript.

Place	Date	Hour	Summary of Events and Information	Remarks and references to Appendices
Wednesday Continue	25th 1916		Unfortunately Sergt Welding became a casualty almost as soon as he leapt our trench and the position coming of our numerous heavy fires and not made the first impulse anticipated. The platoon, which was ably led by Sen Sergt Stanman, although also exposed to considerable fire, successfully carried forward and eventually carried more successes in reaching a bombing position from where they were able to throw bombs into the enemy trench. A number of the enemy were seen running away from this more trench on the advance of A- Sen. Stanman more than states the position being in that several of our own men and many of his wounded men indifferently, several others who had been hit were on the ground — many very slightly. More were sent up from supports in support but the platoon took, not retained support. Being unaware, owing to the obscurity due to smoke & trench mortar fire and enemy machine gun fire, that more were being wounded, or 2 the subsequently — In the afternoon our left company "D" pushed forward with a view to occupying castles down distance in front. This move was met with enemy effective and were obliged to return to our lines. During this operation two men were killed — Of major of Battalion from relieves by 2-17th London who arrived about 9 P.m and was completed by 11.45 P.m. Battalion moved back to billets in NEUVE EGLISE. Sunny this affair the following Casualties were sustained — 1 officer T. SWEET-ESCOTT, 2nd Lieut. C. G. HARRISON and 3 other ranks wounded — 1 other rank killed — Our mater Sergt* The day was fine —	

Army Form C. 2118.

WAR DIARY
or
INTELLIGENCE SUMMARY.
(Erase heading not required.)

Place	Date	Hour	Summary of Events and Information	Remarks and references to Appendices
Linnenton	26.4		This day. Disposition of Battalion unchanged. Enemy artillery very active shelling roads and approaches - moon enabled 16 Battalion front line snipers to snipe on two or three places causing him inconvenience to transport moving forward with supplies. Very dark night after. Rain and heavy wind.	
Friday	27th		This day. Disposition of Battalion unchanged. Situation normal. Transport moves to huts at LOCRE CHATEAU. Lieut Colonel CECIL HUNTER LITTLE D.S.O. Somerset Light Infantry joins the Battalion and assumes command.	
Saturday	28.4		Steady rain from about 5.45am to 11 am. Attack by 30th Division on enemy position was launched at 5.25 am. On our right 2-1/2 Divisions pushed an offensive patrols with a view to occupying ONTARIO FARM - MORTAR FARM - KRUISTRAAT CRATER - but were unable to do so on account of enemy opposition. About 6.30 pm our Battalion sent forward to our front line which has now been vacated by London Regt. which has in the meantime successfully occupied its objective attempted this morning.	

WAR DIARY or INTELLIGENCE SUMMARY

Army Form C. 2118.

Place	Date	Hour	Summary of Events and Information	Remarks and references to Appendices
Sunday	19/8/16		About 5.30 a.m. 2.17th London Regt. again pushed forward and successfully occupied a position along MESSINES Ridge, having encountered little opposition — our Battalion having received orders to return to final objective to HOUTHEM, moved forward about 6 am in following order, our left to our right — Front line — 2 Platoons each of J. a. B. Coys. Support line — 2 " " " " " " 2 Coys in Reserve. The final objective was reached about 3.30 m by which time the Battalion was holding a line along YPRES – COMINES Canal from HOUTHEM to Lock 3. About 1300 yards. Advance now having been resumed to return our Southern Battalion to Battalion moved up to fill in the gap — On the front objective was realised it was found that the 41st Division on our left were being forced back by enemy machine gun & rifle fire — Our two left companies J. and a. were ordered to hold the enemy and this enabled the 41st Division to regain their Kruh. with our left and establish him and got Ranger on our right 3 our companies paint J. a. b. 15 — our left to our right — Snipers were observed in some machine guns from very ordinary but our men were now "sniper" - a number of enemy our men continued all night - Heavy our supplies were taken by bombers to MESSINES Cross Roads and thence to the Battalion by pack animals.

Army Form C. 2118.

WAR DIARY
or
INTELLIGENCE SUMMARY.
(Erase heading not required.)

Instructions regarding War Diaries and Intelligence Summaries are contained in F. S. Regs., Part II. and the Staff Manual respectively. Title pages will be prepared in manuscript.

Place	Date	Hour	Summary of Events and Information	Remarks and references to Appendices
Monday	30th		Enemy were continued shell about 10 a.m. about which time Transport returned to lines at LOCRE CHATEAU — Worked in making drainage gateway outside about 4 pm when enemy put into trench with 4.2 at about 15 cans about one mile N.E. of HOUTHEM ; trench or ca rifles — Brigade ammunition in dug outs and shelters —	
			Signed Basil Major for O.C. 2. S Lancashire Rgt	

50A
13 sheet

WO 52

2nd. Battalion South Lancashire Regt.

War Diary

1st to 31st Oct. 1916

12 Pages

Army Form C. 2118.

WAR DIARY
or
INTELLIGENCE SUMMARY.
(Erase heading not required.)

Instructions regarding War Diaries and Intelligence Summaries are contained in F. S. Regs., Part II. and the Staff Manual respectively. Title pages will be prepared in manuscript.

Place	Date	Hour	Summary of Events and Information	Remarks and references to Appendices
	10/16			
Sunday	1. Oct.		This day - Battalion disposition unchanged - are occupied much shelter by enemy - Transport moved from LOCRE CHATEAU to area 600 yards north west of HOUTHEM - Very dark wet night -	
Monday	2. Oct.		Still another day - Disposition unchanged - Shelling by enemy at intervals -	
Tuesday	3. Oct.		This day - Disposition unchanged - Occasional shelling - Occasional shelling day and night - much aeroplane activity -	
Wednesday	4. Oct.		This day - Disposition unchanged -	
Saturday	5. Oct.		Still another day - not eventful one - During the night 5th-6th the Brigade relieves the 103rd Brigade in the line - Battalion remains as Brigade Reserve in present station - Occasional activity in the both day and night - many guns being moved forward - Whilst this move during the night 5.6 Oct works put back our lines.	

D. D. & L., London, E.C.
(1034) W1 V3300/P713 750,000 3/16 E 2688 F. atms/C2118/16

WAR DIARY
or
INTELLIGENCE SUMMARY.
(Erase heading not required.)

Army Form C. 2118.

Instructions regarding War Diaries and Intelligence Summaries are contained in F. S. Regs., Part II. and the Staff Manual respectively. Title pages will be prepared in manuscript.

Place	Date	Hour	Summary of Events and Information	Remarks and references to Appendices
	Sunday 5 Oct. 1916		Fine day. Battalion dispositions unchanged – Individuals attacked – Several enemy shells fell in vicinity of transport lines – no casualties but other ranks men now to frontline –	
	Monday 6 Oct.		Fine day. During the evening the Battalion moved forward to front line in relief of 6th Royal Irish Regt. – First company moved off at 5.45pm – last half at 6.40pm – Relief completed at 10.15pm by which time relieved Battalion had withdrawn – our own Brigade wounded during relief – Battalion disposed as follows – D Company left front – C centre – A right – B support – North west of WERNICQ – Battalion on flanks – our left 7-8 Royal Inniskilling Fusiliers – our right – 7th Rifle Brigade – Supplies taken forward by Battalion transport to TURPIN early party rifles – Supplies about 1½ miles N.W. of WERNICQ CROSSING.	
	Tuesday 7 Oct.		Fine day – Dispositions unchanged – Enemy artillery very active from 3.45 am to 5.30 am – remainder of day normal with usual intermittent shelling – Boche arras, especially in vicinity of transport lines, shelled rather heavily during the evening –	

Army Form C. 2118.

WAR DIARY
or
INTELLIGENCE SUMMARY.
(Erase heading not required.)

Instructions regarding War Diaries and Intelligence Summaries are contained in F. S. Regs., Part II. and the Staff Manual respectively. Title pages will be prepared in manuscript.

Place	Date	Hour	Summary of Events and Information	Remarks and references to Appendices
	Wednesday 9 Oct		Rather dull day - General distribution unchanged. Our patrols active day and night - Several enemy machine guns and T.M.s located - observing nothing of importance to rnts - From about 6 pm to 7.30 pm enemy persistently shelled the village of HOUTHEM and vicinity - all transport held up during this time - Relief supplies were successfully taken forward under cover arrangements.	
	Thursday 10 Oct		During the night 9th - 10th enemy artillery very active in Battalion sub. sector. B Company withdrew one platoon slightly to conform to general line owing to Company advancing their line about 200 yards - Our patrols active all day and night - During the day our artillery and T.M.s carried out several shoots & cut enemy wire. Rather dull day -	
	Friday 11 Oct		Also dull day - Disposition of Battalion unchanged. During the night 10-11th, one platoon from B Company attempted a raid on CRUCIFIX FARM about 1000 yards West of WERVICQ - with a view to obtaining identification of enemy - Party never got near the objective the following artillery barrage, unfortunately the fell short preventing party from proceeding - when barrage lifted party moved forward but was driven by machine without success. Several casualties were sustained.	

Army Form C. 2118.

WAR DIARY
or
INTELLIGENCE SUMMARY.
(Erase heading not required.)

Instructions regarding War Diaries and Intelligence Summaries are contained in F. S. Regs., Part II. and the Staff Manual respectively. Title pages will be prepared in manuscript.

Place	Date	Hour	Summary of Events and Information	Remarks and references to Appendices
	Friday 11 Oct continued		About same time two Platoons from B Company attempted a raid on enemy trench about 500 yards North of CRUCIFIX FARM, with the same object in view. The barrage was also short causing Platoons to become disorganised - as barrage lifted Platoons reorganised and moved forward - a number of enemy were seen running back but none seemed — Platoons sustained a few casualties and inflicting.	
	Saturday 12 Oct		Very dull day - Disposition of Battalion unchanged - Situation normal - Heavy rain commenced about 4 pm and continued all night - During the night Battalion was relieved by the 7th Royal Irish Regt. over 2-3 am. Owing to the Battalion not having our own Sub-Sector relief was slow.	
	Sunday 13 Oct		Relief completed about 1 am - Battalion had been ordered to rendezvous on ridge to a Waggon road about 1 mile West of HOUTHEM. It was found when area was occupied the other units our Battalion was eventually accommodated in area GUN FARM, about 3000 yards further West. Last party arriving place about 3 am - Battalion at rest but very uncomfortable. Less routine and continued all day -	
	Monday 14 Oct		Fine day - Disposition of Battalion unchanged - Position much improved and all ranks much more comfortable -	

Army Form C. 2118.

WAR DIARY
or
INTELLIGENCE SUMMARY.
(Erase heading not required.)

Instructions regarding War Diaries and Intelligence Summaries are contained in F. S. Regs., Part II. and the Staff Manual respectively. Title pages will be prepared in manuscript.

Place	Date	Hour	Summary of Events and Information	Remarks and references to Appendices
	Tuesday 15 Oct 1918		Dull day - heavy mist - Disposition unchanged - Barrage in progress - Heavy rain during the night -	
	Wednesday 16 Oct		Very wet day - Disposition unchanged -	
	Thursday 17 Oct		Still unsettled day. Disposition unchanged. Barrage over enemy 5 hr. purposes 5 min.	
	Friday 18 Oct		Very fine day - Battalion left GUN FARM at 7.30 am - marching now TENBRIELEN and WERVICK reaches REEKE about noon, halting for the day - all ranks accommodated in houses and German huts - Warning orders received to march to be continuous tomorrow -	

WAR DIARY or INTELLIGENCE SUMMARY

Army Form C. 2118.

Place	Date	Hour	Summary of Events and Information	Remarks and references to Appendices
Battalion	19 Oct.		Battalion left REEKE at 10.30 a.m. — marching East along road to LYS. via BOUSBECQUE — RONCQ and MONT D'HALLUIN to TRIEZ CAILLOUX, reaching there about 2 p.m. and was accommodated in large billets. Thin during the march — men optimistic and cheery. The country through which the Battalion marched, and which had been evacuated by the enemy offered a marked contrast to that in which it has been operating so long — Bishops were none in less intact. The country showed with sign it was in comparison to what we had been accustomed for so long, and a number of civilians were seen. During the night 19/20th Oct. our aviators few reconn. for march to be continued.	
	20 Oct.		Bright sunny day — rain by evening, rain again — Battalion left TRIEZ CAILLOUX at 10.30 a.m. — marching via MONT HALLUIN — CROIX ROUGE — STERHOEK — AELBEKE — to ROLLEGHEM, arriving about 3 p.m. and billeted. All villages through which the Battalion marched were decked out with flags etc and the inhabitants were most enthusiastic. Traces of fighting could be seen here and there and several dead horses were lying on the roads.	

WAR DIARY
or
INTELLIGENCE SUMMARY.
(Erase heading not required.)

Army Form C. 2118.

Instructions regarding War Diaries and Intelligence Summaries are contained in F.S. Regs., Part II. and the Staff Manual respectively. Title pages will be prepared in manuscript.

Place	Date	Hour	Summary of Events and Information	Remarks and references to Appendices
Sunday continued	20 Oct		As the Battalion approached ROLLEGHEM a number of houses were seen on fire. Damage by shell was slight — and seemed to have been done to houses east of the village — we were given an open line to advance, and the inhabitants said the enemy had left only yesterday —	
Monday	21 Oct		Bn made slow march from now — Battalion hqs ROLLEGHEM at 9 am — the 89th Brigade became strung out. 9th & 21st Brigades moved forward and established themselves on a line forming East — LENFER right — HELCHIN left — Bn Battalion being at the line of LENFER — HELCHIN. The Battalion was successful but the objective was successfully reached. We also the Battalion remained in position all day and night —	
Tuesday	22 Oct		NNW progress — fine afternoon and evening. Orders came to Battalion to continue the advance and cross the river ESCAULT by means of a pontoon bridge erected by R.E.'s during the night at C5.a.4.5. in front of village of HELCHIN. At 06.00 hours two platoons of 'A' company crossed the river and established themselves on each flank — Owing to heavy fire from enemy machine guns these two platoons were forced to withdraw and further attempts to cross the bridge proved a company sustaining a number of casualties —	

Army Form C. 2118.

WAR DIARY
or
INTELLIGENCE SUMMARY.
(Erase heading not required.)

Instructions regarding War Diaries and Intelligence Summaries are contained in F. S. Regs., Part II. and the Staff Manual respectively. Title pages will be prepared in manuscript.

Place	Date	Hour	Summary of Events and Information	Remarks and references to Appendices
	Tuesday 22 Oct continued		Day of utility harassing fire from hostile frequently during the day but no further rapid movement took place — During the evening the disposition of companies was changed as follows — "B" company moved forward from support over all posts of "A" and "C" companies — "E" company also moved forward from support into the area round GAVRE about 1000 yards West of HELCHIN — "A" and "C" companies on whose withdrawal to support about 3000 yards further West.	
	Wednesday 23 Oct		Fine day — Disposition of Battalion unchanged — Considerable enemy machine gun and artillery throughout the day — During the morning it was found that the pontoon bridge constructed by the R.E. had been damaged by enemy shell fire — Our artillery shelled enemy positions at frequent intervals — Orders received for the evacuation of another pontoon bridge on site of one destroyed by enemy shell fire — our "A" & "D" company to cross the river and establish themselves on eastern side —	
	Thursday 24 Oct		The following is a copy of the report on the operations of "D" company — Officer Commanding Company — Lieut. S.W. BOAST, M.C. — At 01.30 hours one platoon of "D" company was in position on West Side of the ESCAUT awaiting Construction to cross — At 01.50 hours the bridge was complete and	

D. D. & L., London, V.C. 6 (1919) Wt.(V.5300/P713 750,000 3/19 H.2638 Forms/C2118/16

WAR DIARY or INTELLIGENCE SUMMARY

Army Form C. 2118.

Place	Date	Hour	Summary of Events and Information	Remarks and references to Appendices
Thursday 24th Oct continued		08.05	Lance Nk Malone crossed in charge of some guns. P.T. NOLAN, 2nd Platoon in with us on N.E. division slept S.E. bank of river and met with no opposition to north. He with us on N.E. division along S.E. bank of river and met with no opposition until reaching a lonely farm at C5a.10.40, where the Platoon comm. number about movement from a horse about 100 yards further along its new track and also transverse fire from the main railway S.W. though C6a. and C5b. On moving past was treated at C5a.90 am. This was marked. Another of the capture of two prisoners. One of the enemy men also seen running from the farm. Enemy patrol was encountered the machine gun. Also were fired on but were is now known. The Platoon further along the same track with the initiative of placing the Platoon S.E. in C5b. On reaching C5b.05 the Platoon came under heavy machine gun fire from about C5b.3.6 and from the road running from C6a to C5a. On turning the machine gun impossible to get any further forward owing to heavy machine gun fire the Platoon withdrew to C5a.90.80 and established a screen from post to post over a rifle section line and installed the two Lewis guns at C5a.90.75 and C5a.90.70. Throughout the dug in with the intention of hitching on to the previous screen on its main. a screen Platoon had crossed and established posts at C5a.80.60, C5a.80.55 and C5a.60.20 - A Second Platoon also crossed the river and formed a defensive flank on the right to cover the bridge - At 01.00 Bren the enemy opened very heavy shell fire on the old banks of the river. Mainly H.E. - Our new position came under any heavy fire - The bridge to which the Platoon had crossed was made impassable. Sn. O.C. Company then ordered a withdrawal to the N.W. bank of the river and bridge at C4a.41. Platoon came over in ones - This further shower into memory as the bridge this morning -	

Army Form C. 2118.

WAR DIARY
or
INTELLIGENCE SUMMARY.
(Erase heading not required.)

Instructions regarding War Diaries and Intelligence Summaries are contained in F. S. Regs., Part II. and the Staff Manual respectively. Title pages will be prepared in manuscript.

Place	Date 1915	Hour	Summary of Events and Information	Remarks and references to Appendices
	Friday 25 Oct.		Rather dull day. During the morning our artillery bombards actively on our left and enemy "downs" fire - enemy artillery rather inactive. Followed changes in disposition took place during the morning - A Company moved forward to "outposts" line in relief of B Company - C Company moved forward to from support in relief of D. No one of C company on relief supplies to relieve outposts - Bombardier during night. No casualties. Situation quiet.	
	Saturday 26 Oct.		After four hours day - General Situation very quiet but a large number of our aeroplanes were very active - During the evening a change took place in Battalion disposition - A Coy and B Coy moved forward from case support and took our post on front line from two companies of 7th Royal Scots Regt. on left of our original front. A Company and D Coy all been relieved by 3/4th Londons Regt. moving our original line. A company on relief interior to move on U.22.a and 21.f. D Company move from reserve billets to case support in vicinity of CAMPAGNE.	

Army Form C. 2118.

WAR DIARY
or
INTELLIGENCE SUMMARY.
(Erase heading not required.)

Instructions regarding War Diaries and Intelligence Summaries are contained in F. S. Regs., Part II. and the Staff Manual respectively. Title pages will be prepared in manuscript.

Place	Date	Hour	Summary of Events and Information	Remarks and references to Appendices
	Saturday 26 Oct 1918		"B" Company did not move - Battalion Head quarters and Transport remained at original position all ways composed by about 11 pm - no casualties -	
	Sunday 27 Oct		Quiet day, not afternoon firing by enemy - General situation during the enemy the Battalion was relieved by 14th Argyll and Sutherland Highlanders our 1st Battalion Rifle Brigade composed by about 9.30 pm - Battalions on night withdrew to area about one mile north of TUDDERNOORDE. Bivouacing in this area our supplies owing to the large number of artillery units in the area - all roads very much blocked -	
	Monday 28.10.18		Fine day - Battalion at rest.	
	Tuesday 29 Oct		Fine day - no change in disposition - Battalion at bivouac - About 6 pm enemy aeroplane dropped a few bombs in vicinity of Battalion Transport - no casualties -	

Army Form C. 2118.

WAR DIARY
or
INTELLIGENCE SUMMARY.
(Erase heading not required.)

Instructions regarding War Diaries and Intelligence Summaries are contained in F. S. Regs., Part II. and the Staff Manual respectively. Title pages will be prepared in manuscript.

Place	Date	Hour	Summary of Events and Information	Remarks and references to Appendices
	Wednesday 30 October 1918		Very fine day – Disposition unchanged – Training continued. Enemy aeroplanes again very active about 5-30 p.m.; bombs being dropped in the vicinity of RUDDERVOORDE. Fine night	
	Thursday 31 October		Fine day – No change in disposition. Batt⁰ bathed at ROLLEGHEM during the day. Lt. Colonel CHARLES CYRIL STAPLETON MANCHESTER REGT joined and assumed command of the Batt⁰ vice Capt R.M. ROBERTSON MC. Dull cloudy night	

W. Stapleton
Lieut Colonel
Commdg 2nd Lancashire R

2nd. Battalion South Lancashire Regiment

1st to 30th November 1915

War diary

51A
sheet

Army Form C. 2118.

WAR DIARY
or
INTELLIGENCE SUMMARY.
(Erase heading not required.)

Instructions regarding War Diaries and Intelligence Summaries are contained in F. S. Regs., Part II. and the Staff Manual respectively. Title pages will be prepared in manuscript.

Place	Date 19/8	Hour	Summary of Events and Information	Remarks and references to Appendices
	Friday 1. Mar.		Fine day – no change in disposition – Companies at training –	
	Saturday 2 Mar.		Fine day – Disposition unchanged – Training continued –	
	Sunday 3 Mar.		Fine day – Disposition unchanged – Training suspended – Divine Service – Warning order received for Brigade to be prepared to move forward in relief of Nov. of 90th Brigade –	
	Monday 4 Mar.		Fine day – about 11 am enemy commenced to shell the area occupied by Battalion Headquarters – A and B Companies and Transport. This continued till about 2 pm – on these shells a direct occupied by transport dirricks, one man being wounded – beyond this there was no other casualty or damage – Battalion moved into Brigade Reserve in Area O.21.22.27 a & b. 26 a & b. 29 a & b – about 3 miles north of SAINT GENOIS – L. Company moved off about 2 pm – running into Units at 15 minute intervals, in following order – B.A.D. Lewis gunners – workers and battle limbers accompanying companies & in the remainder Transport moving to new area at 3 pm – move completed by about 5 pm – Battalion was billeted in hutts –	

WAR DIARY or INTELLIGENCE SUMMARY.

Army Form C. 2118.

(Erase heading not required.)

Place	Date	Hour	Summary of Events and Information	Remarks and references to Appendices
	Tuesday 5 Sept.		Very wet day – Battalion dispositions unchanged –	
	Wednesday 6 Sept.		Exceptionally wet day – no change in dispositions –	
	Thursday 7 Sept.		Fine dull day – Battalion moved forward to relieve 2/16th London Regiment under following arrangements – B Company left billets at 2.15 p.m. – assuming sub. units at 15 minute intervals in following order – A, C, D Coys. Battalion Headquarters – B Company took over Q. Company 2/16th London Regt. area with one platoon established just on eastern side of stream about 2 miles east of MOEN – A and C companies were in support in vicinity of RAAPTORF about 1 mile N.W. of B Company – D Company in support reserve at TAAPESTRAAT about 1½ miles north of MOEN – Battalion headquarters about ¾ mile north of MOEN – Battalion arrived – no enemy opposition –	

WAR DIARY or INTELLIGENCE SUMMARY

Army Form C. 2118.

Place	Date 1918	Hour	Summary of Events and Information	Remarks and references to Appendices
	Friday 6 Nov		Weather dull day. Disposition of Battalion unchanged. General situation quiet. Our patrols very active day and night. During the night "B" Company endeavoured to cross River Schelde on a small raft such capable of holding 2 men. Considerable opposition was encountered and raft was sunk all on raft got into dinghy & got that "B" Company established itself on the opposite bank. They occupied the village of ESCANAFFLES. Prior to this operation a hostile post, holding a crossing of a subsidiary stream, had first to be rushed; this was successfully carried out at 10/pm by a patrol of "B" Company under 2nd Lieut. Houghton, 3 prisoners and a machine gun being captured.	
	Saturday 9 Nov		Very fine day. On 10 am B Company was ordered to cross the river in support of "B" Company which was at the same time ordered forward. Another mile & with later the Battalion was moved to 1500 yds. of pursuit of its enemy who was in full retreat and by nightfall was billeted on line RENAIX – AUTRYVE 1000 yards East of WATTRIPONT. Transport moved during the night – Owing to all bridges having been destroyed by enemy Company situation had to be erected. This caused considerable delay and the actual advance of rations was eventually effected by means of pack animals. Bed fast night.	

WAR DIARY
or
INTELLIGENCE SUMMARY.
(Erase heading not required.)

Army Form C. 2118.

Place	Date	Hour	Summary of Events and Information	Remarks and references to Appendices
Sunday	10th Nov.	About 9.30 a.m.	Forward movement continued. Battalion occupying ELLEZELLES; orders from Bing[?] Adv[?] to establish outposts on the line [struck through] ELLEZELLES - [struck through] in this vicinity. Captain K.M. BOURNE M.C. and one other rank were wounded by a shell from enemy field gun. Transport moved to TER STOOKT, about 1½ miles South of RENAIX. Supplies taken forward to Battalion during the night.	
Monday	11 Nov.	About 9 a.m.	Information from Division to the effect that an Armistice had been signed and all advance or move forward the Battalion.	
		About 11 a.m.	the Battalion moved in Brigade Reserve forward with orders to march to AULNOIT, via ELLEZELLES. On arrival in the vicinity of FLOBECQ these orders were changed and motors came to billets in FLOBECQ. Battalion holding point were at once sent out and Battalion eventually all were billeted by about 5 p.m. During the march enthusiasm was shown by the inhabitants, and on arrival in FLOBECQ the people were much excited and gave the troops an extraordinary welcome. The Band of the Battalion performed in the square of the town much to the satisfaction of the inhabitants. The day generally was dull[?]	

Army Form C. 2118.

WAR DIARY
or
INTELLIGENCE SUMMARY.
(Erase heading not required.)

Instructions regarding War Diaries and Intelligence Summaries are contained in F. S. Regs., Part II. and the Staff Manual respectively. Title pages will be prepared in manuscript.

Place	Date	Hour	Summary of Events and Information	Remarks and references to Appendices
	Tuesday 12 Nov.		Very fine day – Battalion in billets at FLOBECQ.	
	Wednesday 13 Nov.		Fine day – Disposition unchanged – Sub-units at training –	
	Thursday 14 Nov.		Fine bright day – Battalion moved from FLOBECQ to RENAIX – Bgde first moved at 10.10 am arrived later about 1 pm and occupied billets –	
	Friday 15 Nov.		Very fine day – Battalion in billets at RENAIX – Warning orders received for move tomorrow –	
	Saturday 16 Nov.		Fine bright day but cold and frosty – Battalion left RENAIX at 6 am and marched to HELCHIN arrived about 2 pm and billets for the night – accommodation in billets.	
	Sunday 17 Nov.		Very fine day – cold and frosty – Battalion left HELCHIN at 10.40 am for LUINGNE arriving about 1.30 pm being accommodated in billets –	

Army Form C. 2118.

WAR DIARY
or
INTELLIGENCE SUMMARY.
(Erase heading not required.)

Instructions regarding War Diaries and Intelligence Summaries are contained in F. S. Regs., Part II. and the Staff Manual respectively. Title pages will be prepared in manuscript.

Place	Date 1918	Hour	Summary of Events and Information	Remarks and references to Appendices
Monday	18 Nov.		Dull day - Some rain - Disposition of Battalion unchanged - at rest.	
Tuesday	19 Nov.		Dull day - Fog at night - Disposition unchanged - Training in progress -	
Wednesday	20 Nov.		Dull frosty day - Disposition unchanged - Bryan Church Parade Thanksgiving Service -	
Thursday	21 Nov.		Very fine day - Disposition unchanged - Training continues -	
Friday	22 Nov.		Fine bright day - Disposition unchanged. Training continues -	
Saturday	23 Nov.		Fine bright day - Disposition unchanged - Battalion bathed - Bands proceeded to TOURCOING to take part in a ceremonial parade in connection with the handing over the second army flag to the MAIRE of TOURCOING -	
Sunday	24 Nov.		Fine day - Disposition unchanged - Training suspended - Divine Service -	
Monday	25 Nov.		Dull wet day - Disposition unchanged - Battalion route march -	
Tuesday	26 Nov.		Rather dull day - Disposition unchanged - Training continues.	

Army Form C. 2118.

WAR DIARY
or
INTELLIGENCE SUMMARY.
(Erase heading not required.)

Instructions regarding War Diaries and Intelligence Summaries are contained in F. S. Regs., Part II. and the Staff Manual respectively. Title pages will be prepared in manuscript.

Place	Date 1918	Hour	Summary of Events and Information	Remarks and references to Appendices
	Wednesday 27 Nov.		Fine day - Dispositions unchanged - Battalion paraded in service dress, short coats - 11 am for march to MOUSCRON. Strength of march past battalion 15 officers and 15 other ranks. Orders received for move of Brigade to ST. OMER area by march route, commencing tomorrow.	
	Thursday 28 Nov.		Very wet day - Battalion left LUINGHE on 9 am and marched to LINSELLES arriving about 1.15 p.m. Billets in billets by 1.30 p.m. - all ranks very wet.	
	Friday 29 Nov.		Dull and unsettled - Battalion left LINSELLES on 9 am - marching via QUESNOY to LA PREVOTÉ, back of ARMENTIERES, arriving about 1 pm. Battalion accommodated in German huts - all huts very damp. Rain commenced about 2 pm and continues for several hours. Very cold night.	
	Saturday 30 Nov.		Still cold day - Battalion left LA PREVOTE at 8.40 am, marching via HOUPLINES - ARMENTIERES - SAILLY SUR LA LYS - LA GORGUE - and to LESTREM about 3.30 pm and surprise billets. A halt was made from 12 noon to 1 pm in the vicinity of SAILLY	

Army Form C. 2118.

WAR DIARY
or
INTELLIGENCE SUMMARY.
(Erase heading not required.)

Instructions regarding War Diaries and Intelligence Summaries are contained in F. S. Regs., Part II. and the Staff Manual respectively. Title pages will be prepared in manuscript.

Place	Date	Hour	Summary of Events and Information	Remarks and references to Appendices
Saturday continued	30		and dinner served. The march was a long one but all ranks marched well. The common plans through which the battalion passed were in absolute ruins as the result of shell fire.	

C. Witts Lt. Colonel
Commdg. 2. S. Som. R.

Vol 52

52.A

2nd. Battalion South Lancashire Regiment.

War diary — 1st to 31st December 1915

5 pages.

Army Form C. 2118.

WAR DIARY
or
INTELLIGENCE SUMMARY.
(Erase heading not required.)

Instructions regarding War Diaries and Intelligence Summaries are contained in F. S. Regs., Part II. and the Staff Manual respectively. Title pages will be prepared in manuscript.

Place	Date	Hour	Summary of Events and Information	Remarks and references to Appendices
Sunday - W. Ste.	1/10/16		Battalion & left LESTREM at 9.20am, marching via MERVILLE and CALONNÉ arrives at ST. VENANT about 12.30pm and occupies billets. Accommodation very poor owing to the town having been badly damaged by shell fire. Still day - none are cold.	
Monday 2. Ste.			Still day - Battalion left ST VENANT at 9.30am, marching via STEENBECQUE STATION - SERCUS - ST. LEDGER, reaches LYNDE at 1.20pm. Great difficulty was experienced in billeting as accommodation was very indifferent - men very uncomfortable -	
Tuesday 3. Ste.			Still day - marches to rain - Battalion is not at LYNDE. Efforts made to improve billets -	
Wednesday 4. Ste.			Weather dull day - Battalion disposition unchanged - Day devoted to cleaning up generally -	

Army Form C. 2118.

WAR DIARY
or
INTELLIGENCE SUMMARY.
(Erase heading not required.)

Instructions regarding War Diaries and Intelligence Summaries are contained in F.S. Regs., Part II. and the Staff Manual respectively. Title pages will be prepared in manuscript.

Place	Date 1916	Hour	Summary of Events and Information	Remarks and references to Appendices
	Thursday 5 Dec.		Still day. Disposition unchanged. Companies at disposal of company commanders.	
	Friday 6 Dec.		Still cold day. Disposition unchanged. Training in progress.	
	Saturday 7 Dec.		Very fine bright day. Disposition unchanged. Training continues.	
	Sunday 8 Dec.		Fine bright day. Disposition unchanged. Battalion at rest.	
	Monday 9 Dec.		Fine day. Disposition unchanged. Training continues.	
	Tuesday 10 Dec.		Fine day. Disposition unchanged. Training continues.	
	Wednesday 11 Dec.		Dull day. Some rain. Disposition unchanged. Training continues.	
	Thursday 12 Dec.		Still wet day. Disposition unchanged. Companies employed in filling in trenches in Battalion area.	

Army Form C. 2118.

WAR DIARY
or
INTELLIGENCE SUMMARY.
(Erase heading not required.)

Instructions regarding War Diaries and Intelligence Summaries are contained in F. S. Regs., Part II. and the Staff Manual respectively. Title pages will be prepared in manuscript.

Place	Date 1916	Hour	Summary of Events and Information	Remarks and references to Appendices
	Friday 13 Dec.		Wet day. Dispositions unchanged. Filling in trenches continues.	
	Saturday 14 Dec.		Still unsettled day. Dispositions unchanged. Companies at disposal of company commanders.	
	Sunday 15 Dec.		Fine day. Dispositions unchanged. Battalion at rest.	
	Monday 16 Dec.		Fine day. Slight rain. Dispositions unchanged. Training continues.	
	Tuesday 17 Dec.		Fine day. Dispositions unchanged. Filling in trenches continues.	
	Wednesday 18 Dec.		Still unsettled day. Considerable rain. Dispositions unchanged. Training continues.	
	Thursday 19 Dec.		Fine day. Cold. Dispositions unchanged. Filling in trenches continues. Heavy rain during the night.	
	Friday 20 Dec.		Fine day. Rather cold. Dispositions unchanged. Training continues.	
	Saturday 21 Dec.		Fine day. Cold. Dispositions unchanged. Brigade ceremonial parade.	

Army Form C. 2118.

WAR DIARY
or
INTELLIGENCE SUMMARY.

(Erase heading not required.)

Instructions regarding War Diaries and Intelligence Summaries are contained in F. S. Regs., Part II. and the Staff Manual respectively. Title pages will be prepared in manuscript.

4

Place	Date 1918	Hour	Summary of Events and Information	Remarks and references to Appendices
	Sunday 22 Dec.		Dull and unsettled - heavy rain during afternoon and evening. Disposition unchanged. Battalion at rest.	
	Monday 23 Dec.		Wet and squally morning - Fine afternoon - Disposition unchanged. Training continues.	
	Tuesday 24 Dec.		Dull and unsettled - Wet during the afternoon - Fine night, very cold. Battalion column arrived from Regimental Depot in charge of Lieut. W. O. NEESHAM and 2nd Lieut. F. BOAST.	
	Wednesday 25 Dec.		Fine bright morning. Battalion ceremonial parade to receive and salute the colours, followed by Divine Service.	
	Thursday 26 Dec.		Fine day - Disposition unchanged. Battalion at rest.	
	Friday 27 Dec.		Still unsettled day - Rather cold - Training in trenches continues.	
	Saturday 28 Dec.		Very wet day - Disposition unchanged.	

Army Form C. 2118.

WAR DIARY
or
INTELLIGENCE SUMMARY.
(Erase heading not required.)

Instructions regarding War Diaries and Intelligence Summaries are contained in F. S. Regs., Part II. and the Staff Manual respectively. Title pages will be prepared in manuscript.

Place	Date	Hour	Summary of Events and Information	Remarks and references to Appendices
5	1918			
	Sunday 29 Dec		Still and unsettled – very boisterous – Disposition unchanged – Battalion at rest	
	Monday 30 Dec		Still and unsettled – considerable rain during the day – Battalion route march.	
	Tuesday 31 Dec		Fine day – slight rain – Disposition unchanged – Training continues –	

C. Little
Lieut. Colonel
Commanding 2nd. South Lancashire Regiment

30

2nd Battalion South Lancashire Regiment

1st to 31st January 1919

War diary

5 pages.

53 A
6 sheets

WAR DIARY
or
INTELLIGENCE SUMMARY.
(Erase heading not required.)

Army Form C. 2118.

Place	Date	Hour	Summary of Events and Information	Remarks and references to Appendices
	Wednesday 1 Jan 1919		Fine day – cold – wet night – Battalion still in billets at LYNDE. Trench felling continues –	
	Thursday 2 Jan		Fine day – heavy rain during the night – Disposition unchanged – Trench felling continues. Warning orders received for move of Battalion on 4th –	
	Friday 3 Jan		Still an unsettled day – very windy – wet night – Disposition unchanged – Battalion preparing to move –	
	Saturday 4 Jan		Fine day – cold wind – Battalion left LYNDE at 10.30 am and marches to RACQUINGHEM, arriving about noon and occupies billets – wet night –	
	Sunday 5 Jan		Very wet day – Battalion halts at RACQUINGHEM –	
	Monday 6 Jan		Fine day – rather cold – Battalion still halts at RACQUINGHEM –	

WAR DIARY
or
INTELLIGENCE SUMMARY.
(Erase heading not required.)

Army Form C. 2118.

Instructions regarding War Diaries and Intelligence Summaries are contained in F. S. Regs., Part II. and the Staff Manual respectively. Title pages will be prepared in manuscript.

Place	Date	Hour	Summary of Events and Information	Remarks and references to Appendices
	Tuesday 5 Jan 1916		Fine day. Cold. Disposition unchanged. Orders received for Battalion to move tomorrow to BOULOGNE by motor transport.	
	Wednesday 6 Jan		Fine day but very cold. Battalion, less transport, left RACQUINGHEM in motor lorries at 10 a.m. for BOULOGNE about 4 miles short of BOULOGNE. When orders were received to proceed to No 10 Convalescent Camp for accommodation, where it arrived about 6 p.m. Several lorries breaking down caused delay to convoy.	
	Thursday 7 Jan		Very stormy day. Disposition of Battalion unchanged. Very wet and stormy night.	
	Friday 8 Jan		Cold, boisterous day. Frequent heavy showers. Disposition unchanged. Orders received for Battalion to move to OSTROHOVE CAMP near BOULOGNE.	
	Saturday 9 Jan		Squally and cold. Battalion left No 10 Convalescent Camp, ECAULT, 10 a.m. marching via PONT de BRIQUES to OSTROHOVE CAMP where it arrived about 1 p.m. The Battalion now organises into 5 Wings and Headquarters, with 2 Wings attached from 6th Inniskilling Fusiliers and 1 Wing from 2-17th Lancers. Kit - 20 "B" Group No 1, District "Reserve" motor or scheme for dealing with Officers and men arriving from other units, to be sent to England for demobilisation. At the same time the demobilising of all ranks of the Battalion itself which contains some time ago, is being continued, men being sent away practically every day.	

Army Form C. 2118.

WAR DIARY
or
INTELLIGENCE SUMMARY.
(Erase heading not required.)

Instructions regarding War Diaries and Intelligence Summaries are contained in F. S. Regs., Part II. and the Staff Manual respectively. Title pages will be prepared in manuscript.

Place	Date	Hour	Summary of Events and Information	Remarks and references to Appendices
	Sunday 12 Jan 1919		Cold dark day - considerable rain - Disposition unchanged - Preparation in progress for dealing with men expected to arrive for demobilization.	
	Monday 13 Jan		Fine day - rather wet - Disposition unchanged. Parties for demobilization arrived and men drew suits by various things.	
	Tuesday 14 Jan		Cold windy day - Disposition unchanged - Further parties arrives for demobilization. Wet stormy night.	
	Wednesday 15 Jan		Very wet stormy day - minimum by night - Disposition unchanged - Demobilization work continues -	
	Thursday 16 Jan		Dull very stormy - much heavy rain at frequent intervals all day and night. Disposition unchanged. Work in connection with demobilization continues -	
	Friday 17 Jan		Weather much improved - Disposition unchanged - Demobilization work continues -	

Army Form C. 2118.

WAR DIARY
or
INTELLIGENCE SUMMARY.
(Erase heading not required.)

Instructions regarding War Diaries and Intelligence Summaries are contained in F. S. Regs., Part II. and the Staff Manual respectively. Title pages will be prepared in manuscript.

4

Place	Date 1916	Hour	Summary of Events and Information	Remarks and references to Appendices
	Saturday 18 Jan		Very fine bright day – cold – Disposition unchanged	
	Sunday 19 Jan		Very fine day – Disposition unchanged	
	Monday 20 Jan		Miserable day – very cold and windy – Disposition unchanged	
	Tuesday 21 Jan		Fine day – very wet – Disposition unchanged	
	Wednesday 22 Jan		Fine day – very wet – frosty night – Disposition unchanged	
	Thursday 23 Jan		Very cold day – Disposition unchanged	
	Friday 24 Jan		Cold frosty day – Disposition unchanged	
	Saturday 25 Jan		Cold day – Disposition unchanged – snow during the night	
	Sunday 26 Jan		Very wet day – Disposition unchanged	
	Monday 27 Jan		Wet miserable day. Disposition unchanged – snow at night	

WAR DIARY
or
INTELLIGENCE SUMMARY.
(Erase heading not required.)

Army Form C. 2118.

Place	Date	Hour	Summary of Events and Information	Remarks and references to Appendices
	Tuesday 28 Jan 1919		Still unsettled day - very cold. Disposition unchanged	
	Wednesday 29 Jan		Very cold and frosty - Disposition unchanged	
	Thursday 30 Jan		Very cold - freezing hard - Disposition unchanged	
	Friday 31 Jan		Very cold day - hard frost - Disposition unchanged	

C. Alle
Lieut. Colonel.
Commanding 2nd S. Lancashire Regt

CONFIDENTIAL.

WAR DIARY OF

2nd. Bn. South Lancs. Regt.

FROM 1st February, 1919 TO 28th February, 1919.

Army Form C. 2118.

WAR DIARY
or
INTELLIGENCE SUMMARY.
(Erase heading not required.)

Instructions regarding War Diaries and Intelligence Summaries are contained in F. S. Regs., Part II. and the Staff Manual respectively. Title pages will be prepared in manuscript.

Place	Date 1919	Hour	Summary of Events and Information	Remarks and references to Appendices
	Saturday 1st Feb.		Battalion with 2nd/1st on OSTROHOVE CAMP - BOULOGNE - organised as No. 1 Group. Stopforth Division under some arrangements as on 11th January for dealing with officers and other ranks passing this Port for demobilisation. Snowy most of the day - very cold.	
	Sunday 2 Feb		Very cold - severe frost at night. Disposition unchanged.	
	Monday 3 Feb		Fine - very cold day. Disposition unchanged.	
	Tuesday 4 Feb		Still day - muggy and inclined to rain. Disposition unchanged.	
	Wednesday 5. Feb.		Heavy fall of snow. Disposition unchanged.	
	Thursday 6 Feb		Bright thaw day. Camidiville thaw. Disposition unchanged. Severe frost at night. Freezing hard.	
	Friday 7 Feb		Bitterly cold day. Freezing hard. Disposition unchanged.	

Army Form C. 2118.

WAR DIARY
or
INTELLIGENCE SUMMARY.
(Erase heading not required.)

Instructions regarding War Diaries and Intelligence Summaries are contained in F. S. Regs., Part II. and the Staff Manual respectively. Title pages will be prepared in manuscript.

Place	Date 1919	Hour	Summary of Events and Information	Remarks and references to Appendices
	Saturday 8th Feb.		Battalion still at OSTROVO CAMP. Weather very cold but hot sun at midday	
	Sunday 9th Feb.		Very cold. Disposition unchanged.	
	Monday 10th Feb.		Very cold still. Disposition unchanged. Reinforcements arrived at Camp. 1 Bandmaster 29 O.R. all handover of the 2nd South Lancashire Regt.	
	Tuesday 11th Feb.		Warmer during the day but frost in the evening. Disposition unchanged.	
	Wednesday 12th Feb.		Much warmer, a distinct thaw. Disposition unchanged.	
	Thursday 13th Feb.		Still warm. Reinforcements of 6 offr. 8/185 O.R. arrived this morning from the 2/4 battalion of the regiment. Disposition unchanged	
	Friday 14th Feb.		Weather fine. Disposition unchanged.	

Army Form C. 2118.

WAR DIARY
or
INTELLIGENCE SUMMARY.
(Erase heading not required.)

Place	Date 1919	Hour	Summary of Events and Information	Remarks and references to Appendices
	Saturday 15th Feb.		Battalion still at Ostrokov Camp. Warm, but some rain. Disposition unchanged.	
	Sunday 16		Very wet day. Disposition unchanged.	
	Monday 17th		Fine and warm all day. Disposition unchanged.	
	Tuesday 18th		Fine morning but very wet afternoon & evening. Disposition unchanged.	
	Wednesday 19th		Fine day but rain in the evening & night. Disposition unchanged.	
	Thursday 20th		Very wet day. Disposition unchanged.	
	Friday 21st		Fine morning, but very wet afternoon & evening. 2 Offrs & 81 O.R. arrived as reinforcements from the 1/5th Battalion of the regiment. 4 Offrs & 8 O.R. arrived as reinforcements from the 2/4th Battalion of the regiment	

Army Form C. 2118.

WAR DIARY
or
INTELLIGENCE SUMMARY.
(Erase heading not required.)

Instructions regarding War Diaries and Intelligence Summaries are contained in F. S. Regs, Part II. and the Staff Manual respectively. Title pages will be prepared in manuscript.

1919

Place	Date	Hour	Summary of Events and Information	Remarks and references to Appendices
	Saturday Feb. 22.		Battalion still at Ostrohove Camp. Very wet all day. Disposition unchanged.	
	Sunday Feb. 23.		Fine and warm. Disposition unchanged.	
	Monday Feb. 24.		Fine day but very wet night. Disposition unchanged.	
	Tuesday Feb. 25		Fine all day. Disposition unchanged.	
	Wednesday Feb. 26.		Fine morning. Very wet afternoon. Disposition unchanged.	
	Thursday Feb. 27.		Fine day, very wet night. One officer reinforcement from the 2/4th Battalion of the regiment reported today.	
	Friday Feb. 28.		Wet morning, but fine afternoon. Disposition unchanged.	

C. Ville
Lt. Col.
O.C. 2nd Batt. S. Lanc. Regt.

1st S. Lancs. Duplicate

Vol 55

55A
5 sheets

WAR DIARY
or
INTELLIGENCE SUMMARY.
(Erase heading not required.)

Army Form C. 2118.

Place	Date	Hour	Summary of Events and Information	Remarks and references to Appendices
	Sunday 1st March		Fine all day. Battalion still at Abrahms Camp. Disposition unchanged.	
	Sunday 2nd March		Fine morning. Showery in the afternoon & evening. Disposition unchanged.	
	Monday 3rd March		Wet day. Dispositions unchanged. Very foggy on the English Channel at night.	
	Tuesday 4th March		Wet day and very wet night. Reinforcements of 10 offs. & 231 o.r. arrived from the 1/5 Batt. King's Shropshire Light Infantry, and one officer from the 2/4 Batt. S. Lanc. Regt.	
	Wednesday 5th March		Very wet day and night. Dispositions unchanged.	
			Showery weather. Dispositions unchanged. Showery day. Dispositions unchanged.	

Duplicate

Army Form C. 2118.

WAR DIARY
or
INTELLIGENCE SUMMARY.
(Erase heading not required.)

Instructions regarding War Diaries and Intelligence Summaries are contained in F.S. Regs., Part II. and the Staff Manual respectively. Title pages will be prepared in manuscript.

Place	Date	Hour	Summary of Events and Information	Remarks and references to Appendices
Saturday	March 1st		Showery. Battalion still at Ostrolow camp. Trenches unchanged.	
Sunday	"	9th	Weather stormy. Trenches unchanged.	
Monday	"	10th	Fine day. Trenches unchanged.	
Tuesday	"	11th	Weather showery. Trenches unchanged.	
Wednesday	"	12th	Wet day. Trenches unchanged	
Thursday	"	13th	Fine day. Wet night. Trenches unchanged.	
Friday	"	14th	Wet day. Fine evening with good sunset.	

Army Form C. 2118.

WAR DIARY
or
INTELLIGENCE SUMMARY.
(Erase heading not required.)

Instructions regarding War Diaries and Intelligence Summaries are contained in F. S. Regs., Part II. and the Staff Manual respectively. Title pages will be prepared in manuscript.

Place	Date	Hour	Summary of Events and Information	Remarks and references to Appendices
	1919.			
	Saturday Mar 15.		Battalion still at Octshove Camp. Fine & warm all day. Disposition unchanged.	
	Sunday Mar. 16.		Very fine & warm day. Much cooler at night. Disposition unchanged.	
	Monday Mar. 17.		Fine & warm all day. Disposition unchanged.	
	Tuesday Mar. 18.		Fine and warm all day. Wet at night. Disposition unchanged.	
	Wednesday Mar. 19.		Heavy dull day. Yet somewhat successful night. Disposition unchanged.	
	Thursday Mar 20.		Showery all day. Disposition unchanged.	
	Friday Mar. 21.		Fine but dull. Disposition unchanged.	

Duplicate

Army Form C. 2118.

WAR DIARY
or
INTELLIGENCE SUMMARY.
(Erase heading not required.)

Instructions regarding War Diaries and Intelligence Summaries are contained in F. S. Regs., Part II. and the Staff Manual respectively. Title pages will be prepared in manuscript.

Place	Date	Hour	Summary of Events and Information	Remarks and references to Appendices
Saturday	March 22		Battalion still at Othokove camp. Fine all day & night. Disposition unchanged.	
Sunday	" 23		Fine all day. Cold night. Disposition unchanged.	
Monday	" 24		Fine all day, but very cold. Disposition unchanged.	
Tuesday	" 25		Fine all day & night. Very cold. Very cold piercing wind. Disposition unchanged.	
Wednesday	" 26		Fine but cold. Reinforcements of 59 other ranks from 1/1 Batt. Shropshire Light Inf. arrived to-day.	
Thursday	" 27		Very wet and stormy morning. Fine and sunny in the afternoon. Disposition unchanged.	
Friday	" 28		Fine all day. Disposition unchanged. Heavy fall of snow in the night.	

Duplicate

Army Form C. 2118.

WAR DIARY
or
INTELLIGENCE SUMMARY.
(Erase heading not required.)

Instructions regarding War Diaries and Intelligence Summaries are contained in F. S. Regs., Part II. and the Staff Manual respectively. Title pages will be prepared in manuscript.

Place	Date	Hour	Summary of Events and Information	Remarks and references to Appendices
Saturday	29		Battalion still at Ookthan camp. Still enemy slightly on the wrong. Guns & heavy of Guns. Position unchanged.	
Sunday	30		Coy. rel. slight camp. fell about mid-day very slight. Battle of Ball. Detonations unchanged.	
Monday	31		Coy. rel. camp. still same as J. Fine with are was till of transm. Situation unchanged. The centre of 1/5 Bn. of the regiment, consisting of 14 officers & 147 men with Transport, stores &c. arrived at the camp at a 2.30 hrs this morning. During the forenoon at which the battalion lay been at Ookthan camp, the following have passed through the camp for demobilization. OHP 3094 OR 14-5185	

C. Little
Lieut. Col.
Commdg. 2nd Btn. S. Lanc. Regt.

60TH DIVISION
179TH INFY. BDE

2/17
2/17TH BN LONDON REGT
~~JUN 1919 - SEP 1919~~
1918 JUN   1919 SEP

FROM EGYPT
60 DIV
180 BDE

Box 2336

89/30

Vol I

Confidential

War Diary

of the

2/7th Battalion London Regiment

From 1st June 1918.

To 30th June 1918.

[signature] Lieut Col
Commanding 2/7th Bn London Regt.

Army Form C. 2118.

WAR DIARY
or
INTELLIGENCE SUMMARY.
(Erase heading not required.)

Place	Date	Hours	Summary of Events and Information	Remarks and references to Appendices
KANTARA	1/6/18	0500	Battalion detrained at KANTARA from LUDD	JWA
	2/6/18		Weekly Military Biogh 44 O.R. arrived. Total admitted to hospital Week ending June 2nd 14 O.R. 573861 Rfn RUDDLE A.T. died in hospital	JWA
	3/6/18		Company Training. Physical Drill, Musketry, Gas drill. 2/Lt GREENWICH + 29 O.T. left/m PORT SAID for embarkation to PORT SAID for MARSEILLES	JWA
	4/6/18		Company Training 2/Lt B.J. CHAPMAN 6th Rif Royale reported for duty	JWA
	5/6/18		Companies inspected m/Gas helmet fittings. 2/Lt J.S. 25 O.R. reported. Rep Ling N. Walton with Eype.	JWA
	6/6/18		Company Training	JWA
	7/6/18		Company Training 14 O.R. reported for duty. 2/Lt W A. BULLOCK reported for duty	JWA
	8/6/18		Company Training Church Parade. Lieut Counter to Hospital Week Ending June 9th 3 O.R.	JWA
	9/6/18		Bnght 23 O.R. reported for duty.	JWA

Army Form C. 2118.

WAR DIARY
or
INTELLIGENCE SUMMARY.
(Erase heading not required.)

Instructions regarding War Diaries and Intelligence Summaries are contained in F.S. Regs., Part II. and the Staff Manual respectively. Title pages will be prepared in manuscript.

Place	Date	Hour	Summary of Events and Information	Remarks and references to Appendices
KANTARA	10/6/18		Company Training	A.I.F.
	11/6/18		Company Training	A.I.F.
	12/6/18		3 off. 8 o.r. reported for duty	A.I.F.
	13/6/18		Company Training	A.I.F.
	14/6/18		Reinforcement of 10 o.r. reported for duty	
	15/6/18	0900	Loading up preparatory to move from KANTARA WEST to ALEXANDRIA	A.I.F.
		1740	Battalion Marched to Station	A.I.F.
		2110	Battalion left KANTARA Station by train	A.I.F.
ALEXANDRIA	16/6/18	0540	Arrived ALEXANDRIA Embarked on H.M.T. CANBERRA	A.I.F.
		0930	Sick admitted to Hospital for week ending June 16th 5 o.r. Embarkation Strength 30 officers 630 o.r.	

WAR DIARY
or
INTELLIGENCE SUMMARY.

(Erase heading not required.)

Army Form C. 2118.

Place	Date	Hour	Summary of Events and Information	Remarks and references to Appendices
~~16-18/6/18~~ ALEXANDRIA	17/6/18		On board H.M.T. CANBERRA	App B
	18/6/18	13.30	H.M.T CANBERRA sailed.	App.
	19/6/18		Physical drill. Boat stations & alarm posts.	App.
At Sea	19/6/18		Physical drill	App.
At Sea	20/6/18		Physical drill	App.
At Sea	21/6/18	11.30	Convoy attacked by Submarine.	App.
		13.00	Arrived TARANTO	
		15.30	Entered inner harbour	
TARANTO	22/6/18	14.00	Disembarked & marched to South Camp CIMINO	App.
TARANTO	23/6/18		Washing Clothing. Seven other ranks admitted to Hospital	App.
	24/6/18	13.00	Entrained at CIMINO Siding	App.
		15.07	Train departed	

WAR DIARY
or
INTELLIGENCE SUMMARY.

(Erase heading not required.)

Army Form C. 2118.

Place	Date	Hour	Summary of Events and Information	Remarks and references to Appendices
In Train	25/6/18	10.00	Halte Repas at FOGIA	JMD
		19.00	Halte Repas at CASTELAMARA	JMD
	26/6/18	10.00	Halte Repas at FAENZA	JMD
	27/6/18	06.00	Halte Repas at SAVONA	JMD
		17.00	Halte Repas at VENTIMIGLIA	JMD
	28/6/18	07.45	Halte Repas at MIRIMAS	JMD
		15.05	Halte Repas at LE TEIL	JMD
	29/6/18	06.05	Halte Repas at PARAY LE MOINAL	
		18.15	Halte Repas at MALESHERBES	
	30/6/18	12.45	Halte Repas at NOYELLES	
		19.00	Detrained at AUDRUIQ Sick admitted to Hospital 13 or	JMD
OUEST MONT		23.45	Arrived at Rest at OUEST MONT. Strength including Transport 31 Officers 636 or	

Murphy/tayl. Project lady
Lieut Col. 2/1/yh Battn. London Regt.

Confidential

War Diary

of

2/17th Battn London Regiment

1st – 31st July 1918

CONFIDENTIAL

WAR DIARY

of

1/17th Battalion London Regiment

From 1st July 1918. To 31st July 1918.

[signature]
Lieut. Colonel
Commanding 1/17th Battalion London Regiment.

Army Form C. 2118.

WAR DIARY
or
INTELLIGENCE SUMMARY.
(Erase heading not required.)

* Instructions regarding War Diaries and Intelligence Summaries are contained in F. S. Regs., Part II. and the Staff Manual respectively. Title pages will be prepared in manuscript.

Place	Date	Hour	Summary of Events and Information	Remarks and references to Appendices
OUEST MONT	1/7/18		Interior economy	
	2/7/18	11 am	Inspection of Companies by B.G.C. and address to Officers	
		12:50 pm	Physical Training	
	3/7/18	8 am	Physical Drill. Specialist classes in Lewis Gun & Bombing	
		9" "	Box Respirators	
		11 am	Bayonet fighting. Specialist Box Respirator training for employment	
			Musketry	
		1 pm	Range Practice for all Companies	
		4 pm		
	4/7/18	9:30 am to	Gas lectures and Demonstration by Divisional Gas Officer at Divisional Gas school. Attendance 4 in command & NCOs attached to Companies during	
			Battalion Training as in 3/7/18 and Tactical Schemes by Companies	
		4:30pm	in afternoon. Special Bayonet fighting Class for NCOs.	
			Capt W.O. E.J. WELSHER M.C. C.F. (Presbyterian) is attached to us from 2/7/18.	
	5/7/18	8 am	Special Gas training for whole Battalion. Lectures & demonstrations as per Appendix.	
		11:50	Divisional Gas Officer	

Army Form C. 2118.

WAR DIARY
or
INTELLIGENCE SUMMARY.
(Erase heading not required.)

Instructions regarding War Diaries and Intelligence Summaries are contained in F. S. Regs., Part II. and the Staff Manual respectively. Title pages will be prepared in manuscript.

Place	Date	Hour	Summary of Events and Information	Remarks and references to Appendices
OUESTMONT	5/7/18	4pm to 6pm	Range Practice for whole Battalion.	
"	6/7/18	9am to 1pm	Special Pro Musketry to complete Skeleton of 5/7/18	
		2pm to 5pm	Recreational Training	
	7/7/18	11am	Church Service	
	8/7/18	10am	Battalion moved by march route to BERTHEN LINE. 5 officers reconnoitred BERTHEN LINE	
	9/7/18	7am	Battalion continued march arriving at (Sheet 27. I.4.0.0.0) N6 a S.6. remaining in fields until 7pm when march was continued to (Sheet 27.I.6.0.0.0) Q 8. C & D 14. a 0.8. Battalion arrived at 2 am on 10/7/18 and were billeted in above areas. 5 more officers reconnoitred BERTHEN LINE	Billets for night 97R
Sheet 27. I.4.0.0.0 Q 8 & 27 a	10/7/18	9am to 4pm	Section, Section, Company + Platoon S/G reconnoitred BERTHEN LINE all Platoon Commanders	

WAR DIARY / INTELLIGENCE SUMMARY

Army Form C. 2118.

Instructions regarding War Diaries and Intelligence Summaries are contained in F. S. Regs., Part II. and the Staff Manual respectively. Title pages will be prepared in manuscript.

(Erase heading not required.)

Place	Date	Hour	Summary of Events and Information	Remarks and references to Appendices
108 c + 7 d	11/7/18	6 am	Physical training. Box Respirator Drill. Parades	
		6.30 am	Specialist Instruction. O.C. Companies	
		8 am	Breakfast	
		9 am	Parades	
		9.45	Lecture with all Junior Officers to emphasise importance of Inspection & improvement	
		11 am	Drills	
		11.30	Lectures Officers & all Platoon Commanders & NCOs per Platoon reconnoitres BERTHEN LINE	
	12.7.18	8 am	Proceeded as for 11/7/18 H.B.S.	
		9.30 am	B/ Coy moved to BOESCHEPE to work under C.R.E. cutting corn in front of BERTHEN LINE	
	13.7.18	1 pm	Parties manning BERTHEN LINE by Battalion. Remained in position till 11 am 13.7.18.	
			Inspected by B.G.C. whilst in position. A/C Platoon nominated to work in the chalk quarries.	
			Join new officers reported for duty viz 2/Lt G.G. BURT	
			" 2/Lt D. M.J.	
			" H. G. BOURNE	
			" W. G. HILLIDGE	
	13.7.18		Usual Economy	
	14.7.18	9 am	Church Parade Service	
	15.7.18	6 am	Usual Economy	

Army Form C. 2118.

WAR DIARY
or
INTELLIGENCE SUMMARY.
(Erase heading not required.)

Instructions regarding War Diaries and Intelligence
Summaries are contained in F. S. Regs., Part II.
and the Staff Manual respectively. Title pages
will be prepared in manuscript.

Place	Date	Hour	Summary of Events and Information	Remarks and references to Appendices
BECOURT	15/7/18	1.30 p.m	Inspection of Brigade by S.O.C. 2nd Army. Draft of 58 men reported for duty.	
	16/7/18	8 a.m	C.O. with Company Commanders went round BERTHEN LINE with S O C 30th Division. Inspected Scheme of Company Commanders at P. 28 & 7.9.	
			Draft of 2/Lt & 4 O.R. reported for duty. 2/Lt E. THOMAS reported for duty with 2/Both DLI Coy.	
		9 a.m	Training as in previous days.	
		12 noon		
	17/7/18	9 a.m	Training as usual	
		12 noon	C.O. & 2 i/c call to Commanders wanted to Assembly positions for counter attack R11 d centre Produce alarm, Batts moved to Assembly Positions returning to billets at 9 p.m. 187/1/6	
		11.30 p.m		
	18/7/18	6 p.m	Inspection of H.Q. & lent draft by B.G.C.	
	19/7/18	9 a.m to noon	Training as usual. Staff rides with B.G.C. C.O. & 2 i/c rode to boundaries of attack.	
		2 to 5 p.m		
			1 Officer & 60 O.R. examining ground in front of Assembly Position	
	20/7/18		1 Officer & Company training as usual + 1 Officer + Company on Range + Go training + draft 4.p.	
	21/7/18		NIL	
	22/7/18		Training as usual. C.O. 2 i/c + Coy Comdrs reconnoitre new countries boundaries R11 d centre	86

WAR DIARY or INTELLIGENCE SUMMARY

Army Form C. 2118.

Place	Date	Hour	Summary of Events and Information	Remarks and references to Appendices
BOOTH L	23/7/18		Training & manual in afternoon. Inspection by G.O.C. 30th Division at 10 AM	
	24/7/18	2 pm	Battalion moved by march route to area W. of BOESCHEPE. Bath +D's at Q.12, Q.11.5 left at R.5.C.9. & R.9.A.5. Shop orderlies and some night cookers staying in Rest area HQ at Q.5.1.8. Brig HQ finishing at 6 am 26.7.18	
			O.C. 2/17th under instruction advanced Bn HQrs at R.10.d.7.1 under 202 field coy RE one by orderlies with constantly advanced party	
	25/7/18		8 OR instructed under training — 2 men wounded by shell fire.	
		9 pm	4 pm Instructed some of Adm under 60.1.9.9.4 30 MG Battalion + Off + 89 k. pers 7.M.G attended	
		8 am	3 pm Instructed some by Adm under with C.O. (Rifle wiring)	
	26/7/18	11 am	R.S.C. sent by C.T.n to note a when instance with C.D.	
			In evening Bn left that night owing to inspection advanced Bde HQ's one Co. continued work on front of MONT NOIR SW.T.F 22 SW M.26 c.8.8.	
	27/7/18	9 am	8 Officers reconnoitre ground in front of MONT NOIR line in dispn	
			1 Coy continuous work from same lines as before	
	28/7/18		" " " 2 Ors wounded Ds + have for shelter	
	29/7/18		" " Enemy busy	
	30/7/18		4 Coy	
	31/7/18		5 " Co's entrance at 89. Bde HQ, See WD +	

Arthur Maufe Lieut. Col.
Commanding 2/17th Battn. London Regt.

CONFIDENTIAL

WAR DIARY

of

1/17th Battalion London Regiment

FROM 1st August 1918. TO 31st August 1918.

[signature]
Lieut. Colonel
1/17th Battalion London Regiment

[stamp: 17TH BATTN. THE LONDON REGIMENT.]

Army Form C. 2118.

WAR DIARY
or
INTELLIGENCE SUMMARY.
(Erase heading not required.)

Instructions regarding War Diaries and Intelligence Summaries are contained in F. S. Regs., Part II. and the Staff Manual respectively. Title pages will be prepared in manuscript.

Place	Date	Hour	Summary of Events and Information	Remarks and references to Appendices
Q.12.c.9.6 S.P.3.c.	1/8/18	6 am to 6 pm	"D" Coy worked with 202 Field Coy R.E. at LIEUT F.A.B. R.10.4.7.2 from. Remaining Coys worked during day.	A/R
Malines Wood 27 S.E.12.S.W.	2/8/18	6 am to 3 pm	A/B/C Coys worked with 171 Tunnelling Coy at MONT VIDAIGNE	A/R
		3 pm	D Coy continued work with 202 Field Coy R.E.	
		9 pm	Battalion relieved by 1/23 2nd LONDON REGT moved to LE CARREAUX sheet 27 O.13 d.+.q.	A/R
LE CARREAUX	3/8/18		Training 6 hours in wiring, Patrolling & Range work. Machine Gunners.	A/R
			Inspection of Brigade Representatives for Army Rumble Scheme at TERDEGHEM	A/R
"	4/8/18	5.30 pm	BRIGADE Church Parade. Army Church Parade at TERDEGHEM	
"	5/8/18		Training as on 3/8/18. C.O. attended lecture reorganization by Inspector General of Training at TERDEGHEM. 2/Lieut E.J.O. BIRD & 2/Lieut W.H. SMITH returned to duty from 2nd Army 2nd LONDON REGT	A/R
		3 pm	Lecture by Divisional Intelligence Officer on Intelligence to all Officers N.C.O.'s 2/Lieut N.R. STONE from 4th Bn 2/3rd Bn LONDON REGT. reported for duty	A/R
"	6/8/18		Training as on 5/8/18. Sixth Command course to training area	A/R
"	7/8/18		"	
"	8/8/18		6 officers attended lecture reorganization of I.G.T. at TERDEGHEM	A/R

WAR DIARY
or
INTELLIGENCE SUMMARY.

Army Form C. 2118.

Place	Date	Hour	Summary of Events and Information	Remarks and references to Appendices
LE CARREAUX	9/8/18		Training as before. Remainder of Officers attended lecture demonstration by I.G.T. 2 Off. 160 OR 1st Bn reinforcements reported 15/7/18 Suffering from work in MONT VIDAIGNE. 4 Reinf: 27 OR	
	10/8/18	8pm	Battalion moved by route march to Brigade Reserve at BOESCHEPE. 4 Reinforcements & Personnel BERNEQUE Bn Reception Camp	
BOESCHEPE londres sheet 27 JE + 28 SW R 9 b + d	11/8/18		C.O. proceeded to WISQUES for 2nd Army C.O.'s course. Major C.G.ROSS assumed command. OC Coys visited O.P's on MONT VIDAIGNE N21a Training in small parties in Patrolling, wiring, Camp Duties & tactical exercises. MC Bath.	
	12/8/18		All Platoon Cdrs visited O.P.s on MONT VIDAIGNE. Training as on 11th	
	13/8/18		Training as on 12th. OC Coys + 2nd iC Dc's went up to front line KOUDEKOT SECTOR. LOCRE 1/10000 N21a	
	14/8/18	9pm	Bath. Bn BOESCHEPE & took over front line KOUDEKOT SECTOR from 2nd Bn. SLANCS REGT. A Coy 4 front B Coy Rt Support. C Coy Left Front. D Coy Left Support	
	15/8/18	3am	Relief complete. Quiet day.	
			2 Officer Patrols went out during night along whole front	
	16/8/18		Quiet day	
	17/8/18	2.45am	Enemy raided left post of A Coy. Enemy strength about 15. All posts known casualties 1 officer wounded 3 OR killed, 2 missing wounded to hospital. Enemy casualties: 1 wounded prisoner. 2 missing presumed killed. 2 missing died during night 17/8 - 18/8 patrols sent Attempted enemy raid on A Coy. left front during night 18/19 - 7/8 patrols the front line repulsed. B Coy relieved A Coy during August 18/19. Patrols for 7/8 2 Lancashire N6 Fusiliers	
	18/8/18		Quiet day in front line.	
	19/8/18		9/8 2 Royal Fus came up to relieve	

WAR DIARY or INTELLIGENCE SUMMARY

Army Form C. 2118.

(Erase heading not required.)

Place	Date	Hour	Summary of Events and Information	Remarks and references to Appendices
KORTEBEEK SECTOR	20/8/18	1.30pm	Relief complete. Bn to Brigade Res. BOESCHEPE. C.O. rejoined Bn.	
		10 pm	HQ & 2 Coys (A & D) moved to support line at MT VIDAIGNE (All sections full).	
	21/8/18	2 am	Attack on HILL 77 by 89 + 90 Brigades. D Coy 2/17 London supplies carrying parties B+C Coy carried out training in wiring, practice, range practice, musketry, platoon schemes at BOESCHEPE. B+C continued	
	22/8/18		HQ A+D remained in support. D Coy supplying carrying party.	
	23/8/18		B+C Coy continued training as on 22.	
		10 pm	HQ+A Coy relieved to BOESCHEPE. B Coy remainder at MT VIDAIGNE working for Brigade. C OR killed whilst working with 171 Tunnelling Coy.	
	24/8/18	2 am	Enemy counter attacked transportation on Hill 77. B Coy casualties 7 killed 6 wounded from HE fire at 7pm. Enemy aeroplane dropping bombs.	
	25/8/18	9 pm	Bn left BOESCHEPE to relieve 7/8 R.INNIS. FUS in front line. Casualties from shelling + gas before relief. A Coy 2 OR wounded B Coy 19 OR wounded.	
	26/8/18	4:15 am	Relief complete. C Coy in Res. Trench. B Coy right front. D Coy right support & supported front companies day. Enemy patrols active during night, having much improved.	
	27/8/18		Quiet day. A Coy pushed up 2 left front by Beaute. C Coy in front line front companies. 2 Platoon S. M.G.s position dropping in. A Coy front being sniped.	

WAR DIARY
or
INTELLIGENCE SUMMARY.
(Erase heading not required.)

Army Form C. 2118.

Place	Date	Hour	Summary of Events and Information	Remarks and references to Appendices
LOCRE 1/10773	28/8/18	2 am	3 by slightly wounded. Casualties. A by 1 OR wounded. 3 Officer patrols out during night 28/8/18 during stopping in White Chalet front Battn 7 OR wound	
	29/8/18		Quiet day. Large fires seen during afternoon behind enemy lines. 6 Patrols out during night to ascertain if enemy had withdrawn with negative result	
	30/8/18	5 p.m.	Information received that enemy was withdrawing. String off in patrols closely supports pushed out to gain touch with enemy & to escort the M.G.S.C. to ZOEGLOVE FARM reaching 3.30 p.m. Rear Guard occupied in chasing optima objective from DRANOUTRE Mill FORNYTH FARM to STIL 3.1. Enemy offered slight resistance on causualties 2 OR wounded. 2 Prisoners taken 1 enemy wounded. 1 enemy light M.G. taken. Patrols sent out from the line during night Reconnoitring for Ground gained. Very little prisoners gained	
	31/8/18	7 am	2 Bn Lancs Regt passed thro our line to continue advance. We followed in support of 1500 yds distance. Our Bn halted for night in position S.6 c Std. Rn 140 = CROYDON FARM	

Commanding 2/7 Battn London Regt

Confidential

Alan Queeny
of
2/7th Battn London Regt.

Shewn 10-9-18

To 30-9-18

J.S.4
89/30

Confidential

War Diary

of

2/17th Battalion London Regiment

From 1st September 1918   To 30th September 1918

[signature]
Major
Commanding 2/17 Battn London Regt

Army Form C. 2118.

WAR DIARY
or
INTELLIGENCE SUMMARY.

(Erase heading not required.)

Instructions regarding War Diaries and Intelligence Summaries are contained in F. S. Regs., Part II. and the Staff Manual respectively. Title pages will be prepared in manuscript.

Place	Date	Hour	Summary of Events and Information	Remarks and references to Appendices
S5a 2.3	1/9/18		Battn in Support to 2nd Bn S. Lancs Regt. Companies situated in S6c+d & S12a.	AEU
M34 d		12 noon	Battn withdrew to area M34d.	
		9 pm	Battn ordered forward to Bde Reserve at WORMLOW CAMP S12 C. Major C.G. ROSS assumed command of the Battalion.	AEU
S12 C	2/9/18	8 am	Battn moved to area T1a. Brigade in support to 21st BDE. Companies employed on Salvage work.	AEU
T1a	3/9/18		Battn took up defensive line from DONEGAL FARM to T7 central. Coys disposed in depth with one platoon in trenches. Bivouac area shelled with H.E & Gas during night. Casualties 10.R. killed. 10.R. wounded. Reconnaissances sent forward to Battn in line.	AEU
	4/9/18		Battn engaged on Salvage work & interior economy. Reinforcement 1 Officer.	AEU
	5/9/18		As for 4/9/18. Further reconnaissances sent to line in front of WULVERGHEM. Preparations made for attack on MESSINES RIDGE at dawn on 6th inst. Reinforcements 8 O.R. Casualties 9 O.R. wounded (Gas).	AEU
	6/9/18	3 pm	Battn withdrew to bivouac area at S4 & 9.2 Outpost line from ROMP FARM to FOXGLOVE FARM supplied by 'D' Coy (2nd Lt D.M DOWNES)	AEU

WAR DIARY
or
INTELLIGENCE SUMMARY.

Army Form C. 2118.

(Erase heading not required.)

Place	Date	Hour	Summary of Events and Information	Remarks and references to Appendices
S.4.d.9.2	7/9/18		Companies training under Coy arrangements - 1 Platoon per Coy engaged on Salvage work in J.35. Company Officers & 1 representative per Platoon up to reconnoitre line from U.7.b.6.6. to SPRING WALK T.6.d.0.8.	AEll
	8/9/18	7.30 pm	Battn. moved forward to take over line from 2nd R.I.R. and 2/16th London Regt.	AEll
T.6.c.5.3	9/9/18	3am	Relief complete. "A" Coy (left) "B" Coy (centre), "D" Coy (Right) & "C" Coy (Support). Nightly Patrols out on each Coy front. 4 O.R. wounded	AEll
T.6.c.5.3	10/9/18	4.45 am	Fighting patrols endeavoured to establish themselves in enemy trenches & were strongly resisted. During night patrols gained valuable information and took two P.W.'s. "C" Coy relieved "A" Coy in left out-sector. 2 off. 2 O.R. wounded. 2 O.R. missing	AEll
	11/9/18		Patrols very active throughout night. Heavy shelling by enemy	AEll
	13/9/18		Patrol activity - Enemy artillery again active 2 O.R. wounded	AEll
	13/9/18		Patrol activity - Artillery both enemy & own active. 1 O.R. wounded	AEll
	14/9/18		Relieved by 7th R.I.Rif. 1 O.R. wounded	AEll
	15/9/18	4.30 am	Relief complete Battn. moved into Bde Support position at LOCRE CHATEAU	AEll
M.25.c		3.30 pm	Battn. moved with Bde into Divisional Reserve at BOESCHEPE	—

Army Form C. 2118.

WAR DIARY
or
INTELLIGENCE SUMMARY.
(Erase heading not required.)

Instructions regarding War Diaries and Intelligence Summaries are contained in F. S. Regs., Part II. and the Staff Manual respectively. Title pages will be prepared in manuscript.

Place	Date	Hour	Summary of Events and Information	Remarks and references to Appendices
BOESCHEPE	16/9/18		Reorganisation and interior economy. 3 Offs Reinforcements training. 10R wounded (Gas) 10R wounded.	AEU
	17/9/18		Open warfare, Patrols &C.	AEU
	18/9/18		Training during morning - Presentation of Medal Ribbons by Corps Commander.	AEU
M26a	19/9/18	7.30 pm	Bde moved support at MT NOIR.	AEU
M20a	20/9/18	11am	Bn HQ moved to SOVIET FARM. Coys engaged on salvage work and training.	AEU
	21/9/18	15.55	Coys engaged on training & salvage.	AEU
	22/9/18	7.30	Coys engaged on training & salvage work. Battn moved to ULSTER CAMP.	AEU
M35c 62	23/9/18	7 pm	Coy training. 1 Coy lived in NEUVE EGLISE Line. 30R wounded Gas.	AEU
	24/9/18		As for 23/9/18. 10R wounded, 10R wounded Gas.	AEU
	25/9/18	7.30 pm	Battn moved up to relief 2nd Ch Lanc.s in Left Position WULVERGHEM SECTOR: "C" Coy on Left, "D" Coy Centre, "B" Coy Right. "A" Coy in reserve. 10R wounded.	AEU
		11 pm	Relief complete.	
N27d 1.7	26/9/18		Patrol activity during night. Bn H.Q. shelled during evening (casualties NIL.	AEU

Army Form C. 2118.

WAR DIARY
or
INTELLIGENCE SUMMARY.
(Erase heading not required.)

Instructions regarding War Diaries and Intelligence Summaries are contained in F. S. Regs., Part II. and the Staff Manual respectively. Title pages will be prepared in manuscript.

Place	Date	Hour	Summary of Events and Information	Remarks and references to Appendices
M27d.1.7	27/9/18		Preparations for advance to be carried out on 28th inst.	AEL
	28/9/18	5.30 a.m.	B, D & C Coys advanced under cover of artillery, T.M. & M.G. barrage against the following enemy strongpoints respectively ONTARIO FARM, MORTOR FARM, KRUISTRAAT CRATER & CRATER inflicting severe losses upon the enemy capturing 13 Germans, 2 M.G. & much material	
		6.30 p.m.	Under cover of further bombardment advance was continued towards MESSINES WYTSCHAETE RIDGE. 3 Coys advanced with 1 platoon forward, two in close support and 1 in reserve despite strong resistance from M.G. rifle fire and the difficulties of the country over which Coy had to pass & the darkness of the night the attackers advanced steadily finally gaining their objective 300 yards E of WYTSCHAETE-MESSINES RD taking 1 Colonel & capturing 1 field gun, 2 M.G's 4 T.M. & great quantities of war material. Before dawn. Casualties 10 OR killed 2 offs. 41 O.R wounded. Consolidation of objective.	AEL
	29/9/18	6.20 a.m. 7 p.m.	2nd S Lancs passed through & advanced on YPRES COMMINES CANAL Concentration of Battn about 027. Casualties 6 OR killed 50 R wounded	AEL
026d22	30/9/18		Battn concentrated about 026 & d	AEL

W.Bom Major
Commanding 2/17 Lancs Regt

(A7930). Wt. W12839/M1293. 75,000. 1/17. D.D. & L., Ltd. Forms/C2118/11

Vol 5

CONFIDENTIAL

WAR DIARY

of

2/17th BATTALION LONDON REGT.

1st October 1918 — 31st October 1918

[signature] Lieut-Col.
Commanding 2/17th Batt: London Regt.

1/11/18.

WAR DIARY or INTELLIGENCE SUMMARY

2/17th London Regt.
Oct. 1918
Army Form C. 2118.

Place	Date	Hour	Summary of Events and Information	Remarks and references to Appendices
O.26.d.2.2	1/10/18	—	Battalion moved into DIVISIONAL SUPPORT at QUAD FARM O.30.d.4.9. Remainder of day devoted to interior economy.	A.E.W.
O.30.d.4.9	2/10/18	0900	Battalion in DIVISIONAL SUPPORT. Day devoted to interior economy, baths etc. Defensive position along WAMBEEK STREAM reconnoitred by Coy Commanders.	A.E.W.
—do—	3/10/18		Training — Range & Grenade Practice, Open warfare & patrolling. Routes to Battn. in line reconnoitred & approximates of all units down to platoons. Selection of Camp Defence position.	A.E.W.
—do—	4/10/18		Training as for 3/10/18. Further reconnaissance of Defensive Line N. of WAMBEEK STREAM — Dispositions arranged.	A.E.W.
—do—	5/10/18		Commanding Officer & Coy Commanders to AMERIKA to reconnoitre position in line to be taken over from 8th Scottish Rifles.	A.E.W.
		1900	Battn. moved up to relieve 8th Scottish Rifles in line, taking over Bienfort also BLOKSTRAAT CART to Q.13 central which 21st INF BDE was to take over. 9/OR's rejoined Battn. from Divnl. hospital a/c 1 Officer reinforcement. Casualties 1OR wounded.	A.E.W.
P.12.d.6.8	6/10/18	0030	Relief completed — 21st INF BDE extended their left to Q.13.C.3.7 only. Orders received & cancelled later to extend Battn. front and take over part of front held by 1/15th R.I.F.	A.E.W.
		2200	Reconnoitring patrols out on Battn. front with view to discovering the nature of the ground, sty. of enemy wire & locate enemy M.G. & rifle posts. Battn. HQ shifted during night. Casualties 1OR wounded (Shell Shock NYDN)	

Army Form C. 2118.

WAR DIARY
or
INTELLIGENCE SUMMARY.
(Erase heading not required.)

Instructions regarding War Diaries and Intelligence Summaries are contained in F. S. Regs., Part II. and the Staff Manual respectively. Title pages will be prepared in manuscript.

Place	Date	Hour	Summary of Events and Information	Remarks and references to Appendices
P12d 6.8	7/10/18	a.m.	7/8th Bn Royal Inniskilling Fusiliers relieved Newfront and 10th over Battn front up to Q13c 37. Vicinity of Battn Headquarters shelled intermittently during the day & night. Battn moved in BDE RESERVE in Re TENBRIELEN area.	S.G.M.
P22 ·A·9·3	8/10/18	0155	Relief complete. Battn HQ opened at P22 A.9.3. Battn engaged cleaning area & improving accommodation. Routes reconnoitred to Battn in line. Defensive line round bivouac area. Selected & occupied lightly. Battn area heavily shelled by Gas & H.E. during night. Casualties 3 o.r. wounded, 5 o.r. wounded gas poisoning.	S.G.M.
do	9/10/18		Reconnaissances to front line continued. Battn engaged in Salvage & improving accommodation. Area shelled continuously, particularly during night. Casualties 1 off. 14 o.r. wounded gas poisoning.	G.H.
do	10/10/18		Reconnaissances continued. Battn engaged in Salvage, improving area, & digging bombardment shelters. Slight shelling during day. Heavy shelling with Gas & H.E. during night. Casualties 2 o.r. wounded gas poisoning.	G.H.
do	11/10/18		Advance parties of 2/5 London Regt. arrived to take over. Marked decrease in shelling both by day & night.	G.H.

WAR DIARY
or
INTELLIGENCE SUMMARY.

(Erase heading not required.)

Army Form C. 2118.

Place	Date	Hour	Summary of Events and Information	Remarks and references to Appendices
T22 & 93.	12/10/18	800	Commenced move to O.19 d y 2, Divisional Reserve Area.	Q.84
O.19 d y 2.	do	2230	Move completed, Batt Hq opened at O.19 d.y.2.	Q.84
do	13/10/18		Day devoted to cleaning areas, improving accommodation, ordinary economy. Reinforcements 42 o.r.	Q.84
do	14/10/18		C.O.'s inspection of companies. Training - P.T. Bayonet fighting, Range practices, rifle bombing.	Q.84
do	15/10/18		Training - P.T. Bayonet fighting, close order drill, Range practices rifle bombing. Reinforcements. 2nd Lt J.H. Mincliffe & 2nd Lt W.N. Skayper.	Q.84
do	16/10/18		Training as for 15/10/18.	Q.84
do	17/10/18		do	Q.84
do	18/10/18	0615	Reinforcements 143 o.r. Batt. commenced move to REEKE area Q21a.	Q.84
Q21a.21.	do	1130	Move completed, Batt Hq opened at Q.21 a.2.1.	Q.84
do	19/10/18	1045	Commenced move to PONT D'MALLOIN area, X.H.	Q.84
X.H.c.3.5	do	1430	Move completed, Batt Hq situated at X+c 3.5.	Q.84
do	20/10/18	1130	Commenced move to ZEVECOTEN area S.Y.	Q.84
S.Y.a.3.2.	do	1400	Move completed, Batt Hq situated at S.Y.a 3.2.	Q.84

Army Form C. 2118.

WAR DIARY
or
INTELLIGENCE SUMMARY.
(Erase heading not required.)

Instructions regarding War Diaries and Intelligence Summaries are contained in F. S. Regs., Part II. and the Staff Manual respectively. Title pages will be prepared in manuscript.

Place	Date	Hour	Summary of Events and Information	Remarks and references to Appendices
S 4 a 3.2.	21/10/18	0900	Commenced forward move to L'ENFER area, C.3. "D" Company acting as advance guard to pass through 90th Brigade.	
U 25 d o 3	do	1130	Pass through 2/14 London Regt. Batt. Hq. established at U 25 d o 3.	
C 3 c 6.6.	do	1225	Advance guard reached L'ENFER C 3 c 6.6.	
C 4 a 2.0	do	1530	Advance guard reached R. SCHELDT at C 4 a 2.0 established posts from C 3 d 3.0 to C 4 b 1.7 along near bank. Heavy sniping & M.G. fire encounted from further bank. Shelling heavy but erratic. Advance guard unable to find a crossing over SCHELDT. Casualties 4 o.r. killed, 20 wounded.	G.R.¹
U 26 d 9.9	22/10/18	0530	Batt. Hq. moved to U 26 d 9.9. Remainder of Batt. unchanged. Batt. on left attempted to cross SCHELDT by means of pontoon bridge. In event of their succeeding, "C" Coy would follow as advance guard to 2/4 Batt. crossing by same bridge. Attempt was unsuccessful, owing to heavy shelling & M.G. fire on approaches to Bridge. Reinforcement Lieut W.T James M.C. Casualties 1 o.r. wounded.	G.R.¹
C 4 a 5.2	22/10/18	0015	R.E. constructed pontoon bridge raft across SCHELDT to enable "C" Company to effect crossing in conjunction with Batt. on our left. Patrols crossed river to reconnoitre route across marsh at C 4 & C 10.	G.R.¹
do	do	0400	2 Platoons "C" Coy crossed SCHELDT by means of pontoon raft at C 4 a 5.2. No route found across marsh. Batt. on left unable to cross owing to bridge being damaged, so "C" Coys 2 platoons returned to N. bank of SCHELDT at 0530 hrs. Casualties 1 o.r. wounded, 2 missing	

(A7092). Wt. W12859/M1293. 75,000. 1/17. D. D. & L., Ltd. Forms/C.2118-14.

Army Form C. 2118.

WAR DIARY
or
INTELLIGENCE SUMMARY.
(Erase heading not required.)

Instructions regarding War Diaries and Intelligence Summaries are contained in F. S. Regs, Part II. and the Staff Manual respectively. Title pages will be prepared in manuscript.

Place	Date	Hour	Summary of Events and Information	Remarks and references to Appendices
C.H.a.2.0	23/10/18	1900	"D" Coy relieved by "A" Coy in outpost line, "D" Coy moving back to reserve billets at BOIS JACQUET.	GW
C.H.a.5.2	do	1825 to 0200	Patrols of "C" Coy crossed SCHELDT to reconnoitre, reconnoitred roads, obtained considerable opposition, encountered from M.G. posts, no route found.	
do	24/10/18		R.E. constructed footbridge to take place of pay. Foot bridge across SCHELDT constructed by R.E.	
C.H.d.4.8	24/10/18	0400	"C" Coy withdrawn to billets in BOIS JACQUET area.	GW
C.H.n.3.6	do	1830	2 Platoons "A" Company crossed SCHELDT reconnoitred towards LOCK 3, capturing 4 prisoners & 1 M.G. Considerable opposition met with from M.G. enemy put down barrage.	
C.H.a.2.0	do	1900 to 2230	Casualties 3 wounded 1 missing. "B" Coy established standing patrol on S. Bank of SCHELDT, returning 2130hr.	
C.H.a.5.2 & do	25/10/18	1815	"A" Coy relieved by "B" Coy in outpost line, "A" Coy moving into support at 6.	GW
C.H.a.2.0	do	1830	Reinforcements 126. Casualties 1 O.R. killed 1 missing.	
C.H.a.2.0	26/10/18		"A" Company withdrawn to reserve area BOIS JACQUET. "B" Coy H.92 support. Platoons now C.2.3.B.4.5.	aW
			"B" Coy to take over from S. Lancs Regt two platoons in support at GAVRE.	
U.26.C.8.8	27/10/18	2140	D Coy on left relieved by A Coy 5th Bn A+S.H. and moved to an area about C12.2.9 B Coy on right relieved by A Coy 16th Bn Manchester Regt & moved to an area about H.C.1.8.2.9 Bathn HQ 1/c U29.C.9.4. A+B Coys R.H.Q and transport moved to an area E of MEULEBEKE. Casualties 1 O.R. wounded	aW

Army Form C. 2118.

WAR DIARY
or
INTELLIGENCE SUMMARY.
(Erase heading not required.)

Instructions regarding War Diaries and Intelligence Summaries are contained in F. S. Regs., Part II. and the Staff Manual respectively. Title pages will be prepared in manuscript.

Place	Date	Hour	Summary of Events and Information	Remarks and references to Appendices
V29c 9.4	28/10/18	1000	Battn. moved to billets in ROLLEGHEM in Divisional Reserve. Remainder of day devoted to interior economy.	All
T20 1.9	29/10/18		Battn. training – P.T. Musketry, Advance Guards &c. Part of Battalion bathed. Reconnaissances carried out by Company Commanders, Signalling Officers + transport Officer of area V7, 18, 24 (routes, assembly positions and areas of approach to river.	All
T2a 1.9	30/10/18		Battn. training on for 29th inst. Remainder of Battn. bathed.	All
T2a 1.9	31/10/18	1300	Battn. moved to area T7, S12 + 18 in Divisional Reserve. Blankets and clothing cleaned in Foden Truck Disinfector. Battn. HQ established S12 c 3.3	All

Hawkeythhr

CO. 2/1st Bn. London Regt.
Lieut. Colonel
Co. 2/1st Bn. London Regt.

CONFIDENTIAL

WAR DIARY

of

2/17th BATTALION LONDON REGIMENT.

FROM: 1st/Nov/1918   TO: 30th/Nov/1918

O.J. Lamu, Captain,
Commanding 2/17th Battalion London Regt.

WAR DIARY
or
INTELLIGENCE SUMMARY.
(Erase heading not required.)

Army Form C. 2118.

Place	Date	Hour	Summary of Events and Information	Remarks and references to Appendices
S.12 c.4.4.	1/11/18	—	Batt. employed cleaning up, special interior economy, improvement of billets &c. Reinforcements 8 o.r.	Q.2.1
do	2/11/18	—	Training. P.T. Range Practice. Steady Drill. Reinforcements 21 o.r.	Q.2.1
do	3/11/18	—	C. of E. Church Parade. No training.	Q.2.1.
do	4/11/18	1000	Battn moved to area near HEESTERT, in support to 4/8 Inniskillings.	Q.2.1
P.28.a.H.3.	do	1800	Batt Hq. established at P.25 a. H. 3.	Q.2.1
Q.18.B.2.1.	5/11/18	1800	Batt. Hq moved to O.18 B.2.1.	Q.2.1.
do	6/11/18	—	Reinforcements 5 o.r.	
do	7/11/18	2000	1/5 Inniskillings relieved by 3/5 Bn. Batt returned to same area. Reinforcements 3 o.r. Batt. gas wilt Exc., Medium 1 Coy of 3/5 London Regt. "B" Coy in line, "A" "C" Coy in reserve. North Hq. established at U.6.d.3.6. Casualties 1 O.R. killed 2 wounded.	Q.3.1.5.
U.6.d.3.6. V.14.d.3.7.	8/11/18	0300	"B" Coy established 1 platoon on N bank of SCHELDT at V.14.d.3.7	
V.15.a.4.9.	do	0500	1 platoon "D" Coy established at V.15.a.4.9. unable to reach SCHELDT owing to heavy opposition from M.G.S, T.M.S & artillery.	Q.2.1.
do	do	1800	"C" Coy relieve "D" Coy, "D" Coy move back to reserve area.	

WAR DIARY
or
INTELLIGENCE SUMMARY.

(Erase heading not required.)

Army Form C. 2118.

Place	Date	Hour	Summary of Events and Information	Remarks and references to Appendices
V15 a. H.3	9/11/18	0100	R.E. constructed footbridges at V15 a. o.6. and V15 a. H.3.	
	do	0300	2 Platoons "C" Coy cross SCHELDT established themselves on S. bank without opposition.	
	do	0900	Remainder of "C" Coy & "B" Coy cross SCHELDT, move to railway line V29 & 30.	Q.91.
			"A" Coy move in support. Battn. Hq. & "D" Coy move to V22 a. 6.6.	
	do	1900	"B" & "C" Coys Head line E of WATRIPONT, W30 b & 15 F7 a. "A" Coy in support. Battn Hq & "D" Coy move to ANSEGHEM. Battn Hq. established at E3 & 5.3.	
D66 7.6	do	1200	"B" Coy handed searchlight, guard by two own flares at D6 6.7.6. Casualties 2 or. Killed. 3 wounded.	
F6 a.0.5.	10/11/18	0600	"B" & "C" Coys Head railway line F2 & 97. Battn Hq. established at WATRIPONT F6 a.0.5.	
	do	1300	Leading Coys reach established line A 5 a. 9.9. - A 5 d.0.2.	Q.91.
A.1.&.2.9.	do		Battn. Hq. established at A.1 & 2.9.	Q.91.
	11/11/18	1215	Battn continued move to FLOBECQ area.	
727 & 5.8.	do	1630	Adv. transport. Battn. Hq. established at 727 & 5.8.	
	12/11/18		Battn. engaged in cleaning billets, cleaning inspection of equipment Stables, Artillery general interior economy. Reinforcement 2 or.	Q.92.
	13/11/18		Inspection of billets, equipment &c. Battn drill under R.S.M. Reinforcements 85 o.r.	Q.93.

Army Form C. 2118.

WAR DIARY
or
INTELLIGENCE SUMMARY.
(Erase heading not required.)

Instructions regarding War Diaries and Intelligence Summaries are contained in F. S. Regs., Part II. and the Staff Manual respectively. Title pages will be prepared in manuscript.

Place	Date	Hour	Summary of Events and Information	Remarks and references to Appendices
Xray B.S.B.	14/11/18	10.00	Batt. commenced move to STOKT area. Move completed 1430 hrs. Batt. Hq. established Xray 4.6.	Q.8.9.
Xray 4.6.	15/11/18		Batt. parade under R.S.M. Reinforcements 4 o.r.	Q.8.9.
do	16/11/18	0430	Batt. commenced move to MOEN area. Move completed 1200 hrs. Batt. Hq. established at Ub a 8.8. Reinforcements 11 o.r.	Q.8.9.
Ub a 8.8.	17/11/18	0845	Batt. move to TOMBROEK area. Move completed Tu a 5.5. Batt. Hq. established Tu a 5.5. Reinforcements 5 o.r.	Q.8.9.
Tu a 5.5.	18/11/18		Batt. parade under R.S.M. Remainder of day devoted to cleaning & repairment of billets, cleaning of equipment &c.	Q.8.1.
do	19/11/18		Commanding Officers parade. Principles of Demobilisation explained. Reinforcements 1 off. 320.r. Bty inspection by M.O.	Q.8.3.
do	20/11/18		Brigade Thanksgiving Service. Reinforcements 1 off. 2 o.r.	Q.8.9.
do	21/11/18		Commanding Officers Parade. Interpreters fielded shortly completion.	Q.8.
do	22/11/18		Route march by bgde. Saluting drawn drill. Interpreters shortly completion. Lecture. Reinforcements 5 o.r.	Q.8.9.
do	23/11/18		Route march by bgde. Drivers dismounted. Interpreters shortly completion. Reinforcements 6 o.r.	Q.8.9.

Army Form C. 2118.

WAR DIARY
or
INTELLIGENCE SUMMARY.
(Erase heading not required.)

Instructions regarding War Diaries and Intelligence Summaries are contained in F.S. Regs., Part II. and the Staff Manual respectively. Title pages will be prepared in manuscript.

Place	Date	Hour	Summary of Events and Information	Remarks and references to Appendices
T14a 3.5	24/11/18		C. of E. & Free Church service morning. Reinforcements 9 off. 9 o.r.	Q.Y.1
do	25/11/18		Inspection of arms, equipment, rifles, saluting, steady drill. Lecture "Billets Discipline".	Q.Y.1
do	26/11/18		C.O.'s parade. Reinforcements 11 o.r. Route march by Coys. C.O.'s parade. Reinforcements 52 o.r.	Q.Y.1
do	27/11/18		Distribution of medal ribbons by G.O.C. Division. Reinforcements 45 o.r.	Q.Y.2
do	28/11/18	09.15	Battalion commenced move to STE BARBE area. Move completed 14.15 hr. Batt. Hq. established at TOURNAI H.A.85.90.	Q.Y.1
	29/11/18	10.00	Move to FONQUEREAU Camp commenced. Move completed 12.15 hrs. Hq established at HAZEBROUCK H.L.60.25.	Q.Y.3
	30/11/18	08.10	Batt. moved to LA GORGUE area. Move completed 14.30 hr. Hq established at HAZEBROUCK 5156.	Q.Y.3

G.H. Mann Lt.Col.
Commg. 2/17 Btn London Regt

907

CONFIDENTIAL

WAR DIARY

of

2/17th BATTALION LONDON REGIMENT

FROM December 1st 1915   TO December 31st 1915

A. Y~~~ /Major
Commanding 2/17th Battalion London Regiment

Army Form C. 2118.

WAR DIARY
or
INTELLIGENCE SUMMARY.
(Erase heading not required.)

Instructions regarding War Diaries and Intelligence Summaries are contained in F. S. Regs., Part II. and the Staff Manual respectively. Title pages will be prepared in manuscript.

Place	Date	Hour	Summary of Events and Information	Remarks and references to Appendices
In the Field	1/12/18	0900	Batt. commenced move to ST VENANT Area. Move completed 1215 hrs.	Q.8.3.
"	2/12/18	0950	Batt. Hq established HAZEBROUCK 5 G.40.h.5.	
"			Batt. commenced move to SERCUS area. Move completed 1315 hrs.	Q.8.3.
	3/12/18		Batt. Hq established at HAZEBROUCK H.F.30.55. Lieut Colonel H.J. Dear.D.S.O having assumed temporary command of 69th Infantry Brigade, Major P.H. TANNER.M.C assumed command of the Battalion.	Appx.
	4/12/18		An advance report was sent in to Brigade, on the conditions of the Battalions Billets. The day was devoted to cleaning up and improving Billets.	Appx.
	5/12/18		Day devoted to physical drill, bayonet fighting, saluting and arms drill. Gas training and Inspection of Box Respirators. The medical officer carried out a routine inspection of Hd of the Battalion.	Appx.
	6/12/18		The Battalion carried out training as on the previous day. The medical officer inspected the remainder of the Battalion for vermin.	Appx.
	7/12/18		The Battalion carried out training as on previous day. One Lewis salvage work was included in the day's training.	Appx.

Army Form C. 2118.

WAR DIARY
or
INTELLIGENCE SUMMARY.
(Erase heading not required.)

Instructions regarding War Diaries and Intelligence Summaries are contained in F. S. Regs., Part II. and the Staff Manual respectively. Title pages will be prepared in manuscript.

Place	Date	Hour	Summary of Events and Information	Remarks and references to Appendices
In the Field (cont'd)	2/12/18		The following decorations were awarded:- CROIX DE GUERRE A L'ORDRE (CORPS) CAPTAIN and ADJUTANT S.P.DAVIES. CROIX DE GUERRE A L'ORDRE (BRIGADE) 573042 C/S/L: PARKER A.E. 'C' COMPANY. CROIX DE GUERRE A L'ORDRE (REGIMENT) 571150 A/Cpl. COLE E. A. COMPANY.	Appx.
	9/12/18		Day's training devoted to 1 hours Salvage work, Inspection of Box Respirators, Rapid Loading & Firing, Company carried out Casualties Range Practices over Company Ranges.	Appx.
	8/12/18		Voluntary Church Parade.	
	10/12/18		The day devoted to firing in Trenches, Visability of trenches was tried, and Guard Duties. The Commanding Officer inspected 'B' Company at 10.00 hr. The Lewis Gun Class fired over Range. 1 officer per Company attended a Lecture at Brigade H.Q.S. on "Demobilisation" at 14.40 hr.	Appx.
	11/12/18		The Battalion commenced move to CLAIR-MARAIS Aerodrome, move completed cup. 12.30 hr.	Appx.

WAR DIARY
or
INTELLIGENCE SUMMARY.

(Erase heading not required.)

Army Form C. 2118.

Instructions regarding War Diaries and Intelligence Summaries are contained in F. S. Regs., Part II. and the Staff Manual respectively. Title pages will be prepared in manuscript.

Place	Date	Hour	Summary of Events and Information	Remarks and references to Appendices
In the Field	12/12/18		The day devoted to Interior Economy and improvements of accommodation. An Excursion Lorry left Batt. H.Q. at 0915 hrs with a party for ST. OMER. Two Journeys were made.	Appx
"	13/12/18		The day devoted to Interior Economy and improvement of Camp. The Medical Officer called out a Venereal Inspection of the Battalion during the day.	Appx
"	14/12/18		The morning was devoted to 1/2 hour's Saluting Drill and Interior Economy.	Appx
"	15/12/18		Voluntary Church Services.	Appx
"	16/12/18		Battalion Parade for Bath turned out Platoon Competition winners, No 8 Platoon.	Appx
"	17/12/18		Training consisted of S.B.R. drill, close order & Arms drill, Physical Training and Games.	Appx
"	18/12/18		The Battalion carried out a Brigade route march in full marching order, under O.S.C. Coys.	Appx
"	19/12/18		Training, same as on 17/12/18.	Appx
"	20/12/18		Training devoted to close order and Arms drill and preparations for Commissioning Parade on 21st inst. The Medical Officer carried out a Venereal Inspection of the Battalion. A Lorry was acted to to the Battalion for Excursions to ST OMER.	Appx

WAR DIARY
or
INTELLIGENCE SUMMARY.

(Erase heading not required.)

Army Form C. 2118.

Instructions regarding War Diaries and Intelligence Summaries are contained in F. S. Regs., Part II. and the Staff Manual respectively. Title pages will be prepared in manuscript.

Place	Date	Hour	Summary of Events and Information	Remarks and references to Appendices
Guth Futh	21/12/18		The Battalion paraded at 0945 hrs for Brigade Communion Service. Voluntary Church services	Appx
"	22/12/18			Appx
"	23/12/18		The day was devoted to Baths at WALLON CAPEL, and disinfecting Barbed wire.	Appx
"	24/12/18		Same as for 23/12/18. An inchuman Party was led journeyed to ST/OMER	Appx
"	25/12/18		Day devoted to Christmas festivities.	Appx
"	26/12/18		The morning was spent in camp cleaning and renovation of defences.	Appx
"	27/12/18		Day devoted to disinfection, camp cleaning and interior economy.	Appx
"	28/12/18		Same as for 27/12/18.	Appx
"	29/12/18		Voluntary Church services. An inchuman Party was led up to ST OMER	Appx
"	30/12/18		The morning devoted to Company training at companies C.O.	Appx
"	31/12/18		The evening was spent in thickening up wire, revetting and renovation of defences.	Appx

C.J. Lang Major
O.C. 2/4th Bn London Regt.

CONFIDENTIAL.

WAR DIARY.

of

2/17th Battalion London Regiment.

From. 1st January 1919.

To. 31st January 1919.

Lieut.Colonel,
Commanding, 2/17th Battalion London Regiment.

WAR DIARY
or
INTELLIGENCE SUMMARY.

Army Form C. 2118.

Place	Date	Hour	Summary of Events and Information	Remarks and references to Appendices
In the Field	1/1/19		The day was devoted to the constructions of defences.	Appendix
...	2/1/19		The day was spent in reconnaissance of Training and defences. The indicated officer inspected half the Battalion for remounts found to be in reserve day.	Appendix
...	3/1/19			Appendix
...	4/1/19		The morning was devoted to Interior Economy & Kit Cleaning. Voluntary Church Parade.	Appendix
...	5/1/19			Appendix
...	6/1/19		The morning was devoted to recreational Training & reconnaissance found as the previous day. No 571124 C.S.M. WARNER J.R. was wounded at D.A.M.	Appendix
...	7/1/19			Appendix
...	8/1/19		The morning was spent in close order Training and reconnaissance of defences. Reconnaissance & W.T. for reconstruction of Line of Battalion.	Appendix
...	9/1/19		Routine same as previous day. The management training ranks were members as lectures, dated 8/1/19.	Appendix
			LIEUT (a/CAPT) S.P. DAVIES SC GREENIDGE 572266 Rfn. ANDERSON G. E Coy. 5/1/19. A Venerect Inspection of the Battalion was carried out.	Appendix

WAR DIARY
or
INTELLIGENCE SUMMARY.
(Erase heading not required.)

Army Form C. 2118.

Place	Date	Hour	Summary of Events and Information	Remarks and references to Appendices
See also Field	11/1/19		The Battalion proceeded by train from EBBLINGHEM Station to BOULOGNE, and arrived at MARLBOROUGH Camp at 17.30 hrs for work in connection with demobilisation scheme. B wing was sent to OSTROHOVE Camp for the same work.	HJDear
—"—	12/1/19		The day was spent in Sunday Routine and general clean up	HJDear
—"—	13/1/19		70 officers and 2053 ORs arrived in the wings at 0600 hrs for demobilisation, and departed at 11.30 hrs for the Boat.	HJDear
—"—	14/1/19		Invited to Brigadier Fenning and General Gorsal by authorisation Lt Colonel	HJDear
—"—	15/1/19		HJ Dear DSO has received Command of the Battalion 15/1/19. The undermentioned Honours were conferred on Belgians	HJDear
—"—	16/1/19		CROIX DE GUERRE LIEUT COLONEL H J DEAR D.S.O 571,013. C.S.M RONET C wing 572,994 RSM MARION A wing	HJDear
—"—	17/1/19		Invited to foresee organisation and preparing the Camps for demobilised	HJDear
—"—	18/1/19			
—"—	19/1/19		Voluntary Church Parades and clearing up Camp.	HJDear

WAR DIARY
or
INTELLIGENCE SUMMARY.

Army Form C. 2118.

(Erase heading not required.)

Place	Date	Hour	Summary of Events and Information	Remarks and references to Appendices
In the Field	20/4/19		Reveries to Sections Reveilley and preparing dress for keen secolised return	Appendices
-"-	22/4/19		34 officers and 1166 O.R's attended an MARLBOROUGH camp for demoralisation	Appendices
-"-	22/4/19		Reveries to sections. Reveilley and Recreations. Training	Appendices
-"-	23/4/19		19 officers and 402 O.R's arrived an MARLBOROUGH Camp for demoralisation 26 -"- 673 -"- departed from -"-	Appendices
			13 O.R's (Personnel) proceeded to U.K. for demoralisation	
-"-	23/4/19		Reveries to Sections Reveilley and Recreations. Training. 13 O.R.s (Personnel) proceeded to U.K. for keen secolised	Appendices
-"-	24/4/19		Voluntary Church Parades. The undermentioned O.R's were awarded the "Meritorious Service Medal"	Appendices
			376604 C.Q.M.S. YOUNG D.N. } Lundan Gazette no 31132 17/4/19.
			570639 Sergt COLE E }
-"-	27/4/19		40 officers and 1178 O.R's arrived an MARLBOROUGH Camp for demoralisation 27 -"- 693 -"- departed from -"-	Appendices
			36 -"- 1175 -"- -"- -"- -"-	-"-
			39 -"- 1194 -"- -"- departed from -"-	-"-
-"-	28/4/19			

Army Form C. 2118.

WAR DIARY
or
INTELLIGENCE SUMMARY.
(Erase heading not required.)

Instructions regarding War Diaries and Intelligence Summaries are contained in F. S. Regs., Part II. and the Staff Manual respectively. Title pages will be prepared in manuscript.

Place	Date	Hour	Summary of Events and Information	Remarks and references to Appendices
In the Field	29/1/19		31 officers and 1176 O.R's arrived at MARLBOROUGH Camp for demobilisation	Appx
			38 -do- -do- 1157 -do- defeated -do-	
	30/1/19		26 -do- -do- 1305 -do- arrived -do-	Appx
			36 -do- -do- 1214 -do- defeated -do-	
			56 O.R's (Part arrivals) -do-	
	31/1/19		36 officers and 1217 O.R's arrived -do-	Appx
			31 -do- -do- 1186 -do- defeated -do-	
			5 O.R's (Part arrivals) -do-	

[signature]

Commanding, 2/17th Battalion London Regiment.
Lieut. Colonel.

CONFIDENTIAL.

--------oo--------

WAR DIARY OF

2/17th Bn.   London Regiment.

FROM 1st February, 1919 TO 28th February, 1919.

--------oo--------

2/17th Battalion London Regiment.

CONFIDENTIAL.

WAR DIARY
of
2/17th BATTALION LONDON REGIMENT.

FROM: 1st FEBRUARY, 1919.   TO: 28th FEBRUARY, 1919.

[signature] Major.
Commanding 2/17th Battalion London Regiment.

WAR DIARY
or
INTELLIGENCE SUMMARY.
(Erase heading not required.)

Army Form C. 2118.

Place	Date	Hour	Summary of Events and Information	Remarks and references to Appendices
Boulogne	1/2/19		Battn. engaged in Demobilization duties 1 Coy Reception Camp, remainder Despatch Camp. No received. Nil	CJL
do	2/2/19		Demobilization 3 Off. 168 O.R. received. 33 Off. 1592 O.R. despatched. 15 Off. 418 O.R. C of E service 0830 hr 1115 hr 1830 hr Presbyterian 0930 hr R.C. 0800 hr	CJL
do	3/2/19		Demobilization 38 Off. 1263 O.R. received 13 Off. 252 O.R. despatched 17 ORs of Batt personnel proceeded to UK for demobilization	CJL
do	4/2/19		Demobilization 33 Off. 1522 O.R. received Nil despatched	CJL
do	5/2/19		do 28 Off. 1289 O.R. do 38 Off. 1413 O.R. do 11 ORs of Battn personnel proceeded to UK for demobilization	CJL
do	6/2/19		Demobilization 20 Off. 868 O.R. received 37 Off. 1516 O.R. despatched 9 ORs of Batt personnel proceeded to UK for demobilization 1 OR do do returned in do 6 ORs do do evacuated to do sick	CJL
do	7/2/19		Demobilization 8 Off. 558 O.R. received 35 Off. 1301 O.R. despatched 6 Off. 145 ORs from 1/1 Batt London reported for duty with this unit	CJL
do	8/2/19		Demobilization 47 Off. 1583 O.R. received 14 Off. 454 O.R. despatched Inspection of Camp and Quarters by Divisional Commander	CJL
do	9/2/19		Demobilization 31 Off. 1676 O.R. received 22 Off. 694 O.R. despatched C of E service 0830 1115 and 1900hr Presbyterian 0930 hr R.C. 0800 hr	CJL

Army Form C. 2118.

WAR DIARY
or
INTELLIGENCE SUMMARY.
(Erase heading not required.)

Place	Date	Hour	Summary of Events and Information	Remarks and references to Appendices
Boulogne	10/2/19		Demobilization 50 off 1582 O.R. received 46 off 1869 O.R. dispatched 17 ORs of Bath personnel proceeded to UK for demobilization	
do	11/2/19		Demobilization 25 off 869 O.R. received 35 off 1659 O.R. dispatched 11 ORs of Bath personnel proceeded to UK for demobilization	
do	12/2/19		Demobilization 49 off 2124 O.R. received 44 off 1591 O.R. dispatched do 14 off 863 O.R. do 28 off 872 O.R. do	
do	13/2/19		4 off ORs from 2/8 Bath London Regt reported for duty with this unit.	
do	14/2/19		Demobilization 17 off 664 O.R. received 45 off 1799 O.R. dispatched do 19 " 1202 " do 18 " 712 " do	
do	15/2/19		15 ORs of Bath personnel proceeded to UK for demobilization 1 OR do do do returned in do 3 ORs do do Invalided to do to sick	
do	16/2/19		Demobilization 33 off 1577 O.R. received 32 off 1164 O.R. dispatched R.C. service 0800 hrs	
do	17/2/19		Demobilization 34 off 1190 O.R. received 36 off 1169 O.R. dispatched 1 Off 11 ORs of Bath personnel proceeded to UK for demobilization 3 ORs do do do returned in do 7 ORs do do invalided to do	
do	18/2/19		Demobilization 38 off 1339 O.R. received 34 off 1433 O.R. dispatched Inspection of Coy equipment by C.O.	

Army Form C. 2118.

WAR DIARY
or
INTELLIGENCE SUMMARY.
(Erase heading not required.)

Instructions regarding War Diaries and Intelligence
Summaries are contained in F. S. Regs., Part II.
and the Staff Manual respectively. Title pages
will be prepared in manuscript.

Place	Date	Hour	Summary of Events and Information	Remarks and references to Appendices
Boulogne	19/2/19		Demobilization 30 off. 1228 o.r. received 27 off. 1336 o.r. despatched 39 ORs of Batt. personnel proceeded to UK for demobilization 1 OR do do for re-enlistment	
do	20/2/19		Demobilization 11 off. do MR o.r. received 25 off. 1162 o.r. despatched do 7. 1107. do 23. 1428. do	
do	21/2/19		16 OR of Batt. personnel proceeded to UK for demobilization	
do	22/2/19		Demobilization 50 off. 1546 o.r. received 18 off. 498 o.r. despatched. 2 off. 149 ORs from 2/10th Batt London Regt reported for duty with this unit. 8 ORs of Batt. personnel proceeded to UK for demobilization sick	
do	23/2/19		Demobilization 22 off. 1052 o.r. received 6 off. 111 o.r. despatched. R.C. service 0800 hr. Presbyterian 1000 hr.	
do	24/2/19		Demobilization 28 off. 1576 o.r. received 46 off. 2051 o.r. despatched 14 ORs of Batt. personnel proceeded to UK for demobilization. 1 OR do do re-enlistment.	
do	25/2/19		Demobilization 11 off. 996 o.r. received 30 off. 1084 o.r. despatched. 24 ORs of Batt. personnel proceeded to UK for demobilization.	
do	26/2/19		Demobilization 37 off. 1629 o.r. received 35 off. 1520 o.r. despatched 21 OR of Batt. personnel proceeded to UK for demobilization 4 ORs do do sick	

WAR DIARY
or
INTELLIGENCE SUMMARY.
(Erase heading not required.)

Army Form C. 2118.

Place	Date	Hour	Summary of Events and Information	Remarks and references to Appendices
Boulogne	27/2/19		Demobilization 27/ff. 301 o.r. received. 22/ff. 741 o.r. dispatched. 2 O.Rs of Batt. personnel proceed to U.K. sick. 1 O.R. do for demobilization	
do	28/2/19		Demobilization 6/ff. 405 o.r. do. 27/ff. 1447 o.r. dispatched. 3 O.R. of Batt. personnel proceeded to U.K. sick	

1/3/19.

A. S. Lamm
Major.
Comdg. 21/7 Batt. London Ryf.

WAR DIARY

of

2/17th BATTALION LONDON REGIMENT.

from

1st March, 1919 to 31st March, 1919.

M.J. Brewer

Major,
Commanding, 2/17th Battalion London Regiment.

15/4/19.

Army Form C. 2118.

WAR DIARY
or
INTELLIGENCE SUMMARY.

(Erase heading not required.)

Instructions regarding War Diaries and Intelligence Summaries are contained in F. S. Regs., Part II. and the Staff Manual respectively. Title pages will be prepared in manuscript.

Place	Date	Hour	Summary of Events and Information	Remarks and references to Appendices
Boulogne	1-3-19	—	20. ORs of this Battalion proceeded to UK for Demobilisation. Capt. W.C. Wilson and Lieut C.P.S. Bradley to UK on Draft Conducting Duty and Leave. 22 Offs 1155 ORs arrived for transfer to UK. 114 Offs 694 ORs despatched to UK.	Mr T. Barrister Major
"	2-3-19	—	6 ORs of this Battalion proceeded to UK for Demobilisation. 5 Offs 103 ORs reported from 1/28d London Regt (1st Cadets) as reinforcements to replace demobilised personnel. 2nd Lts A. Hermelin, R. Beake, V.G. Cornell, W.G. Taylor, R.S. Chote. Corps Commander awards M.M's to 570686 Sgt. Loader, C. 575465 L/Cpl. Leach, D. 575806 L/Cpl. Thomas, R. 23 Offs 788 ORs arrived for transfer to UK. 9 Offs 401 ORs despatched to UK.	
"	3-3-19	—	2/Capt. E.B. Eldridge, M.C. returned from leave to UK. 15 Offs 687 ORs received for transfer to UK. 32 Offs 1554 ORs despatched to UK.	
"	4-3-19	—	28 Offs 902 ORs received for transfer to UK. 22 Offs 783 ORs despatched to UK.	
"	5-3-19	—	No personnel received for transfer to UK. Train expected. 23 Offs 658 ORs despatched to UK.	

Army Form C. 2118.

WAR DIARY
or
INTELLIGENCE SUMMARY.
(Erase heading not required.)

Instructions regarding War Diaries and Intelligence Summaries are contained in F.S. Regs., Part II. and the Staff Manual respectively. Title pages will be prepared in manuscript.

Place	Date	Hour	Summary of Events and Information	Remarks and references to Appendices
Boulogne	6-4-19	—	Lieut-Col. T. J. Doar, D.S.O. returned from leave to UK. 2nd Lt. E.J. Lucas M.C. returned from hospital. 4 O.Rs. of this Battalion to UK for demobilisation.	M. T. Brenner Major
		11.00	6 off, 962 O.Rs despatched to UK. This draft cleans the camp.	
			Coys (B+D) parade as strong as possible for 1 hour rifle and steady drill.	
		14.30	Lewis Gun Class commenced under 2nd Lt. V.C. Gosnell.	
	7-4-19	—	Capt. G.B. Stewart proceeded on draft conducting duty and 14 days leave.	
		12 O.Rs of this Battalion to UK for demobilisation.	
			Training as for yesterday.	
	8-4-19		Training as yesterday.	
			B.D. + Fd. Day booked at 'A' Coy Camp Tinglinghem.	
			Retreat now at 1800 hrs. 1 O.R reinforcement from 1/28th London Regiment.	
	9-4-19		Church Services held in B.R.C.S. hut and Church Army hut.	
		1900	Hymn sing songs in B.R.C.S hut and Church Army hut at 1900 hrs.	

Army Form C. 2118.

WAR DIARY
or
INTELLIGENCE SUMMARY.
(Erase heading not required.)

Place	Date	Hour	Summary of Events and Information	Remarks and references to Appendices
Boulogne	10-4-19.		3 O.R. Invalided to U.K. sick. 2nd Lts V.W.G. Smith, and M.J. Robinson to U.K. for 14 days leave.	
"	11-4-19.		All W.O. & N.COs of B.H.D. Coy parade for Lecture under R.S.M. 2nd Lt. H. Logan proceeded on 14 days leave to U.K.	
"	12-4-19.	1045	Training by 'A' 'B' & 'D' Coys in Football and Hockey fields. 2nd Lt. W.J. Lee. to U.K. on Draft Conducting Duty and 14 days leave. 2nd Lt. A.E.J. Elliott reported from 1/28 Bn. London Regiment (Artists Rifles).	
"	13-4-19.	1015	All 4 Cos of 'A' 'B' & 'D' Coys parade for Adjutants inspection.	
		1030	Battalion parade on Football field. 1 O.R. died in hospital. 1800 to U.K. for demobilisation. 2nd Lieut. W.J. Kildrye returned from hospital. 3 O.R. reinforcements from 1/8th Bath. London Regiment.	
"	14-4-19.		NCOs parade for Adjutants inspection and under RSM for instructional training	

Army Form C. 2118.

WAR DIARY
or
INTELLIGENCE SUMMARY.
(Erase heading not required.)

Place	Date	Hour	Summary of Events and Information	Remarks and references to Appendices
Boulogne	15.4.19	1630	All morning devoted to interior economy. Every man's kit and necessaries thoroughly inspected. Lecture by MrS A. Moff. in B.E.S. Theatre.	
"	16.4.19		A.E.S and Lewis Gun Class. 2/Capt. J. Heynson reported from 1/28th Bn London Regiment (Artists Rifles) & 1 OR 2nd Lt. C. Irving R.C.M. to U.K. on 14 days leave. 2nd Lt. F.H. Dollar M.C. and 118 ORs Reinforcement from 33rd Bn London Regiment. 16 off. 866 ORs arrived for transfer to U.K. Demobilisation re-commences.	
"	17.4.19.		10 off. 460 ORs received for transfer to U.K. 18 off. 701 ORs despatched to U.K.	
"	18.4.19.	1030	Draft from 33rd Bn. Lond. Regt. paraded under R.S.M. 61 off. 1655 ORs received for transfer to U.K. 4 off. 165 ORs despatched to U.K. 1 OR reinforcement from 1/28 Battalion London Regiment (Artists Rifles) Lieut. E.T.A. Evans to United Kingdom leave.	

Army Form C. 2118.

WAR DIARY
or
INTELLIGENCE SUMMARY.
(Erase heading not required.)

Place	Date	Hour	Summary of Events and Information	Remarks and references to Appendices
Boulogne.	19-4-19		19 off. 600 OR received for transfer to UK. 44 off 6 x OR despatched to UK. Draft paraded as for yesterday. Lieuts. J. L. Bancells and CR Brooland reported from 8d Battn. London Regiment.	
"	20-4-19		2/Capt. Awfgord ME. Lieut. W.Y. James, ME. and 2nd Lt. EE. Bupp proceed to the Army of Occupation. Draft paraded as yesterday. 45 off. 1358 OR received for transfer to UK. 34 off 1050 OR despatched to UK. 17 OR to UK for Demobilisation and re-enlistment	
"	21-4-19		Draft paraded as yesterday. 2nd Lt. ETW. Morgan reported from General Base Depot Havre. 1 OR hospital to UK Sick. 43 off 963 OR despatched to UK. 89 off. 1401 OR received for transfer to UK.	
"	22-4-19	1030.	Commanding Officer inspection of Quarters, and necessaries of Draft. 90 off 1820 OR despatched to UK. 68 off. 157 OR received for transfer to UK.	

Army Form C. 2118.

WAR DIARY
or
INTELLIGENCE SUMMARY.
(Erase heading not required.)

Place	Date	Hour	Summary of Events and Information	Remarks and references to Appendices
Boulogne	23.4.19		Lieut. W. Peters returned from leave to U.K. 2nd Lt. P. Ostell reported from 6th Bn. Lond Regt. Lieut. K.Y. Liu and 2nd Lieut. Y. Weld reported from 6th Bn. London Regiment. 2 O.R. to U.K. for demobilisation. Chinese Servants and Keying Ling Kong in BLOs and returned Army Rent. 19 Off. 586 OR received for transfer to U.K. 54 off 1195 OR despatched to U.K.	Jn. T. Moore M.U.
"	24.4.19		6 O.R. to U.K. for demobilisation. 5 OR to U.K. for reenlistment. Lieut. E. Bruno and 2nd Lt. F.Y. Smith reported from 9/10th Bn. London Regt. 2nd Lt. Wm. Sharp promoted A/Capt. and appointed Brigade Education Officer. Capt. W.C. Wilson returned from Draft Conducting Duty and 14 days leave. Wheat now at 1900 tons. Draft hurried in on Saturday. 4 off 86 OR arrived for transfer to U.K. 32 off 1353 OR despatched to U.K.	
"	25.4.19		95 off. 2013 OR arrived for transfer to U.K. 11 off 1017 OR despatched to U.K.	

Army Form C. 2118.

WAR DIARY
or
INTELLIGENCE SUMMARY.
(Erase heading not required.)

Instructions regarding War Diaries and Intelligence Summaries are contained in F. S. Regs., Part II. and the Staff Manual respectively. Title pages will be prepared in manuscript.

Place	Date	Hour	Summary of Events and Information	Remarks and references to Appendices
Boulogne	26-4-19		Draft paraded as for yesterday. 2nd Lts. (A)Metcalf, (A)Robinson, J.S. Kershaw, R.H. Smith, and T.W. Kent to UK demobilised. 5 OR to UK for demobilisation. 2nd Lt. F.H. Fuller, to UK sick. 159 Off. 1832 OR. received for transfer to UK. 64 Off. 20 OR despatched to UK.	
"	27-4-19		Parade as for to-day. Lieut. Att. Yeatesley reported from 1/4th Bn. London Regiment. Capt. r'd Lt. J.J. Parker proceeded to UK on 14 days leave. 115 Off. 597 OR received for transfer to UK. 65 Off. 994 OR despatched to UK.	
"	28-4-19	1030.	Draft paraded as for yesterday. 400 Off. 535 OR received for transfer to UK. 145 Off. 1913 OR despatched to UK. 05E Corp. Inspection of Quarters, Equipment and accessories of draft.	
"	29-4-19		236 Off. 746 OR received for transfer to UK. 50 Off. 1119 OR despatched to UK. Church Services in B.R.S. and Church Army Huts.	

2353 Wt. W3544/1454 700,000 5/15 D, D, & L. A.D.S.S./Forms/C. 2118.

WAR DIARY
or
INTELLIGENCE SUMMARY.
(Erase heading not required.)

Army Form C. 2118.

Place	Date	Hour	Summary of Events and Information	Remarks and references to Appendices
Boulogne	30/4/19		Church Services and hymns sung in R.C.S. and Church Army hut. Belgian Decoration Militaire (2nd Class) and Croix de Guerre awarded to a/Sgt. 570403 Fowler, R.G. (Orderly Room Clerk) 90 O/R 1546 O.R. arrived for despatch to U.K. 31 Off 686 O.R. despatched to U.K.	M. L. Barcauer Major
Boulogne	3/4/19		Draft paraded in Hockey Field under R.S.M. 6 Off 58 OR arrived for transfer to U.K. 64 Off 1064 OR despatched to U.K. Lieut. C.R. Woodland admitted to hospital. Major the Hon. M.J. Barcauer D.S.O. M.C. reported from 33rd B. London Regiment and assumed position of 2nd in command of the Battalion.	

Commanding 1/7th Battn. London Regiment.
Major.

30

2/17th Battalion London Regiment

Vol II

WAR DIARY

OF

2/17th BATTALION LONDON REGIMENT.

FROM. 1st April, 1919.   TO. 30th April, 1919.

2/17TH BATTN.,
THE LONDON
REGIMENT.
No. M 3469.
Date 1st April, 1919.

[signature]
Lieut-Colonel,
Commanding 2/17th Battalion London Regiment.

Army Form C. 2118.

WAR DIARY
or
INTELLIGENCE SUMMARY.
(Erase heading not required.)

Instructions regarding War Diaries and Intelligence Summaries are contained in F. S. Regs., Part II. and the Staff Manual respectively. Title pages will be prepared in manuscript.

Place	Date	Hour	Summary of Events and Information	Remarks and references to Appendices
Boulogne	1/4/19	-	Draft parade for safe arrival etc. 24 off. 757 OR received for despatch to UK. 51 off. 916 OR despatched to UK.	
"	2/4/19	-	Draft parade for standing call etc. 100 off. 1649 OR received for transfer to UK. 52 off. 1115 OR despatched to UK.	
"	3/4/19	-	2nd Lt. D.J. Smith proceeded to UK on 14 days leave. 2nd Lt G.R. Irvine, RAMC RAMC returned from leave to UK. Draft paraded as yesterday. 23 off. 673 OR received for transfer to UK. 74 off. 633 OR despatched to UK.	A.S.Palmer
"	4/4/19	-	2nd Lt R.D.Z. new proceeded to UK on 14 days leave. Bn/Lt R.J. Splatt returned from leave. Major P.A. Landon, M.C. proceeded to UK for demobilisation. 2nd Lt. W.J. Fielding reported to SpO Sy Bde. for staff duties. 9 off. 469 OR received for transfer to UK. 47 off. 1608 despatched to UK.	

WAR DIARY
or
INTELLIGENCE SUMMARY.

Army Form C. 2118.

Place	Date	Hour	Summary of Events and Information	Remarks and references to Appendices
Boulogne	5/4/19		2nd Lt. V.C. Oswald, proceeded on draft conducting duty and 14 days leave to UK. 2nd Lt. A. Grindin returned from leave to UK. 737 2 Offs 546 OR. received for transfer to UK. 13 Offs 534 ORs despatched to UK.	
"	6/4/19		Divine Services in BRCS huts and camp church. 2nd Lt. J.C.L. Harrison proceeded on 14 days leave to UK. 8 OR proceeded to UK for demobilisation and re-enlistment. 91 Offs 1411 OR received for transfer to UK. 20 Offs 544 ORs despatched to UK. Capt. G.H. Parker returned from leave to UK. Capt. W.T. Wilson to UK for demob.	
"	7/4/19		2nd Lieut. W.C. Leighton proceeded on 14 days leave to UK. 2 5 Offs 546 OR received for transfer to UK. 44 Offs 960 ORs despatched to UK.	
"	8/4/19		[illegible] Lieut. [illegible] Reid [illegible] 14 days leave [illegible] 2nd Lt. E.R. Booth to UK for 14 days leave prior to [illegible for demobilisation] 91 Offs 1485 ORs received for transfer to UK. 55 Offs 903 OR. despatched to UK.	

R.J. Browne

Army Form C. 2118.

WAR DIARY
or
INTELLIGENCE SUMMARY.
(Erase heading not required.)

Place	Date	Hour	Summary of Events and Information	Remarks and references to Appendices
Boulogne	9-4-19	—	2nd Lt. R.O. Evans proceeded to 1/28th Bn. London Regt. Army of Occupation. 2 nd Lt. A.E. Jones and O.R. proceed to UK for demobilisation. 2 OR reinforcements from Egypt. 80 Off. 1618 OR. received for transfer to UK. 96 Off. 1153 OR. despatched to UK.	Mr. T. Davies
"	10-4-19		Lieut W. Wright and 9 OR. reinforcements from 1/28th Bn. London Regiment came to UK for demobilisation. 777 Off despatched 5 OR received for transfer to UK. 79 Off. 1473 OR despatched to UK.	
"	11-4-19		Training of staff as usual. 79 Off. 16.? OR received for transfer to UK. 45 Off. 1099 OR. despatched to UK.	
"	12-4-19		34 Off. 646 OR. received for transfer to UK. 77 Off. 1103 OR despatched to UK.	
"	13-4-19		Divine Service in BRCS Tent and Camp Church. 28 Off. 465 OR received for transfer to UK. 36 Off. 1613 OR. despatched to UK.	

WAR DIARY
or
INTELLIGENCE SUMMARY.

Army Form C. 2118.

Place	Date	Hour	Summary of Events and Information	Remarks and references to Appendices
Antwerp	1-4-19		1 Platoon of "B" & "D" paraded for 1 hours rifle drill. 2nd Lieut. D.O.R. Templeman returned from leave to U.K. 17 O.R. 534 O.R. received for transfer to U.K. 28 Off. 826 O.R. dispatched to U.K.	
"	2-4-19		Concert in B.E.F. Theatre by Lunch Circus Co. 25 Off. 369 O.R. received for transfer to U.K. 25 Off. 594 O.R. dispatched to U.K.	
"	16-4-19		Lt. W. B. J. Webster, M.C. proceeded to Base Division Army of Occupation. 2 Lt. H.S. Eberts proceeded on 14 days leave to U.K. 61 Off. 105 O.R. received for transfer to U.K. 19 Off. 107 O.R. dispatched to U.K.	
"	17-4-19		One Platoon of "B" and "D" paraded for 1 hours drill. Lunar Cinema Coy. Show held. [illegible] Queen Alexandra returned from hospital [illegible] 24 Off. 596 O.R. received for transfer to U.K. 71 Off. 782 O.R. dispatched to U.K.	A.T. Brown [?]

Army Form C. 2118.

Instructions regarding War Diaries and Intelligence Summaries are contained in F. S. Regs., Part II. and the Staff Manual respectively. Title pages will be prepared in manuscript.

WAR DIARY
or
INTELLIGENCE SUMMARY.
(Erase heading not required.)

Place	Date	Hour	Summary of Events and Information	Remarks and references to Appendices
Rouloogne	18.4.19		O.C. Engr inspection & practice equipment and necessaries, huts. 7 2/offs 1573 O.Rs arrived for transfer to UK. 12 offs 33 ORs transferred to UK.	*[signature]*
"	19.4.19		2nd Lt. R.D. Draser returned from leave to UK. 22 Offs 690 OR arrived for transfer to UK. 84 offs 1086 OR transferred to UK.	
"	20.4.19		Church Services in B.E.O.S. hut and Camp Church. 2nd Lt. V.C. Gould returned from leave to UK. Also 2nd Lt. L.A.L. Barron. 15 offs 963 ORs arrived for transfer to UK. 26 offs 1579 OR transferred to UK.	
"	21.4.19		Lieut J.B. Carnelle to UK for demobilisation. Two platoons of "D" Coy paraded for drill and bayonet fighting. 12 offs 509 OR arrived for transfer to UK. 15 offs 644 OR transferred to UK.	
"	22.4.19		2nd Lt. R.J.T. Smith returned from leave to UK. 5 offs 529 OR arrived for transfer to UK. 15 offs 964 OR transferred to UK.	

WAR DIARY
or
INTELLIGENCE SUMMARY.

Army Form C. 2118.

Place	Date	Hour	Summary of Events and Information	Remarks and references to Appendices
Boulogne	23/4/19		One platoon of 'B' and 'D' coys paraded for one hours drill. Radio El. Sewed and 10 Ors recruits returned from leave to UK. 11 O/R W/S/R returned for transfer to UK. 2 O/R 90 O/R despatched to UK	[signature]
Boulogne	24/4/19		One platoon of 'B' and 'D' coy paraded for one hours drill. 12 O/R 658 O/R arrived for transfer to UK. 15 O/R 682 O/R despatched to UK. Pte G. B. Chipman returned from leave to UK	[signature]
"	25/4/19		Platoon training and Lewis Gun class commenced. 20 O/R 696 O/R arrived for transfer to UK. 21 O/R 579/1 O/R despatched to UK.	
"	26/4/19		O.C. Coy inspection of Quarters, equipment and necessaries. 2 O/R 170 O/R arrived for transfer to UK. 21 O/R 791 O/R despatched to UK	
"	27/4/19		Divine Service in Camp Church and R.C.S. tent. 1 O/R 96 O/R arrived for transfer to UK. 12 O/R 155 O/R despatched to UK	[signature]

WAR DIARY
or
INTELLIGENCE SUMMARY.
(Erase heading not required.)

Army Form C. 2118.

Place	Date	Hour	Summary of Events and Information	Remarks and references to Appendices
Boulogne	28.4.19		One platoon of 'B' & 'D' paraded for one hour drill. 1 O.R. reinforcement from 1/23rd Battalion London Regiment. KSR's fit to UK for demobilization. ORs invalided to UK sick. 2nd Lieut. KR Reeth to 30th Div. as 'D' tenue. 42 O.Rs 1561 ORs from France & the East for transfer to UK. 1 off 17 OR despatched to UK	~
"	29.4.19		Guard and Fatigue. Our been training. 2nd Lt. KS Coates returned from Liddle. 26 offs 760 OR arrived for transfer to UK. 41 off 484 OR despatched to UK	~
"	30/4/19		Guard and Fatigue. Our been training. 1 off 484 OR arrived for transfer to UK. 65 off 1583 OR despatched to UK	~

LIEUT. COL.
COMMANDING 2/17 BATTN. LONDON REGT

WAR DIARY for the month of May 1919.
or
INTELLIGENCE SUMMARY.
(Erase heading not required.)

Army Form C. 2118.

2/17 London R¹

Place	Date	Hour	Summary of Events and Information	Remarks and references to Appendices
Boulogne	1st		Guard and Lewis Gun Training. 2/Lieut R.D.FRASER Pana 2/Lieut G.T. COX proceeded to England on draft conducting duty. 2/Lieut E.R.SMITH proceeded to England for demobilisation. Capt. T. WHITESIDE (R.A.M.C.) joined unit as Medical Officer. Lieut E. HARMS rejoined unit from leave to U.K. Arrivals 23 Off. 495 O.R. Departures 6 Off. 792 O.R. Casualties 1 O.R. "W" (Acc.)	M. J. Barrau
	2nd		Platoon Training. Arrivals 25 Off. 527 O.R. Departures 12 Off. 522 O.R. Casualties NIL	
	3rd		Interior Economy. Arrivals 56 Off. 2093 O.R. Departures 22 Off. 410 O.R. Casualties NIL	
	4th		Divine Service. Lieut W.H.W. SPENCER proceeded to U.K on leave. 2/Lieut A.G. MARTIN and 2/Lieut W.T.C. LEIGHTON proceeded to U.K for demobilisation. Arrivals 24 Off. 1361 O.R. Departures 45 Off. 529 O.R. Casualties NIL	

Army Form C. 2118.

WAR DIARY
or
INTELLIGENCE SUMMARY.
(Erase heading not required.)

Place	Date	Hour	Summary of Events and Information	Remarks and references to Appendices
BOULOGNE	5		Gun Training. Arrivals 11 Off 560 O.R. Departures 46 Off 1788 O.R. Casualties Nil	
	6		Platoon and Lewis Gun Training. 2/Lieut. T.G. HUTCHINSON, 2/Lieut. S.G. LAMBERT and 2/Lieut. J.M. ANDERSON joined from 23rd Royal Fusiliers. 2/Lieut. E.T. COX returned from conducting duty. Arrivals 10 Off 748 O.R. Departures 16 Off 1686 O.R. Casualties Nil	
	7		Lewis Gun and Guard Training. Arrivals 58 Off 1788 O.R. Departures 110 Off 611 O.R. Casualties Nil	
	8		Platoon and Guard Training. Arrivals 40 Off 684 O.R. Departures 33 Off 750 O.R. Casualties Nil	
	9		Interior Economy. Arrivals 13 Off 700 O.R. Departures 58 Off 1691 O.R. Casualties Nil	M.T. Bascombe

Army Form C. 2118.

WAR DIARY
or
INTELLIGENCE SUMMARY.
(Erase heading not required.)

Place	Date	Hour	Summary of Events and Information	Remarks and references to Appendices
BOULOGNE	10		Games and Platoon Training. Arrivals 64 off 1701 O.R. Departures 29 off 796 O.R. Casualties NIL	M.J. Boscawen
	11		Band Review. 2/Lieut J.I. Fraser, M.C. proceeded to U.K. on 14 days leave. Arrivals 37 off 2559 O.R. Departures 57 off 7130 O.R. Casualties N.K.	
	12		Lewis Gun Training. Lieut Col H.T. DEAR, D.S.O. Commanding Officer proceeded to U.K. on 14 days leave. Major The Hon. M.T. BOSCAWEN, D.S.O, M.C. assumes command of Battalion. Arrivals 29 off 1236 O.R. Departures 36 off 1630 O.R. Casualties NIL	
	13		Platoon Training. 2/Lieut R.D. FRASER proceeded to England for demobilisation. Arrivals 19 off 774 O.R. Departures 29 off 2435 O.R. Casualties NIL	

WAR DIARY
or
INTELLIGENCE SUMMARY.

Place	Date	Hour	Summary of Events and Information	Remarks and references to Appendices
BOULOGNE	14		Lewis Guns Classes, Guard Training. 2/Lieut N.W. PETERS and 2/Lieut A.E.T. ELLIOTT M.C. proceeded to Buchan person on General Course of Training. Arrivals 141 O.R. 1916 O.R. Casualties Nil	
	15		Platoon and Guard Training. 2/Lieut F.D.R.TEMPERMAN, M.C and 2/Lieut PAST H. proceeded to U.K. for demobilisation. 2/Lieut H.F. GEE and 2/Lieut T.W.ELSH proceeded to U.K. for repatriation. Arrivals 24 Off 785 O.R. Departures 38 Off 717 O.R. Casualties Nil	
	16		Lewis Gun Class and Guard Training. Arrivals 25 Off 1869 OR Departures 32 Off 1896 OR Casualties Nil	
	17		Guard Training. Arrivals 52 Off 2201 OR Departures 29 OR 955 OR Casualties Nil	

H.S. Bascomen

Army Form C. 2118.

WAR DIARY
or
INTELLIGENCE SUMMARY.
(Erase heading not required.)

Instructions regarding War Diaries and Intelligence Summaries are contained in F. S. Regs., Part II. and the Staff Manual respectively. Title pages will be prepared in manuscript.

Place	Date	Hour	Summary of Events and Information	Remarks and references to Appendices
BOULOGNE	18		Divine Service. Arrivals 28 off 1047 O.R. Departures 57 off 2111 O.R. Casualties NIL	
	19		Lewis Gun Class. Arrivals 22 off 1256 O.R. Departures 29 off 2205 Casualties NIL	
	20		Gas Training and Lewis Gun Class. Lieut. M.H.W.SPENCER rejoined from leave to U.K. Capt. S.A.GOODGER proceeded. Lieut CR CROSSLAND, M.C. proceeded to U.K. for transpn. Provencan. Lieut B.G. CHAPMAN proceeded to U.K. for repatriation. demobilisation. Arrivals 40 off 1854 O.R. Departures 24 off 1049 O.R. Casualties NIL	
	21		Gas Training and Lewis Gun Class. 2/Lieut T.M. ANDERSON admitted to hospital. Arrivals 25 off 1640 O.R. Departures 43 off 1370 O.R. Casualties NIL	
	22		Gas Training and Lewis Gun Class. Arrivals 21 off 1028 O.R. Departures 23 off 1851 O.R. Casualties NIL	
	23		Gas Training and Lewis Gun Class. Lieut H.R.M.COOK VC proceeded to U.K. on leave. Arrivals 25 off 1663 O.R. Departures 66 off 2249 O.R. Casualties NIL	A.S.Bascomer

Army Form C. 2118.

WAR DIARY
or
INTELLIGENCE SUMMARY.
(Erase heading not required.)

Instructions regarding War Diaries and Intelligence Summaries are contained in F. S. Regs., Part II. and the Staff Manual respectively. Title pages will be prepared in manuscript.

Place	Date	Hour	Summary of Events and Information	Remarks and references to Appendices
BOULOGNE	24		Interior Economy	
			Arrivals 53 off 1032 OR. Departures 24 off 635 OR Casualties Nil	
	25		Divine Service	
			Arrivals 21 off 2261 OR Departures 53 off 1945 OR Casualties Nil	
	26		Platoon Training	
			Arrivals 44 off 647 OR Departures 29 off 719. Casualties Nil	
	27		Guard Training, Lewis Gun Class and N.C.O.s Class	
			Arrivals 38 off 1397 OR Departures 52 off 1298 OR Casualties Nil	
	28		Guard Training and Lewis Gun Class	
			Arrivals 45 off 766 OR Departures 18 off 834 OR Casualties Nil	
	29		Guard Training, Lewis Gun Class and N.C.O.s Class.	
			A football match was played between B Coy. 2/17 Bn London Regt. and B Coy 1/5 S. Lanc. Regt. B Coy. were the winners with the score of 2 goals to One. Arrivals 28 off 1350 OR Departures 30 off 1113 OR Casualties Nil	
	30		Guard Training, Lewis Gun Class and N.C.O.s Class.	
			Arrivals 46 off 1152 OR Departures 31 off 892 OR Casualties Nil	

Army Form C. 2118.

WAR DIARY
or
INTELLIGENCE SUMMARY.
(Erase heading not required.)

Place	Date	Hour	Summary of Events and Information	Remarks and references to Appendices
BOULOGNE	31		Interior Economy. 2/Lieut. F.G. HUTCHINSON proceeded to U.K. on 14 days leave. Arrivals 46 offs 1595 O.R. Departures 47 offs 492 O.R. Casualties Nil. Throughout the month amusements were provided for the demobilisation personnel by entertainments, concerts etc. nearly every evening	A T Boscawen
	4/6/19			

Commanding 2/17 Bn London Regt.

A Payn

2/17 London R¹

WAR DIARY for the month of June 1919 Army Form C. 2118.

INTELLIGENCE SUMMARY.

(Erase heading not required.)

Place	Date	Hour	Summary of Events and Information	Remarks and references to Appendices
Boulogne	1st		Divine Services Arrivals 66 Offs 1341 ORs Departure 6 Offs - 685 OR	
	2nd		Captain J Seymour assumed command of the Battalion vice Major M T Bocawen D.S.O. mc to leave UK Guard Doing, Lewis Gun Training and N.C.O's class 2nd Lieut E J Cox proceeded the UK for demobilization Arrivals 26 Offs 1168 ORs Departures 41 Offs 1107 ORs Casualties Nil	
	3rd		Guard and Lewis Gun Training and N.C.O's class 2nd Lieut A J Shlott proceeded on a Drill course, Etaples Arrivals 20 Offs 655 OR Departures 39 Offs 1596 OR Casualties Nil	
	4th		Guard, Lewis Gun Training and N.C.O's class Arrivals 39 Offs 899 Departures 36 Offs 693 OR Casualties Nil	
	5th		Major W H Baddeley D.S.O M6 reported for duty from 6th E. Surrey Regt and assumed command of the Battalion vice Capt J Seymour Guard training and Lewis Gun Training	

Army Form C. 2118.

WAR DIARY for the month of June.
or
INTELLIGENCE SUMMARY.

(Erase heading not required.)

Place	Date	Hour	Summary of Events and Information	Remarks and references to Appendices
Boulogne	5		Arrivals 117 O/Rs 1327 Departures 55 O/Rs 1250 O/Rs Casualties Nil.	
	6		Interior Economy. Arrivals 60 O/Rs 2041 Departure 52 O/Rs 918 O/Rs. Casualties Nil.	
	7		Guard and Lewis Gun training and NCO's class. Major The Hon MT Boscawen DSO MC rets from leave and resumed command of the Battalion. 2nd Lieut NWG Smith proceeded on 14 days' leave. Arrivals 68 O/Rs 1495 O/Rs. Departure 61 O/Rs 1021 O/Rs. Casualties Nil.	
	8		Revue Service. Arrivals 15 O/Rs 631 O/Rs Departure 72 O/Rs 1856 O/Rs. Casualties Nil.	
	9		Guard and Lewis Gun training, and NCO's class. Arrivals 52 O/Rs 1261 O/Rs. Departure 70 O/Rs 2484 O/Rs. Casualties Nil.	

Army Form C. 2118.

WAR DIARY
or
INTELLIGENCE SUMMARY.

for the month of June

(Erase heading not required.)

Instructions regarding War Diaries and Intelligence Summaries are contained in F. S. Regs., Part II. and the Staff Manual respectively. Title pages will be prepared in manuscript.

Place	Date	Hour	Summary of Events and Information	Remarks and references to Appendices
Boulogne	10th		The Bayonet fighting team of this Battalion chosen to represent the British troops in France and handed at the naval and military Tournament at Olympia.	
			Guard and Lewis Gun training and N.C.O's class.	
			Arrivals 59 Off 1119 OR. Departures 54 Off 1086 OR.	
			Casualties Nil	
	11th		Guard and Lewis Gun training and N.C.O's class	
			Arrivals 50 Off 2468 OR. Departures 57 Off 2452 OR	
			Casualties Nil	
	12th		Lieut-Colonel L.J. Dean DSO resumed command of the Battalion on return from leave	
			Guard and Lewis Gun training and N.C.O's class.	
			2nd Lieut. S.b. Lambert admitted to hospital	
			Arrivals 60 Off 1653 OR. Departures 61 Off 1429 OR.	
			Casualties Nil	

Army Form C. 2118.

WAR DIARY
or
INTELLIGENCE SUMMARY. for the month of June
(Erase heading not required.)

Instructions regarding War Diaries and Intelligence Summaries are contained in F. S. Regs., Part II. and the Staff Manual respectively. Title pages will be prepared in manuscript.

Place	Date	Hour	Summary of Events and Information	Remarks and references to Appendices
Boulogne	13th		Interior Economy.	
			2nd Lieut O W Morgan proceeded on 14 days leave to UK.	
			Lieut H R Macculin returned from leave UK.	
			Arrival. 65 Offrs. 1852 ORs. Departure 56 Offs. 2362 ORs.	
			Casualties NIL.	
	14th		Guard training and NCOs class. A new Lewis Gun class commenced.	
			2nd Lieut W J Lee proceeded to 6th London Regt, Army of Rhine	
			2nd Lieut J.A. Hutchinson returned from leave	
			The football 2nd Knock out competition was played or between	
			Coys found between "B" Coy of the Battalion and "D" Coy of	
			the 1/15th South Lancs Regt. Recd. 3/17th London Regt. 0 1/5 South Lancs 1	
			Arrival. 81 Offs. 3470 ORs. Departure 83 Offs. 2366 ORs. Casualties NIL	
	15th		Divine Service.	
			Arrival 69 Offrs. 2409 ORs. Departure 50 Offs. 1796 ORs.	
			Casualties NIL	

Army Form C. 2118.

Instructions regarding War Diaries and Intelligence Summaries are contained in F. S. Regs., Part II. and the Staff Manual respectively. Title pages will be prepared in manuscript.

WAR DIARY for the month of June
or
INTELLIGENCE SUMMARY.
(Erase heading not required.)

Place	Date	Hour	Summary of Events and Information	Remarks and references to Appendices
Boulogne	16th		Guard and Lewis Gun Training NCO's Class	
			Major Hon M.J. Trefusis DSO MC. proceeded to the UK (Regular Soldier)	
			Arrivals 105 Offs 2611 ORs. Departure 94 Offs 2959 ORs	
			Casualties NIL	
	17th		Guard and Lewis Gun Training	
			Arrivals 24 Offs 1093 ORs. Departure 70 Offs 1988 ORs	
			Casualties NIL	
	18th		Guard and Lewis Gun Training	
			Arrivals 93 Offs 2881 ORs. Departures 67 Offs 2159 ORs	
			Casualties NIL	
	19th		Guard and Lewis Gun Training	
			Arrivals 79 Offs 2127 Departures 39 Offs 960 ORs	
			Interior Economy 19 ORs. proceeded to ADPS for Duty	
	20th		Capt J Seymour proceeded on 14 day leave to UK	
			Arrival 59 Offs 1378 Departure 88 Offs 2938 ORs	
			Casualties NIL	

WAR DIARY
or
INTELLIGENCE SUMMARY.

Army Form C. 2118.

for the month of June

(Erase heading not required.)

Place	Date	Hour	Summary of Events and Information	Remarks and references to Appendices
Boulogne	21st		Guard and Lewis Gun Training	
			2nd Lieut G.V. Wobsley proceeded to the UK for demobilisation	
			2nd Lieut McLambert rtd from Hospital	
			Arrivals 72 Offs 2287 ORs Departure 96 Offs 2877 ORs	
			Casualties Nil	
	22nd		Divine Service	
			Arrival 85 Offs 1893 ORs Departure 60 Offs 1494 ORs	
	23rd		Guard and Lewis Gun Training	
			Lieut H.B Smith returned from leave	
			2nd Lieut K.J Splatt returned from Boulogne Etaples	
			Arrival 55 Offs 1918 ORs Departure 45 Offs 1825 ORs	
	24th		Guard and Lewis Gun Training	
			Arrival 94 Offs 2517 ORs Departure 68 Offs 2214 ORs	
			Casualties Nil	
	25th		Guard and Lewis Gun Training	
			Arrival 44 Offs 616 ORs Departure 73 Offs 2637 ORs	

Army Form C. 2118.

WAR DIARY
or
INTELLIGENCE SUMMARY. for the month of June
(Erase heading not required.)

Instructions regarding War Diaries and Intelligence Summaries are contained in F. S. Regs., Part II. and the Staff Manual respectively. Title pages will be prepared in manuscript.

Place	Date	Hour	Summary of Events and Information	Remarks and references to Appendices
Boulogne	26th		Guard Training and Lewis Gun Class Casualties Nil	
			2nd Lieut A Kennelin admitted to Hospital	
			2nd Lieut H.S Chester proceeded on a Brief leave, Etaples	
			2nd Lieut J.A Ewing and 22 O.R. proceeded to ich on	
			Completion at Naval & Military Tournament, Olympia	
			Arrivals 85 Offrs 1793 O.R. Departure 67 Offrs 1445 O.R.	
	27th		Interior Economy	
			Lieut C.P.S Bradley proceeded on 14 days' leave to the U.K.	
			Arrivals 50 Offrs 1330 O.R. Departures 24 Offrs 740 O.R.	
			Casualties Nil	
	28th		Guard and Lewis Gun Training	
			2nd Lieut Sir Morgan ~~~ returned from leave	
			Arrivals 46 Offrs 946 O.R. Departures 71 Offrs 1740 O.R.	
			Casualties Nil	
	29th		Divine Service	
			Arrivals 140 Offrs 685 O.R. Departures 65 Offrs 1457 O.R.	

WAR DIARY *for the month of June* Army Form C. 2118.

or

INTELLIGENCE SUMMARY.

(Erase heading not required.)

Place	Date	Hour	Summary of Events and Information	Remarks and references to Appendices
Boulogne	30th		Grand Training. A new Lewis Gun Class commenced. Arrivals 61 Offrs 1340 OR. Departures 24 Offrs 972 OR. Casualties Nil.	
			Throughout the month amusements were provided for the demobilised personnel by entertainments, concerts etc. nearly every evening.	
	1/7/1919			

Walter Taylor Lieut-Colonel,
Commanding, 2/17th Battn London Regt.

Army Form C. 2118.

WAR DIARY for the month of July 1919.
or
INTELLIGENCE SUMMARY. 2/17 London Div.

Place	Date	Hour	Summary of Events and Information	Remarks and references to Appendices
Boulogne	1st		Guards training and Lewis Gun Class. Arrived 55 Off's 1181 O.R's. Departures 36 Off's 767 O.R's.	
	2nd		2nd Lieut A.J. Morgan proceeded to G.H.Q., D. & G. R.E. for duty. 2nd Lieut A. Hamblin proceeded to the U.K. for demobilisation. Casualties NIL.	
	3rd		Guard training and Lewis Gun Class. Major W. H. Boddeley DSO, MC, proceeded to UK on 14 days leave Arrived 69 Off's 1593 O.R's. Departures 61 Off's 1439 O.R's. Casualties NIL.	
	3rd		Guard training and Lewis Gun Class. Number of men demobilised in this camp between February 1st and June 30th, 1919 :- 5633 Off's, 165581 O.R's. Arrivals 29 Off's 635 O.R's. Departures 43 Off's 1094 O.R's. Casualties NIL.	
	4th		Interior Economy 2nd Lieut L.B. Poultney proceeded on Draft Conducting Duty	

WAR DIARY
or
INTELLIGENCE SUMMARY.

Place	Date	Hour	Summary of Events and Information	Remarks and references to Appendices
Boulogne	July 4th		and leave to UK 2nd July 1919. Arrivals 48 Offrs 1063 ORs. Departures 59 Offrs 1534 ORs. Casualties NIL.	
	5th		Gunnery Training and two Yun & tear. Lieut W Blight proceeded on 14 days leave to UK. Capt J Seymour returned from 14 days leave to UK. Arrivals 23 Offrs 920 ORs. Departures 51 Offrs 799 ORs. Casualties NIL. Divine Service	SUNDAY
	6th		Arrivals 23 Offrs 981 ORs. Departures 34 Offrs 1283 ORs. Casualties NIL.	
	7th		Gunnery Training and two Yun & tear. Arrivals 14 Offrs 430 ORs. Departures 26 Offrs 966 ORs. Casualties NIL.	
	8th		Gunnery training and two Yun & tear. Arrivals 30 Offrs 809 ORs. Departures 19 Offrs 709 ORs.	

WAR DIARY
or
INTELLIGENCE SUMMARY.

(Erase heading not required.)

Army Form C. 2118.

Place	Date	Hour	Summary of Events and Information	Remarks and references to Appendices
Boulogne	8th		Casualties NIL.	
			Lieut G B Wiman proceed on 14 days leave to UK.	
	9th		2ⁿᵈ Lieut P.R.Y. Canney proceeded to Bayonne France on 7 days leave.	
			Guard training and Lewis Gun class.	
			Arrivals 42 Offrs 1380 OR's. Departures 26 Offrs 442 OR's.	
			Casualties NIL.	
	10th		Guard training and Lewis Gun class.	
			Arrivals 26 Offs 612 OR's. Departures 45 Offs 1525 OR's.	
	11th		Casualties NIL.	
			Interim Economy.	
			Arrivals 14 Offs 544 OR's. Departures 30 Offs 810 OR's.	
	12th		Casualties NIL.	
			A free matinee was given at 1400 hour at the Municipal Theatre, by order by the French Authorities, for British troops.	

WAR DIARY or INTELLIGENCE SUMMARY

Army Form C. 2118.

Place	Date	Hour	Summary of Events and Information	Remarks and references to Appendices
Boulogne	Dec 12		Arrivals 3 Offs 154 ORs. Departures 2 Offs 619 ORs. Casualties Nil.	
	13		Divine Service	
	14		Arrivals 2 Offs 738 ORs. Departures 36 Offs 550 ORs. Casualties Nil.	
			2nd Lieut J A Ewing returned from leave to UK. 2nd Lieut A B Chaplin proceeded on 14 days leave to UK. 2nd Lieut J H Parrott proceeded on 14 days leave to UK. Area Training.	
			Arrivals 60 Offs 1141 ORs. Departures 24 Offs 1512 ORs. Casualties Nil.	
			The Naval Authorities celebrate Peace. All Ranks allowed leave one if camp.	
	15		Drill, Musketry, and heavy gun training. Arrivals 16 Offs 364 ORs. Departures 58 Offs 743 ORs. Casualties Nil.	

WAR DIARY or INTELLIGENCE SUMMARY

Army Form C. 2118.

Place	Date	Hour	Summary of Events and Information	Remarks and references to Appendices
Boulogne	16th		2nd Lieut A. E. J. Elliott, M.C. returned from Brill bonne Burhonsted. Lewis Gun class, Two platoons of "C" Company for inspection and steady drill. Arrival 26 offrs 560 O.R's. Departure 22 offrs 1094 O.R's. Carnation NIL.	
	17th		Major H H Baddeley DSO, MC returned from leave to UK. Infant's Economy. Arrival 24 offrs 963 O.R's. Departure 26 offrs 445 O.R's. Carnation NIL.	
	18th		Attestation of all Rooms in Brown to Battalion Programme for tomorrow, also circular issued by G.H.Q Sports Club entitled "How to spend Joy Day". 2nd Lieut J.E.S. Charles, returned from Brill bonne, Etaples. 2nd Lieut J. M & M hampshire paraded on 14 days leave to UK. 2nd Lieut P.R.Y Panney returned from leave to "Bayonne" Travel	

Army Form C. 2118.

WAR DIARY
or
INTELLIGENCE SUMMARY.
(*Erase heading not required.*)

Place	Date	Hour	Summary of Events and Information	Remarks and references to Appendices
Boulogne	18th		Arrived 19 Offrs 959 ORs. Departures 26 Offrs 56 ORs. Remains N.I.L.	
	19th		"PEACE DAY" There was a "Knock Out" Football Competition between all Companies of the Battalion. "A" Company won. A Cricket Match between Marthinney and Jenkinstown Camps. Marthinney Camp won. Supplied to the men after dinner. All Ranks allowed Passes until mid-night. In the evening there were 2 Bonfires lit on the Sands of Boulogne. Arrivals 26 Offrs 1006 ORs. Departures 26 Offrs 969 ORs. Remains Nil. Divine Service.	
	20th		Arrivals 15 Offrs 623 ORs. Departures 20 Offrs 952 ORs.	

Army Form C. 2118.

Instructions regarding War Diaries and Intelligence Summaries are contained in F. S. Regs., Part II. and the Staff Manual respectively. Title pages will be prepared in manuscript.

WAR DIARY
or
INTELLIGENCE SUMMARY.
(Erase heading not required.)

Place	Date	Hour	Summary of Events and Information	Remarks and references to Appendices
Boulogne	Dec 20th		Casualties NIL.	
	21st		Usual training and leave given to 20 p.c. of Strength. Proceeded on 14 days leave to UK. Officers to cinema matinee at 14:00 this afternoon.	NIL
			Strength of the Battalion	
			into Full Battalion	
	22nd		Annesley 15 Off. 288 O.R's. Departures 16 Off. 898 O.R's. Casualties NIL	
			14 D Bugler returned from leave to UK	
	23rd		Annesley 14 Off. 416 O.R's. Departures 18 Off. 906 O.R's. Casualties NIL.	
			Usual training, known and unknown Gun training	
	24th		Annesley 21 Off. 433 O.R's. Departures 24 Off. 290 O.R's. Casualties	
	25th		to 16 Off 2 Warrant - Bn. taken on Strength of 14th Stationary Hospital.	

2353 Wt. W3544/1454 700,000 5/15 L. D. & L. A.D.S.S./Forms/C. 2118.

Army Form C. 2118.

WAR DIARY
or
INTELLIGENCE SUMMARY.
(Erase heading not required.)

Instructions regarding War Diaries and Intelligence Summaries are contained in F.S. Regs., Part II, and the Staff Manual respectively. Title pages will be prepared in manuscript.

Place	Date	Hour	Summary of Events and Information	Remarks and references to Appendices
Boulogne	24th		Squad training and Lewis Gun class. Arrivals 20 off, 962 OR's. Departures 26 off, 416 OR's. Casualties Nil.	
	25th A.M.		2nd Lieut H. J. Smith proceeded on 14 days leave to U.K. Squad training and Lewis Gun class. Casualties Nil.	
	26th P.M.		Lieut G/R Warren returned from leave to U.K. Helmer men to join on Range under 2 Lieut Y.L. Burrell. Arrivals 26 off, 968 OR's. Departures 21 off, 443 OR's. Casualties Nil. Divine Service.	copy
	27th A.M.		Arrivals 13 off, 468 OR's. Departures 26 off, 634 OR's. Casualties Nil.	
	28th A.M.		2nd Lieut J. H. Connort returned from leave to U.K. Arrivals 30 off, 682 OR's. Departures 16 off, 982 OR's. Casualties Nil.	

Army Form C. 2118.

WAR DIARY
or
INTELLIGENCE SUMMARY.
(Erase heading not required.)

Place	Date	Hour	Summary of Events and Information	Remarks and references to Appendices
Boulogne	29.		A sum of £150 - has been surpassed on first instalment of the Battalion's contribution to the "Old Comrades Association & Benevolent Fund of the 14th Border Regt".	
	30th		A further contribution of £15 - has been forwarded on behalf of the Sergeants' mess, to the same fund. Lieut E Sterne admitted into Hospital. Next SC hamper provided on 1st day leave to UK. Capt. y te Packet provided on 14 days leave to UK. Arrivals 14 Offr. 509. OR's Departures 25 Off. 464 OR's. Casualties Nil	
	30th		2nd Lieut H G Blenkinson returned from 1st day leave UK. Arrivals 24 Offr. 666 OR's Departures 16 Off. 886 OR's Casualties Nil	
	31st		2nd Lieut Y L Youmans proceeded on 1st days leave to UK. Arrivals 17 Offr. 734 OR's Departures 22 Offr. 529 OR's.	

WAR DIARY
or
INTELLIGENCE SUMMARY.
(Erase heading not required.)

Army Form C. 2118.

Place	Date	Hour	Summary of Events and Information	Remarks and references to Appendices
Bologne	31st		Casualties Nil.	
			Throughout the month movements were preserved for the demobilised personnel by cinema, enemas etc., every evening.	
	1/8/1919.			

Walter Marwig
Major,
Commanding, 2/14th Battalion London Regt.

2/17 + Bn London R.

Army Form C. 2118.

WAR DIARY
or
INTELLIGENCE SUMMARY.
For the month of September 1919.

(Erase heading not required.)

Place	Date	Hour	Summary of Events and Information	Remarks and references to Appendices
Boulogne	1st		Casualties — Nil	A.T.M.
	2nd		The 20th (S) Bn The Kings (Liverpool) Regt took over the admin- istration of Malbrow Camp and assumed all responsibility to	
			Annihilation from Newell	
			Casualties — Nil	A.T.M.
	3rd		2/Lieut C.E. Poultney returned from leave 2/9/19	
			G.E. Line	
			ditto	
			Casualties — Nil	A.T.M.
	4th		Casualties — Nil	A.T.M.
	5th		Casualties — Nil Battn. Headquarters moved to Wimille Camp	A.T.M.
	6th		Casualties — Nil	A.T.M.
	7th		Divine Service Casualties — Nil	A.T.M.
	8th		Company Parade	
			Casualties — Nil	A.T.M.
	9th		Casualties — Nil	A.T.M.

M M Mills of Major

Army Form C. 2118.

WAR DIARY
or
INTELLIGENCE SUMMARY.
(Erase heading not required.)

Instructions regarding War Diaries and Intelligence Summaries are contained in F.S. Regs., Part II. and the Staff Manual respectively. Title pages will be prepared in manuscript.

Place	Date	Hour	Summary of Events and Information	Remarks and references to Appendices
Boulogne	10th		Lieut. E.E. Parker proceeded to UK on duty.	N/M.
	11th		Cavalry — Nil.	N/M.
			Bull Parade	N/M.
			Cavalry — Nil.	
	12th		Commanding Officer's Inspection of Subs. Rifles & Equipment	N/M.
			Cavalry — Nil.	N/M.
	13th		Cavalry — Nil	N/M.
	14th		Divine Service	
			Cavalry — Nil.	N/M.
	15th		Lieut. A.R. Blake reported from 30th Division	N/M.
			Cavalry — Nil.	N/M.
	16th		Cavalry — Nil.	N/M.
	17th		Cooks on parade for Commanding Officer's Inspection	N/M.
			Cavalry — Nil.	
	18th		2/Lt. B.B. Pordhey — proceeded to UK for decode.	N/M.
			Capt. J. Seymour proceeded to HQ D.G.R.E.	

W.M.Mulcock Major

Army Form C. 2118.

WAR DIARY
or
INTELLIGENCE SUMMARY.
(Erase heading not required.)

Instructions regarding War Diaries and Intelligence Summaries are contained in F. S. Regs., Part II. and the Staff Manual respectively. Title pages will be prepared in manuscript.

Place	Date	Hour	Summary of Events and Information	Remarks and references to Appendices
Boulogne	19th		Cavalric – Mtn.	M/M.
	20th		Cavalric – Mtn.	M/M.
	21st		Cavalric – Mtn.	M/M.
			Divine Service –	
			Cavalric – Mtn.	M/M.
	22nd		Clothing Parade. Bath Parade. Lt. W.W. Peers struck off strength from 28/2/1919.	M/M.
			Cavalric – Mtn.	M/M.
	23rd		Cavalric – Mtn.	M/M.
	24th		Lt. & H.Q. Smith proceeded on leave to UK	M/M.
			Lt. LC Lambert returned from duty in UK	
			Cavalric – Mtn.	
	25th		Lt. PRP Pavey proceeded to UK on leave.	M/M.
			Cavalric – Mtn.	
	26th		Lt. W.W. Spencer returned from Hospital	
			2/Lt. Ft. Jensen No. proceeded on leave to UK 12.9.19	M/M.
			Cavalric – Mtn.	

W.W. Wood Major

Army Form C. 2118.

WAR DIARY
or
INTELLIGENCE SUMMARY.
(Erase heading not required.)

Instructions regarding War Diaries and Intelligence Summaries are contained in F. S. Regs., Part II. and the Staff Manual respectively. Title pages will be prepared in manuscript.

Place	Date	Hour	Summary of Events and Information	Remarks and references to Appendices
Bialopa	27th		Casualties – Nil.	Nil.
	28th		Divine Service.	
			Casualties – Nil.	Nil.
	29th		Casualties – Nil.	Nil.
				W.T.Nichol Major
				Comdg 2/17th Bn London Regt

30TH DIVISION
89TH INFY BDE

89TH MACHINE GUN COY.
MAR 1916-FEB 1918

30TH DIVISION
89TH INFY BDE

Vol. I

WAR DIARY of 83 COY. MACHINE GUN CORPS

Army Form C. 2118.

or

INTELLIGENCE SUMMARY

(Erase heading not required.)

Instructions regarding War Diaries and Intelligence Summaries are contained in F. S. Regs., Part II. and the Staff Manual respectively. Title pages will be prepared in manuscript.

O.C. 83 Coy. Machine Gun Corps.
T.H. Roberts Capt.

Place	Date	Hour	Summary of Events and Information	Remarks and references to Appendices
HAVRE	10/3/16	7.30 a.m.	Landed. Proceeded to No 1. Camp.	T.H.R
HAVRE	13/3/16	5.30 a.m.	Entrained Point 3 for MERICOURT.	T.H.R
SAILLY LAURETTE	14/3/16	3. a.m.	Entered billets - remained till 18/3/16. 9. a.m.	T.H.R
LA HOUSSOYE	18/3/16	2. p.m.	Entered billets - remained till 29/3/16	T.H.R
—	26/3/16	—	1 OR Died 1 OR to CCS	T.H.R
SAILLY LAURETTE	29/3/16	1.15 p.m.	Entered billets	T.H.R

89 COY. MACHINE GUN CORPS.

From :- Officer Commanding,
        89th Coy Machine Gun Corps.

To :-   O/c A.G's Office,
        The Base.

Forwarding War Diary for March for your information, please.

J H Roxburgh Capt.
O.C., 89 COY. MACHINE GUN CORPS

31 MAR 1916

Vol II April 1916.   89 M G Coy
                                                   VOL 2
Army Form C. 2118.

WAR DIARY of 89 Company
or
INTELLIGENCE SUMMARY. Machine Gun Corps

(Erase heading not required.)

Instructions regarding War Diaries and Intelligence Summaries are contained in F. S. Regs., Part II. and the Staff Manual respectively. Title pages will be prepared in manuscript.

Place	Date	Hour	Summary of Events and Information	Remarks and references to Appendices
SAILLY LAURETTE	7/4/16	—	2 OR Reinforcements from M.G. Base Depot CAMIERS. JMR	
—	10/4/16	—	1 OR Reinforcement " " " " JMR	
—	29/4/16	—	14 ORs (2 Sgts) returned to M.G. Base Depot CAMIERS (Authority A/G's letter No A/6564) JMR dated 8/4/16.	
			4 OR. 2nd Bn Bedfordshire Regt ⎫	
			4 OR. 17th Bn. Kings (Liverpool) Regt ⎬ 89th Inf. Bde. Transferred to 89 Coy MGC.	
			3 OR 19th " ⎪ JMR	
			3 OR 20th " ⎭	
	30/4/16		Moved to BRAY to relieve 63 Coy MGC in Z Sector (MARICOURT)	Operation Order
			8 guns in Z Sector - 4 guns in MARICOURT defences - 4 guns in BRAY JMR	No 4 (Appendix I)

T.A. Cox (WR) Capt.
Comdg 89 Coy M.G.C.

From :— O.C. 89 Coy. Machine Gun Corps
To :— D.A.G 3rd Echelon

Enclosed please find Appendix I of Vol. II of the War Diary of 89th Coy. Machine Gun Corps. Regret that it was omitted with Vol. II. of War Diary of 89th Coy M.G.C. for April, please.

A. N. Broad.
Lieut

for O.C.
89 Coy. M.G.C

2/5/-16.

Appendix. 1
of Vol. 2 of War Diary of 89th Coy.
Machine Gun Corps for April 1916.

V.G (Cont.)
1/123

89th Coy. M.G.C. Operation Order. No. 4
by Capt. J H Roxburgh.
18th April 1916

Reference Maps. Trench Maps - Maricourt - 1/10.000

1/ The 89th Coy. M.G.C will relieve the 53rd Coy. M.G.C. on April 30th 1916.

2/ The 89th Company will leave billets in SAILLY LAURETTE at 6 a.m. on 30th inst. & move to BRAY. No 4 Section will form a rear party.

3/ No.1 Section will relieve guns in Z 1 subsector
No. 3 —   "   "   "   Z 2   —
No. 2 —   "   "   "   MARICOURT defences

4/ Guides for gun teams will be provided at A 22 a 1.5. MARICOURT.

5/ No. 1 Section will leave BRAY at 9.30 a.m.
No. 3 —   "   "   "   10.0 a.m.
No. 2 —   "   "   "   10.30 a.m.

6/ All trench stores will be handed over.

7/ O.C.s Nos 1, 2 & 3 Sections will report to Coy H.Q. BRAY when relief has been completed.

8/ O.C. 89 Coy. will take over command at 4 p.m. 30/4/16.

(Signed)
Copy 1. To 89th Inf. Bde.   J. H. ROXBURGH Capt
— 2. to 53 Coy M.G.C.   Comdg. 89 Coy. M.G.C.
— 3 Retained.   12 noon.

	89th COMPANY, MACHINE GUN CORPS.
	No. V.G.a8.
	Date. 31.5.16.

From:- Officer Commanding,
89th Coy, Machine Gun Corps.

To:- Officer i/c
A.G's Office at the Base.

Forwarding War Diary of this Unit Vol: III for May 1916, for your information, please.

Also Appendices II, III, IV & V please

J H Roxburgh Captain,
Commanding,
89 COY. MACHINE GUN CORPS.

Vol III p.1.
May 1916

WAR DIARY of 89 Company Machine Gun Corps.
INTELLIGENCE SUMMARY

Army Form C. 2118.

Place	Date	Hour	Summary of Events and Information	Remarks and references to Appendices
Reference Maps			62 D. N.E. 1/20,000 (French map) + Appendix No II.	
BRAY (Coy HQ.)	30-4-16	2 p.m.	Guns of 89 Coy M.G.C. had relieved those of 53 Coy in Z Sector. For orders re relief see Method of relief.	APP. I (Vol II Apps)
			No 1 Section paraded in BRAY at 9:30 a.m. with 1 limbered wagon (for men's packs + spare parts etc.) + 4 pack mules (each carrying 1 gun + 1 tripod) + 2 pack mules carrying 6 boxes (belt) of ammunition. (7 belt boxes having been changed the previous night.)	
			They reached SUZANNE at 10·30 a.m., where limbered wagon was left, the men putting on their packs and carrying the spare parts etc. The gun teams moved from this point at intervals of 200 yds. The driver + one man of the gun team led each mule, and they moved up in the bottom of the valley to MARICOURT, where the 1st team arrived at 11·35 a.m. Here it was met by a guide. The other teams followed similarly.	
			No 3 Section followed ½ hour after No 1. Section.	
			No 2 Section followed ½ hour after No 3 Section.	
			System taken over.	
			4 guns in Z1 Subsector - Taken over by No 1 Section Nos. 12, 19, 21 + 26 emplacements.	See Appendix II
			4 guns in Z2 Subsector - Taken over by No 3 Section Nos 3, 4, 6 + 7 emplacements.	— " —
			2 guns in MARICOURT DEFENCES. Taken over by No. 2 Section Nos 28 + 30 emplacements. 2 guns in a killer in School Sr.	— " —
			2 guns resting in BRAY.	

Vol VII - p.2.
May 1916.

Army Form C. 2118.

WAR DIARY of 89 Company Machine Gun Corps.

~~INTELLIGENCE SUMMARY~~

(Erase heading not required.)

Instructions regarding War Diaries and Intelligence Summaries are contained in F. S. Regs., Part II. and the Staff Manual respectively. Title pages will be prepared in manuscript.

Place	Date	Hour	Summary of Events and Information	Remarks and references to Appendices
Z Sector	1-5-16		Transport & Coy H.Q. in BRAY. Telephones from Section H.Q. in MARICOURT to Section H.Q. in Z.1. & Z.2. and Brigade Report Centre. Also from Coy H.Q. to Brigade H.Q. in BRAY. Gun teams change round every 6 days.	JHR
			Left gun in MACHINE GUN WOOD (No 3 emplacement) moved to position in A.P. 7 (no 2 emplacement). gun also moved from No 4 emplacement to no 3.	Appendix II
	4-5-16		Gun by Haystacks (No 7 emplacement) moved at special request of Col: POYNTZ, O.C. 22nd Beds. to position in MERSEA STREET (no. 10 emplacement) with field of fire to front line. New position (no 23 emplacement) sited for "French" gun (no. 21 emplacement) Position for another gun in BREWERY KEEP found (no 32 emplacement) Emplacement (no. 30) on PERONNE ROAD Barrier altered to allow the gun to fire on ground to the S.E.	JHR
	5-5-16	10.a.m.	L/cpl: EATON (No 2 gun in No3 emplacement) fired on a party of about 20 Germans seen leaving their French opposite A.P. 3. The result could not be observed. The gun in MERSEA STREET also opened indirect and overhead fire in conjunction with rapid fire from the front line.	JHR
	6-5-16		Sectional relief of guns carried out. Incoming teams brought gun, French trays, spare parts, oil can cases	

T2134. Wt. W708-776. 500000. 4/15. Sir J. C. & S.

Vol III p.3.

Army Form C. 2118.

WAR DIARY of 89 Company Machine Gun Corps.

INTELLIGENCE SUMMARY

Instructions regarding War Diaries and Intelligence Summaries are contained in F. S. Regs., Part II. and the Staff Manual respectively. Title pages will be prepared in manuscript.

(Erase heading not required.)

May 1916

Place	Date	Hour	Summary of Events and Information	Remarks and references to Appendices
			and cleaning rods.	Appendix "I"
			No 4 Section relieved No 3 Section in ZZ Subsector	
			No 3 " " No 2 " MARICOURT DEFENCES.	
			No 2 " " No 1 " Z.1. Subsector	
			No 1 " " to BRAY.	JHR
0Z Sector	8-5-16		1 O.R. wounded, later died of wounds. Hit by shell during a slight bombardment of MACHINE GUN WOOD.	JHR
	9-5-16		Position (no 31 emplacement) sited for a gun in NORTH PERONNE AVENUE firing N. N.E. & E.	JHR
	10-5-16		gun from 90 Company to be placed in the ADVANCED BREWERY REDOUBT to watch ground to S. of road. Bombardment of german near of front line trenches opposite A.P.2 & AP.3 during the morning. a simple emplacement was made by day in A 15/3 (no 5 emplacement) and the range obtained. An aiming mark was put out for a gap made in the German wire and two stops were fixed marking the limits of traverse on the portion of trench bombarded in the morning. No 2 gun from No 3 emplacement (MACHINE GUN WOOD) was mounted here in the evening with the stereotype attachment on and a sandbag screen in front. at 11:15 p.m., the enemy having been reported repairing their trench, the gun fired & continued to do so at intervals till 1:20 a.m. when patrols were sent out from our line and the germans were unable to mend their wire	JHR

T2134. Wt. W708 –776. 500000. 4/15. Sir J. C. & B.

Vol III. p.4.
May 1916

Army Form C. 2118.

WAR DIARY of 89 Company
of Machine Gun Corps.
INTELLIGENCE SUMMARY

(Erase heading not required.)

Instructions regarding War Diaries and Intelligence Summaries are contained in F. S. Regs., Part II. and the Staff Manual respectively. Title pages will be prepared in manuscript.

Place	Date	Hour	Summary of Events and Information	Remarks and references to Appendices
Z sector	12-5-16		Sectional relief carried out.	
			No 3 Section relieved No 4 Section in Z 2 Subsector	
			No 4 Section relieved No 3 Section in MARICOURT DEFENCES.	
			No 1 Section relieved No 2 Section in Z1 Subsector	
			No 2 Section to BRAY.	
			During the last hours of the night and the early hours of 13th inst. there was a fairly intense bombardment of MARICOURT and especially the valley behind and also the trenches of the 90th Brigade on our right where a hostile raid was attempted.	
			The gun at "French" emplacement (no 21.) fired at intervals into the german wire opposite all night.	App: A II JHR
"	13-5-16		The mine dug out in DONE'S REDOUBT was completed & work was begun on the mined emplacement (no 29) in the same work.	JHR
"	14-5-16		The two reserve guns in MARICOURT DEFENCES searched the german supply dump at CLAPHAM FARM with indirect fire. The position fired from was the sunken road which crosses the orchard in front of BREWERY REDOUBT and runs between LOWESTOFT STREET – NORTH PERONNE AVENUE – and CAMBRIDGE STREET. Angles of elevation and direction were worked out	

T/134. Wt. W708—776. 500000. 4/15. Sir J. C. & S.

Vol VII p.5

WAR DIARY of 89 Company
at
INTELLIGENCE SUMMARY

Machine Gun Corps.

Army Form C. 2118.

May 1916.

Place	Date	Hour	Summary of Events and Information	Remarks and references to Appendices
			from the 1/10,000 map. In the afternoon the positions of the cross heads were marked and the direction laid out by lines of sticks set by means of a prismatic compass.	
			The guns & tripods were brought up at 9.45 p.m. As the position was not in view of the Germans, siege lamps were used for setting & laying the gun. The Clinometer was used to obtain the angle of elevation.	J.H.R.
			The guns were fired at intervals until 12.30 a.m. A whole belt was fired at a time and after each the guns were relaid & reset. Each gun fired 1,000 rounds. A little traversing and searching was allowed for.	
Z Sector	17-5-16		A new open emplacement (no 31) was made in NORTH PERONNE AVENUE to sweep the ground behind the front line in the right of Z1 subsector.	App. II J.H.R.
	18-5-16		Sectional relief carried out.	
			No 2 Section relieved No 1 Section in Z1 Subsector	
			No 1 " " No 4 " " MARICOURT DEFENCES	
			No 4 " " No 3 " " Z2 Subsector	
			No 3 Section to BRAY	
			2 guns moved from billet in SCHOOL St MARICOURT (in reserve) – One to No.29 emplacement in DOFFES REDOUBT.	

Vol III p.6

Army Form C. 2118.

May 1916.

Instructions regarding War Diaries and Intelligence Summaries are contained in F. S. Regs., Part II. and the Staff Manual respectively. Title pages will be prepared in manuscript.

WAR DIARY of 89 Company Machine Gun Corps.

INTELLIGENCE SUMMARY

(Erase heading not required.)

Place	Date	Hour	Summary of Events and Information	Remarks and references to Appendices
2 Sector	19/5/16 20/5/16		The orders to no 32 emplacement in BREWERY KEEP. gun in no 30 emplacement (PERONNE ROAD Barrier) moved to no 31 emplacement in NORTH PERONNE AVENUE. A raid was arranged on Y wood. M.G. emplacements were therefore made in 21 Subsector for 12 guns to fire on the German parapet opposite (nos. 13,15,16,17,18,20,24,25 + 27 emplacements) The raid was abandoned later.	App. II JHR JHR JHR
	23/5/16		8 O.R. reinforcements arrived from CAMIERS.	JHR
	26-5-16		MACHINE GUN WOOD was bombarded. No 1 gun was knocked over but no damage done. A position (no. 8) was chosen in the front line for the gun in MERSEA STREET in consultation with O.C. 21 Coy M.G.C. 1 O.R. reinforcement from CAMIERS.	JHR JHR
	26-5-16	10 p.m.	Indirect fire was opened with 1 gun on the communication French between SUPPORT COPSE + MAUREPAS STA. Position fired from was the same as on the 14th inst. - 500 rounds fired	JHR
	27-6-16		From 1.30 to 2.45 a.m. indirect fire on SUPPORT COPSE by same gun - 1000 rounds fired.	JHR
		3.30 p.m.	1 O.R. wounded (Sgt at SAP gun no 12) Later to 5th C.C.S.	JHR
		12 midnight	89 Coy was relieved by 21 Coy	For orders re relief see JHR App. IV
	28-5-16	8 a.m.	89 Coy arrived in billets in ETINEHEM	--- no move --- App V
		10.30 p.m.	89 Coy arrived in billets in CORBIE	JHR
	29-6-16	1.30 p.m.	89 Coy arrived in billets in AILLY-SUR-SOMME 1 O.R. to 21 C.C.S.	JHR

J. H. Roxburgh Capt.
Comdg 89 Coy
M.G.C.

WAR DIARY.

Appendix 3, (Reference Appendix 2):—

VOL III.   89th Coy, Machine Gun Corps.   MAY 1916.

No 1:— Emplacement in parados, high up, and the alternative position for No 1 Gun (No 2 Emp).

No 2:— Position of No 1 Gun with field of fire as shown. Open emplacement in parapet in corner of bay of trench.

No 3:— Position of No 2 Gun, firing down our wire as shown. Open emplacement on edge of wood, hidden by trees.

No 4:— Open emplacement in parapet, alternative to and with same field of fire as No 3.

No 5:— Open emplacement in parapet with field of fire on enemy line opposite A.P.3. Not a defensive position.

No 6:— "Smugglers Den" – open emplacement behind parados firing as shown. Barrage line of fire fixed by an aiming mark. Position of No 3 Gun.

No 7:— "Haystacks" – emplacement in parapet. Field of fire similar to No 6. Registered on by German Artillery and often shelled.

No 8:— Emplacement only sited. A defensive position to put a Barrage across front of A.P.1. In parapet.

No 9:— Open emplacement in parapet; field of fire to front line. Alternative position to No 10.

No 10:— Open emplacement in parapet. Field of fire to front line. Position of No 4 Gun.

No 11:— Old open emplacement in parapet. Field of fire to Mersea Street. Support position to No 10.

No 12:— "Sap" – open emplacement in parapet firing across A.P1. Can also fire on German front line. Position of No 5 Gun.

No 13:— Open emplacement in parapet for firing on German front line in re-entrant opposite.

No 14:— Original alternative to No 12. Open emplacement in parapet. Subject to shelling.

No. 15:- Open emplacement in communication trench, originally a sap head.

No. 16:- Open emplacement in parapet of support line. To fire on German front and support line - can enfilade some of the communication trenches.

No. 17:- Covered emplacement in old French O.P. to fire on German line.

No. 18:- Open emplacement in side of communication trenches. Good field of fire on German line.

No. 19:- "Forest" - open emplacement behind parados. Field of fire along German front line, as shown, and giving barrage fire across front of No. 23. Deep dug-out near. Position of No. 6 Gun.

No. 20:- Alternative to No. 19; open emplacement in parapet of support line.

No. 21:- Alternative position to No. 23. Open emplacement in parapet, with field of fire along our wire, as shown, but slightly hampered by wire.

No. 22:- Old French emplacement (covered). Used to keep No. 7 Gun in by day for cleaning purposes &c.

No. 23:- Open emplacement in parapet, with very good field of fire, as shown. Position of No. 7 Gun.

No. 24:- Open emplacement in parapet of support line, firing on German front line.

No. 25:- Open emplacement in traverse of communication trench firing on German line. A possible 2nd alternative emplacement for No. 7 Gun.

No. 26:- Covered emplacement at side of sandbag dump. Enfilades German front line at "Y" wood, and can put barrage in front of wire of Brigade on right. Position of No. 8 Gun.

No. 27:- Open emplacement in the side of communication trench, can enfilade German front line at "Y" wood. Alternative to No. 26.

No. 28:- Covered emplacement in bank which forms parapet of fire trench, with very large field of fire, up to our front line and up to behind German support line. Could in an emergency give overhead fire on German front line. Position of No 9 Gun.

No 29:- A mined emplacement in the same bank with similar field of fire, made for muzzle-pivoting mounting. Position of No 10 Gun.

No 30:- Open emplacement in the PERONNE ROAD barrier, Covers road and ground to right. Given over to Lewis Gun.

No 31:- Open emplacement in traverse of communication trench, firing to either side of the trench, on ground to the left of PERONNE ROAD. Position of No 11 Gun.

No 32:- Covered emplacement at the junction of two trenches, made for muzzle-pivoting mounting, to watch ground to the right of the BREWERY REDOUBT. Position of No 12 Gun.

J H Roxburgh Capt
Comdg 89 Coy M.G.C.

APPENDIX No IV of WAR DIARY of 89 COY - MACHINE GUN CORPS.

Vol IV
May 1916

Copy No 1.

Operation Order No 5.
by Capt J.S. Roxburgh   26/5/16

Reference Maps 62 D N.E. 1/20000

1. The 21st Coy M.G.C. will relieve the 89th Coy M.G.C. in S' Sector on the evening of May 29th 1916.

2. Guides from each gun team will be at H.Q. at MARICOURT (Nispero Quarri?) by 8.9pm on 29/5/16

3. Trench Stores S.A.A. in boxes orange candles will be handed over, and receipts taken by the O.C. in charge of gun.

4. Maps — which will be handed over.

5. Gun teams on being relieved will move back independently to H.Q. MARICOURT, where guns & c will be picked up in the lorries.

6. O.C. 21st Coy M.G.C. will take over command from O.C. 89 Coy M.G.C. at 8pm on 29/5/16.

7. H.Q. [?] of 89 Coy will move to BRAY independently of the transport.

J.S. Roxburgh Capt
O.C. 89 Coy
May 26/1916

APPENDIX No V of WAR DIARY of 89 COY - MACHINE GUN CORPS

Vol III
May 1916

Operation Orders No 6

by Capt J H Roxburgh

Ref map Amiens Sheet 17 1/100000

1. 89 Coy will move into Billets in ETINEHEM on the evening of 27.5.16
   An advanced party. Lt. BROAD & Ptes Warren & Spriggs will move off independently at 5pm.

2. No 4 Sect & transport will parade at 5pm & march off

4. No 1, 2 & 3 Sect on being relieved will march to BRAY. Their packs will be carried back by the limbers of 21 Coy. M.G.C. Packs will be put on at BRAY & they will continue their march to ETINEHEM

5. 89 Coy will move into Billets in CORBIE on 28/5/16.

6. Coy will parade at 5.30pm & march off

7. An advanced party Lt BROAD C QMS Roberts Ptes Cartwright & Spriggs will move off independently at 5.30pm

8. 89 Coy will move into Billets in AILLY-SUR-SOMME on 29.5.16

9. Reveille 29.5.16 4.30am Breakfast 5am.

10. Coy will parade at 6am & march off

11. An advanced party Lt BROAD. C QMS Roberts L.Cpl. Burden Pte Gaye & Spriggs + GS Wagon will move off independently as early as possible. They will draw supplies at the cross roads VAUX ST SAUVEUR. ST VAST AMIENS. & then move on to AILLY.

12. The Coy will halt at 8am & fall out. There will be a meal at 12 noon & 3.30pm. Coy will parade at 4.30pm & march on.

Copy No 1 Retained
  "   2 Mr Acheson

J H Roxburgh Capt
Comdg 89 Coy MGC

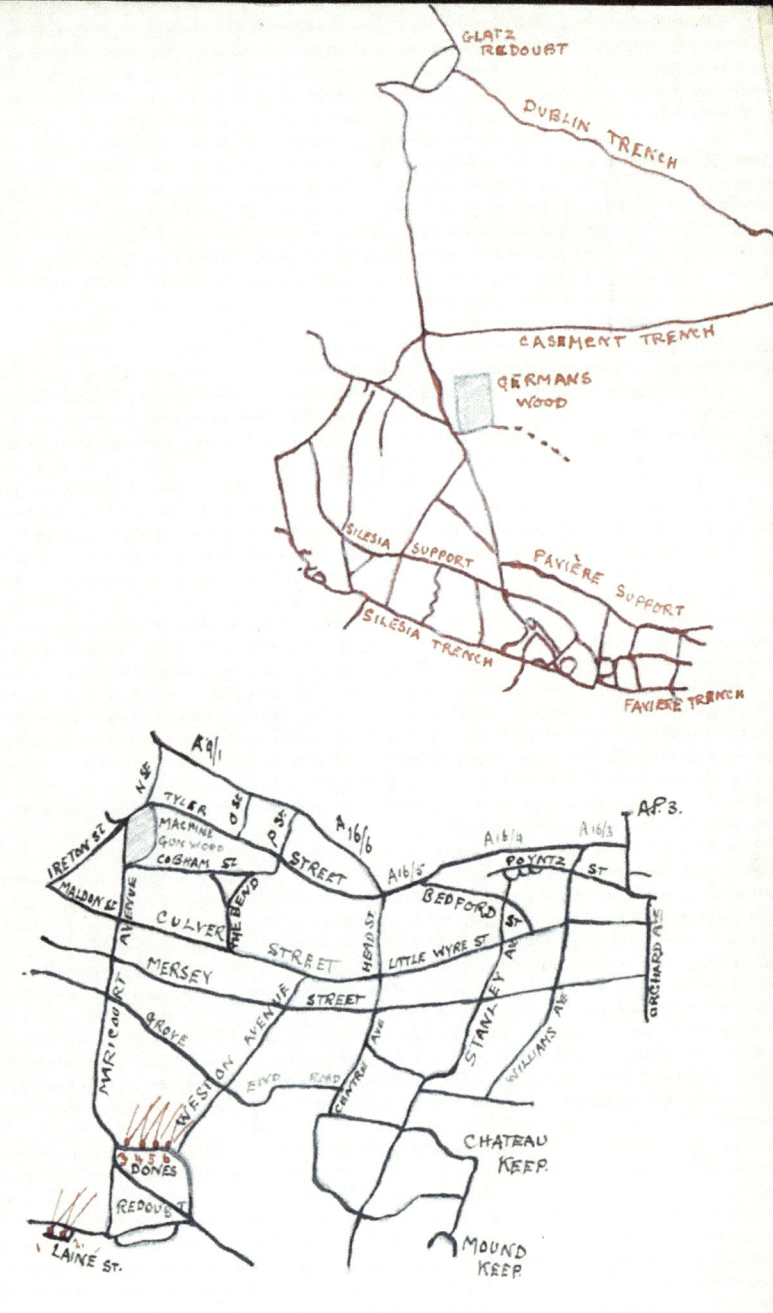

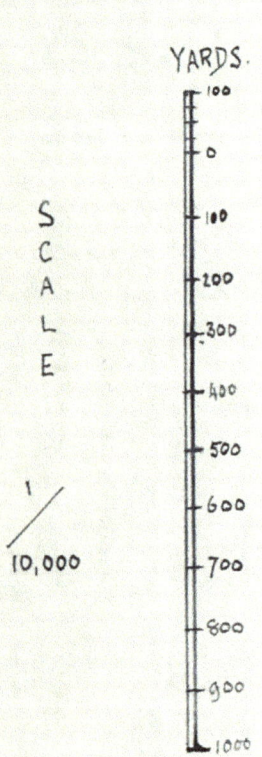

APPENDIX VI

Showing position & Field of Fire
of 6 guns to be used for
Overhead Fire.

1st Target .... SILESIA SUPPORT & FAVIERE SUPPORT
2nd   ———   .... GERMANS WOOD
3rd   ———   .... CASEMENT TRENCH
4th   ———   .... DUBLIN TRENCH

> 89th COMPANY,
> MACHINE GUN
> CORPS.
> No. V.G.a.87
> Date 1.7.16

From:- Officer Commanding
 89th Coy. Machine Gun Corps.

To:- Officer i/c
 A.G's. Office at the Base.

Forwarding the War Diary of this Unit, Volume IV and Appendix VI, for June 1916, for your information, please.

J H Roxburgh   Captain,
 Commanding
89 COY. MACHINE GUN CORPS.

June.
P.1. Vol IV
Vol 4
Army Form C. 2118.

WAR DIARY of 89 Company Machine Gun Corps

INTELLIGENCE SUMMARY

(Erase heading not required.)

Instructions regarding War Diaries and Intelligence Summaries are contained in F.S. Regs, Part II. and the Staff Manual respectively. Title pages will be prepared in manuscript.

June 1916

Reference Maps. Trench Map. MARICOURT 62cNW1 – ypres

Place	Date	Hour	Summary of Events and Information	Remarks and references to Appendices
AILLY-SUR-SOMME	31-5-16		2 OR to C.C.S. (1 wounded mentioned in p.s. Vol III – 1 sick) (1 OR reinforcement)	not notified till later. JHR
AILLY-SUR-SOMME	1-6-16		89 Coy M.G.C. in billets – 1 O.R. reinforcement	JHR
---	1-6-16		1 officer reinforcement	JHR
---	5-6-16	10.30am	Brigade training commented – attack on German trenches opposite Z 2. subsector	JHR
---	11-6-16		Brigade training ceased	JHR
CORBIE	12-6-16	6.30 pm	arrived in Billets	JHR
ETINEHEM	13-6-16	0 p.m.	arrived in No 2 Camp. 1 O.R. to C.C.S.	JHR
BRAY	16-6-16	5.50 pm	89 Coy M.G.C. had completed relief of 89 Coy M.G.C. in new Z Sector (from A.P.3 on right to TALUS BOISE light railway on left.)	
			Guns taken over	
			1 gun in Support in LEXDEN STREET at A.16.a.9.6 firing N.W.	
			1 gun in front line near BEDFORD STREET at A.16.a.48 firing N.W. to N.	
			1 gun in MACHINE GUN WOOD at A.15.b.60.85 firing E. to N.E.	
			1 gun in QUEEN VICTORIA STREET at A.9d 23 firing N.E.	
			1 gun in front line at A.9.a.6.4 firing E. (in next Brigade's sector)	JHR
			2 guns in support in N face of DONES REDOUBT at A.15d.4.4 + A.15d.5.9	JHR
	18-6-16		1 OR reinforcement.	
			2 OR to C.C.S.	

p.2. Vol IV
June 1916

Army Form C. 2118.

WAR DIARY of 89 Company
INTELLIGENCE SUMMARY. Machine Gun Corps

(Erase heading not required.)

Instructions regarding War Diaries and Intelligence Summaries are contained in F. S. Regs., Part II. and the Staff Manual respectively. Title pages will be prepared in manuscript.

Place	Date	Hour	Summary of Events and Information	Remarks and references to Appendices
MARICOURT	19-6-16		2 O.R. to C.C.S. gun in left Brigade's Sector at Aga 54 withdrawn. All Sections in line or at MARICOURT. Those not in the line engaged in preparing positions for overhead fire near DONES REDOUBT. Work chiefly done at night. JHR	See App VI
--	20-6-16		1 O.R. transferred as unsuitable to ETAPLES.	JHR
--	21-6-16		1 O.R. to C.C.S.	JHR
--	22-6-16		Gun teams relieved. No 3 Section put 4 guns in front line. No 1 Section — 2 guns in support in DONES REDOUBT. Remainder on working parties. 1 O.R. to C.C.S.	JHR
--	23-6-16		3 O.R. to C.C.S. 2 gun teams of No 1 Section to start 2 new emplacements in DONES REDOUBT.	
--	24-6-16		1 O.R. returned from C.C.S. – left gun in QUEEN VICTORIA STREET relieved by 21 Coy MGC 1st day of the Bombardment – "U" day	JHR
--	25-6-16	2ᵈᵒ	"V" day. 1 O.R. wounded.	JHR
--	26-6-16	3ᵈᵒ	"W" day 1 O.R. wounded	JHR
--	27-6-16	4ᵈᵒ	"X" day - everything ready. Reserve of gunners i.e. trained personnel from 89th Bde. kept at BRAY. These were used to	

p.3. Vol IV June 1916

Army Form C. 2118.

WAR DIARY of 89 Company
or
INTELLIGENCE SUMMARY. Machine Gun Corps.
(Erase heading not required.)

Instructions regarding War Diaries and Intelligence Summaries are contained in F. S. Regs., Part II. and the Staff Manual respectively. Title pages will be prepared in manuscript.

Place	Date	Hour	Summary of Events and Information	Remarks and references to Appendices
			Raising the personnel of the gun teams to full strength. Also to provide 3 men at each of the 3 dumps for belt filling. In addition to this carrying parties of 4 men per gun were given by the Battalions of the Bde. The Transport extra personnel, Quartermaster Sergt, Storeman, Cook & the remainder of the reserve personnel remained behind at BRAY under the Transport Officer and Company Sergeant Major. 1 O.R. 15. C.C.S. J.H.R.	
MARICOURT 28-6-16			1 O.R. wounded. Originally "Y" day — 5th day of the bombardment. All guns for overhead fire laid & readings for clinometer elevation taken. Auxiliary Aiming marks also put up. Zero arranged for 7.30 a.m. on 29th inst. but cancelled later. J.H.R.	
MARICOURT 29-6-16			6th day of the bombardment. 1 officer to Field Ambulance. 2 O.R. wounded. The weather during the last 3 days was very wet and trenches became very muddy but today was dry. J.H.R.	
	30-6-16		7th day of the Bombardment — 2nd "Y" day — Another fine day. All guns except 3 in front line & those in DONES REDOUBT (covered emplacements) were withdrawn to H.Q. NAPIERS REDOUBT & thoroughly cleaned. 1 O.R. wounded 29/6/16, rejoined.	see Appx VI
		9 pm 11.30 pm	Coy H.Q. moved to DONES REDOUBT. All guns in DONES REDOUBT in position, remainder had reported to their respective C. Os.	

Commdg. 89 COY. MACHINE GUN CORPS J.H.Roxburgh Capt.

From:- Officer Commanding
          89 Coy. Machine Gun Corps.

To:- Headquarters 89th Inf Bde.

Reference your BMA543 & DRO1722
War Diary of this Unit, Volume V for
July 1916, forwarded herewith please

J A Roxburgh Capt
Comdg 89 COY. MACHINE GUN CORPS.

4 AUG 1916

p.1. Vol V

30/July

Army Form C 2118.

WAR DIARY
or
of 89 Company
INTELLIGENCE SUMMARY. Machine Gun Corps

Vol 5

(Erase heading not required.)

Instructions regarding War Diaries and Intelligence Summaries are contained in F.S. Regs., Part II. and the Staff Manual respectively. Title pages will be prepared in manuscript.

Place	Date	Hour	Summary of Events and Information	Remarks and references to Appendices
MARICOURT	1/7/16		"Z" Day – Zero for the attack was fixed for 7.30 a.m. For Operation Orders See App	
		6.30 a.m	A fairly thick mist hung between the lines. Guns were laid by means of clinometers.	THR
		7.28 a.m	Guns in DONES REDOUBT opened overhead fire on German Support line on GERMANS WOOD.	THR
		7.30 a.m		THR
		7.30 a.m	Our front line advanced apparently without any casualties.	THR
		7.35 a.m	Guns in DONES REDOUBT opened overhead fire on CASEMENT TRENCH.	THR
		7.45 a.m	" " " " " " on DUBLIN TRENCH	THR
		8.25 a.m	ceased fire.	
			Meanwhile the enemy had not shelled our positions at all. 2 men were temporarily overcome by fumes from the gun in one of the covered emplacements + were later sent back. A muzzle cup was broken and one muzzle attachment for ball firing worked loose and was shot away	THR
		11.0 a.m	A messenger from Sgt SIDDLE, N.C.O. in charge of 2 guns attached 20th K.L.R. reported his 2 guns in position in Strong Point No 6. and without casualties.	THR
		1.30 p.m	A Sergt from R.E. Smoke Mortar company reported having seen	

p.2 Vol I 1916
July

Army Form C. 2118.

WAR DIARY
of 89 Company
INTELLIGENCE SUMMARY. Machine Gun Corps

(Erase heading not required.)

Place	Date	Hour	Summary of Events and Information	Remarks and references to Appendices
DONES REDOUBT	1/7/16	3.30 p.m.	One of Sergt. Siddle's guns in action in DUBLIN TRENCH just to the right of GLATZ REDOUBT. 1 O.R. from one of the two guns attached to 17th K.L.R. returned to DONES REDOUBT & reported the whole team with the exception of himself to be put out of action (6 O.R. killed 2 O.R. wounded), but that the gun was still in working order & left in charge of a Lewis Gun Sergeant 20th K.L.R. in DUBLIN TRENCH. Brigade Headquarters informed.	J&B / J&B
		6.0 p.m.	Under instructions from Brigade 6 men ordered to be sent from teams, attached to 19th K.L.R. in strong points in our original front line, to STRONG POINT 4. Reserves called up from BRAY.	J&B
		7.30 p.m.	O.C. Company went to Brigade H.Q., where he received instructions to move 2 guns to Strong Point No 1 & 2 guns to Strong Point No 2 from DONES REDOUBT. On his return a messenger reported that the other gun attached to the 17th K.L.R. was safe in DUBLIN TRENCH. 4 guns were sent to Strong Points as detailed above.	J&B
		11.0 p.m.	Position of guns. 2 in reserve in DONES REDOUBT – 4 in strong points in our original	

p3 Vol I
July 1916

WAR DIARY
of 84 Company
INTELLIGENCE SUMMARY. Machine Gun Corps
(Erase heading not required.)

Army Form C. 2118.

Place	Date	Hour	Summary of Events and Information	Remarks and references to Appendices
			front line - attached to 16th K.R.R.	
			2 in Strong Point No 1 att. 2nd Beds.	
			2 in Strong Point No 2	
			2 in Strong Point No 5	
			1 in Strong Point No 6	
			1 in Strong Point No 3 att. 17th K.R.R.	
			1 in Strong Point No 4 att. 17th K.R.R.	
			2 in BRIQUETERIE att. 20th K.R.R.	
DONES REDOUBT	2/7/16	1·0 a.m	15 reserve gunners reported to Coy HQ from BRAY	
		1·30 a.m	6 reserve gunners sent to replace 6 men detached from guns in our front line.	IHR
		8·45 a.m	Report received from Sergt Siddle re guns in BRIQUETERIE. 1 o.R. (Cpl in charge of gun) wounded. at other gun early in morning Ptes REGAN & BAAND were on duty by the gun, the remainder of the team being some distance away + making an alternative emplacement Meanwhile fire of six gunners managed to get down the communication trench running from BERNAFAY	IHR

WAR DIARY or INTELLIGENCE SUMMARY

Army Form C. 2118.

4 L Vol 5
July 1916

Place	Date	Hour	Summary of Events and Information	Remarks and references to Appendices
WOOD			MG our position & one of them threw a grenade & killed Pte BLAND before the gun could be mounted. Pte RIEGAN immediately attacked the party with a revolver & drove them out of the trench, finally dispersing them. It was also reported that the enemy made a counter-attack against the BRIQUETERIE but it was stopped by MG fire & artillery barrage which was very effective. Everyone at BRIQUETERIE reported very fine. JMR	
DONES REDOUBT	2-7-16	1.30 pm	The 4 gun teams of no 4 Section in Strong Points A, B, C & D in our original front line were sent up to relieve teams in BRIQUETERIE & DUBLIN TRENCH. Relief was completed without casualties & gun teams, especially those in BRIQUETERIE were thus enabled to be well dug in by fresh men. JMR	
		7.30 pm	20th Bn K.L.R. took over GLATZ REDOUBT Sector from 21st Inf Bde. 2 reserve guns of no 1 Section sent from DONES REDOUBT to HQ of 20th Bn KLR in Strong Point 2. Thence they moved into positions in NORD ALLEY, from which they could enfilade the ground in front of DUBLIN TRENCH. The 21st Bde MGC also left 4 guns in the Sector to assist in the defence. During the night there was some heavy shelling — casualties 4 killed 4 or 5 wounded. JMR	

p.5. Vol I July 1916

Army Form C. 2118.

WAR DIARY
of 89 Company
INTELLIGENCE SUMMARY. Machine Gun Corps

(Erase heading not required.)

Instructions regarding War Diaries and Intelligence Summaries are contained in F.S. Regs., Part II. and the Staff Manual respectively. Title pages will be prepared in manuscript.

Place	Date	Hour	Summary of Events and Information	Remarks and references to Appendices
DONES REDOUBT	3-7-16		Intermittent shelling during the day. The positions were consolidated. A certain amount of M.G. material (German) found in enemy's line. Most of this was sent up to the 20th Bn. K.R.R. who had a German Machine Gun in action at the BRIQUETERIE.	JHR
	4-7-16	8.0 am	Report received from guns in BRIQUETERIE. 1 Dr. killed, 1 Dr. wounded in early morning. Teams reported very exhausted.	JHR
		9.30 am	2 gun teams of No 2 Section sent from Strong Point 2 and relieved teams in the BRIQUETERIE without loss.	JHR
		4.0 p.m.	Arrangements made with O.C. 28 Company M.G.C. (S African Brigade) for relief. Gun positions to be taken over – 2 guns instead of one at Strong Point 3. 2 guns at BRIQUETERIE 2 guns to be placed at junction of DUBLIN TRENCH & GLATZ REDOUBT 2 guns in NORD ALLEY. Remainder to be in reserve.	JHR
		6.0 p.m.	Message received from O.C. No 5 Strong Point saying all gunners except one knocked out at gun in that Strong Point. Gun undamaged. Reserves sent up.	JHR
		6.30 p.m.	Guns not being taken over by 28 Coy were withdrawn to DONES REDOUBT.	JHR

P.6 Vol I July 1916

WAR DIARY
of 89 Company
INTELLIGENCE SUMMARY   Machine Gun Company

Army Form C. 2118.

Place	Date	Hour	Summary of Events and Information	Remarks and references to Appendices
BOIS DES RIQUIET	4-7-16	9:30 p.m.	S/Limbered wagons arrived to take back guns & stores.	JHR
	5-7-16	2:0 a.m.	@ 28 Coy arrived	JHR
		3:0 a.m.	Relief commenced. The 4 guns of 21 Coy were relieved independently.	JHR
		3:30 a.m.	Guns & teams already withdrawn, moved off to BOIS DES TAILLES.	JHR
		5:30 a.m.	Relief completed - Remainder of company follows.	
			CASUALTIES in BATTLE.	
			<table><tr><td></td><td>M.G. Coy</td><td>Reserve Gunners</td><td>Carriers</td></tr><tr><td>Killed</td><td>8 OR.</td><td>2 OR.</td><td>2 OR.</td></tr><tr><td>Wounded</td><td>4* OR.</td><td>2 OR.</td><td>8 OR.</td></tr></table>	
			* includes 1 OR wounded & removed at Bury	
BOIS DES TAILLES	5/7/16	11: a.m.	Company under canvas. (Tents & bivouacs) - 4 OR. reinforcements.	JHR
	6-7-16		Guns were cleaned & stores overhauled. 1 spare parts + 1 jamming handle for tripod, 1 muzzle attachment for ball firing & muzzle cups + 1 belt filling machine.	JHR
	7-7-16	3:30 p.m.	Limbers were packed ready for move at short notice.	JHR
BOIS DES TAILLES	8-7-16	9 p.m.	89 Coy left BOIS DES TAILLES	JHR
CEYLON WOOD	11:45 p.m.	Arrived & bivouacked in CEYLON WOOD. 2nd Lt. E.J.LAINÉ to 45 C.C.S.	JHR
	9-7-16	9:45 p.m	Left CEYLON WOOD. 2 guns attached to 17th K.L.R. later to Strong Point 1.	JHR

p.7 Vol V
July 1916

WAR DIARY
of 89 Company
INTELLIGENCE SUMMARY. Machine Gun Corps

Army Form C. 2118.

Place	Date	Hour	Summary of Events and Information	Remarks and references to Appendices
JONES REDOUBT	10-7-16	2.30am	Arrived at JONES REDOUBT. 2 guns attached to 19th K.L.R and sent to Strong Point 2.	JHR
		3.15am	Under orders from Brigade H.Q. 2 guns in Strong Point 1 & 2 guns in Strong Point 2 recalled.	JHR
		2.30pm	Warning order received of relief of 19th Inf Bde.	JHR
		9pm	2 guns No 4 Section attached to 20th K.L.R. Later to MALTZ HORN FARM Trench.	JHR
		10pm	2 guns No 2 Section moved off to DUBLIN TRENCH to be in reserve there.	JHR
			4 guns No 1 Section moved off to CASEMENT TRENCH	JHR
	11-7-16	4.50am	Report received from O.C. 4 guns in CASEMENT TRENCH that he has been moved by Bde H.Q. with 4 guns to the BRIQUETERIE.	JHR
		11.15am	2 guns No 2 Section + 2 guns No 4 Section sent to take place of above in CASEMENT TRENCH.	JHR
		7.30am	Report received from O.C. 2 guns attached 20th K.L.R. 1 gun in MALTZ HORN FARM TRENCH where it is cut by BRIQUETERIE - MALTZ HORN FARM road. The other on extreme left of MALTZ HORN FARM Trench. 20th KLR having bombed up the French, consolidated a strong point at S.E.	

Army Form C. 2118.

WAR DIARY
of
INTELLIGENCE SUMMARY. 89 Company
Machine Gun Corps
(Erase heading not required.)

P.S. Vol V
July 1916

Instructions regarding War Diaries and Intelligence Summaries are contained in F. S. Regs., Part II. and the Staff Manual respectively. Title pages will be prepared in manuscript.

Place	Date	Hour	Summary of Events and Information	Remarks and references to Appendices
DONES REDOUBT		11.30pm	corner of TRONES WOOD. A german maxim gun found there & used for firing into GUILLEMONT. Under orders from 89th Bde H.Q. 3 guns of No 3 Section sent up to the BRIQUETERIE. One gun now left in DONES REDOUBT.	JMB JMB
	12/7/16	1.30am	Disposition of guns.— 2 guns No A Section in Front Line in MALTZ HORN TRENCH 4 guns No 1 Section + 3 guns No 3 Section in support at BRIQUETERIE 2 guns No.2 Section in reserve at CASEMENT TRENCH 2 guns No.2 Section + 2 guns No.4 Section in reserve at DUBLIN TRENCH 1 gun No 3 Section in reserve at DONES REDOUBT.	JMB
		6.30am	Report received from Lt A.M.BROAD in charge of 2 guns in MALTZ HORN TRENCH that owing to a strong counterattack by the enemy on TRONES WOOD the 2nd Bn Bedfordshire Regt had been driven back & the 20th Bn.K.L.R. had been compelled to withdraw from the Strong Point at the S.E. Corner of TRONES WOOD The Vickers gun which had been moved into this point was withdrawn without loss but the german gun could not be got away and was therefore battery put out of action.	JMB
		9.10am	Report received from 20th Bn. K.L.R. that Lt A.M. BROAD had been killed by an enemy sniper.	JMB

T.2134. Wt. W708—776. 500000. 4/15. Sir J. C. & S.

Army Form C. 2118.

p.9. Vol V
July 1916

WAR DIARY
of 89 Company
INTELLIGENCE SUMMARY. Machine Gun Corps.
(Erase heading not required.)

Instructions regarding War Diaries and Intelligence Summaries are contained in F. S. Regs., Part II. and the Staff Manual respectively. Title pages will be prepared in manuscript.

Place	Date	Hour	Summary of Events and Information	Remarks and references to Appendices
DONET REDOUBT	12-7-16	11.00 am	10R reported wounded (later died of wounds) from CASEMENT TRENCH	
		5.30 pm	Arrangements made with O.C. 55th Coy M.G.C. for relief. Guns at BRIQUETERIE & MALTZ HORN TRENCH to be taken over.	
DONET REDOUBT	13-7-16	5.45 am	Relief completed. Gun teams marched back to BOIS DES TAILLES leaving 1 man per gun with gun & stores at DONET REDOUBT.	
		9.30 am	Transport for guns arrived & was loaded up. They were shelled on the PERONNE ROAD going back. 2nd Lt C.J. LANE wounded. 2nd Lt C.J. LANE rejoined from CCS.	
			Casualties 10R wounded.	
BOIS DES TAILLES	13-7-16	12 noon	89 Coy in Bivouacs at BOIS DES TAILLES	
BORGIE	14-7-16	3 pm	Arrived in Billets.	
	17-7-16		3 OR reinforcements from CAMIERS. 7149 a/Sgt Q. BUTT awarded MILITARY MEDAL	ALBERT (SOMEBRED SHEET) 1/40000
	19-7-16		12 OR reinforcements from CAMIERS - TB CCS 10R. From CCS 10R.	
HAPPY VALLEY		7.10 pm	Arrived in Bivouacs L36 29	
	20-7-16	12.15 pm	Arrived in Bivouacs at F15 a 18 - 1 Officer REINFORCEMENT.	
F15 a 18	21-7-16		Lt J. CAMPF. arrived at 17 Coy M.G.C. Coy under 1/2 hours notice to move.	
	26-7-16		Practice of attack on German 2nd line SE of GUILLEMONT. 10R to CCS	
F15 a 18	29-7-16	8.45 pm	89 Company moved up into line for attack on 2nd line, in 3 parties + at 3/4 hr intervals	

T2131. Wt. W708—776. 500000. 4/15. Sir J. C. & S.

F.10 Vol V
July 1916

WAR DIARY
or of 89 Company
INTELLIGENCE SUMMARY. Machine Gun Corps

Army Form C. 2118.

Place	Date	Hour	Summary of Events and Information	Remarks and references to Appendices
			Disposition of guns for attack.	
			2 guns No 2 Section attached to 19th K.L.R. (Left assaulting Battalion) under Lt ACHESON	
			2 guns No 2 Section attached to 20th K.L.R. (right assaulting Battalion) under 2nd Lt NICHOLS	
			2 guns No 3 Section attached to 17th K.L.R. (Supporting Battalion) under 2nd Lt LAINE	
			4 guns No 4 Section under 2nd Lt NAWTON to move into GERMAN MALTZ HORN TRENCH as soon as captured & hold the MALTZ HORN FARM ridge at all costs, & if possible give overhead fire & enfilade fire	MAUREPAS 1/20000
			2 guns No 3 Section under 2nd Lt LOCHHEAD to get forward as soon as possible to T 25 D. whence the advance of our troops could be assured by oblique fire on to @ GERMAN 2nd LINE.	
			4 guns No 1 Section to remain in reserve with company headquarters at SUNKEN ROAD (A 4 b 99.30)	
	30.7.16	12.30am	Teams heavily shelled on their way up to assembly position. Transport officer + 2 drivers wounded + 1 mule killed. The enemy used a fair number of gas shells.	
		4.30am	All gun teams were in position.	
		4.45am	Zero hour. Guns attached to Battalions moved forward with them	

P. 11. Vol I
July 1916

WAR DIARY
of 89 Company
INTELLIGENCE SUMMARY. Machine Gun Corps.

Place	Date	Hour	Summary of Events and Information	Remarks and references to Appendices
			There was a very thick mist which not only made it very difficult to keep direction but also made it very hard for gun teams to keep their men together. The 4 guns of no 4 Section after sending men forward to ascertain if the german MALTZ HORN TRENCH was secured were able to get into it at A 6 d. The 2 guns of No 2 Section under 2nd Lt LOCHHEAD also went with these as it was quite impossible for them to carry out their task. These 6 guns found that the german trench there was more of in the nature of a communication trench and a strong point of the enemy remained further down the trench, which ran down into the valley. As from this position they could not effectively hold the ridge, they moved further North into the german trench at A 6 b 29, where they got into position to meet a counter attack from the enemy who were reported massing to the East of GUILLEMONT. Of the guns attached to Battalions, it is very difficult to obtain an accurate account of their action owing to the mist, which prevented the g men from ascertaining their surroundings.	GUILLEMONT 1/20,000 Ordnance map

p.12 Vol V
July 1916

WAR DIARY
or 91 Bg Company
INTELLIGENCE SUMMARY. Machine Gun Corps

Army Form C. 2118.

Place	Date	Hour	Summary of Events and Information	Remarks and references to Appendices
	30-7-16		(a) 2 guns attached No 2 g Section attached 1st K.L.R. (Left assaulting Battalion) Left gun advanced but did not get into action. Finally it fell back with the infantry and got into position at 5.30 a 5.3 with field of fire towards ARROWHEAD COPSE. Right gun under Lt ACHESON advanced and came on a German Strong Point held by a machine gun. After some time they managed to get into action on the light mounting & fired two belts. The Strong Point fell on the arrival of supports from 17th K.L.R., but all the gun team except one man & 2 carriers were wounded. The gun was also put out of action by a bullet which went through the rear cover & penetrated the crank bearings. The remaining gunner managed to get back with gun & tripod to Company Headquarters later in the day. (b) 2 guns attached No 2 Section attached 2nd K.L.R. (right assaulting Battalion) These two guns started at zero under 2nd Lt NICHOLS. After advancing some distance they lost direction & got scattered. 2 guns & 6 gunners under 2nd Lt. NICHOLS finally got back to HAIRPIN BEND (A5d.76.96) whose they reported	GUILLEMONT 1/20,000

p.13. Vol V
July 1916

WAR DIARY
of 39 Company
INTELLIGENCE SUMMARY. Machine Gun Corps.
(Erase heading not required.)

To O.C. 20th K.L.R. & To Company Headquarters. They were reinforced from the Reserves and remained at the HAIRPIN BEND.

(b) 2 guns No 3 Section attacked 17th K.L.R (supporting Battalion) Left gun under 2nd Lt LAINE advanced with the infantry but suffered heavy casualties, 2nd Lt LAINE being killed very soon, 2 men finally reached the front line with gun & bipod but no ammunition. Here they were surprised by a large force of the enemy, which attacked them from very close range. The infantry, 16 in number, fell back, & the gunners were unable to get the gun away, it therefore must have fallen into the enemy's hands.

Right gun advanced some distance with a Lewis gun of the 17th K.L.R. but soon fell back and got into position at A 6 a 65 95. Later in the day the gun was hit & destroyed by shell fire.

During the night 30/31 July the 39th Bde was relieved by the 160th Bde and guns were moved out with the infantry. The guns at No A Section at A 6 t & the gun at S 30 a 53 were relieved by other Vickers guns

p.14 vol I July 1916

WAR DIARY

of 89 Company Machine Gun Corps

INTELLIGENCE SUMMARY

Army Form C. 2118.

Place	Date	Hour	Summary of Events and Information	Remarks and references to Appendices
	31.7.16		On relief the company moved back to its old bivouac at F.15a.18 Officers 1 killed 2 wounded. CASUALTIES	

	Killed	wounded	missing
	O.R.		
M.G. Coy	4	14	3
Reserves	-	-	-
Carriers	-	7	3
Total	4	22	7

	21
	2
	10

Grand Total 36

JHR

T.H.Roxburgh Capt
Comdg 89 M.G. Coy

89th Brigade.

30th Division.

89th MACHINE GUN COMPANY

AUGUST 1 9 1 6

> 89th COMPANY,
> MACHINE GUN
> CORPS.
>
> No. V.G.a.253
> Date. 3.9.16

Headquarters,
    89th Inf. Bde.

Vol. VI (August 1916) of the War Diary of this Unit is forwarded herewith, please.

            T.H. Roxburgh Capt

            Comdg 89 M.G. Coy

Army Form C. 2118.

WAR DIARY

of 89th Machine Gun Company Machine Gun Corps

Vol VI August 1916.

Instructions regarding War Diaries and Intelligence Summaries are contained in F.S. Regs., Part II. and the Staff Manual respectively. Title pages will be prepared in manuscript.

(Erase heading not required.)

REFERENCE MAPS —
FRANCE. Sheet 36cN.W. Trench map 1/20,000
MÉAULTE 62ᴰ N.E.2. 1/20,000
ABBEVILLE 11. 1/80,000
FRANCE 36ᴬ
BETHUNE Combined Sheet 1/40,000

Place	Date	Hour	Summary of Events and Information	Remarks and references to Appendices
F15a.18 MÉAULTE 1/10,000 62ᴅ NE 2	1-8-16		Company in bivouacs. Transport left for HUPPY (2 days march). 1 G.S limbered wagon was kept behind & followed with the cookers of Battalions later.	FRANCE Sheet 36c N.W. Trench map 1/20,000 JHR
	2-8-16		The company moved to HUPPY. Marched to MERICOURT, thence by rail to LONGPRÉ & so by road to HUPPY & followed 20 O.R. reinforcements.	ABBEVILLE 11. 1/80000 JHR
HUPPY	2-8-16	10.0pm	Arrived in billets. 20 O.R. reinforcements & 3 officer reinforcements. Transport rejoined.	JHR
	3-8-16	2.30pm	Moved to MERVILLE by trains from PONT REMY. 4.30 pm	JHR FRANCE Sheet 36ᴬ
Q 20 a	4-8-16	8.45am	Marched to & arrived in billets at BACQUEROLLES FARM near CALONNE.	BETHUNE Combined Sheet 1/40,000 JHR
	6-8-16	—	13 O.R. reinforcements	JHR
R 7 c	9-8-16	4.45pm	Arrived in billets in L'ÉPINETTE. 30th Division becomes divisional reserve.	JHR
	10-8-16		Arrangements in case of attack as follows :- (a) to reinforce right flank. Company moves to VIELLE CHAPELLE R34a2/6 central (b) " " left flank. Coy moves to LES 8 MAISONS R29b central (c) to hold Corps line - guns take up positions as follows:- 3 guns in post of L'ÉPINETTE. 1 gun " " " PARADIS N. - Q18a 1/9. 1 gun " " " PARADIS S. - Q30b 6/8. 1 gun " " " ZELOBES - R.27 e 0/5. 1 gun " " " MESPLAUX N. - X & b 9/2.	JHR

Army Form C. 2118.

WAR DIARY
of 8th Machine Gun Company
INTELLIGENCE SUMMARY
Machine Gun Corps

Vol VI August 1916

Instructions regarding War Diaries and Intelligence P2.
Summaries are contained in F.S. Regs., Part II.
and the Staff Manual respectively. Title pages
will be prepared in manuscript.

(Erase heading not required.)

Place	Date	Hour	Summary of Events and Information	Remarks and references to Appendices
R7c	11-8-16		5 O.R. reinforcements – 9 O.R. returned to M.G.C. Base Depot	JHR
"	12-8-16		3 Vickers guns required to complete arrived from D.A.D.O.S.	JHR
"	13-8-16		1 officer + 1 O.R. reinforcement	JHR
"	17-8-16		2nd Lieut. F.H. POOLEY wounded while attached to 21 M.G. Coy for instruction	JHR
"	- -	7 p.m.	1 O.R. reinforcement	JHR
LE VERTANNOY	18-8-16	11.30 a.m.	Arrived in Billets at W 15 a.	JHR
- -	20-8-16	5 p.m.	1 officer reinforcement	JHR
- -	23-8-16	-	2 O.R. reinforcements (1 Signaller – 1 Artificer)	JHR
- -	24-8-16	4 p.m.	1 officer reinforcement	JHR
GORRE	26-8-16	6 p.m.	Arrived in billets at FAC44 to relieve 21st M.G. Company in GIVENCHY Sector. Advanced party consisting of 2nd Lt. F. GILLIES & the Nos. 1 arrived 12 noon & went into the line to their respective gun positions in order to become acquainted with them before dark. Relieving Sections (No 1 + 2) each comprising 5 gun teams, (reinforced from Reserves) arrived 4 p.m. Relief of 21st M.G. Company commenced at 9 p.m. guides met at PONT FIXE.	JHR
	26-8-16	12.20 a.m.	Relief completed.	JHR

WAR DIARY of 89 Machine Gun Company, Machine Gun Corps.

INTELLIGENCE SUMMARY

Vol. VI August 1916 - p.3

Army Form C. 2118.

Place	Date	Hour	Summary of Events and Information	Remarks and references to Appendices
GORRE.	27-8-16	—	Positions of Guns in GIVENCHY Sector.	Sheet 36 a N.W. 1/20,000

FRONT LINE 1 gun in "Death or Glory" Sap. Weak covered emplacement, firing North along own wire to Salient at 53. A.16.c.04.68.

KEEP LINE holding the ridge on which GIVENCHY Village stands.

1 gun in Orchard Keep S.E. corner A.15.a.90.35. firing across front of SPOILBANK towards BRICKSTACKS. open emplacement.

2 guns in MAIRIE REDOUBT A.9.b.11 (1.) firing S.E. down front of Orchard both open emplacements. (2.) — E.N.E. towards RED DRAGON CRATER

1 gun in GIVENCHY KEEP A.9.c.65 - 3 covered emplacements with small field of fire in all directions.

2 guns in MOAT FARM A.9.c.27 with field of fire N.N.E. to GROUSE BUTTS. 2 covered emplacements + 2 open emplacements (latter used if NEW CUT is manned)

VILLAGE LINE 1 gun in PONT FIXE S. A.14.d.37 - 2 covered concrete emplacements. Field of Fire S.E. from HERTFORD St. to 7th St.

1 gun near WINDY CORNER A.14.a.99.80. - 2 covered concrete emplacements. firing S.E. & also N + N.E.

Army Form C. 2118.

WAR DIARY
or
INTELLIGENCE SUMMARY

of 89 Machine Gun Company

Machine Gun Company.

(Erase heading not required.)

Vol VI August 1916 p.4

Instructions regarding War Diaries and Intelligence
Summaries are contained in F. S. Regs., Part II.
and the Staff Manual respectively. Title pages
will be prepared in manuscript.

Place	Date	Hour	Summary of Events and Information	Remarks and references to Appendices
GORRE	28-8-16		1 gun at LE PLANTIN - A 8 central - strong covered emplacement firing S.E. past HERTS REDOUBT (A8d74) to WOLFE Rd & then onward E. of rising ground to DISTILLERY & Canal Bank.	JHR
--	28-8-16		6 guns in reserve at Coy H.Q. F.4.C.44. Activity normal - M.M.G. did indirect fire nightly from ORCHARD FARM from A15 a 55. R.E. began strengthening emplacement in "Death or Glory" Sap. From 7.30 pm to 7.50 pm the enemy shelled near MOAT FARM heavily. Several shells hit the Keep, the M.G. officers dug out (uncompleted) was hit. 2ND LT. F. GILLIES killed - 2ND LT. A. ROBINSON wounded. Otherwise the night was quiet. Emplacements undamaged.	JHR JHR JHR
--	29-8-16		Quiet day. Work on emplacements & dug outs continued.	JHR
--	30-8-16		Sectional relief carried out. No 3 Section relieved No 1 in KEEP Line. No 4 Section relieved No 2 in Village line, Orchard Keep, & "Death or Glory" Sap.	JHR
--	31-8-16		A very quiet day.	JHR

SECRET

Vol 7

WAR DIARY.
of 89 MACHINE GUN COY.
FOR THE MONTH
of SEPTEMBER 1916
VOLUME VII

> 89th COMPANY,
> MACHINE GUN
> CORPS.
>
> No. Y.G.a.307
> Date. 1-10-16

Headquarters,
    89th Inf. Bde.

Vol VII (September 1916) of the War Diary of this Unit is forwarded herewith, please

J.H. Roxburgh Capt.

Comdg 89 M.G. Company

WAR DIARY
INTELLIGENCE SUMMARY

Vol. VII — SEPTEMBER 1916. of 89 MACHINE GUN COMPANY, MACHINE GUN CORPS. p 1.

Army Form C. 2118.

Place	Date	Hour	Summary of Events and Information	Remarks and references to Appendices
GORRE			REFERENCE MAPS. BETHUNE Combined Sheet 1/40,000. Sheet 36c NW Trench map 1/20,000. Sheet 36 SW Trench map 1/20,000. LENS Sheet 11. 1/100,000	
	1-9-16		89 M.G Company in the line in the GIVENCHY Sector. A quiet day. Our artillery active during afternoon. Night exceptionally quiet except for snipers.	IHR
	2-9-16		Normal day. Enemy artillery active during the night at intervals. Machine Gun played on hostile at intervals at night.	IHR
	3-9-16		Quiet day; much as last.	IHR
	4-9-16		Normal day. Heavy enemy bombardment on point about 100 yards N of A.9.c.2.7. between Sheet 36 c NW & occ 6.30 & 6.50 p.m. Very quiet night.	IHR
	5-9-16		Quiet day. Our artillery fairly active especially firing across canal to S.	IHR
	6-9-16		Enemy's artillery shelled Le PLANTIN + all keeps with 5.9s for half an hour. Trench mortars of both sides busy all day near craters. During the afternoon an emplacement was made in the front line at A.15.c.9.5. in order to fire on the enemy's wire between A.16.a.3.7. and A.16.a.5.6. This wire was cut by our artillery during the day. Our patrols were out until 2 a.m. 7th inst & reported a large working party. On return of patrol our gun fired 1250 rounds while the enemy were from 2 to 5 a.m. A few rifle grenades in retaliation.	IHR
	7-9-16		89 M.G. Company were relieved by 21 M.G Company, who took over our emplacements etc.	

Army Form C. 2118.

WAR DIARY
of 89 Machine Gun Company
Vol. VII
~~INTELLIGENCE SUMMARY.~~ Machine Gun Corps.
September 1916
p 2.
(Erase heading not required.)

Instructions regarding War Diaries and Intelligence Summaries are contained in F. S. Regs., Part II. and the Staff Manual respectively. Title pages will be prepared in manuscript.

Place	Date	Hour	Summary of Events and Information	Remarks and references to Appendices
~~Aug~~ X 30 6 9.	7-9-16.		89 HG Company having been relieved & having left GORRE, arrived in billets at ESSARS.	IAR
W 22.d.2.3.	13-9-16	11.30 am	89 M.G. Company left ESSARS & marched to LOISNE & from there relieved 90 M.G. Company in FESTUBERT Sector. Guns in position as follows :—	
			SUPPORT LINE. 1 gun at R1 at A3c14 firing S.E.	
			1 gun at R1a at A2d72.36 firing N. to BARNTON Rd.	Sheet 36 SW Trench map 1/20,000
			1 gun at R2 at A2b 51 firing S.E.	
			1 gun at R3 at S26 d 63 firing N.E. to PIONEER Rd.	
			1 gun at R5 at S26 d 70.95 firing N.E.	
			1 gun at R6 at S26 c 75.80 firing S.E.	
			1 gun at R7 at S26 b 8.6. by day & moving to S27 b.36. by night to fire S.	
			1 gun at R10 at S20 d 9.7 firing S.E.	
			1 gun at R11 at S21 c.00 95 firing N.E.	
			VILLAGE LINE 1 gun at VL 8 at A 2C 49 firing N. 1 gun at VL14 at S25 b 95 90 firing N.E.	
			1 gun at VL 13 at S26a 16 firing S.E. 1 gun at VL 15 at S19 b 71 firing S.E.	IAR
			Remainder with Coy Headquarters at LOISNE	

Army Form C. 2118.

WAR DIARY
of 89 Machine Gun Company.

Vol VII

~~INTELLIGENCE SUMMARY.~~ MACHINE GUN CORPS.

SEPTEMBER 1916 p. 3.

(Erase heading not required.)

Place	Date	Hour	Summary of Events and Information	Remarks and references to Appendices
W 22 d 23	14-9-16	5 pm	90 M.G. Company relieved 89 M.G. Company in FESTUBERT Sector. The latter left LOISNE & marched to their former billets in ESSARS.	
ESSARS.	15-9-16		LIEUT. H.C. ATKIN-BERRY to Headquarters XI'S Corps for duty.	JMR
	16-9-16	4.30 pm	89 M.G. Company left ESSARS.	JMR
LA MIQUELLERIE		9 pm	Arrived in billets in LA MIQUELLERIE just N.W. of BUSNES	BETHUNE Combined Sheet
	Mag 2/2		2nd LT. F.C. NAWTON (to 45 MG Coy) & 22nd Lt. A.D. NICHOLS (Sick) struck off strength	JMR
	18-9-16	10 am	89 MG Company marched from LA MIQUELLERIE to FILLERS. Entrained at FILLERS & thence to DOULLENS.	JMR
BRETEL		9 pm	Arrived in billets in BRETEL	JMR LENS Sheet 11
	21-9-16	7.15 am	Left BRETEL & joined 89th B.de Column at GEZAINCOURT.	JMR 1/100,000.
VIGNACOURT		1 p.m.	Arrived in billets in VIGNACOURT.	JMR
	23-9-16	11.30 pm	2ND LIEUT. D.D. RICHARDS reported for duty.	JMR
	28-9-16		1 OR killed - 2 OR wounded as a result of MG accident	JMR

B A Roxburgh Capt.
Comdg 89 M.G. Coy.

T.2134. Wt. W708—776. 500000. 4/15. Sir J. C. & S.

vol 8

War Diary

of the 89th Machine Gun Company

for the month of October 1916

Volume VIII

SECRET

Army Form C. 2118.

WAR DIARY
of 89 Machine Gun Company Machine Gun Corps.
INTELLIGENCE SUMMARY
(Erase heading not required.)

Instructions regarding War Diaries and Intelligence Summaries are contained in F. S. Regs., Part II. and the Staff Manual respectively. Title pages will be prepared in manuscript.

Vol VIII — October 1916. p.1.

Place	Date	Hour	Summary of Events and Information	Remarks and references to Appendices
			REFERENCE MAPS. LENS - Sheet 11 - 1/100,000. ALBERT. Combined Sheet - 1/40,000. Sheet 62d N.E. - 1/20,000 Sheet 57c S.W. 1/20,000	Trench Map. RANSART 1/10,000 FONQUEVILLERS 1/10,000
VIGNACOURT.	1-10-16	—	89 M.G. Coy in billets in VIGNACOURT.	J.H.R. LENS Sheet 11 - 1/100,000
"	4-10-16	11 a.m.	Moved by motor busses to MERICOURT l'ABBÉ, thence marched to billets in DERNANCOURT.	ALBERT Combined Sheet
DERNANCOURT	5-10-16		The line N.W. of FLERS reconnoitred.	J.H.R.
	8-10-16	8.20 p.m	3 O.R. reinforcements.	J.H.R.
	10-10-16	8 a.m.	Marched to S 21 b. — Here a mid-day halt was made.	
S 21 b.		6.30 p.m	Marched to Thistle Dump (S.16.a.2.9.) & thence to M 36 b. 5.6. relieved 123 M.G. Coy in the line.	
M 36 b. 5.6.			Dispositions. Front & Support Lines.—	Sheet 57c S.W. 1/20,000
			Left Subsector — No 1 Section...guns at M 17 d 8.0.	
			M 24 a 1.6.	
			M 24 a 3.2.	
			M 24 a 1.5.	
			Right Subsector — No 2 Section...guns at M 24 b 4.5.	
			M 24 b 5.5.	
			M 24 b 8.1.	
			N 19 a 1.5.	

WAR DIARY
of B9 Machine Gun Company.
INTELLIGENCE SUMMARY Machine Gun Corps.

Vol VIII - October - 1916. Title pages p. 2.

Army Form C. 2118.

Place	Date	Hour	Summary of Events and Information	Remarks and references to Appendices
M36 b 5.4	10-10-16		Support - No 3 Section - 2 guns in FACTORY TRENCH at M24 d 7.1 M24 d 0.6.	Sheet 57 c S.W. 1/20,000
			6 guns in reserve at Company H.Q at M36 b 5.6. JHR	
		10 p m	1 gun sent to right subsector to M24 b 3.3. JHR	
	11-10-16	8.30 a.m	Company H.Q. moved to FLERS SUPPORT at M36 a 5.9. JHR	
			Brigade front reduced to M17 d 8.0 to M24 b 4.7. 1.O.R. killed. 1.O.R wounded (later returned to duty) JHR	
			New dispositions. Left subsector as before.	
M36 a 5.9			Right subsector - guns at M24 b 3.3.	
			M 24 b 4.5.	
			M 24 b 5.5.	
			1 gun in support at right Battalion H.Q.	
			Support guns withdrawn to Company H.Q. (M36 a 5.9)	
			Arrangements made for attack on German line on 12-10-16.	
			2 guns No A Section sent to O.C. 2nd of K.L.R. (Support Battalion). JHR	
	12-10-16	7. a. m	Dispositions for attack as follows :- 2 guns No 1 Section attached to 17th K.L.R. (left assaulting Bn).	
			2 guns No 2 Section attached to 2nd Beds. (right assaulting Bn)	
			2 guns No 4 Section attached to 20th K.L.R. (supporting Bn)	

Army Form C. 2118.

WAR DIARY
of 89 Machine Gun Company.
INTELLIGENCE SUMMARY. Machine Gun Corps.

Vol. VIII — October 1916. p. 3

Instructions regarding War Diaries and Intelligence Summaries are contained in F.S. Regs., Part II. and the Staff Manual respectively. Title pages will be prepared in manuscript.

(Erase heading not required.)

Place	Date	Hour	Summary of Events and Information	Remarks and references to Appendices
M 36 a 5.9	12-10-16		2 guns No 1 Section & 2 guns No 2 Section in position at M.17.d.8.0.	Sheet 57c S.W. 1/20,000
			M 24 a 1.6.	
			M 24 b 3.3.	
			M 24 b 4.5.	
			to remain in the front line & hold it at all costs.	
			Remainder in reserve at Company H.Q.	
			1. O.R. wounded - shell shock.	
		2:5 p.m.	Zero hour - guns holding the front line were heavily shelled - Casualties 3 O.R. Other guns could not in most cases get forward for 1 gun with the right Battalion got into action from a shell hole & fired 2 belts. Finally the 4 guns attached to 17th K.L.R. & 2nd Beds. got into position in our old front line. Casualties 2nd Lt W.V. WHEATLEY wounded 2nd Lt E.D. MITCHELL injured - 2 O.R. wounded & 1 O.R. missing. J.H.R.	
		4:30 p.m.	1 gun from 24 b 3.3 fout temporarily out of action by shrapnel & withdrawn for repair. J.H.R.	
		5:30 p.m.	1 gun sent to 17th K.L.R. } and into positions in front line.	
			1 gun sent to 2nd Beds. } J.H.R.	

Army Form C. 2118.

WAR DIARY
of 89 Machine Gun Company. Machine Gun Corps.
INTELLIGENCE SUMMARY

Vol. VIII – OCTOBER. 1916. P. 4.

(Erase heading not required.)

Instructions regarding War Diaries and Intelligence Summaries are contained in F.S. Regs., Part II. and the Staff Manual respectively. Title pages will be prepared in manuscript.

Place	Date	Hour	Summary of Events and Information	Remarks and references to Appendices
M36a5.9.	12-10-16	7.30 p.m.	2 guns No 3 Section sent to 17th K.L.R. & put into positions on the left flank in the front line. They arrived at 9.35 p.m. J.H.R.	Sheet 57cS.W. 1/20,000
		8 p.m.	Gun at M17 d 8.0. buried & temporarily out of action. Withdrawn for repair. J.H.R.	
	13-10-16		Guns back approximately in their old positions. J.H.R.	
		12 NOON	Arrangements made for relief by 21. M.G. Coy. J.H.R.	
		1 p.m.	2 guns attached to 20th K.L.R. Withdrawn to Coy. H.Q. J.H.R.	
		5 p.m.	Relief by 21 M.G. Coy commenced. On relief 89 M.G. Coy moved to BROWN TRENCH M36c2.5. J.H.R.	
			1 O.R. wounded – gassed. J.H.R.	
M36 c 2.5.	14-10-16		89 M.G. Coy in reserve in BROWN TRENCH. 1 O.R. shell shock. J.H.R.	
		2 p.m.	89 M.G. Coy moved to S21b – Still in reserve. Guns were brought back at night by pack mules J.H.R	
S21 b	15-10-16		In reserve at S 21 b. J.H.R.	
	16-10-16		89 M.G. Coy relieved 90 M.G Coy in right sector of Divisional line (N19a 5.9 to N19 b 4.7). J.H.R.	
		3 p.m.	Relief commenced from BROWN TRENCH. J.H.R.	
M30 d 8.5		8.30 p.m	Relief completed. 9 O.R. reinforcements. J.H.R.	
			Dispositions. 4 guns No 4 Section in front line – 3 on left of Bde front a.1 at N19a 9.8 – N19c 2.3	
			4 guns No 3 Section in support in FACTORY TRENCH at M24d 65.20, M24d80.15, N19c.13, N19c 2.3	

Army Form C. 2118.

WAR DIARY
of 89 MACHINE GUN COMPANY INTELLIGENCE SUMMARY. MACHINE GUN CORPS.

Vol VIII - October. 1916.
Title pages p. 5.

(Erase heading not required.)

Instructions regarding War Diaries and Intelligence Summaries are contained in F. S. Regs., Part II. and the Staff Manual respectively. Title pages will be prepared in manuscript.

Place	Date	Hour	Summary of Events and Information	Remarks and references to Appendices
M 30 d 8.5	16-10-16		Remainder in reserve with Company H.Q. at GROVE ALLEY - M 30 d 8.5. J.H.R.	Sheet 57 c. S.W. 1/20,000.
"	17-10-16		Dispositions in front line rearranged as follows:-	
			guns at N 19 a 9.7., N 19 b 17, N 19 b 2.7, N 19 b 3.7.	
			Advanced H.Q. at M 30 a 6.8	
			Arrangements made for covering the attack of 21st Bde on our left on 18-10-16. J.H.R.	
"	18-10-16		2nd LT F. WINTERINGHAM + 2nd LT H.G. FAULKNER reported for duty J.H.R.	
		3.40 a.m.	Zero hour for attack by 21st Inf. Bde. J.H.R.	
			Action by own machine guns:-	
			No 1 gun (N 19 a 9.7) fired on BAYONET TRENCH (N 18 c 5.2 to N 13 d 7.3)	
			No 2 gun (N 19 b 17) fired onto + around LUISENHOF FARM.	
			No 3 gun (N 19 b 27) fired into LE BARQUE.	
			No 4 gun (N 19 b 37) fired on BAYONET TRENCH + later into LE BARQUE. J.H.R.	
		8 a.m.	Message received that No 3 gun team (except for 1 man) i.e. 5 O.R. blown up. This was reported to Bde H.Q. J.H.R.	
		10.15 a.m.	1 gun + team sent from FACTORY TRENCH to front line to replace. These were unable to get up by PIONEER LANE owing to enemy artillery fire. Several attempts were made and at 3.15 pm	

Army Form C. 2118.

WAR DIARY

Vol VIII - October 1916 p. 6

of 89 Machine Gun Company.
Machine Gun Corps.

INTELLIGENCE SUMMARY (crossed out)

(Erase heading not required.)

Place	Date	Hour	Summary of Events and Information	Remarks and references to Appendices
M30 d.8.5.	18-10-16		They succeeded via AEROPLANE TRENCH. 1 gun from the reserve was sent up to FACTORY TRENCH to replace. New gun for front line got into position at N19 a.6.8. JHR	Sheet 57c SW 1/20,000
		10 p.m	4 guns from reserve sent up to report to O.C. 19th K.L.R. 2 put into position in front line at N19 a 30.85 + N19 a.o.8, in near extension of the Brigade front, 2 returned to Coy H.Q. JHR	
	19-10-16		A very wet day. Considerable artillery activity.	
		6.30 p.m	Gun team at N19 b.17 knocked out. Casualties 3 O.R. killed - 2 O.R. wounded. 19th K.L.R. relieved in front line by 20th K.L.R. during night.	JHR
	20-10-16		2 guns No 2 Section in extension of Bde front relieved by 21st Bde. just after midnight. 3 guns No 1 Section relieved 3 guns No 4 Section in front line. The 1 gun of No 3 Section remained in. JHR	
	21-10-16		2nd Lt. F. WINTERINGHAM wounded - shell shock. During the evening 3 O.R. wounded. JHR	
	22-10-16		Normal day. JHR	
		3 p.m.	Relief of 89 M.G. Coy by 8th Australian M.G. Coy. Guns in reserve were relieved first, then guns in FACTORY TRENCH, lastly guns in front line. Owing to weather conditions, tripods + belt boxes were handed over. On relief Sections marched back to MAMETZ WOOD CAMP. Sig. C. JHR	

Army Form C. 2118.

WAR DIARY
of 89 Machine Gun Company
Machine Gun Corps.

Vol. VIII — OCTOBER. 1916. p.7

INTELLIGENCE SUMMARY

(Erase heading not required.)

Instructions regarding War Diaries and Intelligence Summaries are contained in F.S. Regs., Part II. and the Staff Manual respectively. Title pages will be prepared in manuscript.

Place	Date	Hour	Summary of Events and Information	Remarks and references to Appendices
S 19 c	23-10-16		In bivouacs in MAMETZ WOOD CAMP. JHR	
	24-10-16	8:30 a.m.	5 O.R. reinforcements. JHR	ALBERT Combined Sheet 1/40,000
BUIRE	25-10-16	6 a.m.	89 M.G. Coy marched to billets to BUIRE. JHR	LENS 11.1/100,000
	26-10-16	10.55 a.m.	Transport left BUIRE for 2 days journey by road to HALLOY area. JHR	
BUIRE	27-10-16	2 a.m.	89 M.G. Coy left BUIRE. Marched to DERNANCOURT — entrained & was moved to DOULLENS. JHR	
			Arrived in billets in CAUMESNIL.	
CAUMESNIL	28-10-16	1:15 pm	Left billets in CAUMESNIL & marched to POMMIERS. Reconnoitred sector of the line. JHR	
POMMIERS	29-10-16	2 pm	No 1 & 3 Sections marched to BIENVILLERS & BERLES respectively & relieved guns of 138 M.G. Coy in Front & Support line. JHR	Trench Map RANSART 1/10,000
		3 pm	No 2 Section marched to BIENVILLERS & relieved guns in the Divisional Line. JHR	
		6 pm	Relief completed. JHR	
			Dispositions:-	
			Left Subsector. No 3 Section. 1 gun at W.23 c 6.4. firing S.W. to enemy wire & covering our salient at W.29 a.	
			1 gun at W.29 a 5.6. firing E & to QUARRY in W.23 d.	
			1 gun at W.29 a 05.35. firing E & to QUARRY in W.23 d., down valley	
			1 gun at W.28 b 8.1. firing S.E. to our front line. JHR	

Army Form C. 2118.

WAR DIARY
of 89 Machine Gun Company
INTELLIGENCE SUMMARY   Machine Gun Corps

Vol VIII - OCTOBER - 1916. p. 8.

(Erase heading not required.)

Instructions regarding War Diaries and Intelligence Summaries are contained in F. S. Regs., Part II. and the Staff Manual respectively. Title pages will be prepared in manuscript.

Place	Date	Hour	Summary of Events and Information	Remarks and references to Appendices
POMMIER	29.10.16		Right Subsector :- No 1 Section.	Trench maps RANSART & FONQUEVILLERS. 1/10,000
			1 gun at E4b 45.55 firing E.S.E. on German wire & covering our diversed Salient at E 5 c.	
			1 gun at E4d 7.5. firing N.N.E. & enfilading German front line to W 2 g c central.	
			1 gun at E4c 45.25 firing behind our support line.	
			1 gun at F10b 4.6 firing similarly - gun kept at F10b 6.0. & used for indirect fire.	
			Divisional Line :- No 2 Section.	
			1 gun at W 27 a 6.9 firing E. across valley	
			1 gun at W 27 a 6.7 firing N.E.	
			1 gun at E 3 a 05.70 firing N.E. down valley to RAVINE.	
			1 gun at E 2 c 8.3. £ (STONEYGATE S.) firing S.S.E across HANNESCAMPS road.	
			During night 2,000 rounds fired indirect from E 10 b 9.5. on MONCHY-RANSART Rd. - ESSARTS Rd.	
				Enemy Bracks (F 7 b 56 & F 7 b 87) J.H.R
	30.10.16		Quiet day - Coy H.Q. & reserve section moved to BERLES. at W15 c 7.9.	
			During night 1,000 rounds fired indirect from ALSACE VILLA E 3 a 05.70. on MONCHY Rd - W30 A 6.1. J.H.R	

Army Form C. 2118.

WAR DIARY
of 89 Machine Gun Company
INTELLIGENCE SUMMARY

Vol VIII - October 1916

Machine Gun Corps.

p. 9.

(Erase heading not required.)

Place	Date	Hour	Summary of Events and Information	Remarks and references to Appendices
BERLES-AU-BOIS	31·10·16		Guns at E.4.6.4.5.55 & E.4.d.7.5. registered on their barrage lines of fire. Latter covers edge of salient at E.5.e.5.7. Observation good. During the night 2,000 rounds were fired indirect from E.10.b.3. on same targets on night of 29th inst. JAR	French Maps RANSART & FONQUEVILLERS 1/10,000

J.A. Roxburgh Captain.

Comdg. 89 Machine Gun Company
Machine Gun Corps

SECRET

WAR DIARY

OF 89 MACHINE GUN COMPANY

FOR THE MONTH OF

NOVEMBER 1916

Volume IX + Appendices VII/VIII

Army Form C. 2118.

WAR DIARY
of 89 Machine Gun Company
~~INTELLIGENCE SUMMARY~~ Machine Gun Corps.
(Erase heading not required.)

Vol. IX – NOVEMBER 1916.
Part II. Title pages p. 1.

Instructions regarding War Diaries and Intelligence Summaries are contained in F. S. Regs., Part II. and the Staff Manual respectively. Title pages will be prepared in manuscript.

Place	Date	Hour	Summary of Events and Information	Remarks and references to Appendices
			REFERENCE MAPS. TRENCH MAP. RANSART — 1/10,000	
			TRENCH MAP Appendix VIII .... FONQUEVILLERS — 1/10,000	
			1/10,000 (October) — LENS – SHEET 11	1/100,000
W16 c.6.6.	1-11-16.		89 M.G.Coy in the line opposite MONCHY – Guns as in Vol. VIII (October) – Company H.Q. in BERLES. Transport at LA BAZÈQUE farm. Inter sectional relief every 6 days.	JHR
		5.30 p.m.	From 5.30 p.m to 6.30 p.m there was a little M.G. fire into the RAVINE (W 2 2 c), but much less than usual, probably from about W 29 c 4.0.	JHR
		6. p.m.	From 6 p.m to 8 p.m – 500 rounds were fired indirect from position at W 23 c 0.6 at roads W 30 a 8.2 to W 30 c 1.9 and W 30 a 8.2 to W 30 c 6.6. There was no reply.	JHR
—	2-11-16		750 rounds fired indirect from position at W 27 o 6.5 – Targets W 30 c 4.0 – E 6 a 2.4 – E 5 d 9.9. Enemy replied with artillery fire searching for the gun.	JHR
			Gun at E 4 d 45.55 fired during night on sunken road at E 5 c 6.8, where enemy machine gun had been reported by patrols.	JHR
—	3-11-16		Gun at E 4 b 45.55 fired during the night on (a) suspected snipers post at end of salient (E 5 a 2.0) + (b) vicinity of MONCHY Church.	JHR
				30 R reinforcements (transferred from 90 Bgy) JHR
			Indirect fire also carried out on (a) MONCHY – RANSART ROAD + (b) ESSARTS road.	JHR
—	4-11-16		Quiet – Nothing to report.	JHR
—	5-11-16		Emplacement at W 28 b 73 sited for anti-aircraft use.	JHR
—	6-11-16	12 midnight to 1 a.m	Gun at E 4 d 7.5. fired 250 rounds in the vicinity of MONCHY Church.	JHR

Vol. IX — NOVEMBER

WAR DIARY
of 89 MACHINE GUN COMPANY
INTELLIGENCE SUMMARY. MACHINE GUN CORPS.
p. 2.

Army Form C. 2118.

Place	Date	Hour	Summary of Events and Information	Remarks and references to Appendices
W16c 6.8.	6.11.16		Enemy guns active between 5.15 & 6.15 p.m. but quiet during night. JHR	
--	7.11.16		Very quiet — Nothing to report — JHR 3.O.R. reinforcements JHR	
--	8.11.16		Enemy guns very active in the left subsector between 6 and 6.45 p.m., traversing our parapets. JHR 2nd Lt. A.E.BROWN & 2nd Lt. W.G. BORDERO reported from Base Depot. JHR Between 6 and 6.30 p.m. gun at E.30.c.5.70 fired 500 rounds indirect, traversing road from W.30.c.4.0. to E.5.d.o.o. There was no reply. JHR During the night enemy guns were quiet. JHR	
--	9.11.16		Except for a few bursts from an enemy gun into the RAVINE at 10.45 p.m. quiet — JHR	
--	10.11.16		Gun at E.27.a.55.45 fired 750 rounds indirect on road E.5.d.9.9. to E.5.a.2.4. There was no reply. JHR	
--	11.11.16		Enemy machine gun fire into the RAVINE was less than usual. JHR Between 6 and 6.30 p.m. gun at W.23.c.0.6 fired 500 rounds indirect on to roads from E.6.b.53, E.6.c.9.6 and E.6.c.43, vertically searching along each road. As soon as fire was opened, enemy snipers became very active and a few shells came over. Otherwise normal — JHR	

Army Form C. 2118.

WAR DIARY
of 89 MACHINE GUN COMPANY
~~INTELLIGENCE SUMMARY~~ MACHINE GUN CORPS.

Vol IX - NOVEMBER - 1916 p. 3

(Erase heading not required.)

Instructions regarding War Diaries and Intelligence Summaries are contained in F. S. Regs., Part II. and the Staff Manual respectively. Title pages will be prepared in manuscript.

Place	Date	Hour	Summary of Events and Information	Remarks and references to Appendices
W.16.c.6.8.	12-11-16		Quiet. Preparations made for covering fire during gas discharge. All ready by 7.p.m. JHR	
	13-11-16	2.40am	Gas discharged from our front. At 2.47 a.m. 5 guns opened fire on enemy roads as follows:-	
			gun at W23c0.6. on roads E6b5.3 to F1c 9.7.	
			E6c9.6 to E12 b 9.7.	
			E6c4.3 to E12 b 5.2.	
			gun at E4d 7.5. on roads W30 c 4.0 to X26 a 4.4	
			E6a7.6 to X25 d 0.0.	
			and S.W. corner of ADINFER WOOD.	
			gun at E.1b 7.2 on roads W29d 9.6 to W30 a 8.2.	
			W30 e 4.0 to X26 a 4.4.	
			guns at E2a 05.70 ? on area around E5d 9.9	
			E6a 2.4	
			gun at W27 a 55.45	
			W30 c A.O.	
			6,000 rounds fired. Fire was continued till about 4. a.m. — Casualties and damage to guns, emplacements etc. — Nil. — Enemy M.G. fire during the discharge very scattered JHR	

Vol. IX - NOVEMBER 1916.

Army Form C. 2118.

WAR DIARY

of 89 MACHINE GUN COMPANY

INTELLIGENCE SUMMARY.

MACHINE GUN CORPS.

(Erase heading not required.)

Instructions regarding War Diaries and Intelligence Summaries are contained in F. S. Regs., Part II. and the Staff Manual respectively. Title pages will be prepared in manuscript.

P.A.

Place	Date	Hour	Summary of Events and Information	Remarks and references to Appendices
W16.c.6.8.	14-11-16	5.30 a.m.	1000 rounds fired from E.10.b.7.2 on to E.12.b.5.1 to assist a raid made by the Brigade on our right - Quiet day - Nothing to report - JHR	
			Between 6 & 7.15 p.m. Gun at E.3.a.05.70 fired 750 rounds indirect on to E.6.a.5.8. E.6.a.2.3 & E.6.c.0.8. Enemy guns quiet. JHR	
	15-11-16		Quiet day - JHR	
	16-11-16		Quiet day - Slight enemy M.G. activity on left during early hours of the evening JHR	
	17-11-16	6 p.m.	Gun at W.27.a.35.45 fired 1,000 rounds indirect between 6 and 8 p.m. on road from E.6.a.4.9 to E.5.d.9.9. JHR	
		7 p.m.	Gun at E.10.b.9.6 fired 1,000 rounds indirect between 7 & 9.30 p.m. at the QUARRY & cross roads F.7.a.5.3. Enemy guns normal. JHR	
	18-11-16		Quiet day - JHR	
	19-11-16	5.30 a.m.	At 5.30 a.m. sentry on gun at W.29.a.5.6 saw an enemy patrol examining our wire. No reply being given to his challenge, he threw a bomb & patrol replied with 3 bombs & ran back, as he was then also seen by the infantry bombing post on the right of the gun. During "Stand to" the enemy sent over rifle grenades on this part of the French JHR	
			During the morning the 4 guns in the right subsector (E.4.b.45.55, E.4.d.7.5, E.4.c.45.25, & E.10.b.4.6.)	

Army Form C. 2118.

Vol. IX — NOVEMBER — WAR DIARY
of 89 MACHINE GUN COMPANY
1916 —
INTELLIGENCE SUMMARY   MACHINE GUN CORPS.
p. 5.

Place	Date	Hour	Summary of Events and Information	Remarks and references to Appendices
W.16.c.6.8.	19-11-16		and the 2 night guns in the Divisional Line (E.3.a.05.70 and E.3.c.8.3) were relieved by guns of 148 M.G.Coy. The Section H.Q. at BIENVILLERS was also handed over. Relief completed by 11.15 a.m. JHR	For Operation Order see App. VII
		11.15 a.m.	On relief the 2 guns, from the Divisional Line marched to BERLES & hence relieved 2 guns of 21 M.G.Coy in Nobs Walk (W.22.a.30.25 & W.22.a.25.18), and 1 gun in D Post (W.16.d.8.9) JHR	
		6.10 p.m.	The flash of an enemy M.G. was seen at W.29.b.35.55. Work had previously been noted on an emplacement near this point. JHR	
	20-11-16		The whole of No 2 Section (which had come from the old right Section on the 19th inst) relieved 3 guns of 21st M.G.Coy in the new left sector at W.17.b.40.43, W.18.c.4.8, & W.23.c.9.9. Enemy guns not very active. JHR	
		10.30 a.m.	Relief completed. JHR	
	21.11.16		Normal day. JHR	
	22-11-16		At dawn several enemy M.G's traversed our line in an arc between SIORDET TRENCH & NUTS WALK. This fire was accompanied by a heavy Trench Mortar bombardment on the right of our Sector. JHR 2nd Lieut. R.H.W. ROBERTS reported from Base Depot. JHR	App. VIII
	23-11-16		1 gun placed at W.17.a.25.38 in H.Post for indirect fire on enemy front line opposite brigade on our left. Similarly one gun placed at W.23.c.0.6 for indirect fire. JHR 1 gun taken from W.27.a.6.9. JHR	

T2134. Wt. W708—776. 500000. 4/15. Sir J. C. & 8.

Army Form C. 2118.

Vol. IX – NOVEMBER – WAR DIARY
of 89 MACHINE GUN COMPANY
~~INTELLIGENCE SUMMARY~~ MACHINE GUN CORPS.
1916
p.6.

(Erase heading not required.)

Instructions regarding War Diaries and Intelligence Summaries are contained in F. S. Regs., Part II. and the Staff Manual respectively. Title pages will be prepared in manuscript.

Place	Date	Hour	Summary of Events and Information	Remarks and references to Appendices
W.16.c.6.8.	23-11-16		NEW DISPOSITION OF GUNS.	

Right Section 5 guns – *NEVERENDING ST. – W 28 b 8.1.
 Section H.Q. at   NEWARK ST.   – W.29 a 05.35.
 W23 c 0.6.   99 Trench   – W29 a 5.6. } In the Right Subsector – B1.
      Noodles Av.   – W 23 c 6.4
(Team provided from left section) *RAVINE   – W 23 e 0.6.
      NUTS LANE   – W 23 c 9.9.

Left Section 3 guns – TUNNEL SAP   – W 18 c 4.8.
 Section H.Q. on   *SIORDET TRENCH – W 17 b 40.43. } In the Left Subsector – B2.
 FOX LANE at W 17 d 4.2.

Support Section 5 guns *BERLES ROAD – W 27 a 6.7.
 Section H.Q. with Bn HQ   *NOBS WALK i – W 22 a 25.18
 in BERLES   NOBS WALK ii – W 22 a 30.25 } In the DIVISIONAL LINE.
     *D POST   – W 16 d 8.9.
     *H. POST.   – W 17 a 25.38.

It was arranged for guns marked * to fire indirect on points in the enemy's line, thereby being able to put up an indirect fire barrage, as a secondary barrage in case of attack. At night these guns were to fire S.O.S.
            JHR.

Army Form C. 2118.

WAR DIARY
of 89 Machine Gun Company
~~INTELLIGENCE SUMMARY~~
Machine Gun Corps.
(Erase heading not required.)

Vol IX — November — 1916 — p.7.

Instructions regarding War Diaries and Intelligence Summaries are contained in F. S. Regs., Part II. and the Staff Manual respectively. Title pages will be prepared in manuscript.

Place	Date	Hour	Summary of Events and Information	Remarks and references to Appendices
W.16.c.6.8.	24.11.16		Quiet day — Nothing to report. JHR	
	25.11.16	7 p.m.	Gun at D Post fired 500 rounds indirect between 7 & 7.30 p.m. on the enemy's communication & support trenches in area W 24 c 3.0....4.3....1.5....0.3. JHR Enemy guns normal JHR	
	26.11.16	2.30 p.m.	The gun from W 23 c 6.4 was mounted a little way from the emplacement for cooperation with the Medium Trench Mortars. It was however spotted by the enemy's artillery and had to come down. This was chiefly due to the fact that the sun was shining very brightly at the time and there were several enemy planes up. JHR At dawn the gun at SIORDET TRENCH registered on its line for indirect barrage fire. The shots appeared to go well into the German lines. JHR	
	27.11.16		Quiet day — No firing done owing to poor visibility. JHR 2nd Lr F.S.A. REEVES reported from Base Depot JHR	
	28.11.16		Nothing to report — 1 OR rejoined from C.C.S. JHR	
	29.11.16		Quiet day — JHR	
	30.11.16		Casualties during month of November — NIL. in action	

J. H. Roxburgh Captain
Cmdg 89 MG Company

APPENDIX VII — to War Diary Vol IX

89 MACHINE GUN COMPANY.

Copy...1...

Operation Order No.6.
by
Captain J.H.Roxburgh.

Reference Maps.

Trench Maps...FONQUEVILLERS....1/10000.
            RANSART.........1/10000.

1. The 89th M.G.Coy. is to hand over the emplacements in the Right Subsector and the emplacements in the Divisional Line at STONEYGATE SOUTH (E 3 e 8.3) and ALSACE VILLA (E 3 a 05.70.) to the 148th M.G.Coy. on the 19th November.

2. <u>Guides.</u> One guide from each gun team will report to 2nd Lt. Faulkner at the support section H.Q., No.9 Billet BIENVILLERS by 8.45 a.m. 19th inst. He will take them to the meeting place (E 2 c 4.8.).

3. Belt boxes will be handed over at each position, but ALL tripods will be taken out. 60 belt boxes will in return be handed over to us at BIENVILLERS.

4. All maps, range cards, targets & angles for indirect fire will be handed over.

5. On relief the 2 guns of No 1 section at STONEYGATE SOUTH & "ALSACE VILLA", will march to W 21 b 30 BERLES, where guides from 21 M.G.Coy. will be met at 11.30 a.m. They will also get there 1 gun, tripod etc. of No 3 Section.

6. No 1 section will then take over the double gun position in NOB'S WALK and the position at D POST, now garrisoned by 21 M.G.Coy. Belt boxes will be handed over.

7. The H.Q. of the support section (No 1) will then be at Coy. H.Q. BERLES, where the completion of this relief will be reported.

8. No 2 section, on relief, will march to No 9 Billet BIENVILLERS, where guns, stores etc. will be left in charge of a guard until called for by limbers. No 2 section will then march to Coy. H.Q. BERLES.

9. 2 complete limbers will be at BIENVILLERS by 4.0 p.m. 19th inst. to move stores etc. direct to Coy. H.Q. BERLES.

10. On 20th November at an hour to be notified later. No 2 section will relieve 3 guns of 21 M.G.Coy in the new left sector.

11. Receipts will be obtained for all stores handed over.

J.H.Roxburgh.
Captain,
Commanding
89 Machine Gun Company.

Copy No 1...Retained.
       2...No 1 section.
       3...No 2 section.
       4...Transport Officer.
       5...C.Q.M.S.

18-11-16.

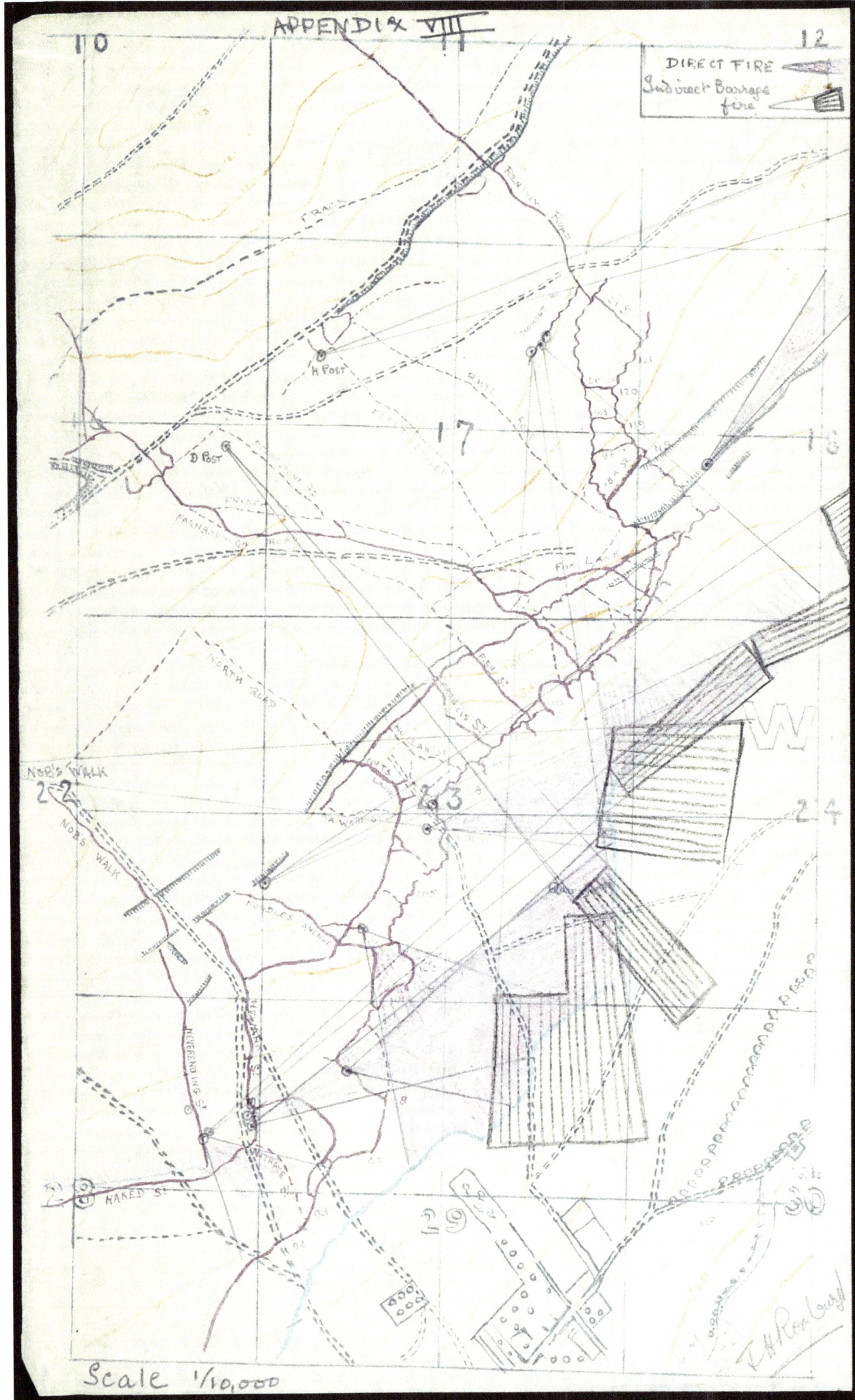

Vol 10

SECRET

WAR DIARY

OF 89TH MACHINE GUN COMPANY

FOR THE MONTH OF DECEMBER 1916

Volume X

Army Form C. 2118.

WAR DIARY
of 89 MACHINE GUN COMPANY.
~~INTELLIGENCE SUMMARY~~ MACHINE GUN CORPS.
(Erase heading not required.)

Vol. X — DECEMBER 1916.

Instructions regarding War Diaries and Intelligence Summaries are contained in F. S. Regs., Part II. and the Staff Manual respectively. Title pages will be prepared in manuscript.

Place	Date	Hour	Summary of Events and Information	Remarks and references to Appendices
			Reference Maps:- Trench Map - RANSART 1/20,000 - FONQUEVILLERS 1/10,000 Appendix VIII - Vol IX (November) 1/10,000 JHR	
BERLES-AU-BOIS W.18.c.6.8.	1-12-16		89 M.G. Coy. in B Sector in front of BERLES-AU-BOIS - Guns as in Vol IX (November). JHR	
			Quiet day - nothing to report. JHR	
			Between 5 & 8 P.M. Gun at W 23 c 0.6. fired 1500 rounds indirect on following	
			Targets — Roads E 6 b 5.3 to F 1 d 5.5.	
			E 6 c 9.6 to F 7 a 5.3.	
			~~Enemy front line.~~ JHR E 6 c 4.3 to F 7 c 0.5.	
			Enemy guns were at first active in reply, one firing into the RAVINE about W 23 a JHR	
	2-12-16	4.15 p.m.	4 guns opened indirect fire on German lines as follows:-	
			(i) Gun at NEVERENDING STREET (W 28 b 8.1.) on German front line W 23 b 88.15 to W 24 a 13.45	
			and W 24 a 42.41 to W 24 a 72.78.	
			(ii) Gun at RAVINE (W 23 e 0.6) on German front line ~~JHR~~ W 18 d 20.22 to W 18 d central.	
			& W 18 d 47.72 to W 18 d 60.85	
			and on french junctions W 24 b 31.76 & W 18 d 70.28. JHR	
			(iii) Gun at NOBS WALK (W 22 a 25.18) on German front line W 24 a 15.43 to W 24 a 43.42.	
			& communication trench W 24 a 56.03 to W 24 a 8.0.	
			(iv) Gun at BERLES ROAD (W 27 a 6.9) on points W 29 d 60.88, W 29 d 10.67, & W 29 d 85.60.	

WAR DIARY

Vol. X – December 1916
of 89 Machine Gun Company – Machine Gun Corps
p. 2.

Army Form C. 2118.

Place	Date	Hour	Summary of Events and Information	Remarks and references to Appendices
W.15.c.6.8.			Bursts were fired until 5 p.m. In all 4,000 rounds were fired. It was impossible to get satisfactory observation. Enemy guns were slightly active in reply. JHR	
	3.12.16	4.15 p.m	2 guns opened indirect fire until 5 p.m. on German lines as follows:-	
			(i) Gun at SIORDET TRENCH (W17 b 40.43) on German front line from W23 d q.5 to W24c 00.25.	
			a. W29 b 5.8. to W29 b 50.45.	
			on Trench junctions :- W29 b 92.86, W29 b 70.66, & W29 b 64.59.	
			(ii) Gun at D POST (W16 d 8.9) on German front line from W23 d 90.35 W24c 00.25.	
			a communication trenches W23 d 92.56 to W24c 14.22.	
			W24c 11.11 to W30 a 22.90.	
			2,380 rounds were fired.	
		4.30 p.m	Gun at W23 c 0.6 fired 1250 rounds indirect until 5.45 p.m on following Targets:-	
			E 6 b 5.3 to F 1 d 5.5.	
			E 6 c 9.6 to F 7 a 5.3.	
			E 6 c 4.3 to F 7 c 0.5.	
			Enemy guns were very active from 3 p.m to 3.45 p.m. Traversing our parapets + firing into the RAVINE. They were also very active between 8+9 p.m firing long bursts Traversing our parapets in B1. JHR	

Army Form C. 2118.

WAR DIARY

of 89 MACHINE GUN COMPANY.

INTELLIGENCE SUMMARY MACHINE GUN CORPS.

Vol. X – DECEMBER – 1916
p.3.

Instructions regarding War Diaries and Intelligence Summaries are contained in F. S. Regs., Part II. and the Staff Manual respectively. Title pages will be prepared in manuscript.

(Erase heading not required.)

Place	Date	Hour	Summary of Events and Information	Remarks and references to Appendices
W15c6.8	4.12.16		Quiet day – Nothing to report. JHR	
–	5.12.16	4.15pm	Gun at H.Post (W17a 25.38) opened indirect fire till 5pm on following targets:— Trench – X7c 28.57. 19 X7d 50.61. Points – X7c 31.83 + X7c 2.9. 12500 rounds fired. Enemy guns moderately quiet. JHR	
–	6.12.16		Quiet day – 3 O.R. reinforcements from Base Depot. JHR	
–	7.12.16	5pm	Gun at W23 c.o.6 fired 1,000 rounds indirect on road E6c8.7 to F7a5.3 and enfiladed Trench E6d 2.9 to F7a 5.3. Enemy replied with a little M.G. fire into the RAVINE. JHR	
–	8.12.16	9.25pm	Gun in 99 Trench (W2q a 5.6) opened fire in conjunction with Lewis Guns on a strong enemy working party located by one of our patrols. A little later the enemy replied with M.G. fire along our front line. JHR	
–	9.12.16		Nothing to report. JHR	
–	10.12.16		Quiet day. JHR	
–	11.12.16	10.30pm	Between 10.30pm & 1.0 am 12th inst. guns at W17 b 40.43 + W23 c.o.6 fired 1250 and 1500 rounds respectively in conjunction with a bombing patrol by 19th K.L.R. Targets were as follows:—	

T2134. Wt. W708–776. 500000. 4/15. Sir J. C. & S.

WAR DIARY

Vol X. December 1916.

of 89 Machine Gun Company
Machine Gun Corps.

Army Form C. 2118.

Place	Date	Hour	Summary of Events and Information	Remarks and references to Appendices
W.15.c.6.8.	12.12.16		Siordet St. on german Support line W24 b 36.76 to W18 d 72.28 and communication trench in rear.	
—	13.12.16	11.0 am	Ravine on Rd W24 a 8.0 and W24 b 05.10. T.M.R. 4 O.R. reinforcements T.M.R. Monchy and the german lines around it were bombarded by our artillery and french mortars. The bombardment lasted for 3 hours 20 minutes and was intense at 11 a.m. and 1.20 p.m. At the two latter times the enemy's trenches & tracks were swept for 3 minutes by our machine guns. Fd orders & targets see Coy Operation Order No 7. From 4.30 pm until 6.20 a.m. 14th inst. these tracks & trenches were kept under fire at irregular intervals for one minute, as detailed in Coy Operation Order No 7 with the exception that no burst could be fired at 8.30, 9.0, 9.55, 10.30 p.m. owing to patrols being out. In all 50,225 rounds were fired. The enemy did not find any gun. At 6 p.m. a raid was carried out by 20th K.L.R. from B1 (right) Subsector. The guns of the night subsector were placed in position to cover the party's flanks, but did not fire, as they had orders only to do so in case of an emergency. After the raid & throughout the night the enemy appeared extremely nervous. Whenever our guns opened fire a large number of very lights would be	App. IX
	14.12.16			

Army Form C. 2118.

WAR DIARY

Vol V — DECEMBER

of 89 MACHINE GUN COMPANY MACHINE GUN CORPS.

1916

p.5

Place	Date	Hour	Summary of Events and Information	Remarks and references to Appendices
W.15.c.6.8.	14.12.16		Sent up down R18 line. Patrols reported working parties + two of the guns of the night entrenched were detailed to sweep the enemy's parapets from various points in the front & support lines. An enemy working party opposite trench 103 was fired on at 1.30 am. 1500 rounds were fired in this manner. JHR	
---	15.12.16	10.30pm	Between 10.30 pm & 1 a.m. gun at SIORDET ST. fired 1500 rounds indirect on German support line — W.24.b.1.5 to W.24.b.36.76 in conjunction with patrol of 19th K.L.R. JHR	
		4.30 pm	Between 4.30 pm & 5.30 pm gun at W.13.c.0.6 fired 1000 rounds indirect on new German trench at W.24.q.92.75 to W.24.b.47.30. JHR	
		7.10 pm	Between 7.10 p.m. & 8.30 p.m. gun at NOB'S WALK (W.22.a.30.25) fired 1000 rounds indirect on targets:— W.24.a.7.0 to W.24.a.8.D. W.24.b.0.3 to W.24.b.0.5 in conjunction with patrol of 19th K.L.R. JHR	
---	16.12.16	6 pm	A gun was placed at W.17.a.99.38 & fired 1000 rounds indirect between 10 & 10.15 pm on enemy front line from W.18.d.5.7 to W.18.d.2.7 in conjunction with a raid by the 2nd Yorks. (21st Bde_on our left). The raiding party started from the RAVINE at W.18.c & the Tunnel emplacement at W.18.c.4.6 was handed over to them for	

Army Form C. 2118.

WAR DIARY
of 89 MACHINE GUN COMPANY.
MACHINE GUN CORPS -

Vol. I. - DECEMBER. 1916.
~~INTELLIGENCE SUMMARY~~
p.6.
(Erase heading not required.)

Instructions regarding War Diaries and Intelligence Summaries are contained in F. S. Regs., Part II. and the Staff Manual respectively. Title pages will be prepared in manuscript.

Place	Date	Hour	Summary of Events and Information	Remarks and references to Appendices
W.15.c.6.8.			use. This gun was moved for the night to a position at W.18.c.15.55. JHR	
---	17.12.16		Quiet day - nothing to report - JHR	
---	18.12.16		Quiet day - JHR	
---	19.12.16		Nothing to report - JHR	
---	20.12.16		Gun in Tunnel Sap at W.18.c.4.8. was permanently moved to W.18.c.45.55, where in addition to firing up the RAVINE it could fire on our wire & the ground in front of it on the north of the RAVINE. JHR	
---	21.12.16		Quiet day - JHR.	
---	22.12.16		Nothing to report. JHR.	
---	23-12-16	5:30 pm	Fire was opened by 6 guns in conjunction with bombardment by heavy artillery on German Trenches and Light Railway in W.24.a. and b. as follows:- (i) Gun at H Post (W.17.a.25.38.) on communication trench W.24.a. 86.85 to W.24.b.8.7. Range - 1500 to 1950 yards - Vertical Searching - (ii) Gun at D Post (W.16.a.8.9) on communication Trench W.24.a.52.60 to W.24.a.95.47. Range - 1500 to 1700 yards. Vertical Searching - (iii) 2 guns at W.22.b.25.65 on Light Railway W.24.b.11.47 to X.19.a.2.4. Range 1800 to 2300 yards. Bracketing fire.	

Army Form C. 2118.

WAR DIARY
of 89 Machine Gun Company, Machine Gun Corps.

Vol. X – December 1916.
p. 7.

(Erase heading not required.)

Instructions regarding War Diaries and Intelligence Summaries are contained in F. S. Regs., Part II. and the Staff Manual respectively. Title pages will be prepared in manuscript.

Place	Date	Hour	Summary of Events and Information	Remarks and references to Appendices
W15 c 6.8.			(iv.) Gun at RAVINE (W23 c 0.6) on Frenchel. W24 a 95.25 to W24 b 30.75 and W24 a 95.30 to W24 b 30.75. Range 1500 to 1700 yards – Traversing fire.	
			(v.) Gun at BIDRDET St (W17 d 40.43) on same target as (iv) – Range 1300 yards – Traversing fire. Intermittent fire was also kept up between 6 & 10 p.m. The enemy sent up a large number of Very lights. – 22,000 rounds were fired. J.H.R.	
	24-12-16		Gun at W29 b 8.1 was moved to W17 d 23.14, as a supporting gun to fire up ravine. J.H.R.	
	25-12-16		Enemy shelled BERLES between 7 & 3 p.m. with guns of all calibres. J.H.R.	
	26-12-16		Quiet day. Enemy machine guns active opposite right subsector between 6 & 7 p.m. J.H.R.	
	27-12-16		BERLES shelled intermittently. J.H.R.	
W15 d 2.2.	28-12-16		Enemy M.Gs active 6 to 7 p.m. & at 6:30 p.m. Coy H.Q. moved to W15 d 2.2. J.H.R.	
	29-12-16	7.25 a.m.	2 O.R. reinforcements from Base Depot. Artillery activity. J.H.R. 2 escaped German prisoners were recaptured by gun team at W2 q 05.35. J.H.R.	
	30-12-16		Usual artillery activity on BERLES. J.H.R.	
	31-12-16		Nothing to report. J.H.R.	

H. Roseboys Capt.
Comdg 89 M.G. Coy.

SECRET.

Appendix X

89th. MACHINE GUN COY. OPERATION ORDER No. 7.

by,

Captain, J.H. ROXBURGH.

Reference Maps:-
   RANSART ....1/10,000.
   FONQUEVILLERS .1/10,000.

Headquarters.
11-12-16.

---

1. A bombardment of the MONCHY Salient by artillery and trench mortars will take place on December 13th. This will be assisted by machine guns.

2. Zero hour will be at 11.0 a.m. The bombardment will be for 3 hours and 20 minutes.

3. From 4.30 p.m. onwards during the night December 13th/14th artillery will sweep roads and tracks in rear of the German lines by bursts of fire at irregular intervals.

4. The following guns will fire rapid on the following targets:

    (a) From ZERO to ZERO plus 3 minutes.
    (b) From ZERO plus 140 minutes to ZERO plus 143 minutes.

    No 8 Gun at W 17 b 40.43 (Siordet Trench) on German front line from W 29 b 2.4 to W 29 b 5.7.

    No 1 Gun at W 28 b 8.1.(Neverending Street) on German front line from E 5 d 4.1 to E 5 a 25.00

    Berles Road Gun and two guns in Nobbs Walk on streets and road junctions in centre of MONCHY.

    Two guns at W 22 b 12.47 and W 22 b 0.2 across the valley running N.E. from MONCHY at TOWER HOUSE (Bracketing fire).

    Three guns in the RAVINE at W 23 c 0.5., W 23 c 1.7., and W 23 c 15.75 on the roads running S.E. from MONCHY from E 6 b 5.3., E 6 c 9.6., and E 6 c 4.3., respectively.

    They will also fire bursts of fire for one minute at the following hours:-
    4.30 p.m., 4.50 p.m., 5.20 p.m., 8.30 p.m., 9.0 p.m., 9.55 p.m.
    10.30 p.m., 11.40 p.m., 12.10 a.m., 1.0 a.m. 1.25 a.m.,
    2.10 a.m., 3.0 a.m., 4.30 a.m., 5.0 a.m., 6.20 a.m.

    The targets will be the same with the following exceptions:
    No 8 Gun at W 17 b 40.43 will fire on roads between X 19 a and RABBIT WOOD.
    No.1 Gun will not fire.

5. No.4 Section will be at the disposal of the O.C.20th.Bn.K.L.R during the night December 13th/14th and will receive special orders.

6. The three guns in the RAVINE will be under the command of 2nd.Lt.Lochhead and will be manned by the team of No 2 Section at present there and two small teams of No 3 Section.

The two guns in W 22 b will be under the command of 2nd.Lt. Faulker and will be brought forward from D and H Posts.

The gun at Berles Road will be under the command of 2nd.LT. Reeves.

The remainder of the Company, who are in BERLES will stand to in their bombardment stations from 11 a.m. to 3 p.m. on December 13th.

7. Watches will be synchronized as soon as possible after 9 a.m. at H.Q. 20th.Bn.K.L.R.

8. Belts will be refilled as quickly as possible after each burst, and guns will be thoroughly overhauled between the day and night firing.

9. Armourer Sgt.Dudley will be at Section H.Q. in the RAVINE and Artificer Burns will be at NOBBS WALK gun to attend to any gun which gives trouble.

10. If any gun is left with only 2 muzzle cups, it will continue to fire without the muzzle attachment and with the fusee spring lowered.

11. The Transport will bring rations to the Company H.Q. at BERLES via POMMIER by 5 p.m. Gun teams of No 1 Section and the gun team at W 17 b 40.43 will draw their rations from there when convenient.

The rations of the remainder of No 2 Section and No 4 Section will be carried to the cookhouse in the RAVINE when suitable by a party detailed from No 3 Section under the command of Sgt.Haycock.

J.H.ROXBURGH.
Captain,
Commanding 89th.MACHINE GUN COY.

Copy No 1. to O.C. No 1 Section.
" " 2. " O.C. " 2 "
" " 3 " O.C. " 3 "
" " 4 " O.C. " 4 "
" " 5 " O.C. 20th.Bn.K.L.R.

SECRET.

APPENDIX TO

89th. MACHINE GUN COMPANY OPERATION ORDER No 7.

by

Captain J.H. ROXBURGH.

Special orders for No 4 Section.

1. On the night December 13th/14th. the four guns of No 4 Section will give covering fire during a raid to be made by the 20th. Bn. K.L.R.

2. O.C. No 4 Section will in conjunction with the 20th Bn. K.L.R. select gun positions for his guns as follows:-

    One gun to cover the right flank - firing on German front line from W 29 a 8.1 to the S.W.
    Three guns to cover the left flank. One firing on the German front line particularly at W 29 b 45.75 and the sap W 29 b 3.6. One firing on German front line from W 29 b 55.82 to N.E. and particularly at the QUARRY. One firing on the support line from W 29 b 75.45 to W 24 c 16.22.

3. Fire will be opened at ZERO minus 5 minutes and kept up intermittently until both the raiding and covering party are in.

4. On completion of the above the guns will be moved to their normal positions.

                                        J.H. ROXBURGH.
                                            Captain,
                            Commanding, 89th. MACHINE GUN COMPANY.

Copy No 1 to O.C. No 4 Section.
Copy No 2 to O.C. 20th. Bn. K.L.R.

Vol XI

CONFIDENTIAL.

WAR DIARY
OF
89th MACHINE GUN COMPANY

JANUARY 1917.
Volume XI.

WAR DIARY
or
INTELLIGENCE SUMMARY

of 89 MACHINE GUN COMPANY, MACHINE GUN CORPS.

Army Form C. 2118.

VOL XI
JANUARY 1917.
p. 1

Reference Maps:- Bondecklof, RANSART-Vimy
FONQUEVILLERS - 1/10,000.
Appendix VIII, VOL IX (Maps - 1/10,000. 1/100,000.
LENS - Sheet 11 - 1/20,000.
Sheet 57d N.W - 1/20,000.

Place	Date	Hour	Summary of Events and Information	Remarks and references to Appendices
BERLES-AU-BOIS W15.C.6.8.	1.1.17		89 M.G Cy. "B" Section in front of BERLES-AU-BOIS - Guns as in VOL X (December 1916). JHR Quiet day - our guns did not fire. Enemy Machine Guns continuously traversed over parapets from 11 p.m to 11.30 p.m. JHR	
"	2.1.17		Nothing to report - quiet day - our guns did not fire. 1.O.R accidentally wounded. JHR	
"	3.1.17		Our Guns did not fire, enemy guns normal. JHR	
"	4.1.17		Our Guns did not fire, Enemy machine gun fired two bursts about 7.10 p.m. Last night, bullets were high - probable target BERLES & POMMIER ROAD. JHR 1.O.R wounded. JHR	
"	5.1.17		Quiet day - our guns did not fire. An enemy machine gun was spotted at W.8.2.6.8.4.0.4. JHR	
"	6.1.17		Nothing to report - quiet day - our guns did not fire. JHR	
"	7.1.17		Our guns did not fire - enemy machine guns normal. During the afternoon Nos 1 and 4 Sections were relieved by two sections of the 147th Machine gun Coy 49 Division. This was completed by 4 p.m. On arrival of the remainder of 147 M.G Coy, No 3 Section (in BERLES) marched to HUMBERCAMP into Billets, & were followed on relief by Nos 1 & 4 Sections JHR	
"	8.1.17		During the afternoon No 2 Section in B.2 Subsector was relieved by one section of 147 M.G. Cy & on relief marched to HUMBERCAMP. 89 MG Coy moved by bus to billets in CAUMESNIL. JHR sheet 57d NW 1/20,000	

Army Form C. 2118.

WAR DIARY

Vol XI

of 89TH MACHINE GUN COMPANY.

INTELLIGENCE SUMMARY

JANUARY 1917   MACHINE GUN CORPS.

(Erase heading not required.)

Instructions regarding War Diaries and Intelligence Summaries are contained in F. S. Regs., Part II. and the Staff Manual respectively. Title pages will be prepared in manuscript.

Place	Date	Hour	Summary of Events and Information	Remarks and references to Appendices
B 29 c 4.8	9-1-17	—	In billets at CAUHESNIL — Training — IHR.	
—	20-1-17	8.30 pm	1 O.R. reinforcement from Base Depot. IHR.	
—	22-1-17		1 O.R. reinforcement from Base Depot. IHR.	
—	25-1-17		3 O.R. reinforcements from Base Depot. IHR.	

J. A. Roxburgh Captain

Cmdg 89 M.G. Company

Appendix X to War Diary

SECRET.   January 1917   Copy No. 8.

96th. MACHINE GUN COMPANY. OPERATION ORDER No 3.

by

Captain J. B. BOARDWELL.

Reference Map   Headquarters,
Trench Sheet 11..1/1   6-1-17.

---

1. The 96th. Machine Gun Company will be relieved by the 147th. Machine Gun Company in R.Sector on the 7th. inst. Jan.

2. On the 6th. inst. two Sections of 147th. Machine Gun Company will arrive at HUMBERCAMP.

3. On the afternoon of the 7th. inst. the above two Sections will relieve Nos. 1 and 3 Sections in the Divisional line and R.1 Subsectors respectively.
   Guides for limbers, provided by Transport, to be at HUMBERCAMP at Noon.
   Guides from each gun team of No 1 and 3 Sections to be at Company H.Q. at 1.30 p.m.

4. On arrival of the above two Sections in HUMBLES, No.3 Section will proceed to " HUMBERCAMP, with Coy. H.Q., less C.O., Ptes. Evans, Mitchell, and Signallers.
   For this move 3 limbers and the cook's cart will be available and will report at the Coy. H.Q. during the afternoon.

5. On relief Nos. 1 and 3 Sections will leave guns, tripods, etc. at Coy. H.Q. in the RAVINE, respectively, under charge of one man, and will proceed to HUMBERCAMP to take over the billets vacated by 147th. Machine Gun Company.

6. On the evening of the 7th. inst. one limber will come to Company H.Q. to take away guns, etc. of No.1 Section and one limber with No.3 Section's rations to the RAVINE, to take away No.3 Section's guns etc.

7. On the 7th. inst. the remainder of 147th. Machine Gun Company will arrive in HUMBLES.

8. On the 7th. inst. the Transport less 3 limbers and cook's cart will move to billets in CAMPAGNE.

9. On the 8th. inst. the remainder of the Company will move to CAMPAGNE.
   The Quartermaster's stores will move by the lorry.
   Further orders will be issued for the remainder.

10. On the afternoon of the 8th. inst. No.2 Section will be relieved in R.2 Subsector.
    Guides to be at Coy. H.Q. at 3.30 p.m.

11. On relief No.2 Section will leave guns etc. at the RAVINE under charge of one man and will proceed to HUMBLES for tea. Thence they will move to HUMBERCAMP.

12. On the evening of the 8th. inst. 1 limber will proceed to the RAVINE to bring away No.2 Section's guns etc. It will then call at Coy. H.Q. and proceed thence to CAMPAGNE, via HUMBERCAMP.

13. Gun boots will be handed over. They must be washed.
    No. 3 Section will provide boots for the Section relieving S 1 Subsector on the 7th.inst.
    No 1 Section will hand over boots in the Divisional Line.
    Nos. 2 and 4 Section will wash their boots on being relieved and hand them in at Company H.Q.

14. Belt boxes will be handed over, as also will all sketches, range cards, and indirect fire targets. Receipts will be obtained and as much information as possible will be given.

15. Great care must be taken that all equipment and spare parts are brought out.

16. 2nd.Lts. Soldero and Roberts will remain in the Line for 24 hours after their sections have been relieved.

                                                 Captain.
                         Commanding, 50th. MACHINE GUN COMPANY.

Copy No.1. Retained.
"   No.2. No.1 Section.
"   No.3. No.2 Section.
"   No.4. No.3 Section.
"   No.5. No.4 Section.
"   No.6. Transport Officer.
"   No.7. War Diary.
"   No.8.
"   No.9. Reserved.

Vol 2

WAR DIARY.

of the 89th MACHINE GUN COMPANY — M.G.C.

For the Month of FEBRUARY.

Volume XII

SECRET

Secret.

> 89th COMPANY,
> MACHINE GUN
> CORPS.
> No. V.G.a.500
> Date. 2.3.17.

Headquarters,

    89th Infantry Brigade.

        Herewith Volume XII for FEBRUARY 1917 + Appendix XI of the War Diary of this Unit for necessary action, please. Kindly acknowledge receipt.

          J. H. Roxburgh.
              Captain

Comdg. 89 COY. MACHINE GUN CORPS.

Army Form C. 2118.

WAR DIARY
of 89TH MACHINE GUN COMPANY
MACHINE GUN CORPS

Volume XII

for FEBRUARY 1917.

(Erase heading not required.)

Instructions regarding War Diaries and Intelligence Summaries are contained in F.S. Regs., Part II. and the Staff Manual respectively. Title pages will be prepared in manuscript.

Place	Date	Hour	Summary of Events and Information	Remarks and references to Appendices
			Reference Maps:- Sheet 57 D-NW 1/20,000	LENS. Sheet 11.
				Trench Map. - NEUVILLE VITASSE 51B S.W. 1 - 1/10,000
				LENS Sheet 11.
				Trench Map. G Sector. APPENDIX XI
CAUMESNIL			89 M.G. Coy in billets in CAUMESNIL - J.H.R. Sheet 57d NW.	
BAQUE 48	1.2.17			
WARLUZEL	3.2.17	2 p.m.	Left CAUMESNIL and marched to billets in WARLUZEL - J.H.R.	
	4.2.17	1 p.m.	Left WARLUZEL and marched to billets in MONCHIET. J.H.R.	
MONCHIET	5.2.17	1 p.m.	Nos. 2+4 Sections left MONCHIET + marched to billets in AGNY. J.H.R.	
		2 p.m.	Nos. 1+3 Sections + Coy HQ marched to billets in BEAUMETZ. J.H.R.	
BEAUMETZ	6.2.17		Transport + Q.M. Stores remained in MONCHIET - J.H.R.	
			Reinforcements 1st A.C. McPHERSON + 2.O.R. J.H.R.	
			G Sector to night of AGNY reconnoitred J.H.R.	
	7.2.17		Nos 2+4 Sections relieved gun teams of 42nd M.G.Coy in gun positions in G Sector Sheet 51B S.W.	
			from M15 a 3.1 to M19 b 9.5. Relief completed 1.30 p.m. J.H.R.	
			Coy HQ moved to M6 L 8.5. J.H.R.	
M6L8.5.			Disposition of guns as follows:-	
			Left Section (No 4)	1 gun at V7 (GOAT POST) - M.14 + 55.65 - firing S.S.W.
				1 gun at V6 (RESERVE LINE) - M.14 a. 8.1 - " S.S.E.
				1 gun at V5 (") - M.14 c 39.90 " S.W.
				1 gun at V12 (AGNY DEFENCES) - M 8d 30.35 " S.W.
			Right Section (No 2)	1 gun at V1 (SUPPORT LINE) - M.14.C. 40.15 " E. across No Man's Land.
				1 gun at V4 (RESERVE LINE) - M 13 d 56.28 - " S.E.
				1 gun at V11 (MILL POST) - M.7 c 32.15. " S.W.
				1 gun at Section HQ. in reserve at M13 c 0.7. J.H.R.
			Enemy guns fairly active during the night on roads in + around AGNY - J.H.Q	

WAR DIARY

of 89TH MACHINE GUN COMPANY MACHINE GUN CORPS.

Vol XII for February 1917 p.2.

Army Form C. 2118.

Place	Date	Hour	Summary of Events and Information	Remarks and references to Appendices
Mqt 8.5	8.2.17		Quiet day – Enemy guns again active during the night. IHR	
" "	9.2.17		Gun in reserve at right Section H.Q. moved to V11 (Mill Post), as a 2nd gun. IHR	
" "	10.2.17		3 more gun positions in AGNY defences taken over from 21st M.G. Coy. For this No 1 Section were brought up. They also took over V12 position & the team of No 4 Section thereby displaced remained in reserve as a working party at M 8 d 40.35. Dispositions now as follows.	

			Left Section. 1 gun at V 6 Right Section. 1 gun at V 1
			              1 gun at V 6 1 gun at V 4
			              1 gun at V 5 2 guns at V 11
			 1 team in reserve as above.	

			Section in AGNY Defences. (No 1.) 1 gun at V 12 – M 8 d 30.35 firing S.W. 1 gun at V 13 – M 8 d 72.25 " S.S.W. 1 gun at V 14 – M 9 c 37.73 " S.E. 1 gun at V 15 – M 9 a 34.26 " N.E. IHR	
" "	10.2.17	6 p.m.	Between 6 & 7 p.m. 3 of our guns at M 14 b 55.82, M 14 b 62.72 & R 18 c 96.66. (Trench Hole FICHEUX) fired 3,000 rounds at intervals on Sunken Road (M 21 c 8.6 to M 21 c 4.1), Trenches (M 21 c 3.5 to M 21 d 00.25) & Dump at M 21 c 71.58. Previous to opening fire enemy transport had been heard. Enemy replied with 2 guns, one from BEAURAINS & one from M 20 c. IHR	
" "	11.2.17		Enemy machine guns active during the morning at our aeroplanes. Sectional relief	

WAR DIARY

of 89th MACHINE GUN COMPANY

~~INTELLIGENCE SUMMARY~~ MACHINE GUN CORPS.

Army Form C. 2118.

Vol XII
for February 1917
p.3.

Place	Date	Hour	Summary of Events and Information	Remarks and references to Appendices
M8 & S5	12.2.17		Carried out during afternoon & evening Brigade front extended to the left to Sap G16 (inclusive) J.H.R	
—	13.2.17		Quiet day - nothing to report - J.H.R Enemy machine guns quieter than usual during the night. J.H.R	
—	14.2.17		Quiet day. 3 searchlights used during night J.H.R Enemy machine guns active till 3.30 a.m. Normal day. Enemy machine guns active between 7.30 & 9.30 p.m. firing over GOAT POST, RESERVE LINE, SUNKEN ROAD and AGNY. J.H.R. Enemy used 2 searchlights at intervals during the night. J.H.R	
—	15.2.17		Normal day - usual machine gun activity at night. J.H.R	
—	16.2.17		2 enemy observation balloons up. Enemy machine guns active from 7.30 to 11.30 p.m. firing over GOAT POST and RESERVE LINE. J.H.R	
—	17.2.17		Normal day. Sectional relief carried out during afternoon & evening J.H.R	
—	18.2.17		Enemy Trench Mortars active during the day. Enemy machine guns slightly active around AGNY during night. J.H.R	
—	19.2.17		Quiet day & night J.H.R 2.O.R. reinforcements J.H.R	
—	20.2.17		Enemy M.G suspected at M16a.5.6. Quiet night J.H.R 4 shells fell in the vicinity of gun at M14C 40.15.	
—	21.2.17	4 pm	Gun at M13 d 56.18 fired 50 rounds registering on No Man's Land at the end of GAME	
		6.15 pm	STREET. Shots fell short. J.H.R	
—	22.2.17	6.15 pm	Normal. V4 gun again registered - Result very satisfactory. J.H.R Between 5.45 & 7 p.m. a considerable number of enemy shells again fell in the vicinity of V1 gun. There are some Trench Mortars behind it. J.H.R Sectional relief carried out in afternoon & evening. In accordance with instructions received the Section coming into reserve remained in billets in AGNY & did not move to BEAUMETZ — J.H.R	

Army Form C. 2118.

WAR DIARY
of 89TH MACHINE GUN COMPANY.
~~INTELLIGENCE SUMMARY~~ MACHINE GUN CORPS.

Volume XII
for FEBRUARY. 1917.

(Erase heading not required.)

Place	Date	Hour	Summary of Events and Information	Remarks and references to Appendices
M & G 8.5	23.2.17		Quiet day & night. J.H.R.	
—	24.2.17		The reserve section moved to SAULTY to attend course at Divisional Infantry School. J.H.R. At 9.30 p.m. and 11.30 p.m. the enemy fired several rifle grenades on our front line at the head of GAME STREET. J.H.R.	
—	25.2.17		Enemy machine guns active during the night. J.H.R.	
—	26.2.17		Enemy machine guns again active during the night, particularly at 11.15 p.m. J.H.R.	
—	27.2.17		Quiet day. Nothing to report. J.H.R.	
—	28.2.17		1000 rounds fired at enemy aircraft during the morning + 1550 rounds during the afternoon. 1 enemy plane flying low across our lines was turned back. J.H.R. Quiet day — 4 O.R. reinforcements. J.H.R.	

J.H.Roxburgh Captain
Comdg 89 Machine Gun Company
Machine Gun Corps.

SECRET

Y/13

WAR DIARY

of the 49th Coy. Machine Gun Corps.

for the month of MARCH 1917.

VOLUME XIII.

Army Form C. 2118.

WAR DIARY
of 89th MACHINE GUN COMPANY -
MACHINE GUN CORPS.

Intelligence Summary (Erase heading not required.)

Volume XIII for MARCH 1917

p.1.

Place	Date	Hour	Summary of Events and Information	Remarks and references to Appendices
AGNY - M.8.b.8.5.	1.3.17.		89 M.G. Coy in the line in G Sector on the night of AGNY. Dispositions as in Volume XII for February 1917. JHR	REFERENCE MAPS:- LENS - Sheet 11 Trench Map - NEUVILLE VITASSE - 51 B S.W.11 - 1 - G Sector - Appendix XI 10 Vol XII — BOISLEUX, 51 B S.W. 3. — 51 B S.W. — 51 C S.E. 10,000. 5,000.
		1.15 a.m.	The enemy fired several sharp bursts from his machine guns. Otherwise quiet. JHR	
	2.3.17		Normal day. Quiet night. JHR	
	3.3.17		Very quiet. JHR	
	4.3.17		From 3.50 a.m. to 4.10 a.m. the enemy bombarded our Front & Support lines between GEM STREET and GATE STREET with Trench Mortar and light Howitzer shells. Gun at V4 position fired 250 rounds at intervals on to No Man's land at the dt of GAME STREET. One shell burst in the entrance to the dug out of V1 position - Casualties 3 O.R. JHR	
		5.15 p.m	Gun at V4 position fired 500 rounds at an enemy aeroplane when fired on, it planed down suddenly behind the German Front line, apparently hit. JHR	
	5.3.17		Nothing to report. JHR	
	6.3.17		Gun at V7 (MILL POST) fired 200 rounds, & gun at V4 fired 250 rounds at enemy aircraft. JHR	
			Between 6 & 7 p.m. two guns fired 3,000 rounds on enemy track from M21 b13 to H28 a o 6. JHR	
	7.3.17		Quiet day. JHR	
	8.3.17		Nothing to report. JHR	
	9.3.17		Quiet day. JHR	
	10.3.17		Nothing to report. JHR	

Army Form C. 2118.

WAR DIARY
of 89th MACHINE GUN COMPANY
~~INTELLIGENCE SUMMARY~~
MACHINE GUN CORPS.

Volume XIII for MARCH 1917.
p. 2.

(Erase heading not required.)

Place	Date	Hour	Summary of Events and Information	Remarks and references to Appendices
M & G. S.	11.3.17		1,100 rounds were fired during the afternoon at enemy aircraft. JHR	
—	12.3.17		Between 6 & 7 P.M. gun at V7 (GOAT POST) fired 250 rounds registering on enemy Saps Y4, Y5, & Y6. The results, as observed from one of our Saps, were very satisfactory. JHR Enemy machine guns particularly active between 6 PM & 8 PM on the left Subsector. JHR	JHR
—	13.3.17		Quiet day. JHR	HEM
—	14.3.17		Quiet day. Nothing to report. 4 I.B. ell. 39 rds fired at hostile aircraft during afternoon.	HEM
—	15.3.17			
—	16.3.17		No 3 Section relieved guns of 31st M.G. Coy in positions on the left of G. Sector. Disposition of guns as follows:— 1 gun at V2 – M9d 50.29. 1 gun at V2a – M9d 55.26. 1 gun at V9 – M9d 38.79. 1 gun at V8 – M9c 08.01.	Capt. T.A. ROXBURGH to Hospital Sick. Lieut. H.E. MIDDLETON assumed Command of Coy. JHR
		12 NOON.	Relief completed by 12 NOON. Enemy machine guns were active during very heavy bombardment last night while a raid by the 18th Bn. Liverpool Regt. was in progress on our left. Our Machine guns fired between 2.50 a.m & 4 a.m as follows:— (1) at T18 C 9.6.6 fired 1,000 rounds on the LAUENBURG REDOUBT. HEM (2) at M13 A 99.49 " 1,000 " " TREUTLEIN WEG. HEM	HEM
	17.3.17		Quiet day; reflection, or flare fires, could be seen behind the enemy lines after each. Between 3 & 4 PM 1 gun at M13 A 56.38 fired 750 rds indirect on to the light railway from M 20 C 95.75 to M 20 C 40.33. HEM	HEM
—	18.3.17		Information received at 8.30 a.m from Brigade Major that enemy had evacuated his trenches in front of us and Owing to the Lilac model's received immediately north from Machine Gun battalion a/cs 28 B/Gaz K.L.R., 2nd Beds and 19th K.L.R. HEM	HEM

Volume XIII for 89th MACHINE GUN COMPANY
WAR DIARY
or
INTELLIGENCE SUMMARY

Army Form C. 2118.

MARCH 1917   MACHINE GUN CORPS.
p. 3.

Place	Date	Hour	Summary of Events and Information	Remarks and references to Appendices
M.9.f.6.5.	18.3.17	1.31pm	Message received from O.C., No. 4 Section, that he had 3 guns placed in MANSFIELD TRENCH from M.20.c.90.75 to M.15.a.15.10 + one gun in support line at M.15.d.30.15, with 3rd Beds.	W/ill
		2.50pm	Message received from O.C., No. 3 Section that 20th K.L.R. had reached SCHLANGAN REDOUBT - holding with a platoon advanced posts at MALABRY TRENCH and MADRAGUE TRENCH and in touch with 2nd Beds at MALPLAQUET TRENCH. Two guns up on this line with two guns in reserve at M.21.b.0.3.	W/ill
		4.55pm	Message received from O.C., No. 1 Section; 19th K.L.R. line ran from M.20.d.9.4 (in HAASMANN WEG) to M.20.d.5.0, with right flank open, owing to Brigade on right not having come up. 3 guns defending this flank from approximately:—	W/ill
			1/ M.20.d.5.0 ⎫	
			2/ M.20.d.2.3 ⎬ all firing towards	
			3/ M.20.c.9.7 ⎭ MALDON LANE.	W/ill
			The fourth gun in reserve at M.20.d.9.4 but probably being advanced during night on to embankment at M.21.c.6.3.	
		6.55pm	Message received from O.C., No. 3 Section that his two front line guns were in positions as last reported. The reserve guns had moved to approximately M.22.a.35.50, the other having been sent up to reinforce the front line. The enemy had been located in small numbers in MERCATE L and the 20th K.L.R. had pushed forward a strong patrol into the village to reconnoitre.	W/ill
		7h.m	Message received from O.C., No. 4 Section from M.21.a.65.65 that he was moving his guns	
			One into LAUENBERG REDOUBT.	
			One " MALPLAQUET TRENCH.	
			One " MADELINE REDOUBT.	
			One " GABEL TRENCH.	W/ill
		8.45pm	Message received from O.F., No. 1 Section that his guns with 2nd Beds were still in the positions previously reported.	

Army Form C. 2118.

WAR DIARY of 89th MACHINE GUN COMPANY

Volume VIII for MARCH - 1917

~~INTELLIGENCE SUMMARY~~
MACHINE GUN CORPS.

(Erase heading not required.)

Instructions regarding War Diaries and Intelligence Summaries are contained in F. S. Regs., Part II. and the Staff Manual respectively. Title pages will be prepared in manuscript.

Place	Date	Hour	Summary of Events and Information	Remarks and references to Appendices
M.6.2.6.5	18.3.17	9.15 pm	Message received from O.C. No. 3 Section that his reserve gun was digging in at M.15.d.9.3. Rations for No. 3 Section were sent to V.3 & carrying sheds by H.Q. Rations from the Section carried them up from there. Rations for 1, 2, & 4 Sections were sent to the H.Q. in A & W personnel & drawn there. Water for 1, 3 & 4 Section was sent up in Petrol Tins viz. 5 tins per Section.	HBW
"	19.3.17	0.45 am	Message received from O.C. No. 3 Section that his reserve gun was mounted at M.28.a.5.7	HBW
		4.15 pm	His front line guns were in position as follows:—	
			One at M.30.c.3.0	
			One at M.30.c.30.70	
			One at M.29.b.80.30	HBW
		4.25 pm	Message received from O.C. No. 1 Section that his guns had advanced as follows:—	
			One to M.36.c.8.7.	
			One to M.36.a.5.3.	
			One to M.36.a.4.6.	
			One to M.30.c.2.2.	HBW
		6.0 pm	Report sent in to Bde. H.Q. that guns of No. 1 & No. 3 Sections were in position as above & guns of No. 4 Section as follows:—	
			One at M.21.d.0.5	
			One at M.27.a.7.1	
			One at M.35.a.2.6	HBW
			One at M.35.b.0.4.	
			Orders received from Brigade H.Q. to withdraw these guns from 2nd Bedo, and the following returned into Coy Reserve:—	
			One gun from M.21.d.0.3.	
			One gun from M.27.a.7.1.	
			One gun from M.35.b.0.4.	HBW

WAR DIARY of 89th MACHINE GUN COMPANY

INTELLIGENCE SUMMARY

Volume VIII
MARCH – 1917
p.5

MACHINE GUN CORPS.

Army Form C. 2118.

Place	Date	Hour	Summary of Events and Information	Remarks and references to Appendices
M.G.C. 5.	19.3.17	10.p.m	Orders received that 19th K.L.R. moved take over the front held by a Batt: of 175th Inf: Bde from right flank of 2nd Bde about M36 A.9.9 along SUNKEN ROAD to about T7 A.9.9 on far side of COJEUL River. O.C. N°2 Section at once got in touch with C.O. 19th K.L.R. and received orders from him to move forward at 6.30 a.m. for this purpose. Arranged for four pack mules to transport at 4.30 a.m. at 89 H.Q. for this purpose. Rations to alter to and up to N°s 1,3,+4 Sections as on previous night. C.O. went forward and visited the Gun teams of N°s 1 and 4 Sections during the day. Message received from O.C. N°3 Section with 20th K.L.R. that he had two Guns in position in reserve line :-	HgM
"	20.3.17	8.25 a.m	One Gun on right flank at M25 c 4.8 and One Gun on left flank at M3 a 4.7.	HgM
		2.a.m	2 a.m. H.G. FAULKNER 1/c N°1 Section wounded in left wrist about 6.0 a.m. & sent to C.C.S. Message received from O.C. N°3 Section that he had had a mule Gun knocked out. Casualty 3 killed and 3 wounded, and asking for another team to take his place. Sent up a team from Reserve three Guns be in action.	HgM
		3.p.m	Message received from O.C. N°2 Section with 19th K.L.R, who went forward at 5 a.m. that he had two Guns in position in front line :-	HgM
			One Gun at M36 a 6.0 and One Gun at 9 b h 7.4.	
		7.p.m	Message received from 2nd Lt W.G. BOLDERO, who took over N°1 Section with 2nd Bedes on 2nd Lt. H.G. FAULKNER, that he had found all covered. His guns were in position along the forward edge of the BEURAINS–BUCQUOY ROAD at approximately.	HgM
			One Gun at M30 c 3.1. One Gun at M36 a 4.9. One Gun at M36 a 6.4. One Gun at M36 a 7.0.	HgM

Army Form C. 2118.

WAR DIARY of 89th Coy

Volume XIII

INTELLIGENCE SUMMARY MACHINE GUN CORPS.

(Erase heading not required.)

Instructions regarding War Diaries and Intelligence Summaries are contained in F. S. Regs., Part II. and the Staff Manual respectively. Title pages will be prepared in manuscript.

MARCH – 1917
h.b.

Place	Date	Hour	Summary of Events and Information	Remarks and references to Appendices
M6b.B.5	20.3.17	7p.m	One Gun of No 4 Section remaining with 3rd Bede was in position at M 35 a 9.6.	H.B.M.
		4pm	Message received from O.C., No 3 Section (giving details of his casualties totaling two guns were in position as follows:-	
			One Gun at M 29 b . 9.2	
			One Gun at M 30 a . 2.8. and	H.B.M.
		...	Two Guns in reserve, August out at M 23 c . 4.9.	
			Message received from O.C., No 2 Section, with 19th K.L.R. that he was in touch with a M.G.O. of 197-Coy M.G.C. on his right, in BOIRY=BECQUERELLE.	H.B.M.
			Two Guns was in position at M 36 c. 9.6. co-operating with night gun of No 1 Section + the left gun was in position at M 36 c. 9.6. co-operating with night gun of No 1 Section + about 30 yards southward of it.	H.B.M.
			Shot Rations, Water, Gun & ammunition up by Pack mules for Nos 1, 2 + 3 Sections of the team of No 1 Section to M 29 d 30.65 (bench mark 76.25) where they were met by ration parties forward. Gun at 7.0 p.m.	H.B.M.
	21.3.17	6.30am	No 4 Section have been relieved during the night by Section from 90th M.G. Coy. and reported their return to Coy H.Q. all correct by 6.0 a.m. Team of No 4 Section also withdrawn and reported at Coy H.Q. all correct by 7.0 a.m.	H.B.M.
		10.0am	Message received from O.C., No 3 Section that his guns had moved forward as follows:-	
			One Gun to M 29 b . B.9. }	
			One Gun to M 35 d 70.65. } Front line	
			One Gun to M 23 c. 4.2. }	
			One Gun to M 29 a. 4.0 } Reserve line.	H.B.M.
		N∞N	Message received from O.C. No 2 Section that he had had 2.O.R. killed by shell	H.B.M.
			Sent forward and visited No 2 & 3 Sections in MERCATEL & BOIRY during the day	H.B.M.
			1 O.R. Reinforcement re-joined from C.C.S. H.B.M. No rations or water sent up.	H.B.M.

WAR DIARY of 89th MACHINE GUN COMPANY.

INTELLIGENCE SUMMARY MACHINE GUN CORPS.

Volume VIII
MARCH - 1917
P.7.

Army Form C. 2118.

Place	Date	Hour	Summary of Events and Information	Remarks and references to Appendices
M.G.C. E.5	21.3.17	3.35 p.m.	Message received from O.C. No 2 Section that his right gun at 36d 8.4 fired 500 rds on the SUNKEN ROADS S.E. of HENIN in T 2 a, about 6.0 a.m.	H.B.M.
		10.30 p.m.	Two Section from 90th M.G. Coy moved up to relieve Nos 2+3 Sections in the line.	H.B.M.
	22.3.17	4.45 a.m.	Wired Brigade H.B. that over relief by 90th M.G. Coy was completed and that guns + teams had reported back to Coy H.B (all correct, Guns, Tripods, ammunition etc., were carried out by limbered wagon from M 26d 30.65 hand mark 76.25) gun positions finally handed over to 90th M.G. Coy guns as follows:-	H.B.M.
			No 3 Section on left :- M 23 a. 4.0. M 23 c. 4.2. M 23 d. 40.65. M 29 b. 8.9.	
			No 1 Section in centre :- M 30 c. 3.1. M 36 a. 4.9. M 36 a. 6.4. M 36 a. 7.0.	
			No 2 Section on right :- M 36 c. 9.6. S. 6 d. 7.4. M 35 c. 20.25 (two guns in reserve)	H.B.M.
		5 p.m.	Sections (4) moved off to Billets at LE FERMONT.	H.B.M.
		6.30 p.m.	Coy H.B. closed at A.G.N. and moved with transport to LE FERMONT.	H.B.M.
		7 p.m.	Coy arrived in Billets at LE FERMONT. H.B., at Billet No 63	H.B.M.
LE FERMONT	23.3.17		In Billets resting, at LE FERMONT. 2.O.R. reinforcements arrived	H.B.M.

Army Form C. 2118.

WAR DIARY
of 89th MACHINE GUN COMPANY,
INTELLIGENCE SUMMARY.
MACHINE GUN CORPS.

(Erase heading not required.)

Volume VIII

Instructions regarding War Diaries and Intelligence MARCH-1917
Summaries are contained in F. S. Regs., Part II.
and the Staff Manual respectively. Title pages
will be prepared in manuscript.   M.B.

Place	Date	Hour	Summary of Events and Information	Remarks and references to Appendices
FERMONT	24.3.17		The Company moved off at 11.0 a.m. to Billets at BASSEUX. Transport following independently owing to having several journeys backwards & forwards, no lorry being available. HCM	
	25.3.17		Arrived at BASSEUX - 12 NOON. Company Billeted in WHITE CHATEAU. Company H.Q., at Billet No. 27 B. HCM	
	26.3.17		In Billets BASSEUX. Company H.Q. moved to Billet No. 57. HCM	
	27.3.17		In Billets BASSEUX. HCM	
	28.3.17		" HCM	
	29.3.17		The Company & Transport moved off at 10.50 a.m. to Billets at BAILLEULMONT. HCM Arrived in Billets at BAILLEULMONT at 12.45 p.m. H.Q. Billet No. 57. HCM	
	31.3.17		A.O.R. reinforcements arrived from M.G.C. Base Depot, CAMIERS. HCM	

H.E. Middleton, Lieut.
Commanding 89 COY. MACHINE GUN CORPS.

Vol 14

War Diary

of

89th Machine Gun Company

For the month of April, 1917

Volume XIV

SECRET

Army Form C. 2118.

WAR DIARY

Volume XIV for of 89th Company
INTELLIGENCE SUMMARY MACHINE GUN CORPS.

APRIL 1917.

No. 1.

Place	Date	Hour	Summary of Events and Information	Remarks and references to Appendices
BAILLEULMONT	1.4.17		89th M.G. Coy in rest Billets in BAILLEULMONT. **REFERENCE MAPS:-** LENS - Sheet 11. - 1/100,000. Trench Map - 51C S.E. - 1/20,000. — " 51B S.W. - 1/20,000. — " 57D N.E. - 1/20,000.	
"	2.4.17		Captain J.H. ROXBURGH returned from Hospital & resumed command of the Company. 2nd Lieut. G.H. WOOD 6th Lancashire Fusiliers (T.F.) seconded M.G.C., joined the Company from M.G.C. Base depôt CAMIERS, & was posted to No.1 Section as subsection officer. 2nd LIEUT. H.G. FAULKNER re-joined the Company from C.C.S., and resumed command of No.1 Section.	
"	3.4.17		Captain J.H. ROXBURGH returned to Hospital - Sick - and LIEUT. H.E. MIDDLETON again assumed command of the Company.	
"	4.4.17	19.0 midnight	Warning order received from 89th Bde that the Company would relieve the 90th M.G. Coy in the line on the night of the 5/6 instant.	
"	5.4.17		O.C. and 4 Section Commanders proceeded at 9.15 a.m. to H.B., 90th Bde in Railway cutting at S3.C.84 to reconnoitre line. Met there at 11.15 a.m. by O.C., 90th M.G. Coy & made all the necessary arrangements to relieve his Company in the following positions the same night. Guides to be at M27.c.8.8 at 4 p.m., N.C.- 1 Gun (called HENIN Post N°5) at N.32.C.45.30. 1 Gun (" HENIN Post N°3) at T.2.1.45.26. 1 Gun (" WATKINS Gun N°1) at T.1.d.1.5. 1 Gun (" WATKINS Gun N°2) at N.31.d.40.45. 1 Gun (on Railway embankment) at S.3.a.9.6. 1 Gun (") at S.3.c.9.4. 4 Gun Teams & guides to be at M.29.c.14.80. at 7.30 p.m. & arrived in BAILLEULMONT at 2.15 p.m., & made necessary arrangements for relief. At 4 p.m., N°1 Section and N°1 & 4 teams of N°4 Section, with Pack mules carrying Guns, Tripods, Spare Parts, Ammunition, Rations, &c after the relief, turned off under 2nd Lt. G.H. WOOD. The above Section & teams arrived back in BAILLEULMONT, in omnibuses received from H.Q. 90th Brigade, 11.15 pm the relief having been perfected for 4 hours.	

Army Form C. 2118.

WAR DIARY

Volume XIV for 89th Company

INTELLIGENCE SUMMARY

of 89th Company MACHINE GUN CORPS.

APRIL 1917

(Erase heading not required.)

Title pages W.9.

Place	Date	Hour	Summary of Events and Information	Remarks and references to Appendices
BAILLEULMONT	6.4.17	4.15 p.m.	No. 1 Section and No. 2 14 teams of No. 4 Section moved off under 2nd Lt G.H.WOOD to relieve the 6 guns of the 90th M.G.Cy as detailed on pages. Guns, tripods, ammunition &c, conveyed by G.S. Limbered Wagon.	W.9.III
		11.30 p.m.	19 iced G.S.Brigade relief of 90th M.G.Cy completed and reported positions of the six guns.	W.9.III
BLAIREVILLE	7.4.17	2 p.m.	Gun at T.9.b.65.26 moved to N.33.c.20.13	W.9.III
		4 p.m.	Arrived in BLAIREVILLE and bivouaced there.	W.9.III
			Nos 2 & 3 Sections and No 2 14 teams of No 4 Section, with Limbers, moved off to bivouac positions in Lindon Road in squares S & C and S.10.a where they remained for 24 hours. Bdy H.Q. remained at BLAIREVILLE.	W.9.III
	8.4.17	12.15 a.m.	Orders received from Brigade H.Q. to move Guns at T.1.b.15 to cross roads N.32.b.7.7 forthwith and report to O.C. "B" Coy 2nd/6th Beds & Herts Regt at that point. Move completed at 4.0 a.m. reported to Bde.	W.9.III
		10 a.m.	Wired Ldn Officer in position and received orders to move to BOIRY-BECQUERELLE with transport Officer in connection with the formation of an advanced dump. Decided on a position at S.12.b.8.7.	W.9.III
S.12.b.8.7		7 p.m.	Moved Bdy H.Q. forward to advanced dug-out at S.4.c.80.15 and reported personally at Bde H.Q. 5.3.c.8.4.	W.9.III
		6 p.m.	No. 16 Platoon 17.O.R. K.L.R. reported. In Bivouacs and was distributed between Sections, who then moved off to their assembly positions as follows :-	
			No. 3 Section in trench ahead M.36.c.8.7.	
			No. 2 Section with 19th OR K.L.R. at T.1.a.10.15. (2 guns).	
			No. 2 Section with 2nd OR Beds at S.11.2.4.7 (2 guns).	
			No. 4 Section " 20th OR K.L.R. at S.6.b.9.1 (2 guns).	
			No. 4 Section " 2.O.R. reinforcements from M.G. Base Depot CAMIERS.	W.9.III
			Dump formed at S.12.b.8.7.	
			Bde known for 89th Bde advance. 5.30 a.m. plus 9 hrs 36 mins	
		4 p.m.	Report received from O.C. No. 3 Section that he had captured two German prisoners in a dug-out at N.32.a.20.99 who were sent under escort to 89 Brigade H.Q.	W.9.III
		5.25 p.m.	Report received from O/c 2nd gun No 2 Section with 2nd Beds that he was still at S.11.b.4.7 with his guns at S.12.b.8.7 (Dunny).	W.9.III
			Two guns of No 4 Section with 2nd Beds at N.27.c.1/4 and N.33.d.30.95 opened cross fire on German trench system in square N.27.d and N.33.c at 2 p.m. plus 9 hrs 36 mins in accordance with Co. No. 2 orders at the jumping day.	W.9.III
		9.30 p.m.	Report received from O.C. No. 3 Section with 19th K.L.R. that he was in position at N.33.d.45.90 + had fired	W.9.III

Army Form C. 2118.

WAR DIARY

Volume XIV of 89th Company

INTELLIGENCE SUMMARY. — MACHINE GUN CORPS.

APRIL 1917.

p. 3.

(Erase heading not required.)

Instructions regarding War Diaries and Intelligence Summaries are contained in F.S. Regs., Part II. and the Staff Manual respectively. Title pages will be prepared in manuscript.

Place	Date	Hour	Summary of Events and Information	Remarks and references to Appendices
S 4 C 80.15	9.4.17	2.30 pm	Report received from O.C. No 1 Section holding HENIN, that in accordance with orders issued on 8th instant, his Guns at N 32 d 5.6 fired 1,250 rounds flanking fire on to the German trench system in squares N 34 b + d, to support the advance of the 2nd Division on our right. HGM. Following casualties reported - LIEUT A. McPHERSON and 2nd LT L.H.G. FAULKNER slightly wounded and remaining at duty. (3 O.R. killed, 4 O.R. wounded. 1 O.R. (Barries) killed and 2 O.R (Gabriel) wounded.) HGM.	
"	"	2.30 pm	Report received from O.C. No 2 Section that his guns were in position from a point N 26 c 4.2 to N 26 c 4.5 and that in accordance with orders previously issued he fired 1,260 rounds flanking fire on to the HINDENBURG LINE, covering the advance of the 89th Brigade. HGM.	
"	"	11.45 pm	Report received from O/C No 2 Section with 2nd Bedfordshire Regt. that he was under orders to move with his two Vickers guns to HENIN and adjust these to O.C. "C" Company HGM.	
"	9.4.17	10.30 am	Message received from 89th Brigade H.Q. that our line was being withdrawn as follows:- N 34.C.C.7. - N 34 c 5.10. and to SUNKEN ROAD N 33 c and T 31 by 19th K.L.R. 2nd K.L.R. withdrawing to N 27 c 35. 6.5 to N 27 c 2.1 and N 26 d 9.0 to N 33 a 2.6. 17th K.L.R. concentrating in road from T.1.a 3.2 another 2.0 to 2nd Bedfordshire Regiment not to move. HGM.	
"	"	11.30 am	Message received from O.C. 2nd Bedfords Regt. that his H.Q. was moving to T.1.a 15.20. HGM.	
"	"	11.30 am	Sent reports to H.Q. 89th Brigade as to position of guns & and asked for further orders as to the employment of No 3 (left) Section. HGM.	
"	"	12.15 am	Sent orders to O.C. No 3 Section to move his guns into such positions as would enable them to cover our front against enemy counter-attack. HGM.	
"	10.4.17	1.50 am	Message received from H.Q. 89th Brigade that a bombardment would start at daylight. HGM.	
"	"	8.0 am	Report received from O.C. No 2 Section that his guns at N 33 b 2.7 and N 33 d 30.95 covered with the advance of the 19th K.L.R. referred to above, during the night, and at 3.30 a.m. had in conformity with them withdrawn his M.G. positions at N 33 c 35.45 and N 33 c 9.2 respectively. HGM.	
"	"	12.30 pm	Message received from O.C. No 3 Section that in accordance with orders issued early in the morning he had moved his 4 Guns to positions as follows:-	

1 Gun to N 26 c 4.3
1 Gun to N 32 a 2.7.4
1 Gun to N 32 a 8.7.4
1 Gun to N 32 c 90.99
1 Gun at N 26 c 2.2   HGM.

with Section H.Q.

A5834 Wt. W4973/M687 750,000 8/16 D. D. & L. Ltd. Forms/C.2118/13.

WAR DIARY

Army Form C. 2118.

Volume XIV. of 89th Company

INTELLIGENCE SUMMARY MACHINE GUN CORPS.

April - 1917

p. 4

Place	Date	Hour	Summary of Events and Information	Remarks and references to Appendices
S.4.c.80.15	10.4.17	12.30 p.m.	From these positions a clear view of the whole of our front could be obtained and the guns could reach all the high ground in front. H.M.	
		5.30 p.m.	Report received from O/C 2 guns N°2 Section with 2nd Bedk Regt. that he had posted one gun in the NAGPUR TRENCH at approximately N.32.d. & 5.60. to fire on aprare N.26 in case of a counter attack. The other gun remaining in reserve at Bn. H.Q., at approximately N.32.c.4.3. He further reported having left in touch with O/C 2 guns N°4 Section with 2nd Bedk Regt whose guns were at approximately N.26.d.9.2. and N.33.d.9.5.9.5. H.M.	
		5.30 p.m.	Report received from O.C. N°1 Section that O/C 2 guns N°4 Section with 2nd Bedk Regt. had his guns at approximately N.27.c.2.5. and N.33.d.3.9. H.M.	
S.12 & 8.7	10.4.17	5.40 p.m.	Orders received from Brigade H.Q., to move Company H.B. forward to HENIN. Did so forthwith. H.M.	
		7.05 p.m.	Arrived at Bn. Dump and made arrangements for moving it forward nearer to HENIN. H.M.	
			Report received from O/C 2 guns N°4 Section with 2nd Bedk Regt. that he was with one of his guns at N.27.c.1.4. 1 O.R. wounded slightly during the morning. H.M. Right gun at N.27.c.65.125. H.M.	
			Report received from O.C. N°3 Section that the guns at N.36 & 2.7 and N.32.c.90.99 had moved to N.26.c.10.05 and N.33.d.10.12 respectively. H.M.	
N.32.c.5.3	10.4.17	10.30 p.m.	Arrived at H.Q. N°1 Section, HENIN, N.32.c.5.3 and established Coy H.Q. there. H.M.	
		9.0 p.m.	Proceeded to Brigade Advanced Report Centre & reported completion of move & position of new H.Q. H.M.	
	11.4.17	12.30 a.m.	Visited Dump at S.12 & 8.7 & found 1 O.R. collected by Brigade & sent N°6 material to unit — returned to unit.	
			arrangements as to his disposal and new him written instructions to H.Q. at BLAIREVILLE made. H.M.	
		2.30 a.m.	Got a gun to Coy H.B., N.32.c.5.3. H.M. Obtained copy of O.O. N°88 from B.A.R.C. en route. H.M.	
		3.15 a.m.	Proceeded to visit O.C. N°3 Section at Bn. H.B., N.26.c.2.2. with D.D.N°89 + remained till 4.30 a.m. H.M.	
		5.40 a.m.	Left Bn. H.B. and proceeded to reconnoitre position for forward Dump. Decided upon T1.a.9.4 approx. & returned to Dump S.12 & 8.7 to move instructions where to move forward to. H.M.	
		6.30 a.m.	Returned to Coy. H.Q., N.32.c.5.3. H.M.	
		10.15 a.m.	Proceeded with O.C. N°1 Section to visit his guns and also visited O.C., N° 2 Section at N.33.c. SUNKEN ROAD H.M.	
		12.30 p.m.	Orders received from Brigade for guns under HENIN to withdraw & proceed at 14K.L.R. to accrue flanks. O.C., 19th K.L.R. and ascertain his wishes. H.M.	
		2.30 p.m.	Section at once proceeded to get in touch with O.C., 19th K.L.R. to report to 19th K.L.R. H.M.	
			N°1 Section moved off from Coy H.B., to report to 19th K.L.R. H.M.	

Army Form C. 2118.

WAR DIARY
of 89th Company
Volume XIV.
INTELLIGENCE SUMMARY. MACHINE GUN CORPS
APRIL - 1917.
p. 5.

(Erase heading not required.)

Instructions regarding War Diaries and Intelligence Summaries are contained in F.S. Regs., Part II. and the Staff Manual respectively. Title pages will be prepared in manuscript.

Place	Date	Hour	Summary of Events and Information	Remarks and references to Appendices
N32 c 5.3.	10.4.17	12 NOON	Report received from O.C. No 4 Section that his left gun had moved to approximately N27 c 4.7. on the left flank of the front line of the 20th K.L.R., with the right gun at N27 c 6.25 as before.	H/W
		5 p.m.	Advanced of 69 Dump from 519 b. 8.7 to T1 a 9.4 completed.	H/W
		8 p.m.	Report received from O.C. No 1 Section that two guns were in position as follows:- 1 gun at T3 b.57 & 1 gun at T3 b.5.5 — in touch with No 2 Section & left 2 guns of 62nd M.G. Coy on right.	H/W
		11 p.m.	1 gun at N33 c 30.05 & 1 gun at T3 b 40.95, with Section H.Q. in a dug-out at N33 c 15.10. Reported positions of all guns by H.Q. and by Dumps to Brigade H.Q., as follows:- Gd gun each at N28 c 4.3 – N28 c 10.5 – N33 c 8.14 and N32 b. 10.12 with Section H.Q. N2 b c.2.2 (No 3 Section) H/W Two guns with 20th K.L.R. at N37 c 4.7 and N37 c 6.25 with Section H.Q., 2nd Redt at N27 d 1.4 and N33 d 3.9 (line) and (two in reserve) N32 c 9.5.80 – N2 a Section. Two guns north 19th K.L.R. at N33 c 6.5.45 and N33 c 9.2 (No 2 Section) and T3 b.37 – T3 b 5.5 – N33 c 30.05 and T3 a 40.95 (No 1 Section). H/W Section H.Q., remaining at N32 c 5.3. 69 Dump at T1a 9.4, approximately.	H/W
	12.4.17	12 NOON	Reported to Brigade H.Q. that guns had moved as follows:- 1 gun at N33 d 3.9 moved to N27 c 1.5 by orders of O.C. 2nd Redo Regt. 1 gun at N27 c 6.25 moved to N27 c 20.55. Two guns in reserve at N32 c 95.80 moved to N32 c 80.75.	H/W
		2.15 p.m.	Orders received for relief immediately by the 19th M.G. Coy, 33rd Division (89 Bde O.O. No 89)	H/W
		3.30 p.m.	Arranged for guides to be at crossroads (N32 c 9/7) as soon as possible.	H/W
		4.0 p.m.	O.C. 19th M.G. Coy arrived at Coy H.Q., discussed relief, proceeded with him to Road Junction T2 a 6/3, to meet his Company & ordered Guides to proceed there from N32 c 9/7.	H/W
		7 p.m.	Relief completed. Coy also sent 14 full belt boxes handed over.	H/W
		7.45 p.m.	Sections, in relief, marched back independently to Railway Crossing S3 c. concentrated there. Dump leaved to BLAIREVILLE.	H/W
S 3 c 2.2.		10.15 p.m.	All Sections having concentrated, Company moved off to billets in BLAIREVILLE.	H/W
BLAIREVILLE		11 p.m.	Arrived in billets at BLAIREVILLE and reported personnel at Brigade H.Q.	H/W
"	13.4.17	9.30 am	Company moved to billets at BASSEUX.	H/W
BASSEUX		12 NOON	Arrived in billets at BASSEUX. H.Q. at billet No 17 a.	H/W
"	14.4.17	7.15 am	Received orders from Brigade H.Q. 6 and 2 Sections to report to VII Corps Machine Gun officer for Anti-aircraft work at FOSSEUX and BEAUMETZ respectively. Detailed Nos 2 and 4 Sections, the former to FOSSEUX at 10 am. and BEAUMETZ at 11 am. respectively, complete with fighting Limbers	H/W

A 5834 Wt. W4973/M687 750,000 8/16 D.D. & L.Ltd. Forms/C.2118/13.

WAR DIARY
Volume XIV of 89th Company
INTELLIGENCE SUMMARY of MACHINE GUN CORPS
APRIL 1917

p. 6

Army Form C. 2118.

Place	Date	Hour	Summary of Events and Information	Remarks and references to Appendices
BASSEUX	14.4.17	12 NOON	Warning Order to move received from Brigade H.Q.	JHR
		3 p.m.	Orders received for move to COUIN at 4.30 p.m.	JHR
		4.30 p.m.	Company with transport moved off to COUIN.	JHR
COUIN	14.4.17	8 p.m.	Company arrived at DAINVILLE and billeted in empty field hospital on COUIN-SOUASTRE Road at North entrance to COUIN.	JHR
	16.4.17		Captain J.H. ROXBURGH returned from Field Ambulance and resumed command of the Company.	JHR
	18.4.17		10 O.R. reinforcements arrived. C.S.	JHR
	21.4.17		3 O.R. rejoined from C.C.S. 3 O.R. reinforcements arrived.	JHR
		7.15 p.m.	Coy paraded + moved off. Met busses at COUIN.	JHR
		9.30 p.m.	Busses moved off + went to DAINVILLE Sta. The Transport moved independently. Coy H.Q. and Coy marched on to ACHICOURT + billeted in dug outs in railway cutting. M.30.a.5.9.1.	JHR
ACHICOURT.	22.4.17		1 O.R. reinforcement arrived. 89th Bde was in reserve in the ACHICOURT–BEAURAINS area, the 90th Bde being in the line & the 21st in support in the NEUVILLE VITASSE area.	JHR
	23.4.17	8 p.m.	As the 21st Bde were moved up into the line, say 89th Bde moved into support in NEUVILLE VITASSE area. Coy left M.30.a.4.5.9.1 + marched to bivouac in N.20.a. The Transport was situated at M.11.d.6.8.	JHR
M.11.d.6.8.	24.4.17	10 a.m.		
		1 p.m.	Orders received to move to N.27.a. Coy H.Q. arrived at N.27.a. of N.27.a.4.7. Guns and ammunition were kept beside the men, and the limbers and animals sent back.	JHR
N.27.a.4.7.		5 p.m.	Rations arrived on pack mules.	JHR
		5.15 p.m.	Orders received to send 1 Section to cooperate with 17th K.L.R. and 1 Section with 20th K.L.R., who were in support and garrisoning the old German front line and the old British front line in N.30. & N.36.a.+c.	JHR
		5.25 p.m.	Nos 1 + 4 Sections moved off + reported at the respective Battalion H.Q.	JHR
		8.40 p.m.	Message received from O.C. No 1 Section that he had placed his guns	

Army Form C. 2118.

WAR DIARY

Vol XIV for 89th MACHINE GUN COMPANY
APRIL 1917   MACHINE GUN CORPS.
p.p.

(Erase heading not required.)

Place	Date	Hour	Summary of Events and Information	Remarks and references to Appendices
N27a 4.7	24.4.17		as follows:- 3 with the Support Companies at N30 c 9.7, N30 a 9.7, N30 c 4.2, + N30 c 8.6. 1 with the reserve company at N30 a 9.7. I.H.R.	
		10.40pm	Message received from O.C. No 4 Section that his guns were as follows:- 3 with the supports at N36 G 3.0, N36 G 4.6, + N30 d 5.2. 3 with the reserve at N35 G 4.7. I.H.R.	
		10.50pm	Reported these positions to Bde H.Q. I.H.R.	
	25.4.17	8.40am	O.C. No 1 Section reported that the gun at N30 c 9.7 had been moved to N30 d 4.7 after consultation with the Battalion commander, as there was a large number of Lewis guns on the left and there was more scope for Vickers guns on the right. I.H.R.	
		10.30am	Orders received that on the night of 25th/26th, 89th Bde would take over the front of the left Battalion of the 21st Bde, and that each of the two Brigades would find their own garrison for the front, support, + the reserve positions of their sectors. For this purpose 4 guns were required for the front line system and 4 for the support, the remaining 8 being in reserve at N27 a. I.H.R.	
			Visited Nos. 4+1 Sections to make the necessary arrangements + saw O.C. 21st MG Coy as to his positions, while O.C. No 2 Section reconnoitred the front line + consulted O.C.s 17th + 20th K.L.R. as to the positions to be occupied in the front line system. O.C. No 3 Section reconnoitred the front of the 21st Bde with a view to overhead fire from the flank on CHERISY during our advance which was expected on the 27th inst. The front line was found to be behind the crest. I.H.R.	

Vol XIV for APRIL 1917 p. 8.

WAR DIARY of 81st MACHINE GUN COMPANY
INTELLIGENCE SUMMARY — MACHINE GUN CORPS

Army Form C. 2118.

Place	Date	Hour	Summary of Events and Information	Remarks and references to Appendices
N27 d 4.7	25.4.17	5:30 p.m.	No 2 Section left N27a and moved up to the front line, relieving 2 guns of 21st M.G. Coy. On account of enemy shelling the relief was considerably delayed. Pack mules carried the guns and ammunition to about O 25 c 6.0, and by making a double journey to this point, 14 boxes per gun were taken up. JHB A dump of belt boxes, S.A.A., oil, and water under the artificers was formed at N 29 c 43.80. JHB	
		8:15 p.m.	At dusk No 4 Section were withdrawn, No 1 remaining in support. JHB AC. No 1 Section reported that during the enemy's shelling he had lost a Tripod, knocked out and 1 killed & 3 wounded. Visited his H.Q. and found he had got another Tripod. JHB The guns of No 2 Section were placed during the night as follows:- 1 at O 25 d 4.0 between front and support lines firing to left front. 1 at O 25 d 7.6 in support line firing to left front and covering O 26 a. 1 at O 25 d 8.8 slightly in front of the support line firing across the front of the 2 right guns and to the left, necessary. 1 at O 25 d 9.9 in a large gap in the support line, laid to the right but with a field of fire to the left as well. JHB	
— N29c43.80	26.4.17	11:50 a.m.	Coy H.Q. was moved to the dump at N 29 c 43.80. JHB	
		12 noon	The gun of No 1 Section at N 30 c 9.7 was moved forward after consultation with the O.C. 20th K.L.R. to a position at O 25 c 0.6. It was accompanied by a Lewis gun and with it formed almost a small strong point between the front and support systems and covered the reverse slope of the ridge, particularly to the left. JHB	
		5:30 p.m.	Message received that Lt. A.C. BROWN, O.C. No 2 Section, had been wounded while visiting his guns. Lt. A. McPHERSON, O.C. No 3 Section, took his place, as information had meanwhile been received that the attack of the 27th inst. had been postponed & the Division would be relieved. Nos 3 & 4 Sections would in all probability remain in reserve. JHB	

Army Form C. 2118.

WAR DIARY

Vol XIV for 89th MACHINE GUN COMPANY
INTELLIGENCE SUMMARY. MACHINE GUN CORPS.
APRIL 1917
p.9

(Erase heading not required.)

Instructions regarding War Diaries and Intelligence Summaries are contained in F.S. Regs., Part II. and the Staff Manual respectively. Title pages will be prepared in manuscript.

Place	Date	Hour	Summary of Events and Information	Remarks and references to Appendices
N.29.c.43.80	26.4.17	6 p.m.	Visited No 2 Section. Decided that it would now be better to move the guns into and in front of the front line, but as Lt McPHERSON arrived at dusk it was decided to leave them where they were till the next day. Information received that the Coy. was to be relieved on the evening of the 27th.	IHR IHR
	27.4.17	9.30 p.m. 10 a.m.	Arrangements for relief made with O.C. 21 M.G. Coy. The front line guns were reconnoitred by one of their Section officers. Visited Nos 2 + 1 Sections & saw O.Cs 17th & 20th K.L.R.	IHR
		3 p.m.	Relief of No 1 Section in support commenced – ammunition was handed over	IHR
		4.30 p.m.	Rations arrived & dump at N 29 c 43.80 removed.	IHR
		5.15 p.m.	Relief of No 1 Section completed	IHR
		6 p.m.	Coy H.Q. moved back to N 27a 4.7	IHR
		8.15 p.m.	Relief of No 2 Section in the front line commenced.	IHR
		10 p.m.	Relief completed.	IHR
N 27 a 4.7			The Coy spent the night at N 27 a. 11 O.R. reinforcements	IHR
	28.4.17	7 a.m.	Coy paraded + moved off to transport lines at M 11 d 6.8. 3 limbers were brought up to carry away guns, tripods etc.	IHR
M 11 d 6.8.		12 noon	Coy paraded & marched to ARRAS Stn + entrained.	IHR
		11.30 pm	Transport moved off on a two days journey to FRAMECOURT, stopping the night at WANQUETIN.	IHR
FRAMECOURT	29.4.17	9.30 pm	Coy detrained at PETIT HOUVAIN + marched to billets at FRAMECOURT	IHR
	30.4.17		1 O.R. rejoined from C.C.S.	IHR

J.H. Rotherham Capt.
Comdg 89 M.G. Coy

Confidential

War Diary

of

89th Machine Gun Company.

for month of MAY 1917

Vol 15

WAR DIARY

Vol XV for MAY 1917
p.1.

of 89th MACHINE GUN COMPANY
MACHINE GUN CORPS.

Army Form C. 2118.

REFERENCE MAPS.

LENS — Sheet 11 — 1/100,000
HAZEBROUCK 1/100,000
Trench Map BELGIUM Sheet 28 N.W. 1/20,000
do. ZILLIBEKE Sheet 28 N.W.4 and 1/10,000
N.E.3 (parts of)

Place	Date	Hour	Summary of Events and Information	Remarks and references to Appendices
FRAMECOURT	1.5.17		89 M.G.Coy in rest billets. 1 O.R. reinforcement. JHR	
FRAMECOURT	2.5.17		In rest billets	
do	3.5.17		In rest billets	
BUIRE	3.5.17		Moved to BUIRE	
HARAVESNES	4.5.17		Moved to HARAVESNES. 1 O.R. reinforcement	
	5.5.17		In rest billets	
	10.5.17		2nd Lt W.G. BOLDERO proceeded on leave to Paris	
	15.5.17		do returned from do	
FRAMECOURT	20.5.17		Moved to FRAMECOURT	
CONTEVILLE	21.5.17		Moved to CONTEVILLE	
	22.5.17		2nd Lt G.H. WOOD went to Hospital	
			Lt D.W. LOCHHEAD went to Hospital	
LESTRESSES	22.5.17		Moved to LESTRESSES	
	23.5.17		In billets LESTRESSES	
THIENNES	24.5.17		Moved to THIENNES	
CAESTRE	25.5.17		Moved to CAESTRE area	
			Captain J.M Roxburgh went to Hospital	
WATOU	26.5.17		Moved to WATOU area	
BRANDHOEK	27.5.17		Moved to BRANDHOEK.	
			Lt D W LOCHHEAD rejoined from Hospital	
	28.5.17		1 OR rejoined from CCS.	

Army Form C. 2118.

Vol. XV for May 1919

WAR DIARY
or
INTELLIGENCE SUMMARY.
of 89th Machine Gun Company.
Machine Gun Corps.

(Erase heading not required.)

Place	Date	Hour	Summary of Events and Information	Remarks and references to Appendices
YPRES	28.5.19		Took over ZILLIBEKE Sector from 92 M.G.Coy. night of 28/29 Inst.	
			Guns as follows:—	
			No.1 Section No.1 gun North Shore L.B.12. I.22.a.65.45. firing E.	
			No.2 gun Mental Grange L.B.13 I.16.c.80.40 do E.S.E.	
			No.3 gun The Fort. L.B.14. I.16.c.35.80 do N.E.	
			No.4 gun Gordon House L.B.10. I.16.B.30.30 do E.	
			No.2 Section No.1 gun Stafford St. R.B.9. I.24.c.30.90 do E.	
			No.2 gun Jump Hole R.B.4. I.24.c.40.30 do N.	
			No.3 gun Redan R.B.3. I.24.d.65.35 do E.	
			No.4 gun Conft Front — I.24.d.40.45 do E.S.E.	
			No.3 Section No.1 gun Strina Wall L.B.10a. I.16.d.80.95 do E.N.E.	
			No.2 gun Senator St. L.B.3. I.19.d.05.84 do E.N.E.	
			No.3 gun Tilly St. L.B.9. I.19.c.46.14. do E.	
			No.4 gun Front Line L.B.4. I.19.B.95.25. do E.N.E.	
			No.4 Section No.1 gun Maple Frt. L.B.1. I.24.a.92.81. do N.E.	
			No.2 gun Wellington Cress. L.B.2. I.19.d.40.40. do E.S.E.	
			No.3 gun Lorring Ameri. L.B.9. I.23.a.65.60 do E.N.E.	
			No.4 gun Maple Cophies — I.24.a.25.23 do S.E.	
	29.5.19		1 O.R. joined from B.E.F.	
	30.5.19		do do	
	30.5.19		Capt J.H. Rookroyd & 2nd/Lt G.H. WOID rejoined from Hospital	

W. Rookroyd Lieut
for Capt Commanding
89 Machine Gun Coy

"Secret"

Vol 16

War Diary

of the 89th Machine Gun Coy
for the month of June 1917.

Volume 16

Headquarters,
89th Inf. Bde

> 89th COMPANY,
> MACHINE GUN
> CORPS.
> 2.5
> 3.7.17

Herewith Volume XVI for JUNE 1917 of the WAR DIARY of this Unit for necessary action.

Kindly acknowledge receipt.

F.H. Roxburgh
Capt
Comdg 89 M.G. Coy

Vol. XVI
JUNE 1919

WAR DIARY of 89th MACHINE GUN COMPANY.
INTELLIGENCE SUMMARY MACHINE GUN CORPS.

Army Form C. 2118.

REFERENCE MAPS

Trench Map. ZILLEBEKE. Sheet 28 N.W.4.
and N.E.3 (parts of) 1/10,000.
Trench Map. BELGIUM Sheet 28. N.W.
1/20,000
BELGIUM and FRANCE Sheet 24. 1/40,000

Place	Date	Hour	Summary of Events and Information
YPRES.	1/6/19		In the line in HOOGE Sector. Gun positions per WAR DIARY.
	2/6/19		Lt. H.E. MIDDLETON. wounded. Vol. XV. fr MAY 1919. 1.O.R. reinforcement rejoined from B.B.S. 1.O.R. killed and 1.O.R. wounded at gun position. I.24.c. 30.90. and 1.O.R. wounded at gun position. I.24.a.25.23.
	3/6/19		150 rounds were fired from anti-aircraft position at T.14.c.46.19 at enemy aircraft. Three gun teams of No.1 Section at I.22.a.05.95, I.16.c.80.90 and I.16.c.35.80, relieved three gun teams of No.2 Section in the Right Sector at I.24.c.30.90, I.24.c.95.35, and I.24.d.90.45. Relief completed by 9 p.m. Guns at T.19.d.40.40 and I.16.b.30.30. Fired 3000 rounds during the night on gaps in enemy wire in front of trenches running from J.13.c. and J.13.c.A.4. to J.19.a.5.5.
	4/6/19		Guns at I.24.c.30.90, and I.24.c.95.35. Fired 500 rounds at hostile aircraft. 1.O.R. reinforcement rejoined from B.B.S. 1.O.R. reinforcement from Base.
	5/6/19		2nd Lt. B.C. ISAACS. M.G.C. and 2nd Lt. N.J. MILLER. M.G.C. joined the Company from Base Depot.

Vol. XVI

Army Form C. 2118.

WAR DIARY
of 89th MACHINE GUN COMPANY.
INTELLIGENCE SUMMARY. MACHINE GUN CORPS.
JUNE 1919
p. 2.
(Erase heading not required.)

Instructions regarding War Diaries and Intelligence Summaries are contained in F. S. Regs., Part II. and the Staff Manual respectively. Title pages will be prepared in manuscript.

Place	Date	Hour	Summary of Events and Information	Remarks and references to Appendices
YPRES.	5/6/19		Guns at I.19.d.40.40, I.16.b.30.30 and I.19.c.46.19 fired 6500 rounds during the night on gaps in enemy wire — same targets as last night. DyS. Guns at I.16.d.80.95 and I.23.a.65.60. fired 2150 rounds during the night on Communication Trenches and Tracks behind the enemy's lines. DyS.	
	6/6/19		1. OR reinforcement rejoined from B.C.S. DyS. Gun at I.24.c.30.40 was knocked out by a direct hit from a shell at 11 h.m. 1. OR killed and 1 OR wounded. DyS. As before 3 guns fired 6000 rounds during the night on gaps in enemy wire, and 2 guns fired 2000 rounds on communication trenches and tracks. DyS. Reserve gun and team at I.16.c.80.90 replaced gun knocked out at I.24.c.30.40 at 5.30 p.m. DyS.	
	7/6/19	4.30 pm	In accordance with orders received from Brigade H.Q., three guns at I.20.a.05.95, I.16.c.35.80 and I.16.b.30.30 of No 2 section were ordered to report to O.C. 2nd Bedfords: at first burnt dug outs in I.24.a. for orders as to covering gaps in our line South of ST. PETER ST. in I.30.B. DyS.	
		9.45 am	Gun at I.24.d.40.45. fired 250 rounds against enemy counter attack SOUTH of OBSERVATORY Ridge. DyS. Guns at I.19.d.40.40 and I.19.c.46.19 fired 5000 rounds during the night on gaps in enemy wire. DyS.	

Vol XVI
JUNE 1919
A.3.

WAR DIARY of 89th MACHINE GUN COMPANY
INTELLIGENCE SUMMARY. MACHINE GUN CORPS.

Army Form C. 2118.

Place	Date	Hour	Summary of Events and Information	Remarks and references to Appendices
YPRES	8/6/19	1am	The three guns which had moved up to cover gaps in our line were in position	DWS
		10am	Received a warning order that we were being relieved on night of 8/9th by 90th M.G. Coy. and 21st M.G. Coy, the former taking over the left half of our front and the latter the right half.	DWS
		4pm	Received an order from Division that only 8 of guns were being relieved, as follows:-	
			By 90th M.G. Coy. Gun at T 16 d. 30. 30.	
			" " T 16 d. 80. 95	
			" " T 19 d. 05. 89	
			" " T 19 b. 95. 25	
			By 21st M.G. Coy. " T 24 a. 92. 81.	
			" " T 24 a. 95. 23	
			" " T 24 c. 95. 35	
			" " T 24 d. 40. 45.	DWS
			The remainder of our gun positions to be vacated as soon as it was dark.	DWS
	9/6/19	2am.	In accordance with these orders, relief was completed by 2am	DWS

Army Form C. 2118.

Vol XVI

WAR DIARY
or
89th MACHINE GUN COMPANY.
INTELLIGENCE SUMMARY. MACHINE GUN CORPS.
JUNE 1919
N.H.
(Erase heading not required.)

Place	Date	Hour	Summary of Events and Information	Remarks and references to Appendices
YPRES.	9/6/19		When relieved, Company Headquarters and the four sections moved back independently to rest billets at K.18.a.9.9. DH	
K.18.a.9.9.	10/6/19		In rest billets. DH	
"	11/6/19		In rest billets. DH	
	12/6/19		Lt. D.D. RICHARDS. Left the Company to take up appointment as an Instructor at GRANTHAM. DH In rest billets. DH	
			Lt. D.W. LOCHHEAD. appointed second in command of the Company. (Authority II Corps telegram N/113. 11.6.19) DH	
	13/6/19		5. O.R. reinforcements from Base. DH In rest billets. DH	
		4 p.m.	Nos. 2 and 4 Sections proceeded on anti aircraft duty to area S.E of POPERINGHE and occupied the following positions:-	
			1 gun at dump. H.14.d.5.8.	
			1 gun at dump. H.13. central.	
			1 gun at N. Atlantic Siding G.10.a.	
			1 gun at S. Atlantic Siding G.10.d.4.4.	
			2 guns at dump. G.29.d.9.4.	
			2 guns at dump. G.21.d.9.5. DH	
	14/6/19		In rest billets. DH	

WAR DIARY or INTELLIGENCE SUMMARY

89th MACHINE GUN COMPANY MACHINE GUN CORPS.

Vol. XVI JUNE 1917 p. 5.

Army Form C. 2118.

Place	Date	Hour	Summary of Events and Information	Remarks and references to Appendices
K.18.a.9.9.	15/6/17		In rest billets. JHR	
			The section relieved by a section of an M.G. Coy of 8th Division. The following positions being taken over by them:—	
			1 gun at dump. H.14.b.5.8.	
			1 gun at dump. H.13.central.	
			1 gun at N. Atlantic Siding G.10.a. JHR	
			1 gun at S. Atlantic Siding G.10.d.9.4.	
			M.G. section arrived back at billets 10 p.m. JHR	
			Relief completed by 9 p.m. JHR	
"	16/6/17		In rest billets. JHR	
"	19/6/17		In rest billets. JHR	
"	15/6/17		In rest billets. JHR	
"	19/6/17		In rest billets. JHR	
"	20/6/17		In rest billets. JHR 20.O.R. reinforcements from Base. JHR	
"	21.6.17		1 O.R. reinforcement from Base. JHR	
"	22.6.17	5.a.m.	Moved to tents in DICKEBUSCH area - H.Q. at H.33.d.28. JHR In reserve. JHR	Sheet 28 N.W.
H.33.d.2.8.	23.6.17		Lt. E.R. TAYLOR to Field Ambulance. JHR 8 men attached from each Battalion of the Brigade for purpose of carrying ammunition and issuing. JHR	
"	27.6.17	2.30 a.m.	Left DICKEBUSCH with 2 Sections Officers & reconnoitred line in OBSERVATORY RIDGE Sector. JHR	
		6.0 p.m.	Coy left camp at DICKEBUSCH & moved to CHATEAU SEGARD to Bivouacs at H.30.a.90.05, relieving the 2 reserve Sections of 21st M Gr Coy. No 2 Section had meanwhile been relieved in anti aircraft positions & moved direct to CHATEAU SEGARD JHR	

Army Form C. 2118.

WAR DIARY
of 89th MACHINE GUN COMPANY
INTELLIGENCE SUMMARY
MACHINE GUN CORPS.

Vol XVI
1st June 1917
p. 6.

Place	Date	Hour	Summary of Events and Information	Remarks and references to Appendices
H 30 a.90.05	27.6.17	9.0 pm	No 3 Section left CHATEAU SEGARD & marched to ZILLEBEKE and relieved right section of 21st M.G. Coy. JHR	
		9.15 pm	No 4 Section followed No 3 relieving left section. JHR	
		12 midnight	Relief completed without casualties. JHR Dispositions as follows:-	
			Right Section:-	
			1 gun at REDAN - R.G. 3 - I 24 d 2.2.	
			1 gun at CRAB CRAWL - I.13.15 - I 24 d 70.45	
			1 gun at ST PETERS ST. - I 24 d 35.25	
			Left Section	
			1 gun at VINCE ST. - L.B.11. - I 24 a 25.40. firing S.E. & for "	
			1 gun at MAPLE FORT - L.B.1 - I 24 a 75.80 - " N.E. "	
			1 gun at LOVERS WALK - I 24 b 30.70 - " E.S.E.& for "	
			1 gun at WELLINGTON CRESCENT L.B.2. - I 17 d 35.45 - " E " for "	
			1 gun at RITZ ST. L.B.9 - I 17 c 50.45 - firing E.S.E. for anti aircraft work.	
			Remaining 6 guns in reserve with Coy Hd qrs at CHATEAU SEGARD JHR	
	28.6.17		Enemy artillery active. 1520 rounds fired at enemy aircraft flying low as follows:-	
		8.55 am	by gun at ST PETERS ST.	
		11 am	LOVERS' WALK.	
		7 pm	LOVERS' WALK. JHR	
			Reserve Sections commenced preparing gun positions for barrage fire behind ZOUAVE WOOD and on slight of BOND ST. This work carried on each night. JHR	
	29.6.17		Enemy artillery more lively. 3650 rounds fired on enemy aircraft as follows:-	
		7.15 am	2 hostile formation flying low over front line was broken up.	
		4.15 pm	2 red planes successfully engaged. One flying over MAPLE COPSE side slipped about 100 ft & flew towards its own lines, appearing to land safely. JHR	
	30.6.17		Normal activity except MGs which were more active. Rain usual from HOOGE. Between 10.45 pm & midnight RITZ ST gun fired 1000 rounds on to area J 13 b 45.32 to J 13 d 9.8. JHR W.Roxburgh Lt. comdg 89 M.G. Coy. JHR

Vol. 17

SECRET.

WAR DIARY
of the 49th Machine Gun Company.
for the month of July 1917.

VOLUME XVII
APPENDIX XI

Army Form C. 2118.

WAR DIARY
of 89th MACHINE GUN COMPANY
MACHINE GUN CORPS

Volume XVII for JULY – 1917 P.1

(Erase heading not required.)

Instructions regarding War Diaries and Intelligence Summaries are contained in F.S. Regs, Part II. and the Staff Manual respectively. Title pages will be prepared in manuscript.

REFERENCE MAPS:—
Trench Map – ZILLEBEKE — 1/10,000
HAZEBROUCK — 5a — 1/100,000
BELGIUM Sheet 27 — 1/40,000
" " 28 — 1/40,000

Place	Date	Hour	Summary of Events and Information	Remarks and references to Appendices
H 30 a 90.05	1-7-17		In the line in the OBSERVATORY RIDGE Sector – For dispositions See Vol XVI for JUNE 1917. Enemy artillery active throughout the day. JHR Usual aerial activity. Our M.G.s fired 1000 rounds on CLAPHAM JUNCTION during the night. 2ND Lt. H. WATTS joined for duty. JHR	
–	2-7-17	2am to 2.15am	The enemy put a very heavy barrage on the night Sector. Our artillery active – chiefly on back areas. Aeroplane activity was above normal – 2,700 rounds were fired by A.A. machine guns at LOVERS WALK and ST PETERS ST. JHR 1 gun placed at I 23 d 68.63. in disused Trench. JHR 1000 rounds fired during the night on the CLAPHAM JUNCTION area. JHR	
–	3-7-17		Enemy artillery slightly less active. 2,000 rounds fired at enemy aircraft during the day. JHR As the enemy was expected to attack, 2 Sections of 90 M.G. Company were sent up to reinforce. 4 guns were placed near our gun at I 23 d 68.63 and 4 guns near ours in WELLINGTON CRESCENT. (I 17 d 35.45).	
–	4-7-17		Enemy artillery quieter. 500 rounds fired at enemy aircraft. JHR	
–	5-7-17		Arrangements for relief made with 55 M.G. Coy – who reconnoitred Re. line. JHR Enemy artillery active against ST PETERS ST & ZILLEBEKE ST. 1000 rounds fired at enemy aircraft. JHR	
–	6-7-17	10.30am	2 LT. N. J. MILLER & 2.O.R. slightly wounded – remained on duty. JHR Normal day. JHR	
–	7-7-17	9 pm	55 M.G. Coy arrived at CHATEAU SEGARD. Relief commenced guides were provided for each Section & Transport from Coy HQ & for each team from ZILLEBEKE. JHR On relief Sections moved back independently to Transport lines at G 24 c 98. Teams were heavily shelled on their way out, near CHATEAU SEGARD. Casualties 1 O.R. killed – 1 O.R. shell shock – 2 mules wounded (1 at duty) JHR Relief completed by midnight. Transport left under Brigade T.O. for march to back area. JHR	
G 24 c 8.8	8-7-17	5.30 am 10.30 am	Coy moved off & marched to RENINGHELST Sta., where it entrained – Proceeded to WATTEN, where it detrained. The 2 Sections of 90 Coy accompanied 89 Coy & regained their unit from here. 89 Coy then marched on to billets in NOTRE DAME FARM, where it arrived at 9 p.m. JHR	
NOTRE DAME FARM	8-7-17 to 18-7-17		In training in RECQUES area. Chief training was in M.G. Barrage work for forthcoming operations. This was done near billets. The picture ground was also used. JHR	

A 5834 Wt. W4973/M687 750,000 8/16 D.D. & L. Ltd. Forms/C 2118/13.

Army Form C. 2118.

WAR DIARY

of 89 MACHINE GUN COMPANY MACHINE GUN CORPS.

INTELLIGENCE SUMMARY

(Erase heading not required.)

Volume XVII for JULY 1917 p.2.

Place	Date	Hour	Summary of Events and Information	Remarks and references to Appendices
NOTRE DAME FARM.	18-7-17	6.30 am	Transport left under Bde. T.O. for move to forward area. JHR	
	19-7-17	12 Noon	Coy moved off and marched to RECQUES & thence (by busses) to LE TEMPLE - (STEENVOORDE area W.)	
LE TEMPLE	24-7-17	9.30pm 6am	Arrived in billets in Farm ½ mile E. of 32D E in LE TEMPLE. JHR Left billets & marched to DALLINGTON CAMP L.35 b.11.5. JHR operation orders issued for forthcoming operations - JHR	
DALLINGTON CAMP	25-7-17 26-7-17 27-7-17		Preparations for moving up into the line were made but this was cancelled at 4·25 pm JHR In rest at DALLINGTON CAMP. Barrage scheme slightly altered. JHR for reinforcement. JHR	See App XI.
— PALACE CAMP	28-7-17 29-7-17	7.16 pm 1 am	Moved to PALACE CAMP H31a 8·8. JHR Nos 1,2,4 Sections moved off & took guns etc into assembly position at STERN ST. JHR	
—	29-7-17 30-7-17	9 pm 9.30 am 3.0 am	No 3 Section moved off to assembly position in CHATEAU SEGARD area No 3. JHR Transport moved to H 27 b 5·3.(Sheet 27) Y. Day. 9 am All Sections in assembly positions. 9pm.	

Events of the 31st will be included in the following months diary

G. H. Coord
2/Lt
for Captain.
Comdg 60th Coy. Machine Gun Corps.

Appendix XI to WAR DIARY Vol. XVII for JULY 1917

Copy 17,
WAR DIARY.

89th Machine Gun Coy. Operation Order No 10.

by
Captain T. W. Roxburgh.

Reference Map. Headquarters.
ZILLEBEKE 1/10,000. 3.7.17.

GENERAL 1. On Z day the 30th Division will attack in the centre of the II Corps from OBSERVATORY RIDGE Sector   The 8th Division will attack on the LEFT. The 24th — do — — " — RIGHT — 18th — — will Support the 30th Div.

OBJECTIVES 2. The BLUE, BLACK, GREEN, and if possible RED lines as shown on MAP (Partial ground).
The 90th and 21st Bdes will attack BLUE & BLACK lines — 53rd (18th Div.) and 89th Bdes — " — GREEN line Boundaries as on MAP.

TASKS of M.G. Coy. 3. Will fall under two headings
    a. consolidation see APPENDIX A
    b. Barrage — " — B.
On completion of attack 89th Bde will hold the line. see appendix C.

INFORMATION 4. Special message forms will be issued with maps NO maps other than these will be carried No maps will be marked. Information about enemy artillery is especially valuable. All messages must be clear, concise, accurate and invariably timed

COMMUNICATION 5. An advanced Report Centre will be established in JACKDAW RESERVE at J 13 d 3.3 and later at J 14 c 58.20. These will always forward any message for Coy. H.Q. Every effort to save runners by sending messages through Battalions must be made.

PERSONNEL 6. 25% of Officers. N.C.O's & men will remain with the Transport as specially detailed

DRESS 7. Officers will wear mens tunics with RED TAPE through the RIGHT shoulder. Packs will not be carried.

TRAFFIC CONTROL 8. All forward movement will be over the open.

RATIONS	9.	All ranks will carry 1 days rations and the IRON RATION. Waterbottles will be filled.
S.A.A.	10.	Every effort will be made to collect all S.A.A. near GUN positions when in the enemy's lines to increase the supply of S.A.A.
ASSEMBLY	11.	The greatest possible care must be taken during X and Y days to prevent the enemy perceiving the concentration of TROOPS. All movement must be reduced to a minimum.
Company H.Q.	12.	At ZERO will be in FENN STREET near Bde H.Q. and will move as soon as possible to the neighbourhood of J.13 d 3.3 where all messages should be sent. Subsequent changes will be notified.
CODE NAMES	13.	All new CODE NAMES must be committed to memory.
S.O.S.	14.	The S.O.S. is a succession of rifle rockets each bursting into 2 RED & 2 GREEN lights simultaneously. until the artillery comply
MISCELLANEOUS	15.	The following MAPS are passed round herewith, and must be specially studied

        MAP of OBJECTIVES shewing DUMPS. H.Qs. etc.
        TRAFFIC ROUTES.
        ENEMY DUGOUTS.
        MAP + NOTES on OBSTACLES.
        BARRAGE LINES.

LECTURE.	16.	The 89th Bde "INSTRUCTIONS for FORTHCOMING OPERATIONS" will also be studied & will form the subject of a special LECTURE by the C.O. on 24th inst. to all N.C.Os. All this information must be passed on to ALL RANKS

T.H. Roxburgh Captain

Commanding 89th Coy Machine Gun Corps.

89th Coy. Machine Gun Corps.

Operation Order No. 10.

APPENDIX A.

CONSOLIDATION.

Section detailed. 1. No 3 Section under Lt A. McPHERSON will advance with the 89th Bde (17th & 20th K.L.R.) for the purpose of consolidating the GREEN LINE.

ASSEMBLY. 2. No 3 Section will move on X/Y night to CHATEAUX SEGARD AREA No 3.
On Y/Z night it will move behind the 20th K.L.R. to the Western end of the PROMENADE getting into position by 2 a.m. Z day.

SYNCHRONIZATION. 3. O.C. No 3 Sect. will synchronize watches with the 20th K.L.R. on Y day.

ADVANCE. 4. No 3 Section will move forward behind the 20th K.L.R. to a forward assembly position in front of MAPLE COPSE by ZERO plus 3.10 hours. No 3 Sect. will advance thence under orders of Lt McPHERSON who will place them on the capture of the GREEN LINE approximately as follows:–

1 Gun at BLACK WATCH CORNER.
1 — — LONE HOUSE.
1 — — NORTHAMPTON FARM
1 — — Junction with 17th Bde on MENIN Rd.

As soon as these are placed, he will report their position to the Battalion Commanders concerned.

REINFORCEMENT. 5. This consolidation will be strengthened by the addition of No 1 Section under Lt FAULKNER who will move up to the GREEN LINE after completing the Barrage and on receiving orders from Bde. H.Q.

ACTION. 6. On arrival O.C. No 1 Section will get into touch with O.C. No 3 Section and arrange to relieve the latter's 2 left guns in order that the 17th K.L.R. may then be supported entirely by No 1 Section and the 20th K.L.R. by No 3 Section.

SUBSEQUENT ACTION. 7. O.C. Nos 1 & 3 Sections must be prepared to move up guns to support & consolidate any further advance made by the infantry from the GREEN LINE.

J. H. Roxburgh
Capt

Comdg. 89th Coy. Machine Gun Corps.

? Machine Gun Company — Operation Order No. 10.
APPENDIX "B".

Preliminary Instructions for Machine Gun Barrage during Future Operations.

SECTIONS DETAILED. 1. ?????? ????? Sections ?? form "A" Battery for Divisional Machine Gun Barrage.
Lt. R.H.V. ROBERTS will command the Battery.
2/Lts. H.G. FAULKNER, N.F. MILLER, E.S.A. REEVES will be in command of Sections.
2/Lts. C.C. ISAACS and H. WATTS will be in charge of carriers.

DIVISIONAL M.G. BARRAGE. 2. The 19th Division will be doing the first barrage on the advance to the BLUE LINE (1st objective). Gun positions in our present trench system.

ASSEMBLY 3. "A" Battery will assemble during X/Y night in STERN TRENCH. During Y/Z night then write if practicable move forward to an assembly position in or near our front line after consultation with O.C. Infantry.

1st ADVANCE. 4. At ZERO the Battery will advance behind the infantry in columns of sections to a position about J13a 76.18 to J13c 77.04 & will fire as follows:-
ZERO + 1.15 to ZERO + 2.10 on line J8 b 72.47 to J9c 31.18.
Rate of fire – 1 belt per gun /? 4 mins.
Communication will be maintained by telephone & runner with 00th Bde. Report Centre at JACKDAW RESERVE J13 d 3.3.

2nd ADVANCE 5. The Battery will then move forward to a position about 400 yards behind the BLACK LINE and on the NORTH of the MENIN Road & will fire as follows:-
From ZERO + 6 hrs 10 mins to ZERO + 7 hrs 40 mins on line J16a 41.84 to J?a 28.00. at ???? rate.
Communication will be secured by telephone & runner with 89th Bde. Report Centre at INVERNESS COPSE J14c 59.24

RECONNAISSANCE 6. The route to be ????? will be reconnoitred by Map & Picture ground ?? ?? aeroplane photographs. Compass bearings will be taken & the ?????? to be traversed will be measured.

POSITION DISC. 7. The Battery will carry a large disc with A painted ?? it. on reaching the barrage position it will be planted where it can easily be seen from the rear.

LIGHT MOUNTINGS. 8. Light mountings will not be carried except ? for ?????? and ???? ??????????? ?? ?? minimum scale.

S.A.A.	9.	Two S.A.A. dumps have been formed, one forward of BOND ST. & the other main one at CHINA WALL. Arrangements are also being made for TANKS to form an M.G. S.A.A Dump at STIRLING CASTLE.
WATER.	10.	One petrol tin of water will be carried for each gun.
OIL.	11.	One waterbottle full of oil will be carried with each gun.
ANGLES.	12.	Calculations for firing & direction will be worked out beforehand, & 2 tables given for each team. The Battery Commander will have his map marked with Q.E. angles & bearings for any target within range from the 2nd Battery position.
AMMUNITION SUPPLY.	13.(a)	All except 3 men per gun will go back under 2nd ISAACS & WATTS & bring up the 2nd supply of S.A.A. from the forward dump.
	(b)	After the 2nd supply of S.A.A. has been brought up 4 men will remain at each gun position for firing & filling belts & the remaining 4 will go back to the forward dump & continue bringing up S.A.A. When this is completed the carriers will return to STERN STREET.
	(c)	As soon as is practicable (probably ZERO + 4 hrs) O.C. No 1 Section will detail Pte. ROBINSON to go back to the main S.A.A. dump & guide up 12 pack mules which will have waited previously at MOATED GRANGE & will carry S.A.A. to the guns. A limber will also accompany these, and will be used in preference if possible. A limber will also bring up S.A.A. if possible & will move from CHATEAU SEGARD under orders of an officer of 21 M.G.Coy. dumping at CLAPHAM JUNCTION
S.O.S.	14.	On receipt of S.O.S. call all guns will open fire at double rate for 15 minutes. On receipt of information that the ZANDVOORDE - POLYGON LINE has been occupied by us, the barrage line will be moved forward to line J.16 a 61.85 to J.16 a 79.00.
CARE of GUNS	15.	Guns can only be kept firing for so long a period as is required if there is the strictest discipline with regards to "points during firing". Locks & barrels must be very frequently cleaned & elevation checked continually. Guns will be thoroughly overhauled when the Barrage is finished, one Gun per section being stripped at a time.

J. H. Roxburgh.

Captain
Comdg. Sqt. Machine Gun Coy

89th Coy. Machine Gun Corps. – Operation Order No. 10.

APPENDIX "C"

Subsequent Action & Eventualities to Consider.

A. O.C. Consolidating Sections must be prepared
   (1). To assist in the capture & consolidation of the BLACK LINE.
   (2). To push guns forward in front of the GREEN LINE, to support the infantry out-posts in the POLYGON – ZANDVOORDE LINE.
   (3). To cover the consolidation of the GREEN LINE with fire, though S.A.A. must be saved as far as possible to meet counterattacks.
   (4). To assist in forming a defensive flank in the event of the 17th Bde (on the right) being held up. In this case the line to be held would be J20 a 0.7 to J14 d 1.2.
   (5). To deal with enemy patrols during the night Z/A.

B. O.C. Barrage Battery must be prepared.
   (1). To turn the fire of his guns onto any point within range on receipt of orders.
   (2). To move forward by Sections whenever possible after firing the Barrage in order to be able to put up a more effective belt of fire & to deal with more distant targets. A suitable position would seem to be J14 c 6.8. Company H.Q. will also probably be with the Battery H.Q.
   (3). To alter his S.O.S. Barrage line on receipt of information that our patrols have secured the POLYGON-ZANDVOORDE Line.
   (4). To assist in the formation of a defensive right flank, as in Para A (4), by a new barrage line.
   (5). To harrass the enemy during Z/A night – consisting of GHELUVELT Chateau area J16 d, J16 a 8.1, J16 a 9.3, J16 a b.9.
   (6). To replace any of the consolidation guns knocked out. Battery guns will in turn be replaced by guns from 226 M.G. Coy.

J. H. Roxburgh.

Captain
Commanding 89th Coy. Machine Gun Corps.

War Diary

Copy No 3 on Bdry

FIRE ORGANIZATION TABLE -

89 M-G- Coy.

Section	'A' BATTERY			Target.	Time and Rate.	Remarks.
	Gun	Bearing (Mag)	Elevation	J 8 b 40.20 to J 8 d 95.00.	J 13 a 76.18 to J 13 c 77.94.	2 Taps right and left.
No 1.	No 4.	67°	3° 10'		1. ZERO + 1 hr. 15 mins. to ZERO + 2 hrs. 10 mins. at FULL rate.	
	No 3.	69°	3° 16'			
	No 2.	71°	3° 25'			
	No 1.	73°	3° 32'			
No 2	No 1.	74°	3° 35'		2. ZERO + 2 hrs. 10 mins. to ZERO + 6 hrs. 20 mins. at HALF rate. Gun by section.	
	No 2.	75½°	3° 45'			
	No 3.	77°	3° 50'			
	No 4.	78°	3° 52'			
No 4.	No 1.	79°	3° 55'			
	No 2.	40°	3° 55'			
	No 3.	42°	3° 55'			
	No 4.	43°	3° 54'			

J. H. Roxburgh
Captain
Commanding 89th Machine Gun Coy.

2/

FIRE ORGANIZATION TABLE.

89. M.G. Coy

Section	Gun	Bearing (mag)	Elevation	Target	Time and Rate	Remarks
No 1	No 4	89°91'	4°7'	J16a 41.94. to J16a 28.00.	ZERO + 6 hrs. 20 mins. to ZERO + 7 hrs 40 mins. at FULL rate. Subsequently on S.O.S. at DOUBLE rate.	J14c 6.8 to J14a 55.12. 1 Tap right and left.
No 1	No 3	88°92°	4°7'			
No 1	No 2	91°93°	4°7'			
No 1	No 1	94°	4°7'			
No 2	No 1	93°	3°31'			
No 2	No 2	93¾°	3°31'			
No 2	No 3	94½°	3°31'			
No 2	No 4	95½°	3°31'			
No 4	No 1	96°	3°29'			
No 4	No 2	97°	3°29'			
No 4	No 3	99°	3°29'			
No 4	No 4	99°	3°29'			

A BATTERY

J.W. Roxburgh Capt.

96/18

Secret.

War Diary

of the 89th Company Machine Gun Corps
for the Month of August 1917.

Volume XVIII

Army Form C. 2118.

WAR DIARY
of 89th MACHINE GUN COMPANY MACHINE GUN CORPS.
INTELLIGENCE SUMMARY

Volume XVIII
for August 1917 p.1.

Instructions regarding War Diaries and Intelligence Summaries are contained in F.S. Regs. Part II. and the Staff Manual respectively. Title pages will be prepared in manuscript.

(Erase heading not required.)

Place	Date	Hour	Summary of Events and Information	Remarks and references to Appendices
I 17 d 1.1	31.7.17	3.50 a.m	Zero hour – "A" Battery moved forward very shortly after Zero from STERN St. & reached the German front line without casualties. There however they came under heavy fire. They got forward as quickly as possible to their battery position by JACKDAW RESERVE but not without casualties. 1 gun was hit. 2 Lieut. E.S.A. REEVES & 2nd Lt. B.C. ISAACS were wounded & approx. 10 OR casualties. On reaching the Battery position, O.C. battery received an urgent message from 90th Inf. Bde. for every available Machine Gun to be pushed up to the front line to meet an expected counter-attack. Accordingly he determined to push forward & with his 12 guns to hold the embankment of the MENIN road about J 13 b 21. This was done & more casualties were sustained. On reaching the embankment word was received that the enemy were massing in NONNE BOSCHEN and a few belts were fired into or on to this target. Meanwhile No 3 Section had worked its way up to the same embankment without casualties. One gun was immediately pushed forward with the leading infantry & finally got into a position in a shell hole in the front line at about J 13 d 85.75. The other 3 guns were got into positions later at J 13 d 8.6, J 13 d 75.50, J 13 d 65.30 (approx.) A second supply of belt boxes was brought up to A Battery. During the evening the following moves took place:– No 2 Section to positions covering the front of the 19th K.R.R.	Trench Map ZILLEBEKE – 1/10,000 HAZEBROUCK – 50 – 1/100,000 BELGIUM – Sheets 27 & 28 1/40,000

A 584 Wt. W4973/M687 750,000 8/16 D. D. & L. Ltd. Forms/C.2118/13.

Army Form C. 2118.

WAR DIARY
of 89th MACHINE GUN COMPANY
INTELLIGENCE SUMMARY. MACHINE GUN CORPS.

Vol. XVIII
for August 1917 p. 2.

(Erase heading not required.)

Instructions regarding War Diaries and Intelligence Summaries are contained in F. S. Regs., Part II. and the Staff Manual respectively. Title pages will be prepared in manuscript.

Place	Date	Hour	Summary of Events and Information	Remarks and references to Appendices
I.17.d.11	1-8-17		down to & including the MENIN road. Only one of these guns was actually with the front line as good fields of fire could be obtained from behind. No 1 Section (now 3 guns) to support at J.13.c.87.18, J.13.a.9.0 and J.13.b.45.78. No 4 Section moved to positions in JACKDAW ROW. These positions were held till 3-8-17. Casualties 31-7-17 — Killed 2 O.R. & 2 carriers wounded 3 off. * 20 O.R. & 12 carriers	J.H.R. J.H.R. J.H.R. * 1 Shell shock 2nd Lt. H. WATTS.
	2-8-17		In position as above. Weather very bad. Casualties killed 1 O.R. wounded 3 O.R. & 5 carriers.	J.H.R.
			As above. Casualties killed 1 O.R. & 1 carrier wounded 1 O.R. (gas — effect of mustard oil shells on 29/30th — blisters)	J.H.R. J.H.R.
	3-8-17		One gun knocked out by shell fire.	J.H.R.
			As above.	J.H.R.
	4-8-17	7 am	No 2 Section relieved by a section of 54th M.G. Coy.	J.H.R.
G.24.b.30		12.30 pm	The remainder of the Coy was relieved or withdrawn. On relief Coy moved to CHATEAU SEGARD area & thence by 'bus to Camp at G.24.b.30.	J.H.R. J.H.R.
EECKE	5-8-17	1 pm	Moved by Train (transport by road) to EAESTRE & marched thence to billets in farm ½ mile north of EECKE on the STEENVOORDE EECKE road.	J.H.R.
	6-8-17		Lieut. W.A. KINGDON reported as reinforcement with 25 O.R. (from Base)	J.H.R.
	7-8-17	7 am	Marched by road to MERRIS area. Billeted on right of road East of S in MERRIS	J.H.R. J.H.R.

Army Form C. 2118.

WAR DIARY
or INTELLIGENCE SUMMARY

of 89th MACHINE GUN COMPANY.
MACHINE GUN CORPS.

Volume XVIII
for August 1917
p.3.

(Erase heading not required.)

Instructions regarding War Diaries and Intelligence Summaries are contained in F. S. Regs., Part II. and the Staff Manual respectively. Title pages will be prepared in manuscript.

Reference Map: BELGIUM Sheet 28 1/40,000

Place	Date	Hour	Summary of Events and Information	Remarks and references to Appendices
MERRIS	9-8-17		1 OR reinforcement - IHR	
S8 d.6.6.	10-8-17	3 pm	Marched by road to camp near BAILLEUL at S8 d 6.6. IHR	
	14-8-17		4 OR reinforcements IHR	
	15-8-17		1 OR rejoined from C.C.S. IHR	
	16-8-17		1 OR rejoined from C.C.S. IHR	
	20-8-17		Lt. A. McPHERSON to go to HQ Coy to take command. IHR Capt. J.H. ROXBURGH to U.K. on leave - Lt. H.G. FAULKNER took command pending the arrival of Lt. D.W. LOCKHEAD from M.G. Course CAMIERS.	
			On rest Breath. H.G.F.	
	21-8-17		On rest Breath. T.O.R. from 17th Bn K.L.R. reported on convoy. H.S.F.	
	22-8-17			
	23-8-17/8.30am		Marched by road to DRANOUTRE area. (Relieved 2nd DIVIS 19th G Pozières at M36.a.9/3) H.S.F.	
DRANOUTRE	23.6.17 4 pm		1 Officer & 1 O.R. reinforcement. (rec'd A.S. Sayers) P.F. Inbourne. H.S.F.	
	24.8.17		On breath in Divisional Reserve. LT. D.W. LOCKHEAD returned from M.G. Course Camiers and assumed command of the Company in the absence on leave of Capt. J.H. ROXBURGH. Infy	
	25.8.17		In Billets in Divisional Reserve. Infy	
	26.8.17		do. Infy	
	27.8.17		do. Infy	
	28.8.17		Marched to Lonegal Farm. N.31.d.8.4. - In support area. Infy	
N.31 d.8.4.	29.8.17		In Billets in support to Division Infy	
	30.8.17		do Infy	
	31.8.17		do Infy	

J.W. Lockhead Lieut
For O.C. 89th Coy M.G. CORPS.

SECRET.

WAR DIARY OF
89th MACHINE GUN COMPANY,
for the month of SEPTEMBER 1917

VOLUME XIX

Vol 19

Army Form C. 2118.

WAR DIARY or INTELLIGENCE SUMMARY

Vol XIX

of 89TH MACHINE GUN COMPANY.
MACHINE GUN CORPS.

(Erase heading not required.)

for SEPTEMBER 1917 p.1.

Instructions regarding War Diaries and Intelligence Summaries are contained in F. S. Regs., Part II. and the Staff Manual respectively. Title pages will be prepared in manuscript.

Place	Date	Hour	Summary of Events and Information	Remarks and references to Appendices
N.31.d.8.7.	1-9-17-		In support 15 Divn. at DONEGAL FARM. Capt. J H ROXBURGH assumed command on rejoining from leave. 3 O.R. reinforcements. JHR	Reference Maps – WYTSCHAETE 1/10,000 WERVICQ 1/10,000 BELGIUM sheets 27428 1/40,000
	2-9-17	6.30 pm	Line of HOLLEBEKE Sector reconnoitred. JHR Coy moved off & relieved guns of 111th Coy as follows:- 2 guns No.4 Section at 011 c 0.0 firing S.E. under 2nd Lt BOLDERO 4 guns No.3 Section on front edge of ROSE WOOD 4 guns No.1 Section at DENYS FARM under Lt. H.G. FAULKNER 2 guns No.4 Section at 016 c 44.24 firing E.& N.E. 4 guns No.2 Section at 021 c 9.7 firing E. Coy H.Q. at 09 a 7.2. in the DAMM STRASSE. under Lt R.H.W. ROBERTS. 2 guns 226th Coy at 016 c 66.90 2 guns " at 015 d 25.60 } also attached. JHR	
09 a 7.2.	3-9-17	11 pm	Relief completed. JHR Reconnoitred right positions with O.C. 90th M.G. Coy- preparatory to relief. JHR Enemy artillery fairly active. JHR	
	4-9-17	9.30 a.m.	Coy H.Q. moved to DENYS FARM. JHR 4 guns at DENYS FARM fired 1000 rounds testing SOS lines at dawn. JHR Enemy artillery active in RAVINE WOOD. In the evening 2 guns of 016 c 44.24, 4 guns at 021 c 9.7 and 2 guns (226 Coy) at 016 c 65.90 were relieved by guns of 90 M.G. Coy. 2 guns (226 Coy) at 015 d 25.60 were withdrawn. On relief 2 guns No.4 Section from 016 c 44.24 relieved 4 guns No.3 Section in ROSE WOOD. Nos 2 & 3 Sections returned to the Transport Lines at KEMMEL. 10 R. reinforcement. JHR	
015 c 96.70	5-9-17	8.45 am 6.45 pm	250 rounds fired at enemy aircraft. JHR 250 rounds fired at enemy aircraft. JHR	
	6-9-17		From 11 pm to 3 am enemy artillery very active, chiefly on RAVINE WOOD & DENYS WOOD. JHR From midnight to 4 a.m. 1000 rounds fired indirect on area 018 a. JHR	

A.5834 Wt.W4973/M687 750,000 8/16 D.D.&L.Ltd. Forms/C.2118/13.

Army Form C. 2118.

WAR DIARY
or
INTELLIGENCE SUMMARY.
(Erase heading not required.)

Vol. XIX of 89TH MACHINE GUN COMPANY.
for SEPTEMBER 1917   MACHINE GUN CORPS.
p. 2.

Place	Date	Hour	Summary of Events and Information	Remarks and references to Appendices
O15b9 6.70	7-9-17		Between midnight & 4 a.m. 1500 rounds fired on area O18a. Enemy artillery fairly quiet.	JHR
	8-9-17		Between midnight & 4 a.m. 1500 rounds fired on area O18a. Lt J.H. GARDNER + 1 O.R. reinforcement.	JHR
			2 guns in ROSE WOOD moved forward to a position at O10d 37.45 to fire S.E. 2 guns moved up from DENYS FARM to replace them.	JHR
	9-9-17		Between midnight & 4 a.m. 1500 rounds fired on area O18a.	JHR
		4.30 pm	400 rounds fired on enemy aircraft.	JHR
			Intersection relief carried out, No.2 Section relieving No.4 in the 4 forward positions + No.3 Section relieving No.1 in support.	JHR
	10-9-17		2 guns in ROSE WOOD moved our 4 relieved 4 guns of 90th M.G. Coy. - one taking over BUG FARM post at O16c 65.90 and one FLEA FARM post at O16c 44.24. 1 O.R. reinforcement.	JHR
	11-9-17	1.30 am	The S.O.S. indirect barrage line was altered.	JHR
		3.0 am	Gun at BUG FARM fired 500 rounds as enemy appeared to be firing heavily on its front. Guns at DENYS FARM registered new S.O.S. line with 500 rounds.	JHR
			1 of the guns at O11a 00 moved into SUPPORT FARM post at O11c 42.97 which was taken over from the infantry, field of fire being as before.	JHR
	12-9-17	3 am	500 rounds fired on S.O.S. line for registration.	JHR
			Enemy artillery rather more active.	JHR
	13-9-17		500 rounds fired on S.O.S. line during night. from RAVINE guns O10d 37.45. No.1 Section brought up to do intense harassing fire. Positions prepared at O16 04 + O10d 73.55.	JHR
	14-9-17		Enemy artillery active particularly at night.	JHR
	15-9-17	9 pm	No.1 Section fired intense for 10 minutes on Lock 5 area.	JHR
		1.0 am		HOLLEBEKE CHATEAU area JHR
		4.0 am		Tracks in P7C area JHR
			In all 8,000 rounds were fired.	JHR
		1.30 pm	500 rounds fired on enemy aircraft.	JHR
			No.1 Section prepared positions for 6 guns at O11a 06.40 to fire a flanking barrage to assist advance of 19th Divn on our left. No.4 Section relieved No.2 in the forward positions. 1 O.R. reinforcement	JHR JHR

A 5834 Wt. W4973/M687 750,000 8/16 D. D. & L. Ltd. Forms/C.2118/13.

Army Form C.²

WAR DIARY
of 89TH MACHINE GUN COMPANY
INTELLIGENCE SUMMARY.
(M)ACHINE GUN CORPS.

Vol XIX for SEPTEMBER 1917 p.3.

Instructions regarding War Diaries and Intelligence Summaries are contained in F.S. Regs., Part II. and the Staff Manual respectively. Title pages will be prepared in manuscript.

(Erase heading not required.)

Place	Date	Hour	Summary of Events and Information	Remarks and references to Appendices
015b96.70	16.9.17	—	No1 Section carried on night firing programme – Bursts were fired at 10pm, midnight, & 3am – 6,000 rounds were fired. Work on the battery position continued. JHR	
—	17.9.17	—	Usual night firing programme carried out by No1 Section. JHR	
—	18.9.17	—	No1 Section fired 8,000 on targets as before. 2nd Lt. C.A. LOCKE reported on being posted as reinforcement. JHR	
—	19.9.17	—	Usual night firing programme. All preparations for barrage complete. Night firing for night 19/20th was carried out from the battery positions & was as usual. JHR. All guns in position by dusk. JHR	
—	20.9.17	5.40am	Our Zero hour. 8 guns specially detailed opened fire in accordance with O.O. No 11. See Appendix XII guns detailed to cover the raid also fired as ordered. JHR	
		9am	Report received from O.C. No1 Section that attack appeared to be going well. Our troops in HESSIAN WOOD. JHR. Those battery was heavily shelled for the first 3/4 hour but not after that. JHR	
		7.25pm	S.O.S. Signal sent up. all guns fired. JHR	
		8.8pm	Situation quiet. JHR. 2 guns No 4 Section returned to their original position at 010d 37.45. JHR	
			Casualties. 1 O.R. Killed – 2 O.R. Slightly wounded. JHR.	
—	21.9.17	—	At dawn a heavy barrage was put up. Our guns fired JHR. No2 Section relieved No 4 who relieved No.3. JHR	
—	22.9.17	7am	During the night a very heavy night firing programme was carried out. JHR Barrage battery (No1 Section) & ammunition limbers withdrawn & normal conditions resumed. Since Zero on 20-9-17 202,000 rounds were fired. JHR. At D.W.LOCHHEAD to England for a course. JHR	
—	23.9.17	—	Normal day. JHR.	
—	24.9.17	—	Fairly quiet. JHR.	
—	26.9.17	—	No firing carried out as Battalions were moving JHR. Arrangements made for barrage on HOLLEBEKE CHATEAU P7c 9.1.34 ⅔	
—	26.9.17	—	Normal. JHR. Arrangements for barrage cancelled. JHR	
—	27.9.17	—	Normal. JHR	
—	28.9.17	—	Enemy active at night. One of the guns at 010d 37.45 to 011c 05.50. JHR arrangements made for barrage on HOLLEBEKE CHATEAU P7c 9.1.34 ⅔	

Army Form C. 2118.

WAR DIARY
or
INTELLIGENCE SUMMARY

Vol XIX for 89th MACHINE GUN COMPANY.
SEPTEMBER. MACHINE GUN CORPS -
1917
p.4.

(Erase heading not required.)

Places	Date	Hour	Summary of Events and Information	Remarks and references to Appendices
O15b 46 70	28-9-17		Inter Section relief carried out. No 3 Section relieved No 2 in the forward positions + No 1 relieved No 4 in the support. THR	
	29-9-17		Normal. Enemy artillery rather active in early morning THR	
	30-9-17		Normal. THR	

T.A. Rowland Capt.
Comdg 89 M.G. Coy.

89 M.G. Coy. Operation Order No. 11   SECRET:
             by
         Capt. J.H. Roxburgh   Appendix XII to Vol IX
                                          of WAR DIARY
                                          19-9-17

1. INTENTION. On 20th September 1917 the troops on our left will attack. The attack will be supported by flanking fire from 16 Machine guns of 30th Divn. as follows:—
   (a) 6 guns - 89 Coy } firing a flanking barrage moving from a line
       6 guns - 90 Coy } O6d 25.30 - P1 a 6.8 to a line O6d 75.00 - P1 d 8.6.
   (b) 2 guns - 89 Coy - firing on HOLLEBEKE chateau.
       2 guns - 90 Coy - "   " area - P7c 9.4.3.4.
   16 guns - 37th Division ┐
   4   " - 19th ——————   │ will also assist.
   6   " - 19th M.M.G.   ┘

2. DISPOSITIONS. Lt H.G. FAULKNER & No1 Section (6 guns) will carry out (a) from positions about O11a 1.4.
   Lt. W.G. BOLDERO & 2 guns No 4 Section (moved from positions at O 10d 2.5) will carry out (b) from about O 10d 8.6.
   The remaining defensive guns will keep their present positions & 2 more guns will be placed in DENYS Farm (see para 9).

3. ACTION. Guns in para 1. will fire at full rate from Zero to Z+ 2.30hrs in accordance with tables already issued. to Z+ 3.30hrs
   From half Z+2.30 hrs guns of No1 Section only will fire at half rate 6° right of their S.O.S. lines & afterwards will relay on their S.O.S. line.

4. SUBSEQUENT ACTION. From Z+ 3.30 hrs onwards fire will be opened according to the tactical situation & on receipt of the S.O.S.
   Fire will be opened from Z+5 hrs to Z+5.30 hrs while troops further on the left advance to their 2nd objective.

5. GUNS OF OPPORTUNITY. The forward defensive guns will keep a sharp look out for any favourable targets, which must be engaged at once.

6. ASSEMBLY. Guns mentioned in para 1. will assemble on the evening of the 19th inst & report to DELBSKE Farm when they are ready. They will take 1 extra day's rations.

7. Coy H.Q. Coy HQ will be at DELBSKE Farm until further notice. Communication thence to Nos 1 & 4 Sections will be by runner.

8. DISTINCTIVE MARKS. Our attacking troops can be distinguished by yellow patches & black & yellow flags.

9. MINOR OPERATIONS. In addition to the above, a raid will be made by the 19th K.L.R on the TWINS & the 2nd Beds. on O12 c 3.7.
   This will be covered by M.G. Fire from 30th Division.
   89 Coy will fire on BOMB FARM & CENTRE FARM with 4 guns.
   For this purpose 4 guns at DENYS FARM will be used. They will fire from Z+11 min. to Z+45 min. at full rate (1 belt per 4 min).

10. S.A.A. Guns firing the barrage (para 1.) will have 20 belts & 2 boxes S.A.A. + 3 barrels per gun. Any further supply of S.A.A. will be through ROSE WOOD DUMP.

11. RESERVES. Any guns knocked out during operations will be replaced from DENYS FARM.

12. ZERO etc. Zero hour will be notified later. Watches will be synchronized on the evening of 19th.

                                    J.H. Roxburgh
                                          Capt.
                                    Comdg 89 M.G. Coy.

Details for 89 MG Coy - 6 guns in flanking barrage of 30th Divn.

Gun No.	Position	Target	Contours in metres Gun	Contours in metres Target	V.I. yards	Q.E.	Range for Q.E.	Bearing grid	Rate of fire	Rate of Traverse	Remarks	Aerial Range
No 1 89 Coy	O.11.a 06.40	066 80.18 to Pic 76.30	50	38	-13	4°18'	2000	65°				2075
				25	-27½	6°50'	2275	79°		1° in 2 min		2375
No 2 89 Coy	O.11.a 06.42	066 98.31 to Pic 97.35	50	42	-9	5°	2130	64°				2175
				24	-28	6°35'	2380	79°		1° in 2 min		2475
No 3 89 Coy	O.11.a 06.44	Pid 15.45 to Pid 15.42	50	43	-8	5°39'	2250	64°				2275
				25	-27½	7°28'	2500	79°		1° in 2 min		2575
No 4 89 Coy	O.11.a 08.46	Pid 32.57 to Pid 37.48	50	42	-9	6°19'	2350	63°				2375
				25	-27½	8°21'	2610	79°		1° in 3 min		2675
No 5 89 Coy	O.11.a 08.43	Pid 48.70 to Pid 57.54	50	41	-10	7°2'	2450	62°				2475
				25	-27½	9°23'	2720	79°		1° in 3 min		2775
No 6 89 Coy	O.11.a 11.42	Pid 6.8 to Pid 8.6	49	39	-11	7°50'	2550	62°				2575
				24	-27½	10°30'	2840	79°		1° in 3 min		2875

Details of Special guns assisting Flanking Barrage of 30th Div.

Gun No.	Position	Contour in metres. Gun.	Target.	V.I. yards.	Q.E.	Range for Q.E.	Bearing-grid.	Rate of fire.	Traverse.	Remarks.	Actual Range
No 7 89 Coy.	O.10.d 73.55.	47	HOLLEBEKE CHATEAU 24.	-25	4°42'	2080	73½° to 80°	1 belt per 3 min.	Inwards Traversing	Cones overlap 55 yds. Depth of combined 90% Zone = 255 yds = depth of target.	2200
No 6 89 Coy.	O.10.d 75.62.	47	HOLLEBEKE CHATEAU 24.	-25	5°21'	2200	79½° to 73°	—	—	Fire to be supplemented by direct fire of 2 guns at 0.11.a.08.40.	2300
No 7 90 Coy.	O.11.c 12.42.	42	P7c 94.34 23.	-22	6°7'	2330	90°	—	Inwards Traversing to 2° right.	Depth of 90% Zone = 170 yards.	2400
No 8 90 Coy.	O.11.c 12.41.	42	P7c 94.34 23.	-22	6°7'	2330	91½°	—	Inwards Traversing to 2° left.		2400

S.O.S. Barrage - 89 M.G. Coy   Appendix XIII
                                 13 Vol XIX - War Diary

GUN POSITION	TARGET OR BARRAGE LINE	RANGE (yds) TARGET	RANGE (yds) OWN TROOPS	HEIGHT (metres) Gun Target	HEIGHT (metres) O.T.	Q.E.	Clearance (yds)	True Bearing (centre)	Traverse (Right & Left)	Remarks
SUPPORT FARM O11c 42.97	O18c 76.68 to O18c 50.39	1660	900	47 35	30	2°20'	38	137½°	3½°	
MARBLE ARCH O11a 0.0.	O18a 80.25 to O18c 80.00	1950	1200	57 33	35	3°26'	55	137°	3°	
OLIVE STREET O11c 05.50	O18a 78.09 to O18c 77.68	1600	920	43 33	31	2°12'	32	121½°	3½°	
RAVINE GUN O10d 27.45	O18a 79.45 to O18a 78.09	1800	1200	45 29	30	2°47'	42	109°	3°	
DENYS FARM (left) O15G 90.77	O12 a 80.20 to O18a 80.82	2450	1825	50 24	29	6°22'	107	87°	2½°	
DENYS FARM (right) O15G 90.70	O18 a 80.82 to O18a 79.45	2450	1850	49 26	30	6°28'	108	91°	2½°	
BUG FARM O16c 65.90	O12d 66.96 to O12c 80.60	2250 to 2750	1550	47 25	28	5°4' to 9°11'	87	68°	VERTICAL SEARCHING	
FLEA FARM O16c 44.24	O12 c 80.60 to O12 c 80.20	2450	1750	53 24	29	6°18'	125	64°	3°	
	30-9-17									

WAR DIARY

of the 89TH MACHINE GUN COMPANY

for the month of OCTOBER 1917 –

Volume XX

SECRET

258.
1-11-17-

Headquarters
89th Inf. Bde.

Herewith Volume XX of the WAR DIARY of this Unit, for necessary action, please.

Kindly acknowledge receipt.

F.H. Roxburgh
Capt.
Comdg 89 M.G. Coy.

WAR DIARY
of 89th MACHINE GUN COMPANY — INTELLIGENCE SUMMARY. MACHINE GUN CORPS —

Vol. XX   for OCTOBER 1917   p.1.

Reference Map. WYTSCHAETE/Moore JHR

Place	Date	Hour	Summary of Events and Information	Remarks and references to Appendices
O.15.b.96.70.	1-10-17	5 a.m.	89 M.G. Coy holding the line in the HOLLEBEKE Sector — for dispositions see Vol XIX for SEPTEMBER. JHR	
			Hostile artillery active from 5 a.m. to 5.45 a.m. JHR	
		5.10 a.m.	4,000 rounds fired on SOS call. JHR	
	2-10-17		Normal day. JHR	
			Hostile artillery active in the early morning. JHR	
	3-10-17		800 rounds fired at E.A. flying low over our lines. JHR	
	4-10-17	5 a.m.	Normal day — Inter Section relief — 2 O.R. reinforcements from 21 M.G. Coy & 5 O.R. from 41 M.G. Coy. JHR	
	5-10-17		S.O.S. sent up on Left. Otherwise nothing to report. JHR	
	6-10-17	12.40 a.m.	Quiet day — Enemy M.Gs very quiet. JHR	
	7-10-17		S.O.S. sent up on right front — Our guns fired 5,000 rounds. JHR	
	8-10-17		Enemy active in the early morning but quiet during the day. Poor observation. JHR	
			Enemy artillery active in the morning while observation was good. gun at Support Farm + gun at Marble Arch relieved by 2 guns of 90 M.G. Coy. These 2 guns came to DENYS FARM, relieving 2 guns of No 2 Section, which in turn relieved 2 guns of 226 M.G. Coy at O.22.a.3.7 and O.22.a.3.9. JHR	
	9-10-17		Normal day. JHR	
	10-10-17		Quiet day — Inter section relief. 5,000 rounds fired at dusk + dawn 11-10-17 on enemy Backs. JHR	
	11-10-17		Enemy attitude normal. 5,000 rounds fired at dusk + dawn 12-10-17 on enemy Backs. JHR	
	12-10-17		Enemy activity slightly below normal — M.Gs very quiet — 1,000 rounds fired at E.A. JHR	
	13-10-17		Quiet day — 500 rounds fired on enemy aircraft. JHR	
	14-10-17		Normal — JHR	
	15-10-17		Enemy more active during night — Quiet day — JHR Lt. H.G. FAULKNER appointed 2nd in command of 24 M.G. Coy. JHR	
	16-10-17	5 a.m.	Our MGs fired 2,000 rounds on enemy Backs. O.18.c. until 6 a.m. Inter section relief at dusk. JHR	
	17-10-17	12.15 a.m.	Our MGs fired 4,000 rounds on enemy Backs until 12.45 p.m. JHR	
	"	7.15 p.m.	Our M.Gs fired 2,000 rounds on Backs in the vicinity of PILL FARM (O.24.a) until 9.15 p.m. JHR	
	18-10-17	8 p.m.	Our M.Gs fired 2,000 rounds on Backs in O.18.a. until 9 p.m. JHR	
	19-10-17		Enemy artillery active during afternoon + evening. JHR	
	20-10-17	5 a.m.	Our MGs fired 2,000 rounds on Backs in O.18.c. until 6 a.m. JHR	
			2,500 rounds fired at E.A. during day. Enemy artillery active from 2.30 p.m. to 4 p.m. JHR	

WAR DIARY

of 89th Machine Gun Company

INTELLIGENCE SUMMARY. Machine Gun Corps.

Vol. XX.
1st OCTOBER 1917
p. 2.

Army Form C. 2118.

(Erase heading not required.)

Instructions regarding War Diaries and Intelligence Summaries are contained in F.S. Regs., Part II. and the Staff Manual respectively. Title pages will be prepared in manuscript.

Place	Date	Hour	Summary of Events and Information	Remarks and references to Appendices
D15b 96.70	21.10.17	5 am	Our M.G's fired 2,000 rounds on PILL FARM until 6 a.m. Enemy artillery very active during the day. 1500 rounds fired at low flying enemy aircraft.	JHR
—	22.10.17	5.10 am	Our MGs fired 2,000 rounds on PILL FARM until 6 a.m. Enemy artillery again active. DENYS FARM received special attention from 9.15 to 9.45 am, 10.30 to 10.45 am, & 2.30 to 2.45 p.m. JHR Intersection Relief	JHR
		6.30 pm	Our M.Gs fired 2,000 rounds on PUMP FARM & SPUD FARM until 7.45 p.m. JHR	
—	23.10.17		Enemy shelling mostly on night section's front. JHR	
—	24.10.17	11.12 am	Our M.Gs fired 2,000 rounds on enemy tracks in O18 d. JHR 42,000 rounds on O18 c from 9.20 pm to 10.40 pm	JHR
—	25.10.17		Enemy artillery again more active during day. JHR 2 O.R. reinforcements JHR	
—		7 pm	Our M.Gs fired 2,000 rounds on tracks in D12.c. till 8 p.m. JHR	
—	26.10.17		Normal day. JHR	
—	27.10.17	3.30 am	Our M.Gs fired 2,000 rounds on tracks in O18 b. JHR Hostile artillery considerably more active JHR	
—		7.15 pm	Our MGs fired 2,000 rounds on tracks in O24 a. until 7.45 p.m. JHR	
—	28.10.17		DENYS FARM received continuous attention from 8 pm until 5 am. from 4.2 & 5.9 s. JHR Normal day. 1 O.R reinforcement from Base JHR Intersection relief JHR	
—	29.10.17	1 am	Our MGs fired 2,000 rounds on tracks in O24 a. until 2 am JHR Hostile artillery again active JHR	
—	30.10.17	5.10 am	Our MGs fired 2,000 rounds on tracks in O18 c & d. until 5.40 am. JHR	
—		noon	1 O.R killed O.R. RANKINE GUN D10 d 37.45. Normal day JHR 4 O.R. reinforcements JHR	
—	30.10.17	11 pm	Our MGs fired 2,000 rounds on PILL FARM & tracks in O24 a until midnight JHR	
—	31.10.17		Normal day. 1 O.R reinforcement of 2nd Lt. E. FIELD reported on posting to 89 MGCoy JHR Our MGs fired 2,000 rounds between 10.40 p.m. till 11 p.m. and 11.15 p.m. & 11.40 p.m. JHR	

J.A. Roxburgh
Capt.
Comdg 89 MGCoy

Vol 21

WAR DIARY.

OF THE 89th MACHINE GUN COMPANY.

FOR THE MONTH OF NOVEMBER 1917.

Volume XXI

SECRET

WAR DIARY

Army Form C. 2118.

of **89TH MACHINE GUN COMPANY**, **MACHINE GUN CORPS**

Vol XXI

INTELLIGENCE SUMMARY for NOVEMBER 1917 P.1.

Reference Maps: WYTSCHAETE — 1:14,000
ZILLEBEKE — 1:10,000
HAZEBROUCK — 1:100,000
BELGIUM — Sheets 27 & 28 1:40,000

Place	Date	Hour	Summary of Events and Information	Remarks and references to Appendices
O15 & 6.70	1-11-17		89 M.G. Coy holding the line in the HOLLEBEKE Sector. For disposition see Vol XX for OCTOBER. JHR Normal day. 2,000 rounds fired by No 17 gun on S.O.S. line between 8.10 p.m & 9 p.m; 9.30 p.m & 9.40 p.m; 9.50 p.m & 10 p.m. JHR	
	2-11-17		Quiet day. JHR	
	3-11-17	5 a.m	2,250 rounds fired on D.24.d from VERNE ROAD until 5.30 a.m. JHR Inter Section relief carried out. JHR	
		8 p.m	2,000 rounds fired on O.18.d until 9 p.m. JHR	
	4-11-17		Quiet day. 2 enemy planes flew over low at 4.30 p.m & were fired on. JHR RAVINE GUN (No 21) fired 1,000 rounds on S.O.S line from 5.40 p.m to 6.10 p.m. JHR Enemy M.Gs active at night. JHR	
	5-11-17		Quiet day. Enemy aeroplanes active from 11 a.m to 3 p.m on our right front. JHR Enemy M.Gs again active at night. JHR	
	6-11-17	4.15 a.m	Our M.Gs engaged O.18.d until 4.30 a.m — 1000 rounds fired JHR Normal day with considerable aerial activity. JHR	
	7-11-17	1.30 a.m	1000 rounds fired by OLIVE TRENCH GUN (No 22) until 1.45 a.m on S.O.S. line. JHR Rifles & rifle & fairly active during day. JHR	
	8-11-17		1000 rounds fired from 4.15 a.m to 4.30 a.m on O.18.d. JHR 2 machines brought down during morning JHR 2,000 rounds fired from 8 p.m to 9 p.m on O.18.d. JHR Inter Section relief carried out. JHR Intermittent fire kept up on ORKNEY TRENCH throughout the night. JHR	
	9-11-17		Quiet day. JHR	
	10-11-17		2,000 rounds fired from 10 p.m to 10.15 p.m on PILLEGREMS FARM. JHR	
	11-11-17		Normal day. Usual night firing. JHR	

Army Form C. 2118.

WAR DIARY
or
INTELLIGENCE SUMMARY

of 89TH MACHINE GUN COMPANY
MACHINE GUN CORPS.

(Erase heading not required).

Vol XXI for NOVEMBER 1917 p.2

Place	Date	Hour	Summary of Events and Information	Remarks and references to Appendices
0156.70	12-11-17		Normal day. Arrangements for relief made with O.C. 14th & 15th Australian M.G. Coys. JHR	
	13-11-17		Section officers of 15th A.M.G. Coy reconnoitred the line. Nos 1 went in in advance. JHR Nos 1,5,4 & 6 guns (VERNE ROAD) relieved at dusk by 2 guns of 14th A.M.G. Coy. JHR	
	14-11-17		Gun at BUG FARM (No 18) knocked out by shellfire. 2 O.R. wounded (accidental) JHR Quiet day. Very poor observation. Relief of remaining guns by 15th A.M.G. Coy commenced at 2.30 p.m. & completed by 5 p.m. On relief the Coy moved into billets in LOCRE. JHR I.O.R. reinforcement. JHR	Belgium Sheet 27
LOCRE	15-11-17		In billets in LOCRE. JHR	
LOCRE	16-11-17	8 pm	Moved off from LOCRE - by bus to the STEENVOORDE area. JHR	
J2a d 7.8	17-11-17		Two billets (and tents) at J2a d 7.8. JHR In near billets. JHR	
	23-11-17 25-11-17		Reconnoitred the ZILLEBEKE Sector (GHELUVELDT) preparatory to going in. JHR Nos 1 & 2 & 8 guns (No 1 & 3 Sections) went by bus to the forward area & thence into the line in advance. JHR Teams for the line left STEENVOORDE	ZILLEBEKE 1/10000
	26-11-17	6.30 pm	Thence into the line by lorry to own arrived ZILLEBEKE 3 p.m. relieving 118 M.G. Coy. JHR Relief complete. JHR	
STIRLING CASTLE	27-11-17		Remainder of the Coy moved to LA CLYTTE. JHR Disposition on the line as follows :- No 3. Section H.Q. - J2a R 9.3. Forward Section 1 gun (G) at J21a 4.2 firing S.E. 1 gun (H) - J21 c 0.3 " N.E. 1 gun (J) - J21 c 8.9 " S.E. 1 gun (K) 4th gun at J21c03 firing S. Support Section No 1. Sect HQ - J19 b 59. 1 gun (D) at J21 a 3.9 firing N.E. 1 gun (E) with D gun at J21 a 9.9 firing S.E. 1 gun (A) at J21 a 04 firing E. 1 gun at STIRLING CASTLE in reserve. Coy HQ J19 b 5.9. JHR	

Army Form C. 2118.

WAR DIARY
or
INTELLIGENCE SUMMARY.

Vol XXI of 89TH MACHINE GUN COMPANY. MACHINE GUN CORPS.

for NOVEMBER 1917. Title pages p 3.

(Erase heading not required.)

Place	Date	Hour	Summary of Events and Information	Remarks and references to Appendices
Tig S.9.	27-11-17		Enemy artillery active during the night. Desultory fire during day. T+R	
	28-11-17		Enemy artillery very active in the morning; chiefly on J 21 a+b. D+E guns moved to J15 c. 0.2 firing as before. T+R	
	29-11-17		Enemy artillery again very active. T+R	
	30-11-17		Fairly quiet morning; enemy active in the afternoon. Quiet night. T+R	

WH Roxburgh
Capt
89th Machine Gun Company

Comdg 89th Machine Gun Company

SECRET

H 22

War Diary Vol XXII
of the
89th Machine Gun Company
for the month of
December 1917.

Army Form C. 2118.

WAR DIARY
or
INTELLIGENCE SUMMARY.

(Erase heading not required.)

89 MACHINE GUN COMPANY
MACHINE GUN CORPS.

VOL XXII
DEZEMBER 1917

Place	Date	Hour	Summary of Events and Information	Remarks and references to Appendices
	1.12.17		89 M.G. Coy holding line in ZILLEBEKE Sector (GHELUVELDT) Dispositions in line as [before] in VOL XXI. (27.11.17). Enemy artillery very active. 4 O.R. Reinforcements. PLS	ZILLEBEKE 1/10,000 GHELUVELDT 1/10,000
	2.12.17		Quiet day. PLS	
	3.12.17		Attack in PILLER HOEK WOOD resulting in enemy artillery activity. Enemy machine guns very active at night. 2 O.R. Reinforcements. PLS	
	4.12.17		15,000 rounds fired. No 3 Position blown up. PLS	
	5.12.17		Intermittent firing by M.G's during night. Enemy artillery active. PLS	
	6.12.17		5000 rounds fired. Inter Company relief with 206 M.G.Coy carried out. PLS	
	7.12.17		Night firing carried out. Enemy artillery active. PLS	
	8.12.17		Enemy artillery active against MENIN Road. T.M's and M.G's active during night.	
	9.12.17		Enemy artillery quiet. Enemy T.M's and M.G.'s active.	
	10.12.17		Enemy artillery quiet. Enemy T.M's active at night.	
	11.12.17		Trenches.	
	12.12.17		DO	

WAR DIARY
or
INTELLIGENCE SUMMARY.

(Erase heading not required.)

Army Form C. 2118.

SQ M E Cy

Place	Date	Hour	Summary of Events and Information	Remarks and references to Appendices
	13.12.17		Trenches [ZILLEBEKE] P13	
	14.12.17		Do P13	
	15.12.17		Do P13	
	16.12.17		Do 10R Reinforcement P13	
	17.12.17		Do 10R Reinforcement. P13	
	18.12.17		Do Lt A.J.SAYER to Base; Lt P L STOCKLEY posted as 2i/c P13	
	19.12.17		Do P13	
	20.12.17		Do P13	
	21.12.17		Do P13	
	22.12.17		Do P13	
	23.12.17		Do P13	
	24.12.17		Do P13	
	25.12.17		Do Sq M E C took command of Group [Sq M E Cy and 226 M E Cy from] 12h	
	26.12.17		Do P13	
	27.12.17		Do	

Army Form C. 2118.

WAR DIARY
or
INTELLIGENCE SUMMARY.
(Erase heading not required.)

89 M.F.Cy:

Instructions regarding War Diaries and Intelligence Summaries are contained in F. S. Regs., Part II. and the Staff Manual respectively. Title pages will be prepared in manuscript.

Place	Date	Hour	Summary of Events and Information	Remarks and references to Appendices
TRENCHES	28-12-17		PSS	
do	29-12-17		PSS	
do	30-12-17		PSS	
do	31-12-17		PSS	

SECRET.

W.M. 23

War Diary

of the 69th Machine Gun Company

For the month of January 1918

Volume XXIII

Army Form C. 2118.

WAR DIARY of 89th MACHINE GUN COMPANY MACHINE GUN CORPS.

INTELLIGENCE SUMMARY

VOL XXIII
JANUARY 1918 P.1

(Erase heading not required.)

REFERENCE MAPS	
HAZEBROUCK	1/100,000
AMIENS	1/100,000
ST QUENTIN	1/100,000

Place	Date	Hour	Summary of Events and Information	Remarks and references to Appendices
	1-1-18		89 M.G. Coy holding line in ZILLEBEKE SECTOR P/S	
	2-1-18		Trenches P/S	
	3-1-18		Trenches P/S	
	4-1-18		Trenches P/S	
	5-1-18		Trenches P/S 2Lt. H.T. MORGAN JOINED for duty from Base P/S	
	6-1-18		Relieved by 60 Inf. Coy. P/S	
			1 O.R. killed in shell fire P/S	
HEURINGHEM	7-1-18		Company moved by train to HEURINGHEM P/S	
"	8-1-18		In billets P/S	
"	9-1-18		In billets P/S	
"	10-1-18		In billets P/S	
"	11-1-18		Moved by rail to CACHY P/S	
CACHY	12-1-18		In billets P/S	
	13-1-18		Moved to GUILLAUCOURT P/S	
GUILLAU-COURT VRELY	14-1-18		Marched to VRELY P/S	
	15-1-18		In billets. One O.R. reinforcement from CaC S P/S	
	16-1-18		In billets. One O.R. reinforcement from CaC P/S	
	17-1-18		do do Base P/S	
			In billets P/S	
	18-1-18		Company marched to GUERBIGNY P/S	
GUERBIGNY	19-1-18		Company marched to BEAULIEU-LES-FONTAINE P/S	

WAR DIARY of 99 MACHINE GUN COMPANY

INTELLIGENCE SUMMARY. MACHINE GUN CORPS

Vol XXIII
JANUARY 1918. P.2.

Place	Date	Hour	Summary of Events and Information	Remarks and references to Appendices
BEAULIEU LES FONTAINE	20.1.18		In billets. 1 OR rejoined from Base. PS	
	21.1.18		In billets. PS	
	22.1.18		In billets. 9 OR reinforcements from Base. PS	
	23.1.18		In billets. Lieut W.G. BOLDERO rejoined from C.C.S. PS	
	24.1.18		In billets. PS	
	25.1.18		In billets. PS	
	26.1.18		In billets. PS	
	27.1.18		Company marched to DAMPCOURT PS	
	28.1.18		Company marched to NOUREUIL PS	
	29.1.18		Company relieved 338 Reg (French) in LA FÈRE Sector: 8 guns taken	PS located at
	30.1.18		in F war positions. PLS	87 M.G.C.
	31.1.18		Company in line at LA FÈRE PLS Sectn: HQ at PARGNIERS:	

Vol 24

MEME
Bill Diary
Vol. XXIV

SECRET

WAR DIARY
or
INTELLIGENCE SUMMARY

Army Form C. 2118.

Vol. XXIV of 89th MACHINE GUN COMPANY. MACHINE GUN CORPS.

For FEBRUARY 1918. p.1

Place	Date	Hour	Summary of Events and Information	Reference maps	Remarks and references to Appendices
	1-2-18		89th M.G. Coy holding the line in the LA FÈRE sector. For disposition see Vol. XXIII for January 1918. RwR	ST QUENTIN - 18 - 1:100,000 FRANCE 66 D NE - 1:20,000 FRANCE 62 B SW - 1:20,000 FRANCE 66 C NW - 1:20,000 FRANCE 66 C SW - 1:20,000	FRANCE 66 C SW.
	2-2-18		Quiet day. RwR		
	3-2-18		Enemy artillery very quiet. RwR		
	4-2-18		1 M.G. Section relief carried out. RwR		
	5-2-18				
	6-2-18		Zone byn shelled in FARGNIER ratio 3am. Otherwise quiet. RwR		
	7-2-18		Day very quiet. Hostile aeroplane active during afternoon. RwR Section officers and No 1 of 206 M.G. By came into the positions, prior to taking over the line. RwR.		
	8-2-18		Nos 2 and 4 Sections 89th M.G. Coy were relieved by 206 by at 8pm and 9pm respectively. RwR Remainder of the Coy in the same Section on relief, moved back to billets at CREPIGNY.		
	9-2-18		Moved by road to rest billets at QUESMY. RwR		
	10-2-18		Moved by road to billets at GOLANCOURT. RwR		
	11-2-18		Moved to rest billets at ESMERY-HALLON. RwR		
	12-2-18 to 19-2-18		In rest billets. RwR		
	20-2-18				
	21-2-18		Marched to billets at DOUCHY. C.O. reconnoitred the line in ST QUENTIN Sector. RwR		
	22-2-18		Section officers and Nos 1 of Nos 1 and 3 Sections moved into the line from to taking over the Sector. RwR		

Army Form C. 2118.

WAR DIARY of 89th MACHINE GUN COMPANY
INTELLIGENCE SUMMARY. MACHINE GUN CORPS

Vol XIV
Part II.
Title page FEBRUARY 1918
p. 2.

Place	Date	Hour	Summary of Events and Information	Remarks and references to Appendices
	23-2-18		Nos 1 and 3 Sections took over the following positions in the ST QUENTIN Section from 109 M.G. Coy. Right Section. No 13 3 guns A4d 3.4, 3.6 and 3.6. Left Section. No 15 2 guns A5a 2.3 and 2.5. No 14 1 gun A4a 3.3	66 C.N.W.
	24-2-18		Sector very quiet at night. An enemy aeroplane dropped bombs on ST QUENTIN. Ref	
	25-2-18		Very quiet day. The following changes were made in the gun positions taken up on the 23rd. 2 of the No 13 guns were moved to A10d 1.4 - 1 of No 13 guns to join No 14 A4a 3.3. No 16 1 gun S2a 2.2. No 17 2 guns S2c 9.05 and 9.1. No 18 1 gun S28a 15.3. Ref. No 16 gun withdrawn to 1 gun No 18 gun at S28a 5.3. Ref	62 B S W
	26-2-18		Very quiet day. Ref	
	27-2-18		Enemy attitude quiet. Great aerial activity on both sides. Ref	
	28-2-18		Message was received at 12 noon to take "Preparatory action" in accordance with Defence Scheme. Six guns were in reserve at Coy H.Q. Two of these were sent up to the redoubt 66 C N.W. M. LEFINE DE DALLON. All guns stand ordered to "Stand By". Ref	FRANCE

Robertson Roberts
Lieut.
89th M.G. Coy.

~~3 ARMY TROOPS~~

30 DIV

89 BDE

89
TRENCH MORTAR BTY

1915 SEP. TO 1916 APL

37 Div
110 Bde
III Bde 121/
6973

3rd Army

A.P.

89th Trench Mortar Batty.

Sept 15

large % of french mortar shells
which failed to explode & pieces

Army Form C. 2118

Instructions regarding War Diaries and Intelligence Summaries are contained in F.S. Regs., Part II. and the Staff Manual respectively. Title Pages will be prepared in manuscript.

WAR DIARY
or
INTELLIGENCE SUMMARY
(Erase heading not required.)

Place	Date	Hour	Summary of Events and Information	Remarks and references to Appendices
In the Field	Sept 17 1915	8.30 p.m.	The 89th Trench Horta Battery (off firing at too great a distance from the 1½" Battery) came into action. Went into the Trenches held by the 6th Bn the Leicester Regt. 110th Inf. Brigade, in front of BERLES au BOIS. was attached to 110th Inf. Brigade owing to the trenches held by 110th Brigade	
" "	Sept 18 1915		Built alternative emplacements in the trenches held by 6th Bn. The Leicester Regt. with ranges from 120x–325x.	
" "	Sept 19 1915		Constructed Bomb proofs and Shelters both for men and guns.	
" "	Sept 20 1915	9.30 a.m.	Fired with light bombs on German positions opposite trench Rs 4 held by "A" Company 6th Bn The Leicester Regt. Out of six bombs two failed to explode. Quantities of timber and earth were seen to fly into the air from German Trench. The enemy replied with 15 whiz bangs, but no damage was done.	
" "	Sept 21st 1915	9 a.m.	Fired six heavy bombs from a position in a cutting off communication trench running parallel with the BERLES-MONCHY Road at a range of 125x. One failed to explode. The remaining five did damage to the enemy's wire & parapet.	
" "	Sept 22 1915	10.30 a.m.	Six light bombs were fired from position behind Rs 4 held by 6th Leicesters. One failed to explode but five did material damage to enemy's dugouts and parapet. The enemy replied with seven whiz bangs but did no damage.	
" "	" "	11 a.m.	Three heavy bombs were fired from position near BERLES-MONCHY Road, at the enemy's machine gun emplacement in sunken road. Range 180x. Two of the bombs failed to explode.	
" "	" "	3 p.m.	Six heavy bombs were again fired from this position. Two failed to explode. The other four cut the enemy's wire and blew up some dugouts to the amount of timber was seen to fly into the air. The enemy did not reply.	
" "	Sept 23 1915		No rounds were fired, as there was not an unlimited supply of bombs.	
" "	Sept 24 1915	6.20 a.m.	Six light bombs were fired from position behind Rs 4 at the enemy's first line. Three failed to explode, range 285x. The others were effective on enemy's trench.	
" "	" "	11 a.m.	Six heavy bombs were fired from position on BERLES-MONCHY Road at enemy's machine gun emplacement, range 125x. One failed to explode. The other five exploded in wire entanglement round machine gun emplacement.	
" "	Sept 25 1915	7.30 a.m.	The enemy searched for the Trench Horta position with whiz bangs but failed to locate them. Nine bombs were fired at enemy's position on BERLES-MONCHY Road parting with whiz bangs. Four bombs failed to explode and six exploded but there was no proof that the machine gun emplacement of the remaining five were effective on machine gun emplacement. Puts one of action	

WAR DIARY or INTELLIGENCE SUMMARY

Army Form C. 2118

(Erase heading not required.)

Instructions regarding War Diaries and Intelligence Summaries are contained in F. S. Regs., Part II. and the Staff Manual respectively. Title Pages will be prepared in manuscript.

Place	Date	Hour	Summary of Events and Information	Remarks and references to Appendices
In the Field	Sept 26th 1915	7 a.m.	Eight light bombs were fired from position behind BL4 held by A Coy 8th Bn The Liverpools eg.f. On first 13 exploded and four were effective. Two dropping in the trench and five in the parapet. The enemy replied with a few rifle grenades but did no damage. An alternative emplacement was made in communication trench joining B.3, B.5 to enable the Battery to fire heavy bombs into this part of the German line.	
" "	Sept 27th 1915	7.15 a.m.	From the new emplacement in communication trench joining B.3, B.5. Three heavy bombs were fired on enemy's trench. The first two failed to explode, the third blew in the enemy's parapet.	
" "	"	11.45 a.m.	In conjunction with the 8th Liverpools rifle grenade party, eight light bombs were fired on the enemy's trench opposite B.4. Four failed to explode and four burst on the trench. It was not ascertained what damage was done. The enemy replied with rifle grenades and bombs.	
" "	"	4.5 p.m.	The enemy fired 16 Lozell battery with two aeroplane arrow aerial torpedoes and about eight other shells. About 6 or 8 these burst within 30' of the position of the Battery but no damage was done.	
" "	Sept 28, 29, 30		For these days no ammunition was expended as the battery has only a few bombs on hand and it was thought advisable to keep a small reserve.	
	Oct 1st/15			

W.R. Bradshaw Lt. M'Leuiots
O.C. 89th Trench Mortar Battery.

WAR DIARY *or* **INTELLIGENCE SUMMARY**

89/2 TRENCH MORTAR BATTERY

Army Form C. 2118.

From 12th April 1916 to 30th April 1916

Place	Date	Hour	Summary of Events and Information	Remarks and references to Appendices
POULAINVILLE	1916 12 Apl	3 pm	Unit formed. Personnel proceeded to XIII Corps Trench Mortar School POULAINVILLE for instruction in Stokes 3" Trench Mortar Gun. Strength of Unit:- 2nd Lieut. B. NEWTON (from 2 BEDFORDSHIRE REGT) in command, 2nd Lieut. W. LINDSAY and 24 O.R. B.L. (from 17th KINGS LIVERPOOL REGT), 12 O.R. from 2 BEDFORD REGT. and 12 O.R. from 19th KINGS LIVERPOOL REGT. B.L.	
do.	19 Apl	1 pm	Left XIII Corps Trench Mortar School. B.L.	
SAILLY-LAURETTE	19 Apl	4 pm	Went into billets at SAILLY-LAURETTE. B.L.	
do.	20 Apl	11.30 am	Left billets and went into billets at MARICOURT. B.L.	
MARICOURT	do	8 pm	Personnel and 4 guns arrived at MARICOURT taking 4 guns and relieved the 53/2 TRENCH MORTAR BATTERY. B.L.	

Bernard Newton 2 Lieut.
O.C. 89/2 Trench Mortar Battery.

Army Form C. 2118.

WAR DIARY
or
INTELLIGENCE SUMMARY 89/2 TRENCH MORTAR BATTERY.

(Erase heading not required.)

VOL. II.

Place	Date	Hour	Summary of Events and Information	Remarks and references to Appendices
MARICOURT	1916 29 Apr (5:35 a.m.)		The Battery remained at MARICOURT during this period and constructed tunnel emplacements behind the front line. R.L.	
	25 May 7 a.m.		Left MARICOURT, taking 6 mortars after being relieved by 21/2 TRENCH MORTAR BATTERY. R.L.	
AILLY SUR SOMME	26 May 11 a.m.		Arrived at billets in this village and immediately entered upon a special course of training. R.L.	

Bernard Weston Keith
OC 89/2 Trench Mortar Battery.

Vol. 2. copy May June 30
Army Form C. 2118.
89 T M B
Vol 2 q 3

WAR DIARY
or
INTELLIGENCE SUMMARY

Place	Date	Hour	Summary of Events and Information	Remarks and references to Appendices
MARICOURT.	MAY.		Work carried out on tunnel emplacements	
	16.5.16.		Orders received to prepare for Minor enterprise on 21.5.16. bh.	
	19.5.16		Three emplacements prepared on the left of Z, entrance. bh.	
	20.5.16.		New orders received to protect left flank of raiding party. Three new positions prepared in MARICOURT WOOD, near the SQUARE & CROUCH ST. bh.	
	21.5.16	8.00 a.m.	Minor enterprise cancelled. bh.	
MERICOURT LOCK S.S. 16.	do.	7.30 a.m.	Battery proceeded to MERICOURT LOCK. bh.	
		3.00 p.m.	Battery proceeded by barge to AILLY-SUR-SOMME. bh.	
AILLY-SUR-SOMME	26.5.16	11.00 a.m.	Arrived at AILLY-SUR-SOMME, & went into billets, pending training at SAINTE SAUVEUR. bh.	

Winded of Lieut.
for OC 89/1 T M B.

Vol. 3.   Copy.

Army Form C. 2118.

WAR DIARY
or
INTELLIGENCE SUMMARY
(Erase heading not required.)

Instructions regarding War Diaries and Intelligence Summaries are contained in F. S. Regs., Part II. and the Staff Manual respectively. Title Pages will be prepared in manuscript.

Place	Date	Hour	Summary of Events and Information	Remarks and references to Appendices
AILLY-SUR-SOMME	4.6.16	9.0.a.m.	Dug trench at SAINTE SAUVEUR for purpose of a Stokes Display before Brigade. W.	
	5.6.16 to 10.6.16		Took part in Brigade training for attack in German trenches north of MARICOURT. Carried out practice firing on the training area. W.	
	11.6.16		Took part in final rehearsal of the Special Training. W.	
	12.6.16	9.0 a.m.	Entrained at AILLY-SUR-SOMME. W.	
HEILLY	12.6.16	12. noon	Retained at HEILLY. W.	
ETINEHEM	do.	2.0 p.m.	Proceeded to ETINEHEM CAMP. No 2. arriving at 5.0 p.m. W.	
	15.6.16	—	89/1 & 89/2 TRENCH MORTAR BATTERIES become one unit, with title 89th TRENCH MORTAR BATTERY. W. Lieut. B. NEWTON, 4th BEDFORDSHIRE REGT. assumed command of combined unit. W.	
MARICOURT	16.6.16	4.30 a.m.	Marched to BRAY in the forenoon, & in afternoon proceeded to MARICOURT to relieve 90th Trench Mortar Battery, in Z.1 subsector of MARICOURT DEFENCES. W.	
	30.6.16	7.0 p.m.	In accordance with 89th Brigade Operation Order, the battery took up their positions in the Russian Saps, the right section of the battery in the sap at AP 3, & the left section at AP 4, in the trenches north of MARICOURT. W.	

Lindsay, Lieut.
for O.C. 89th T.M.B.

Army Form C2118. fifty

WAR DIARY
or
INTELLIGENCE SUMMARY
89th TRENCH MORTAR BATTERY.
(Erase heading not required.)

Vol II

Instructions regarding War Diaries and Intelligence Summaries are contained in F.S. Regs., Part II. and the Staff Manual respectively. Title Pages will be prepared in manuscript.

Place	Date	Hour	Summary of Events and Information	Remarks and references to Appendices
TRENCHES N. of MARICOURT	1916 1st July		The Battery took part in the BATTLE of the SOMME - remaining in the trenches until relieved on 5th July by 1st S.A. Trench Mortar Battery at 5.30 a.m. B.L.	See appendix No 1.
BOIS DESTAILLES	5th July		After the close of the Battery marched to the BOIS DESTAILLES arriving in camp at 8.30 a.m. and remained here until night of 8/9 July. B.L.	Ref. Map. FRANCE. Sheet 62 D. N.E. Edition 2. 1:20,000.
TRIGGER WOOD	8 July	11.50 p.m.	Arrived here and bivouaced for one night, leaving the next day at 9 p.m. B.L.	
MARICOURT	9 July	11.30 p.m.	Arrived at MARICOURT. The Battery remained here until 13th July, in cellars. B.L. On the night of 12/13 July a Stoke Rifle B 3 ammt rounded two stokes. These were belonged to the 17th Bn. Kings (L'pool) Regt. and was attached to the battery as carriers. B.L.	
	13th July	11 a.m.	Marched from MARICOURT. B.L.	
BOIS DESTAILLES	13th July	3 p.m.	Arrived here and stayed under canvas for one night. B.L. Left for CORBIE at 11 a.m. 14 July. B.L.	
CORBIE	14 July	3 p.m.	Arrived here in billets, remaining until 19th July. B.L. Left for HAPPY VALLEY at 1 p.m. 19 July. B.L.	
HAPPY VALLEY	19 July	7 p.m.	Arrived at HAPPY VALLEY and bivouaced for one night leaving the next day at 10 a.m. B.L.	
CITADEL	20 July	12 noon	After arriving here the battery was in reserve (corps) until 29 July. During this time the men bivouaced on the south side of TRICOURT. Map reference Sheet 62 D. N.E. F.15.2.3.8. 1:10,000 B.L.	
CITADEL	29 July	6 p.m.	The battery left the bivouac & proceeded to the trenches. B.L.	
TRENCHES	29 July	10.30 p.m.	Arrived at position in trenches. B.L. Battery took part in attack on German 2nd line, GUILLEMONT - MAUREPAS area. B.L.	See appendix No 2.
CITADEL	30 July 31 July		Left trenches at 4.30 a.m. and proceeded to the CITADEL bivouacing on the same site as on 20 July. B.L.	

Army Form C. 2118.

WAR DIARY
of
89th TRENCH MORTAR BATTERY
INTELLIGENCE SUMMARY
APPENDIX No 1.

(Erase heading not required.)

Instructions regarding War Diaries and Intelligence Summaries are contained in F.S. Regs., Part II. and the Staff Manual respectively. Title Pages will be prepared in manuscript.

Place	Date	Hour	Summary of Events and Information	Remarks and references to Appendices
Battle of the SOMME	by B.NEWTON Lieut.		At the commencement of the Battle of the SOMME (1st July 1916) the battery consisting of 8 howitzers was placed in position in Russian Saps immediately on the right flank of the British Trench Mortar Army, at a distance of 120 yards in front of our first line of troops, with the 89th Infantry Brigade. The 39th French Division was on our right and the 21st Infantry Brigade on our left. Seventy two carriers were placed in position near advanced ammunition dumps under the command of 2nd Lieut F.E.BOUNDY. A reserve of 15 men was left in cellars at MARICOURT. The battery consisted of the following: Lieut. B.NEWTON, 2nd Lieut. A.ROBINSON, 2nd Lieut. F.E.BOUNDY, and 2nd Lt. W.LINDSAY and Interior D.R. We first took 4 the battery was a hurricane bombardment of the German front line and support trenches directly those occupied by the 89th Infantry Brigade, viz. A10d.25.50 to A10c.0.8, lasting from - 8 zero to the time the first wave of the attacking infantry reached a position 10 yards in the rear of the emplacements. At the conclusion of this bombardment the right section - four howitzers - gun howitzers with 2nd Lieut. A.ROBINSON came under the command of the 17th. Bn. KINGS (L'POOL) Reg'. And then moved forward after the fourth wave of our infantry had passed them to the German support trench immediately opposite taking up a defensive position in case of a counter attack. No light plank writing on found A10C.1.6. A cell however was made upon this section before being relieved - but one hostile prisoner received a direct hit from an enemy shell and was totally destroyed - one man being slightly wounded. The left section of four howitzers accompanied by the following officers Lieut. B. NEWTON and 2nd Lieut. W.LINDSAY found difficulty in firing owing to parts of the emplacements, which had been extended to increase, and the rate of fire was much impeded. On arrival after the order "cease fire" had been given a loud explosion occurred in the sap and the sap shaft and possibly an enemy shell was the cause of this but was probably that caused by one firing off. The result of this explosion was	Ref. Maps: FRANCE Sheet 62 N.W. Edition 2. B.

2449 Wt. W14957/M90 750,000 1/16 J.B.C. & A. Forms/C.2118/12.

WAR DIARY
89th TRENCH MORTAR BATTERY.
INTELLIGENCE SUMMARY — APPENDIX No.1. cont'd.

(Erase heading not required.)

Army Form C. 2118.

Place	Date	Hour	Summary of Events and Information	Remarks and references to Appendices
Battle of the SOMME (cont'd)			one man killed and four wounded. One howitzer was totally destroyed and two others buried. Both were afterwards recovered and found to be undamaged. One howitzer was sent to the German front line at 13 9 minutes after Zero, accompanied by 2nd Lieut. W. LINDSAY to reinforce the MONTAUBAN–MARICOURT ROAD, the minute after Zero, accompanied by 2nd Lieut. W. LINDSAY to reinforce from the O.C. 2nd Bn. KING'S (L'POOL) REGT. under whose command the section had now come. This howitzer was eventually brought forward and sent to the same position on the first in the Sunken line, also 250 rounds of Ammunition. Led him stored in a safe dump in the vicinity.	
1916 2 July	11.50 p.m.		The third howitzer was not discovered until the next morning. At this hour the O.C. 20 K&R. asked for two howitzers, one to be sent to the BRIQUETERIE as there was a sign of the Germans counter attacking. There was at once sent forward with two officers and 90 rounds of ammunition. Whilst making emplacements further howitzers for new emplacements. On the evening of 2nd July (8 pm. to 11.30 pm. the enemy very heavily shelled the BRIQUETERIE and our new front line until 5-9'3. All the men of one of the detachments were wounded as while on – Lt. No.1844 Pte. HILL W. remained on duty for four consecutive hours. A second bombardment looking on. Lens commenced at 12.30 am. the next morning – 3rd July during which two more men were wounded. During this bombardment their party was almost all withdrawn from the extreme right flank when the shelling was very bad little line was held by a party of bombers, two machine guns and two Stokes howitzers. In the morning of the 4th July very heavy shelling was	
4 July	6.30 pm.		Again Experienced at its through the GLATZ REDOUBT. (A.4.4.2.9.) where they stayed until being relieved at 5 am S. July by the 1st SOUTH AFRICAN T.M. Battery. During this period various in action the following casualties occurred: Battery 1 killed 14 wounded, carriers 1 killed 1 wounded, all O.R. B.h.	

2449 Wt. W14957/M90 750,000 1/16 J.B.C. & A. Forms/C.2118/12.

WAR DIARY or INTELLIGENCE SUMMARY

Army Form C. 2118.

89th TRENCH MORTAR BATTERY.

APPENDIX No 2

Place	Date	Hour	Summary of Events and Information	Remarks and references to Appendices
Battle of the SOMME by Capt. B. NEWTON	1916 30 July	5 a.m.	On the night of 29/30 July the battery was placed in position in trenches - the right section S.E. of TRONES WOOD - the left section at the HAIRPIN. A.5.d.9.9. Part of the 89th Infantry Brigade was successful that day. The 39th -French Division was on our right and the 90th Infantry Brigade on left. The personnel of the battery was:- Capt. B. NEWTON, 2nd Lt. F.E. BOUNDY, 2nd Lt. W. LINDSAY, 2nd Lt. D. MURRAY (the latter attached to Supervise ammunition dump) and 4 O.R. together with 40. O.R. attached as carriers of ammunition. The right section of the battery with 2nd Lt. F.E. BOUNDY was attached to the 19th. KINGS (L'pool) REGT and was under the command of the O.C. that battalion. The left section with Capt. B. NEWTON and 2nd Lt. W. LINDSAY was attached to the 20th. KINGS (L'pool) REGT and was under the command of the O.C. that battalion. The right section were ordered to move forward behind the fourth wave of the attacking infantry and take up a position of defence behind of the German line running from GUILLEMONT to WEDGE WOOD. The section moved forward received, introuté, (in a dense fog) of this direction owing to left, a captured German trench. 2nd Lt. F.E. BOUNDY was hit by a bullet - death being instantaneous. The section proceeded still further and formed their two mortars in position the third and the other captured trench. One hour afterwards a party of some eighty Germans were noted seen approaching the position and another range was too short for the mortars - rifle fire was opened on them by the men of this section. The Germans disappeared into shell holes and when our men had thoroughly surrounded they came forward and gave themselves up - 17 wounded and 15 unwounded men were taken prisoner. At 4 p.m. this section received orders to take up a position in the trench running from S.30.d.5.0. to S.30.d.5.7. where they remained until 5 a.m. 31 July having then received orders to proceed to the CITADEL near FRICOURT.	Ref: MAP MAUREPAS 1:20,000

WAR DIARY 89th TRENCH MORTAR BATTERY.

INTELLIGENCE SUMMARY

APPENDIX No 2. cont'd.

Army Form C. 2118.

Place	Date	Hour	Summary of Events and Information	Remarks and references to Appendices
Battle of the Somme cont'd 1916	30 July	4.30 a.m. 31.9. July	The left section placed in position at the HAIRPIN (A5.d.9.9.) received orders to fire on MALTZ HORN FARM - south, steps but owing to the depth of the initial (30x)first the target movement visited & no rounds were fired. On the infantry were unable to reach their objective (WEDGE WOOD inclusive to B2.d.4.8.) the mortars of the section moved out forward but took up a defensive position behind the HAIRPIN. When they remained until orders were received to proceed to the CITADEL. The section left the trenches at Buring the attack the following casualties occurred in the battery. Killed 2Lt F.E. BOUNDY. 1. O.R. Wounded 10. O.R. R.L.	Ref. Map MAUREPAS. 1:20,000.

vols
84 TMB

Scan

War Diary
of
84th Trench Mortar Battery
for the month of
August 1916
Volume 3

VOL. III.   89th TRENCH MORTAR BATTERY.   Army Form C. 2118.

WAR DIARY
or
INTELLIGENCE SUMMARY
(Erase heading not required.)

Instructions regarding War Diaries and Intelligence Summaries are contained in F. S. Regs., Part II and the Staff Manual respectively. Title Pages will be prepared in manuscript.

Place	Date 1916	Hour	Summary of Events and Information	Remarks and references to Appendices
CITADEL	2 Aug.		The Battery remained from 31 July in bivouac F.15.a.3.b (Sheet 62 D NE) until 2 Aug. and left at 4.45 a.m. on that date proceeding to MERICOURT Station where they entrained at 6 p.m. and proceeded by rail to LONGPRÉ arriving at 10.30 p.m. and bivouacked on the station B.h.	MAP. REF. N.E. EUROPE Sheet No. 3.
	3 Aug.		Left LONGPRÉ at 4.45 a.m. and marched to HUPPY arriving at 10.30 a.m. At 4.45 p.m. the Battery marched to PONT REMÉ and entrained at 7.45 p.m. the train leaving at 8.50 p.m. B.h.	BÉTHUNE Central Sheet
MERVILLE	4 Aug.		Detrained at MERVILLE at 4 a.m. + marched to CALONNE arriving at 6 a.m. in billets B.h.	
CALONNE	4 Aug.		The battery remained here until the 9th inst. resting and reorganising B.h.	
do	9 Aug	2.30 pm	Left billets at CALONNE and marched to FOSSE B.h.	
FOSSE	9 "	4.30 pm	Arrived in billets and carried on with training B.h.	
do	13 "		The battery was made up to strength by transfer of 13 O.R. from the reserve personnel and 9 O.R. from battalions in the Brigade. B.h. 1 O.R. from the 2nd Batt. KINGS LIVERPOOL REGT was attached for duty. B.h.	
do	18 Aug.	9 am.	2nd Batt. C BERWITZ 20th Batn. KINGS LIVERPOOL REGT. was attached for duty B.h. Battery left FOSSE and marched to billets at PONT L'HINGES arriving at 11.30 a.m. B.h.	
			24 O.R. were sent to battalion for training to form a new reserve personnel. B.h. 2nd Lt. C BERWITZ two R/ofs and 2 O.R. proceeded to 30th Brd. T.M. School for instruction. B.h. 2nd Lt. C BERWITZ was accidentally wounded at the Brd. School. B.h.	
PONT L'HINGES	20 Aug		2nd Lt. W.H.HUGHES 20th Bn. Kings L'pool Regt. and 2nd Lt. N.B FEARN 17th Bn. Kings L'pool Regt. were attached to the battery for duty. B.h. 2nd C R.MUNRO Kings L'pool Regt. struck off strength 9 BATTERY. B.h.	
do	26 Aug	10 am.	Battery left billets at PONT L'HINGE's and marched to billets at GORRE arriving at 12.30 A.m. B.h.	
GORRE	27 Aug.	9 am.	The Battery relieved 21st. T.M. BATTERY in the GIVENCHY SECTOR. Seven mortars being taken into the line. B.h. 2nd Lieut. W.H.HUGHES and 2nd Lieut FEARN proceeded to 30th Brd.	See Appendix No. 1.
	30 Aug		Trench Mortar School for instruction B.h. 2nd Lieut. W.H. HUGHES left Brd. T.M. School, and with 5. O.R. proceeded to 1st. Army School of Mortars at CLARQUES. B.h.	

WAR DIARY or INTELLIGENCE SUMMARY

Army Form C. 2118.

VOL. III

89th. TRENCH MORTAR BATTERY.

APPENDIX. No. 1.

Place	Date	Hour	Summary of Events and Information	Remarks and references to Appendices
TRENCHES GIVENCHY SECTOR	1916 27 Aug to 31st Aug	B. NEWTON Capt.	The relief of the 21st. T.M BATTERY was completed at noon on 27. Aug. From this time until 31st Aug. an intermittent bombardment was carried on - well over 100 shells per day being fired on to selected spots in the enemy trenches, with good effect. Six mortars were stationary in emplacements and one was kept in reserve and to be used for firing in other parts of the Sector by a mobile detachment. On 29th. a heavy thunderstorm flooded part of the emplacements restricting the firing owing to the softening of the ground. Many rounds were fired in retaliation to enemy mortars and rifle grenades - our mortars on every occasion having the better of the duel. Our offensive appeared to worry the enemy considerably and on and on various occasions he directed the hostility of our emplacements to a heavy bombardment with howitzers and field guns in which his heavy T. Mortars joined. No casualties occurred however. The following is now the strength of the Battery:— Officers. Capt. B. NEWTON, 2nd Lieut. W. LINDSAY. 2nd Lieut. W. H. HUGHES, } attached 2nd Lieut. N.B. FEARN } O.R. 46. Total 50. B Newton Capt.	